JCMS Annual Review
of the European Union
in 2015

Edited by

Nathaniel Copsey
and
Tim Haughton

General Editors: Michelle Cini and Amy Verdun

WILEY
Blackwell

This edition first published 2016

Registered Office
John Wiley & Sons Ltd, The Atrium, Southern Gate, Chichester, West Sussex, PO19 8SQ, UK

Editorial Offices
350 Main Street, Malden, MA 02148--5020, USA
9600 Garsington Road, Oxford, OX4 2DQ, UK
The Atrium, Southern Gate, Chichester, West Sussex, PO19 8SQ, UK

For details of our global editorial offices, for customer services, and for information about how to apply for permission to reuse the copyright material in this book please see our website at www.wiley.com/wiley-blackwell.

Wiley also publishes its books in a variety of electronic formats. Some content that appears in print may not be available in electronic books.

Designations used by companies to distinguish their products are often claimed as trademarks. All brand names and product names used in this book are trade names, service marks, trademarks or registered trademarks of their respective owners. The publisher is not associated with any product or vendor mentioned in this book.

Library of Congress Cataloging-in-Publication Data

ISBN 978-1-119-27971-6
ISSN 0021-9886 (print) 1468-5965 (online)

A catalogue record for this book is available from the British Library.

Set in 11/12.5 pt Times by Toppan Best-set Premedia Limited
Printed in Singapore

1   2016

CONTENTS

JCMS 2016 Volume 54. Annual Review pp. 5–7   DOI: 10.1111/jcms.12437

Editorial

Is Crisis the New Normal? The European Union in 2015

TIM HAUGHTON[1]
University of Birmingham

Crisis appears to be the new normal for the European Union. The images of a drowned child refugee from Syria on a European beach, Greek protestors with banners proclaiming όχι! ('no!') and political leaders linking arms on a Parisian street following a terrorist attack stick in the memory. They underline the persistent challenges facing the EU and its Member States related to identity, prosperity and security. The problems afflicting the EU in 2015, however, also highlighted the challenges of governance and perennial questions concerning the locus of decision-making power and responsibility in the EU and its Member States.

Greece was central to the two principal dramas of the year: the eurozone and migration. The eurozone's travails continued, but whilst other countries such as Portugal, Spain and Ireland had exited their bailout programmes, Greece remained within it and its crisis entered its most alarming stage. Two elections and a hurried referendum set Greece on a collision course with its creditors. A Syriza-led government was elected in January 2015 on a ticket opposing austerity. The leading figures of the new administration, Prime Minister Alexis Tsipras and Finance Minister Yanis Varoufakis, became the poster boys of the challenge to austerity. July's hasty referendum and the overwhelming 'no' to austerity that it produced had little lasting impact. By the year's end, Tsipras led a new government that implemented another austerity package very similar to that rejected so overwhelmingly in July. For all the turmoil, protracted negotiations, demonstrations, threats and exchanges of harsh words, Greece remained in the eurozone.

The year began and ended with terrorist atrocities in Paris. Twelve were murdered in the attack on the satirical magazine *Charlie Hebdo* in Paris in January. November's coordinated attacks across six sites in the French capital, including the crowded Bataclan theatre, left 130 dead. News that some of the November terrorists had travelled to Paris from Belgium across an open border posed questions about internal security within the Schengen area.

Tragic as the terrorist attacks in France were, for the European Union as a whole the year 2015 is likely to be remembered most for the migration crisis. The flow of refugees and irregular migrants did not begin in 2015 (Monar, 2015), but the summer of 2015 saw the flow increase dramatically. More than a million people made the journey to the EU over the course of 2015 – a three- or four-four fold increase on 2014. Irregular migration

---

[1] My co-editor Nathaniel Copsey is on leave from academia working as Head of the Europe Research Group at the Foreign and Commonwealth Office.

6

on this scale exposed the gap between EU policies and the willingness, as well as capacity, of the Member States to implement them. It also demonstrated a variety of opinions within the Member States as to what should be done – and who should do it.

Migration on such a large scale led to calls for the new arrivals to be distributed between Member States, particularly since the great majority were headed for just one country: Germany. Redistribution of migrants according to quotas was pushed through despite the opposition of the Czech Republic, Hungary, Romania and Slovakia, but implementation of the measure proved more difficult. Responses to the refugee crisis in transit countries included building fences to keep people out and laying on transport to move people on. Both contravened the spirit of Schengen and free movement. Moreover, these national responses and the summits convened to find solutions to the refugee crisis demonstrated that, for the most serious matters, the European Union remains intergovernmental.

In the background of the year's many dramas, business-as-usual saw the launch of severally potentially significant developments, including plans for the regulation of the Digital Single Market, the creation of an Energy Union and the establishment of a Capital Markets Union. The Five Presidents' Report on the deepening and 'completion' of Economic and Monetary Union by 2025 was also released. Despite the endorsement of the Presidents of five EU institutions – Jeroen Dijsselbloem (Eurogroup), Mario Draghi (ECB), Jean-Claude Juncker (Commission), Martin Schulz (European Parliament) and Donald Tusk (European Council) – the two key players for the future of the eurozone were missing: Chancellor Angela Merkel and President Francois Hollande. Unless and until France and Germany can agree a common strategy for the reform of the eurozone, plans for the future of the euro are unlikely to progress very far.

Lastly, 2015 was the year in which the Conservative party won the May General Election in the UK. Victory for Prime Minister David Cameron meant the implementation of the promise made in 2013 to hold an in-or-out referendum on membership of the EU (Copsey and Haughton, 2014). The referendum of 23 June 2016 and the renegotiation of the terms of membership secured in the February 2016 European Council that preceded it will be covered in next year's *Annual Review*.

This is our eighth issue of the *JCMS AR* as editors. We have continued our policy of commissioning a number of special contributions from leading scholars in the field, alongside our regular authors almost all of whom have continued for another year. We would like to express our thanks to Ana Juncos who stepped down this year after seven years of sterling service.

We invited Tanja Börzel of the Freie Universität in Berlin to deliver this year's *Annual Review* lecture at Europe House in London. Given the challenges of governance posed by the eurozone and migration crisis, she examined two salient questions: how much Europe is necessary for effective and legitimate governance in Europe amid enduring crises; and, is more or rather less European integration the answer to Europe's governance failures? In an echo of the call made in Loukas Tsoukalis's (2011) *Annual Review* lecture a few years ago, her contribution argues that Europe's problem is not too little integration. Indeed Börzel maintains that the way forward is not about 'more' or 'less' Europe. Rather, it is about creating a new kind of EU governance that tackles the problem of redistribution between, and within, the Member States.

The theme of politicization is core to the *Annual Review* lecture and is the focus of Hanspeter Kriesi's contribution. He argues that the politicization of European integration is not only time-dependent, but also embedded in national political conflict structures. These vary systematically between three European regions: the Northwest, the South and the East of Europe. In order to understand the impact of contemporary crisis conditions on the politicization of European integration, he maintains, we have to take into account how these crisis conditions are linked to the underlying region-specific national conflict structures.

Following previous issues of the *Annual Review* in which William Paterson (2011) examined Germany as a 'reluctant hegemon', Christian Lequesne (2013) explored the consequences of a new Socialist President in the Elysée and Sonia Lucarelli (2015) explained why Italy's attitude towards the EU has shifted from 'True Love to Disenchantment', it seemed appropriate for this year's *Annual Review* to contain a contribution examining the Member State at the heart of many of the major events of the year: Greece. In his analysis, Kevin Featherstone argues the combined challenges facing Greece in 2015 pose a conundrum that is existential in nature for the EU: 'a trilemma in which the external leadership of reforms via conditionality confronts national democratic choice and the operational deficiencies of weak domestic institutions'.

We would like to thank all the contributors to this issue of the *JCMS Annual Review* for their efforts and efficiency in producing such excellent copy within the usual tight time timetable, the copy editor Rachel Cameron and Rae Ann Susulin-Perez and the team at Wiley for their hard work during the production phase. Finally, we would also like to thank the editors of the *JCMS*, Michelle Cini and Amy Verdun, for their continuing support.

References

Copsey, N. and Haughton, T. (2014) 'Farewell Britannia? "Issue Capture" and the Politics of David Cameron's 2013 Referendum Pledge'. *JCMS*, Vol. 52, No. s1, pp. 74–89.

Lesquesne, C. (2013) 'A New Socialist President in the Elysée: Continuity and Change in French EU Politics'. *JCMS*, Vol. 51, No. s1, pp. 42–54.

Lucarelli, S. (2015) 'Italy and the EU: From True Love to Disenchantment'. *JCMS*, Vol. 53, No. s1, pp. 40–60.

Monar, J. (2015) 'Justice and Home Affairs'. *JCMS*, Vol. 53, No. s1, pp. 128–43.

Paterson, W. (2011) 'The Reluctant Hegemon? Germany Moves Centre Stage in the European Union'. *JCMS*, Vol. 49, No. s1, pp. 57–75.

Tsoukalis, L. (2011) 'The JCMS Annual Review Lecture: The Shattering of Illusions – and What Next?' *JCMS*, Vol. 49, No. s1, pp. 19–44.

JCMS 2016 Volume 54. Annual Review pp. 8–31   DOI: 10.1111/jcms.12431

From EU Governance of Crisis to Crisis of EU Governance: Regulatory Failure, Redistributive Conflict and Eurosceptic Publics*

TANJA A. BÖRZEL
Freie Universität Berlin

Introduction

Financial crisis, euro crisis, Greek crisis, Crimean crisis, Ukraine crisis, Syria crisis, migration crisis – even the greatest optimist cannot deny that Europe has been suffering through a whole series of crises ever since the Lehman Brothers bank collapsed in 2008. EU scholars and pundits agree that Europe has failed to govern the multiple crises because the European Union has been too weak to prevent the breakdown of banks, contain sovereign debt, generate economic growth, create new jobs, promote stability and democracy in its Southern and Eastern neighbourhood, stop transnational terrorism, and fight climate change. Some even argue that the EU has not only failed to provide solutions but that is actually part of the problem undermining the capacity of its Member States to effectively and democratically govern their markets and societies in the 21st century (Majone, 2014; Scharpf, 2015). Although some Eastern European governments may have been most outspoken in claiming that not more but less Europe is the only way to get out of the various crises and avert catastrophe in the future, Dutch, Danish and British politicians, however, have voiced similar arguments supporting David Cameron's symbolic request to exempt the UK from the goal of 'an ever closer union' in the preamble of the Treaties to avoid Brexit.

How much Europe is necessary for effective and legitimate governance in Europe amid enduring crises? Is more or rather less European integration the answer to Europe's governance failures? This contribution will argue that Europe's problem is not too little integration. The EU has the power to take action. The Fiscal Pact, the Six-Pack, the European Stability Mechanism, the Banking Union, the sanctions against Russia, the Association Agreement with Ukraine, reallocation quotas for refugees, more than €10 billion for assisting countries inside and outside the EU to cope with the migration flows – these are only some of the more prominent measures the EU has adopted in response to the crises over the past few years. Sceptics contend that this is too little too late, particularly in the current crisis. Yet, whether the new laws and institutions will be sufficient is hard to tell as long as they have not taken effect. While the Member States have made significant legal and financial commitments at the EU level, many of them have shown little inclination to follow up and comply. This is particularly evident with regard to the attempts of the EU to tackle the

*I am grateful to Tim Haughton, Nat Copsey, Thomas Risse, Michael Blauberger, Katharina Holzinger, and Beate Kohler for their very useful comments and suggestions on earlier versions of this contribution. This *JCMS Annual Review* lecture was delivered on 12 May 2016 at Europe House in London.

historic influx of migrants. Funds are not paid, refugees and asylum-seekers not accepted, laws not implemented and enforced. The EU does not so much lack the capacity to take binding decisions; it is its Member States that do not comply with these decisions. I will use the euro crisis and the failure of the EU to deal with the migration flows to argue that at the heart of Europe's crises lies a growing commitment-compliance gap, which has exacerbated the regulatory deficits of EU governance in these two core areas of the European integration project. The failure of Member States to put policies they agreed upon at the EU level into practice has its cause in euro-nationalists dominating the politicization of EU policies and institutions, which have been empowered by the way in which the Member States sought to solve the euro crisis. The growing contestation of, and opposition to, the EU and its policies *per se* is not the problem. Nor is it the return of nationalism in Europe or the lack of a European public sphere. Instead of an outright rejection of European integration, we see the mobilization of illiberal, nationalist ideas of Europe, which are exclusionary, xenophobic and anti-Islam. I will argue that this euro-nationalism not only undermines the legitimacy but also the effectiveness of EU governance. It has been fuelled by the mix of Member State negotiation and competition in the shadow of supranational hierarchy, which has worked for the EU as a regulatory state but which is not suitable for dealing with the redistributive issues that have come to dominate important areas of European integration. In fact simply extending the EU's governance mix from regulatory to redistributive policies is likely to further undermine its effectiveness and legitimacy.

In order to develop this argument, the contribution proceeds in three steps. The first part will analyze how the EU has adjusted its governance mix to cope with the euro crisis. Drawing on my previous work, I will demonstrate that the euro crises management resulted in a strengthening of supranational centralization on the one hand and intergovernmental co-ordination in the shadow of supranational hierarchy on the other. The second part will show that the EU has invoked this governance mix to deal with its next crisis caused by the historic influx of migrants and refugees. While it has been able to generate substantial commitment to taking action, the EU faces growing non-compliance problems at the domestic level. I will argue that the refusal of Member State governments to honour their financial and legal commitments is mostly due to increasing politicization driven by the rise of populist forces that mobilize illiberal, nationalist ideas of Europe against the redistributive effects of many EU crises policies.

The contribution concludes with some considerations on how to solve the EU's governance crisis. Rather than pursuing a functionalist strategy of deepening European integration, I will argue that the post-functionalist EU is in need of a new governance mix. Supranational centralization and supranational joint decision-making may be appropriate for regulatory policies. When applied to redistributive issues, however, they fail to generate sufficient social acceptance at the domestic level. Seeking to depoliticize redistributive policies by delegating them to supranational institutions, such as the European Central Bank, the European Commission and a European Border and Coast Guard has backfired. The transfer of political authority to EU institutions, which results in a loss or at least severe constraints on national sovereignty, has fuelled opposition to an increasingly intrusive and undemocratic EU empowering eurosceptic populist forces at both ends of the political spectrum. Rather than being principally opposed to the European integration project, they advocate ideas of an exclusionary, nationalist EU that protects the national sovereignty and cultural heritage of its Member States. These illiberal ideas challenge the effectiveness and the legitimacy of both EU policies and EU institutions. What is necessary is a strengthening of cosmopolitan voices in the politicization of the EU and its policies that appeal to the Europeanized identities of EU citizens based on shared values of solidarity, liberty and humanity, to upgrade the European common interest and scale up solidarity among Europeans.

I. The EU's Changing Governance Mix: More of the Same

Some EU scholars argue that the EU has been in crisis for the past 40 years starting with the eurosclerosis in the 1970s and early 1980s. Crisis arose whenever the Member States resisted (further) transfer of political authority to the EU level or opposed EU interference into their domestic affairs even though joint action at the EU level appeared to be clearly needed (Tömmel, 2016). In the attempt to 'escape from deadlock', the EU developed new modes of governance, such as the Open Method of Coordination (Héritier, 1999). But overall, the Member States have institutionalized different combinations of competition and negotiation in the shadow of supranational hierarchy.

Varieties of EU Governance

To overcome Member State resistance against the harmonization of regulatory standards in the creation of the internal market, the Member States resorted first to framework legislation setting common goals and basic rules and procedures leaving it to Member States to implement their own policies. Compliance with EU framework legislation is monitored by the European Commission and the European Court of Justice (ECJ), while enforcement ultimately lies with the Member States. The subsequent extension of the EU's regulatory competencies and qualified majority voting since the Single European Act in 1986 facilitated the use of the Community Method or what I refer to as supranational joint decision-making, which the Lisbon Treaty of 2010 made the default mode of governance applying to almost all policies of the single market and in the framework of justice and home affairs.

Second, the Member States delegated political authority to independent supranational agencies. The European Commission and the European Central Bank can set and enforce legally binding decisions without requiring the consent of the Member States. This supranational centralization does not only apply in competition and monetary policy. Since the 1990s, the Council has increasingly tasked the Commission with the adoption of EU laws (König et al., 2012). Such delegated or tertiary legislation (Junge et al., 2015) can be adopted by the Commission under the implementing powers given to it by the Treaties (Article 291 TFEU), or under the delegated powers provided by earlier legal acts. It usually involves the further elaboration or updating of standards and technical issues. They are passed through the so-called comitology procedure, which involves committees consisting of Member State representatives with voting power and the Commission which sets the agenda and chairs the committee meetings. Decision-making happens behind closed doors and is in stark contrast to the adoption of legal acts under supranational joint-decision-making; the European Parliament has the right to comment on whether a draft exceeds the implementing powers of the Commission but has no power to amend or reject the directive.

Third, the principle of mutual recognition established by the ECJ in 1979 with its seminal *Cassis de Dijon* decision allows high-regulating Member States to maintain their regulatory standards but prevents them from using those standards as non-tariff trade barriers against low-regulating Member States. It constitutes the framework for a moderate regulatory competition between the Member States in the shadow of supranational hierarchy since EU law mandating the opening of national markets generates competitive pressure not only on domestic companies but also on public regulation within the Member States (Sun and Pelkmans, 1995, pp. 68–69). At the same time, the principle of mutual recognition constrains the dynamics of a race to the bottom by requiring that states (implicitly) agree on minimum standards. It thereby significantly expands the shadow of supranational hierarchy in the single market since the dismantling of non-tariff barriers does not require the consent of the Member States – unlike the harmonization of national standards at the EU level. This form of 'horizontal transfer of sovereignty' (Nicolaidis and Shaffer, 2005) also travelled to other areas where it serves as a functional equivalent to supranational joint decision-making. It has been increasingly invoked in justice and home affairs, for example, in the area of asylum and immigration policy or criminal law, where the national regulations of Member States are too divergent to allow for agreement in the inter- and transgovernmental negotiation systems (Schmidt, 2007). The principle of mutual recognition facilitates cross-border law enforcement since different national standards with regard to criminal codes can no longer obstruct judicial co-operation between Member States (Lavenex, 2007).

Fourth, transgovernmental networks help supranational, national and subnational public actors to informally co-ordinate their interests and reach agreements through the exchange of resources and arguments. The shadow of supranational hierarchy generated by majority rule in the Council and judicial review of the ECJ significantly influences the dynamics and outcomes of inter- and transgovernmental negotiation systems. On the one hand, the perceived threat of a majority decision in the Council increases the willingness of governmental actors to come to an agreement. On the other hand, inter- and transgovernmental actors have to make sure that their agreements are likely to stand up to scrutiny by the Commission and the ECJ. The parameters set by their interpretation of European law are not always oriented towards mere market liberalization and free competition but may also support market-correcting policies. The 'dual mechanism of anticipated reactions and the fleet in being' (Scharpf, 1997, p. 200) is particularly prevalent in the single market but also has an impact on other policy sectors, such as the environment, social policy and tax policy (Héritier and Lehmkuhl, 2008).

These transgovernmental networks also help to fill the 'regulatory gap' at the EU level, when Member States have been reluctant to transfer regulatory authority to the EU level and instead delegated them to independent regulatory agencies or ministries at the national level (Coen and Héritier, 2006). National regulatory authorities have formed informal networks to exchange information and develop 'best practice' rules and procedures to address common problems (Coen and Thatcher, 2008). While these regulatory and operational networks may be open to the participation of private actors (for example, providers and consumers), they are transgovernmental rather than transnational in character (Eberlein and Grande, 2005). Even if the Member States have not delegated regulatory competencies to the EU, transgovernmental networks operate under the shadow of supranational framework regulation, which 'regulates the regulators' (Eberlein and Grande, 2005, p. 98) by setting minimum requirements for the regulatory regimes in the Member States (Levi-Faur, 1999).

If It Ain't Completely Broken, Don't Fix It!

The EU's governance mix has evolved over time developing different varieties of inter- and transgovernmental negotiation and regulatory competition in the shadow of supranational hierarchy (Börzel, 2010, 2012). Economic and monetary union (EMU) combines supranational centralization in the form of delegating the authority to make monetary policy to the European Central Bank (ECB) with the intergovernmental co-ordination of national economic policies in the Eurogroup to safe-guard macroeconomic stability in the shadow of the Stability and Growth Pact and the Excessive Deficit Protocol Procedure on the one hand and the competition of national economic systems in the internal market on the other. Asylum and migration policy mixes supranational decision-making to set common standards on the treatment of asylum seekers and refugees in the Schengen passport-free area and regulatory competition in the shadow of supranational hierarchy to facilitate cross-border law enforcement.

Both governance regimes have been criticized for Member States giving up rather than transferring political authority to the EU level. Monetary union deprives euro countries of key instruments of macroeconomic management without, for example, providing the EU with the ability to contradict the effects of cheap credit availability resulting from the uniformity of ECB interest rates (Scharpf, 2015, 2016; Streeck and Elsässer, 2016). In a similar vein, the Schengen states abolished internal border controls without creating a common external border control and a common administration to handle asylum seekers and refugees. Despite these birth defects, however, the euro and Schengen appeared to work well enough.

Warnings that the governance mix of EMU failed to ensure sufficient convergence among surplus and deficit countries were ignored (Bayoumi and Eichengreen, 1993; Scharpf, 2015; Streeck and Elsässer, 2016) and demands by Spain, Italy and Greece for burden-sharing dismissed (Thielemann and El-Enany, 2010). The Stability and Growth Pact and the Excessive Deficit Procedure Protocol were to impose fiscal discipline on the Member States to prevent spillover effects from unsustainable national deficits. Re-admission agreements with neighbouring countries were to limit the number of asylum seekers to be handled by the Member States in charge of protecting the EU's external borders.

Only when the EU was hit by the collapse of US real estate banks in 2008, and after Libya and Syria collapsed in 2011, respectively, did the Member States have to acknowledge the deficits of the regulatory governance mixes. Since the EU lacked the political authority for a forceful response to both crises, Member States have resorted to unilateral action – bailing out their domestic banks, stopping the registration of refugees and asylum seekers, passing them on to their neighbours, taking them on without registration, and closing off their borders.

EU Crisis Management by Default

Since EMU and the Schengen regime have deprived the Member States of core instruments to mitigate external asymmetric shocks, unilateral action has done little to manage the crises. Consequently, and rather reluctantly, Member State governments sought to find common solutions at the EU level. To prevent the breakdown of the eurozone and protect the common currency against future challenges, the euro countries established a whole set of supranational institutions which constitute the most far-reaching deepening of European integration since the creation of EMU in 1999 – without even touching the Treaties. Rather than fundamentally changing the previous governance mix by establishing a 'new intergovernmentalism' (Bickerton *et al.*, 2014), the Fiscal Compact, the European Stability Mechanism, the Banking Union, the Macro-economic Imbalance Mechanism, and the European Semester reinforce supranational centralization and inter- and transgovernmental co-ordination as the two main governance modes of EMU, placing the latter under a strict shadow of supranational hierarchy.

Certainly, the European Council has played a key role in making decisions in response to the crisis (Bickerton *et al.*, 2014; Puetter, 2014). However, this does not necessarily imply a weakening of supranational institutions (Fabbrini, 2013; Nugent and Rhinard, 2016).[1] The Commission was tasked with transforming Member State decisions into technical proposals for legislative measures including the Six Pack and the Two Pack adopted by supranational decision-making, that is, the ordinary or special legislative procedure. The Macro-economic Imbalance Mechanism and the European Semester substantially strengthen the budgetary and macroeconomic surveillance capacities of the Commission (Savage and Verdun, 2016). Tightening the rules for fiscal discipline of the Stability and Growth Pact and giving the Commission the power to monitor Member State fiscal activities and sanction excessive deficits and debts cast a substantial shadow of supranational hierarchy over the intergovernmental co-ordination of economic, fiscal and budgetary policies that formally remain the political authority of the Member States, but supranational rules and surveillance severely limit Member State discretion.

In a similar vein, the Banking Union creates supranational banking rules (single rulebook) and centralizes banking supervision in the hands of the ECB to avert market failure by banks.[2] The so-called Single Supervisory Mechanism provides for the monitoring and enforcement of a common regulatory framework formed by a series of directives adopted under supranational decision-making, including the Capital Requirements Regulation and Directive implementing the Basel III capital requirements for banks, the Deposit Guarantee Scheme Directive regulating deposit insurance, and the Bank Recovery and Resolution Directive, which establishes the Single Resolution Mechanism and the Single Resolution Fund to regulate and finance the restructuring of troubled banks (de Rynk, 2016). With the European Commission, the ECB obtained comprehensive surveillance powers, which comprise full access to bank data and the right to carry out onsite inspections. The new system takes away Member State authority for financial supervision under the Lamfalussy Process, which provided at best a 'light touch' regulation (Quaglia, 2010).

Strengthening supranational centralization and placing intergovernmental co-ordination under a shadow of supranational hierarchy may be a rupture with the past approach of centralized monetary and decentralized economic policy (de Rynk, 2016). Yet, it is fully in line with the EU's default strategy to deepen integration in the face of Member State resistance against a transfer of political authority to the EU level by supranational centrali-zation (*cf.* Chalmers *et al.*, 2016b). This also applies to the changing role of the ECB, which in a similar vein to the Commission has transformed from a technocratic supranational agent with a very specific mandate into a political actor taking monetary decisions with redistributive consequences, such as quantitative easing or purchasing government debt

---

[1] See Dinan's contribution to this volume.
[2] See Hodson's contribution in this volume.

on secondary markets, but being shielded against political and electoral accountability (Chang, 2016, p. 493).

The changes in the EU's governance mix are also a far cry from calls for a genuine social and political union, which would have the legal and fiscal authority to protect and support specific social rights (Habermas, 2013). The incremental adjustments of the previous governance mix not only raise questions about its effectiveness in preventing future crisis (Scharpf, 2016). They also heighten problems of legitimacy since supranational centralization and intergovernmental co-ordination in the shadow of supranational hierarchy hardly provide for the democratic control and participation the German Constitutional Court demands and EU scholars deem necessary to counter increasing euroscepticism among EU citizens (Fasone, 2013; Hix, 2015; Risse, 2015b).

Whether the reform of the existing governance mix will suffice to protect the eurozone against future external shocks is beyond the scope of this contribution. What is of interest here is that the default strategy of the EU to respond to the refugee crisis by resorting to supranational centralization and inter- and transgovernmental co-ordination in the shadow of supranational hierarchy has not worked. Quite the contrary: I argue attempts at depoliticizing controversial issues by supranational centralization silencing public controversies over EU policies and EU institutions have backfired turning the 'constraining dissensus' (Hooghe and Marks, 2009) into euroscepticism (Grande and Kriesi, 2014). The politicization of the EU as a polity by populist politicians mostly on the right has not only made it impossible for Member State governments to agree on creating new supranational institutions, such as a European Border and Coast Guard, or supranational rules for intergovernmental co-ordination, such as institutionalized reallocation quota, it also undermines their compliance with decisions already adopted under supranational joint decision-making or intergovernmental co-ordination – bringing the entire Schengen system down.

II. The Commitment–Compliance Gap: From Regulation to Redistribution

The combination of negotiation and competition in the shadow of supranational hierarchy has prevented and corrected market failures (on the EU model of regulatory governance see Eckert, 2011; Finger, 2011). Yet, it has clear limits when dealing with issues of redistribution. In (re-)distributive policy areas, such as taxation of mobile capital, employment, social policy or economic governance, the Member States have been very reluctant to resort to supranational joint decision-making and supranational centralization in order to counteract politically undesired outcomes of the internal market. At the same time, EU market and monetary integration impedes the Member States in maintaining such functions. The single currency largely deprives the Member States of their core instruments for national macroeconomic stabilization, while the fiscal austerity rules put serious constraints on state expenditures. Softer modes of governance (intergovernmental negotiations and competition) are unlikely to respond to this 'European problem-solving gap' (Scharpf 2006, p. 855), elucidated once again by the financial crisis.

Masking Redistribution

The imminent threat of sovereign debt has been contained and there are signs that the economies of the crisis countries are recovering, with the exception of

Greece.[3] Yet, the South of Europe continues to suffer from long-term developmental problems. So far 'hard' supranational centralization to discipline the banking sector and Member State spending policies has done little to narrow the gap between the EU's Northern core and its Southern (and Eastern) periphery since they do little to tackle the structural weaknesses that hold back Spain, Portugal, Greece and Italy's capacity to grow and adjust to economic shocks (European Commission, 2016b).[4] This would require the EU to address the overall low governance capacities of creditor countries, their poor education and skills, weak productivity performance and very poor multi-factor productivity scores (Bohle and Greskovits, 2012; Molina and Rhodes, 2008; van Ark *et al.*, 2013). The failure to do so has increased the democratic legitimacy deficit of the EU by insulating political decisions from institutional and electoral accountability, both at the EU and the national level (Scharpf, 2015; Streeck and Elsässer, 2016; de Wilde *et al.*, 2016). What is more, rather than alleviating the social costs of the euro crisis, the reformed EU governance mix interferes with domestic economic and social policy producing or at least exacerbating redistributive effects that are now attributed to the EU (Hix, 2015; Polyakova and Fligstein, 2016; Scharpf, 2015). Through their financial guarantees, assistance and interventions, the ESM and the ECB, directly or indirectly, have engaged in massive redistribution among and within the Member States. The euro crisis has definitely turned EMU into a redistributive issue by increasing the scale and the visibility of redistribution.

To be sure, EMU has never been a purely regulatory issue. While the Member States could not agree on supranationalizing economic, fiscal and budgetary policies, it was clear that overcoming the diverging economic performance between Northern surplus and Southern deficit countries would require some financial transfer by the former to help the latter raise productivity (Streeck and Elsässer, 2016). The structural funds were to provide fiscal assistance to buffer economic and social adjustment costs imposed by the internal market (George and Bache, 2001; Hooghe, 1996), and later the common currency. However, with Eastern enlargement, the Southern European euro countries had to increasingly share the funds with the new Member States in Central and Eastern Europe. Maintaining their initial level of financial transfer would have required an increase of the EU budget from 1 to 4 per cent of EU GDP, which the net payers and surplus euro countries rejected insisting that competitiveness could only be improved by austerity and structural reforms to become self-sufficient (Streeck and Elsässer, 2016, pp. 17–19). The drop in EU financial assistance for the deficit countries was at least partly compensated by access to cheap credit, which, however, was used for consumption rather than investment (Scharpf, 2015).

When the deficit countries had to go into sovereign debt to bail out their troubled banks, the surplus countries came to the rescue. Cheap credit was made conditional on the implementation of austerity programmes, stringently enforced fiscal restructuring and structural reforms, overseen by the International Monetary Fund, the European Commission and the European Central Bank. To support Member States with substantial public debt, two temporary rescue funds were set up in 2010, the European Financial

---

[3] See Featherstone's contribution to this volume.
[4] In the Country Reports published in the framework of the European Semester 2016, the European Commission considers these structural weaknesses the key challenge for the recovery and growth potential of European economies. Available online at: http://ec.europa.eu/europe2020/making-it-happen/country-specific-recommendations/index_en.htm. Last accessed: 27 February 2016.

Stabilization Mechanism (EFSM), guaranteed by the European Commission through the EU budget, and the European Financial Stability Facility (EFSF), which was guaranteed by the eurozone members. These temporary lending facilities were replaced in 2012 with the European Stability Mechanism (ESM), a permanent European emergency fund with a lending capacity of €500 billion. The various bailout mechanisms and rescue packages have turned the EU by all practical means into a transfer union – despite the 'no bailout clause' (Article 123 TFEU). 'The prohibition on international compensation payments in the Maastricht Treaty is no more than pro forma: with significant performance differences between countries joined in a monetary union, there is no way around some sort of inter-country redistribution' (Streeck and Elsässer, 2016, p. 8). Many argue that the installed transfer mechanisms are not enough to deal with the economic and social costs of the euro crises and the structural reforms the creditor countries demand in return for their financial solidarity. In order to help Member States equalize the regional effects of asymmetrical shocks and raise the productivity of deficit countries, the EU needs to become a truly fiscal union replacing intergovernmental economic policy co-ordination under 'soft law' (Hodson and Maher, 2001) with a common taxation, pension and employment insurance system (Scharpf, 2015; Streeck and Elsässer, 2016). Moreover, the EU would have to make sure that the Member States engage in stronger redistribution at the domestic level. Inequality and social exclusion are not only - and increasingly less - an issue between but rather within the Member States (Copsey, 2015). The required redistribution would be of such magnitude that the economic growth in surplus countries would no longer suffice to pay for the fiscal transfers. Nor would the necessary transfer of political authority find sufficient support among political elites and mass publics in Europe given that the distribution of the adjustment burden between creditor and debtor countries in the Euro crisis has already been the most divisive conflict (Genschel and Jachtenfuchs, 2016b).

Unwilling to change the treaties to give the EU substantial redistributive authority, the Member State governments have sought to depoliticize redistributive issues by masking them behind regulatory policies (Genschel and Jachtenfuchs, 2016a). Regulatory policies do have redistributive implications (Wilson, 1980). Yet these are mostly felt at the implementation stage and concealed by imposing the same obligations on all Member States (Majone, 1994). As a result Member States have found it less difficult to transfer regulatory authority to the EU level and to agree on common regulatory policies. Not surprisingly then, the creditor countries have framed the euro crisis as a regulatory issue, a problem of too lenient fiscal and budgetary rules and too lax enforcement (Chang, 2016, p. 495). The solution, hence, is not fiscal transfer but compliance with stricter austerity rules and structural reforms enforced by the Commission and the ECB, which will enable debtor countries to become self-sufficient. Financial assistance is only a temporary means to buffer adjustment costs and help build reform capacities.

Yet, regulatory governance is ultimately inadequate to deal with redistributive issues (Majone, 1994), particularly if it seeks to mask them instead of addressing them head on. The euro crisis marks 'the end of the Eurocrats' dream' (Chalmers et al., 2016a) of ever closer harmonization through technocratic integration. The failure to recognize the need for a different governance mix to tackle redistribution that does not rely on supranational centralization and limits supranational joint decision-making has further politicized the EU as a system of governance whose democratic credentials are not only questioned by populist politicians and citizens rallying against the socioeconomic effects of the crisis but by the constitutional courts of several Member States, which have reserved the right to review and, if necessary, nullify changes in the EU's governance mix (Fabbrini, 2014; Joerges, 2016). As a result, the willingness of Member States to comply with EU austerity rules and procedures is waning. Greece may ultimately have no choice since it is insolvent.[5] But the governments in Portugal, Spain and Ireland have demanded more flexibility for example in assessing Member States' budget and growth policies. So have France and Italy, which never fully complied with the EU's deficit rules in the first place. It remains to be seen to what extent the financial markets will instill budgetary discipline. The EU itself has only limited authority and capacity to enforce its laws and decisions. The reliance on Member State enforcement authorities allowed the EU to externalize compliance costs but turned '[n]ational administrations into both … vehicles for securing its goals and the central impediments to realising them' (Chalmers *et al.*, 2016b, p. 9). The massive redistributive effects of EU regulatory governance on the domestic level have exacerbated the divergence between EU decision-making and enforcement capacities.

Open non-compliance with supranational rules does not only render EU law ineffective; it fuels the politicization of the EU between compliant and non-compliant Member States (Genschel and Jachtenfuchs, 2016b, p. 50). While the former denounce the illegitimate interference with national democratic sovereignty, the latter emphasize that the EU is a community of law, in which *pacta sunt servanda*. The EU had been a latent cleavage in most of the Member States before the euro crisis (Hooghe and Marks, 2009). However, the politicization of EU policies and institutions has not only intensified since the EU has been confronted with a growing influx of migrants and refugees, many claim that it is also nationally segmented dividing EU citizens along national boundaries (de Wilde *et al.*, 2016; Genschel and Jachtenfuchs, 2016b, p. 49; Polyakova and Fligstein, 2016). We still lack the data to measure how Europeanized the politicization of migration actually is. I will argue below that the biggest challenge for EU governance is that politicization is dominated by populist positions advocating illiberal, nationalist ideas of Europe that do not principally oppose the EU but promote an EU that is different from the liberal modernization project that has been constitutive for European integration so far.

Populist forces have not been able to constrain supranational centralization of monetary policy and the building of a strong shadow of supranational hierarchy over intergovernmental co-ordination of economic policy. Member State governments successfully managed to depoliticize and shield decision-making against public scrutiny and silence public debates by avoiding treaty reforms, using secondary legislation (for example, Six Pack, Two Pack), establishing treaties outside the EU framework (for example, the Fiscal Compact), and delegating decision-making powers to non-majoritarian, technocratic supranational bodies (for example, Banking Union) (Genschel and Jachtenfuchs, 2016b, p. 54; Grande and Kriesi, 2016, p. 399; Howarth and Quaglia, 2013; Schimmelfennig, 2014, p. 336).[6] Yet, the successful attempts of Member State governments at managing the euro crisis by 'integration by stealth' (Majone, 2005) have come at a price to be paid once the next crisis hit. When controversial EU policies are isolated from political and electoral accountability, citizens, political parties and interest groups redirect their opposition and discontent with these policies towards the EU as a polity as such contesting its legitimacy to make such policies in the first place (Mair, 2007).

---

[5] See Featherstone's contribution to this volume.
[6] See Kriesi's contribution to this volume.

Figure 1: Identification with the EU (EU Average, 2004–15)

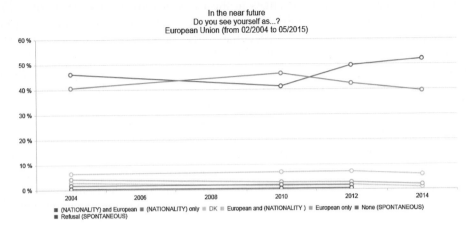

Source: Eurobarometer data base. Available online at: http://ec.europa.eu/COMMFrontOffice/
PublicOpinion/index.cfm/Chart/getChart/chartType/lineChart//themeKy/41/groupKy/206/
savFile/190. Last accessed: 24 February 2016.

Defying Redistribution

Given the seeming success of integration by stealth in mastering the euro crisis, the Commission and the Member States resorted to the same strategy to cope with the historical influx of migrants. Yet this time they were not able to use supranational centralization to depoliticize redistributive issues by masking them behind regulatory policies. This is not only because migration and refugee policies touch upon core issues of state sovereignty and national identity which are particularly likely to get politicized (Genschel and Jachtenfuchs, 2016b, p. 52). The failure of the EU to come to terms with the redistributive implications of the euro crisis have empowered euro-nationalist positions in many Member States to an extent that their governments are not only constrained in making commitments at the EU level for joint decisions but lack the political support to comply with them domestically.

In particular citizens hit worst by the euro crisis have felt that the EU has failed to provide supranational solutions to problems caused by European integration (Polyakova and Fligstein, 2016, p. 61). The EU not only stopped being part of the solution. For many citizens particularly in Southern Europe it has become part of the problem (Majone, 2014; Scharpf, 2015).[7] As a result European citizens have increasingly turned to their national governments to provide solutions and protect their interests. This has not, however, resulted in a nationalist backlash as claimed by Polyakova and Fligstein (2016). Most Europeans still believe that the crises require European rather than national solutions (Risse, 2014). Nor do survey data support a surge of nationalist identities, that is, growing numbers of Europeans who identify exclusively with their nation-state (see Figure 1). With the exception of summer 2010, the identification levels with the EU have increased or remained stable during the euro crisis, including in the debtor countries (Risse, 2014). This should not be too surprising since the literature has found no evidence for a strong

---

[7] See Kriesi's contribution to this volume.

impact of the EU and its institutions on the Europeanization of national identities (*cf.* Checkel and Katzenstein, 2009).

Whether the 'Europeanization of national identities is sufficient to sustain carefully crafted (re-)distributive policies on the European level' (Kuhn and Stoeckel, 2014; Risse, 2014, p. 1208;) is still debated in the literature (Polyakova and Fligstein, 2016; Streeck and Elsässer, 2016). In early 2016, a majority of 57 per cent of EU citizens continued to support EMU and more than two thirds of EU citizens still wanted a common European policy on migration.[8] I argue that the effectiveness and legitimacy of EU governance is undermined by the growing politicization of the EU that is not so much anti-Europe or nationally segmented but dominated by appeals to illiberal, nationalist ideas of Europe which are exclusionary and anti-Islam. Acknowledging that the politicization of the EU and European integration is a cyclical rather than a linear process and differs across (groups of) Member States,[9] political conflict over the EU has intensified in public media and party competition (de Wilde *et al.*, 2016; Grande and Kriesi, 2016; Statham and Trenz, 2014). With the euro crisis citizens have not only become more aware of and worried about EU governance, their attitudes have become more polarized rather than being neutral, ambivalent or indifferent towards the EU (de Wilde *et al.*, 2016). Arguably, the level of politicization is not as unprecedented as some scholars argue (de Wilde *et al.*, 2016; Grande and Kriesi, 2016; Risse, 2015a; Schimmelfennig, 2014, p. 322); nor does it necessarily have to constrain further integration as claimed by post-functionalists (Hooghe and Marks, 2009) or undermine the EU's output legitimacy by paralyzing EU decision-making (Scharpf, 2009, 2015). Replacing 'politics without policy' (Schmidt, 2006) with 'politics about polity' (de Wilde *et al.*, 2016, p. 14) in the Member States can strengthen democracy by enabling citizens to make better informed choices as well as by fostering diffuse support for and identification with the EU (Follesdal, 2015; Harrison and Bruter, 2015). Hence, politicization can both promote and impair the deepening and broadening of European integration depending on certain scope conditions (de Wilde *et al.*, 2016; Genschel and Jachtenfuchs, 2016b; Grande and Kriesi, 2016; Risse, 2014; Zürn, 2012).

The crisis of EU governance is not caused by politicization *per se* nor by its national segmentation. The eurozone crisis and the migration flows have been framed as European issues of common concern and have been debated in transnationally interconnected public spheres (Risse, 2014). However, the growing politicization of EU affairs is dominated by a peculiar type of 'politics about polity', which takes place along the 'cosmopolitan-nationalist' cleavage. This new cultural cleavage emerged as a consequence of globalization (Grande and Kriesi, 2016). Rather than being a 'pro- and anti-EU cleavage' (Grande and Kriesi, 2014, p. 191), it counters liberal ideas of Europe, embodied by the values of the enlightenment, such as human rights, democracy, the rule of law and the market economy, with nationalist and xenophobic ideas of Europe based on an essentialist interpretation of the continent's Christian heritage (Risse, 2010).[10] An emerging 'cleavage coalition' (Grande and Kriesi, 2014) of eurosceptic political forces on the radical right of the political spectrum have exploited the cosmopolitan-nationalist cleavage that pitches

---

[8] Available online at: http://ec.europa.eu/COMMFrontOffice/PublicOpinion/index.cfm/Chart/getChart/themeKy/29/groupKy/180. Last accessed: 29 February 2016.
[9] See Kriesi's contribution to this volume.
[10] See Kriesi's contribution to this volume.

the winners from globalization and European integration against its losers (Fligstein, 2009; Kriesi *et al.*, 2008). Using euro-nationalist frames and claims advocating an exclusionary and anti-globalist 'fortress Europe', the Front National in France, the United Kingdom Independence Party (UKIP), the Party for Freedom in the Netherlands, the Freedom Party Austria (FPÖ), the Sweden Democrats, the Danish People's Party, the Alternative for Germany (AfD), Hungary's Fidesz, and increasingly Poland's Law and Justice Party (PiS) have managed to mobilize the fears, the discontent and the frustrations of those Europeans who perceive themselves as the losers of European integration pressures more broadly speaking. This euro-nationalist mobilization feeding on the 'politics of fear' (Wodak, 2015) takes place in transnationally interconnected public spheres and has been increasingly successful in electoral politics because supporters of cosmopolitan Europe have sought to silence debates on EU affairs rather than defend liberal values (Grande and Kriesi, 2014).

As expected by post-functionalism, the dominance of euro-nationalist positions in the politicization of EU affairs has increasingly impaired an upgrading of the common European interest (Hooghe and Marks, 2009; Mair, 2007). The 'constraining dissensus', which had replaced the 'permissive consensus' in the past two decades, is increasingly turning into opposition not so much against Europe *per se* but against the liberal values, including solidarity, liberty and humanity, around which the European project has been constructed. Member States were able to circumvent domestic opposition in the euro crisis by supranational delegation. At the same time, however, their attempts at depoliticizing the management of the euro crisis empowered populist forces advocating an illiberal, nationalist Europe as a result of which governments are not only constrained but increasingly prevented from reaching common European solutions necessary to tackle the migration and refugee challenges rather than merely seeking to externalize them.

Interestingly, the governance failure of the EU in coming to terms with the migration flows is not only and maybe not even be primarily related to deadlock in decision-making. Between the end of September 2015 and end of April 2016, the Member States agreed on a whole set of joint measures aiming at 'sharing the responsibility' (Council of the European Union, 2015b) for the refugees who had already entered the territory of the EU on the one hand and managing future migration flows on the other.[11] Action was taken by supranational decision-making, drawing on the EU's legal framework for a common asylum and migration policy. Core measures include the Asylum, Migration and Integration Fund (AMIF) set up for the period 2014–20 with a total of €2.4 billion for the management of migration flows by the Member States, including registration, integration and return; the adoption of a common list of safe countries of origin; the real-location of 120,000 'persons in clear need of international protection'; the establishment of additional hot spots in Italy (five) and Greece (six); and the deployment of an additional 165 Frontex experts to Greece and Italy to help with the registration of refugees (Council of the European Union, 2015b; European Commission, 2015a, 2015b, 2015c, 2015d, 2015e; European Parliament/European Council, 2014, 2015). The three EU agencies operating on migration-related issues (Frontex, the European Asylum Support Office/EASO and Europol) also received a reinforcement of 120 new staff.[12]

---

[11] See Monar's contribution to this volume.
[12] Draft Amending Budget No. 7 to the General Budget 2015 (30 September 2015). Available online at: http://opac. oireachtas.ie/AWData/Library3/FINdoclaid061015_172233.pdf. Last accessed: 27 February 2016.

Regarding the stronger protection of the EU's external border, the rescue of refugees and the fight against human trafficking and smuggling, the EU created a new military operation (EUNAVFOR MED) in the Mediterranean Sea in May 2015, and tripled the budget for its already existing operations, Triton and Poseidon in December 2015 (Council of the European Union, 2015a; European Commission, 2015g).

To support third countries that host refugees or are located on major migration routes to the EU, the EU earmarked more than €2 billion within the framework of its European Neighbourhood Policy and Development Cooperation, respectively, including the launching of the Madad Trust Fund for Syria (€654 million) in December 2014 and the Emergency Trust Fund for Africa (€1.8 billion) in November 2015 (Directorate General for Developmental Cooperation of the Italian Ministry of Foreign Affairs and International Cooperation and the European Commission on Behalf of the European Union, 2014; European Commission, 2015f). To help Greece and other Member States struggling with the influx of refugees, in March 2016 the Commission unveiled plans for a refugee emergency fund of €700 million to be disbursed over the next three years. Rather than national governments, the assistance targets aid organizations on the ground, such as UN agencies and non-governmental networks.[13]

In October 2015 the EU agreed to assist transit countries in the Western Balkans, which are current or potential candidates for EU membership, with a plan containing no fewer than 17 points, aimed at building additional reception capacities along the Western Balkan route and stepping up national and co-ordinated efforts to return migrants not in need of international protection with the help of EU financial and technical assistance (Commission and the Heads of State or Government of Albania, 2015). One of the points also refers to an EU–Turkey Joint Action Plan to help Turkey host, register and re-admit migrants and control its borders with Greece and Bulgaria in return for financial assistance, visa liberalization, and the opening of new chapters in Turkey's accession process, which has stalled for almost 10 years. The original €1 billion for setting up six additional refugee camps in Turkey were stepped up to a €3 billion Facility for Refugees at the EU–Turkey summit on 29 November 2015, when the Joint Action Plan was activated (European Commission, 2015h).

These are only the most important measures, the vast majority of which the EU adopted in less than three months under EU primary and secondary law. The co-ordinated European response, however, has failed to reach a fair sharing of responsibility for 'register and process those in need of protection, and to swiftly return those who are not to their home countries or other safe third countries they have transited through' (European Commission, 2016a, p. 3). Maybe, over €10 billion and a series of legal measures are insufficient to accomplish these goals. However, we will probably never know because Member States have squarely refused to put most of them into practice.[14]

Denmark opted out of the AMIF while the other 27 have been slow in implementing projects. Some Member States amended their lists of safe countries of origin, adding for example the Western Balkan countries; others, however, still (at the time of writing) do not even foresee the notion of safe countries in their national legislation, despite the legal obligation under the Asylum Procedures Directive. By April 2016, only 615

[13] *EUobserver*, 2 March 2016.
[14] For the most recent assessment of the progress or lack thereof see European Commission (2016a).

refugees and asylum seekers had been relocated. Slovakia and Hungary challenged the reallocation scheme at the ECJ, Slovenia and Croatia refused to take any refugees and asylum seekers at all, the UK had no obligation because it opted out of Schengen but agreed to take 20,000 from Syria directly. So did Ireland, which offered to accept 20 on a voluntary basis. The remaining 19 Member States made available in total a mere 4,575 places (European Commission, 2016a, Annex 2). Only three of the additional 11 hot spots are operational: two in Italy and one in Greece at the time of writing (European Commission, 2016a, p. 8–9). As of April 2016 the Commission is still waiting for the Member States to send additional experts for Frontex and European Asylum Support Office (European Commission, 2016a, p. 9). Funding pledged by the Member States outside their obligation under the EU budget has not fully been met. Of the €654 million committed to the Madad Trust Fund for Syria, €594 million has come from the EU budget, but only €60.5 million from 19 Member States. The Trust Fund for Africa is approaching the €1.8 billion pledged, but funding from the Member States that is to match the EU's contribution amounts to under €82 million (European Commission, 2016a, p. 7).

Most of the 17 points on which the European Council and the Western Balkan countries had agreed in October 2015 were rendered obsolete by the meeting 'Managing Migration Together' of the Austrian government and nine Western Balkan countries in Vienna on 24 February 2016 to which neither Greece nor any representative of the EU were invited (Bundesministerium für Inneres der Republik Österreich, 2016). In the absence of a European solution, the governments agreed that national measures had to be taken to tighten border controls. Instead of creating reception capacities for 50,000 refugees along the Balkan route and providing temporary shelter, food, water and sanitation for people in need, Croatia, Slovenia and Serbia followed the example of Austria and introduced daily caps for people allowed to apply for asylum or transiting to other countries. Macedonia has effectively closed its border to Greece, only letting in a limited number of refugees from Syria and Iraq every day. This comes close to the 'Plan B' the four Visegrad Countries (V4) called for in their meeting with the heads of government of Macedonia and Bulgaria on 15 February 2016, shifting the EU's external border to Greece's with Macedonia and Bulgaria in the event of Greece not being able to control its border with Turkey.[15] The co-ordinated unilateralism of the Western Balkan candidate countries and some Member States, including Austria, the V4 and Bulgaria, is building up a humanitarian crisis in Greece, where thousands of migrants remain stranded.

Regarding the EU–Turkey Joint Action Plans, on which all hopes for a common European solution appeared to rest in spring 2016, neither the Member States nor Turkey had implemented any of their commitments during the first three months after the agreement had been reached (European Commission, 2016a, pp. 18–19). No money had been transferred to Turkey given the reluctance to tighten the control of its borders with Greece, take on criminal networks of traffickers and smugglers or re-admit migrants. To tackle the issue of non-implementation, the EU signed an agreement with Turkey on 18 March 2016 introducing a 'one in, one out' policy. In exchange for each 'irregular' migrant that Turkey takes back from Greece, the EU will resettle one Syrian refugee from Turkey. Moreover, the EU allotted another €3 billion to help Turkey provide temporary protection for Syrians. The up to 72,000 Syrians will be resettled according to a

---

[15] Available online at: https://euobserver.com/migration/132277. Last accessed: 27 February 2016.

reallocation scheme agreed by the EU for the 120,000 refugees. In the first two weeks of April, some 500 refugees were sent back from Greece to Turkey and an equivalent number of Syrians resettled in the EU. More than ten times the number of new refugees arrived on Greek islands during that time. Most of them immediately filed for asylum, so did many of the 50,000 already stranded in the country after the closure of the Western Balkan route. Greek authorities will have to process thousands of applications and provide the applicants, who have the right to appeal in court, with a place to stay. Whether the economically battered country, whose asylum system has been so deficient that the European Court of Human Rights ruled that EU Member States must not return people there, will be able to cope is an open question. Next to employing 4,000 additional judges, case officers, translators and border guards, Greece will have to establish the necessary administrative and legal procedures and turn its already ill-equipped hot spots (asylum processing facilities) into proper reception facilities and detention centres. The EU and the other Member States have promised to provide 2,300 experts and will foot most of the €300 million the operation is estimated to cost. Yet, the legal responsibility and administrative burden has been again placed on Greece instead of sharing equally among the Member States. Moreover, it remains to be seen how many of the Member States will be willing to accept Syrian refugees to be resettled from Turkey. Finally, it is unclear what will happen if the refugee flows return to their previous routes through Libya into Italy. While the number of migrants crossing the Aegean from Turkey into Greece has declined, those crossing to Italy have more than doubled since the EU–Turkey agreement entered into force. We will have to see whether European courts will accept Turkey as a safe country to which migrants can only be returned under EU law. Libya will certainly not be deemed safe. Austria has already announced tighter checks on its border with Italy in anticipation of a surge of migrants. And on 5 May 2016, the Commission agreed to extend select internal border controls introduced by Austria, Germany, Denmark and Sweden for another six months due to a lack of effective external controls by Greece.

Europe has never seemed further away from a joint solution. The non-compliance with commitments Member States have made over the past six months has resulted in the breakdown of the Common European Asylum System and total defiance of the Schengen rules. Greece and Italy as Member States of first entry stopped registering and accommodating migrants some time ago. They never really managed to return migrants not qualifying for asylum or refugee status to their country of origin (European Commission, 2016a, pp. 9–10). Returning migrants to Greece as a country of first entry (Dublin transfers) has not been possible since 2010 not least because the European Court of Human Rights and the European Court of Justice have raised concerns about the human rights situation (European Commission, 2016a, p. 10). This is one of the reasons why the German government in September 2015 unilaterally decided not to turn back any migrants at its border. Whether this decision encouraged even more migrants to make their way to Europe is an open question. However the use of daily caps to restrict access and the building of razor-wire fences to stop them altogether are violations of both EU Schengen rules and international law.

To be fair non-compliance with the Common European Asylum System had been a problem before the historical influx of migrants and refugees hit the EU. In 2015 the Commission took legal action against virtually all Member States for not applying the five directives the EU had adopted between 2001 and 2011 to provide minimum standards on asylum procedures, reception conditions for asylum seekers, temporary protection and recognition of refugees and the deportation of illegal migrants as well as the Dublin and Eurodac fingerprinting regulations (European Commission, 2016a, pp. 19–20).

In the face of blatant non-compliance with existing EU laws and decisions the Commission has pushed for supranational centralization. In addition to turning the EASO into the 'European Union Agency for Asylum' with new powers to monitor and evaluate Member States' policies, it called for the creation of an EU Border and Coast Guard Agency (EBCG) to replace the European Agency for the Management of Operational Cooperation at the External Borders of the Member States of the EU (Frontex) (European Commission, 2015i). It will monitor the EU's external borders to ensure that EU legal standards for border management are implemented. In order to strengthen its surveillance capacity, the staff of Frontex will be doubled and a rapid reserve pool of border guards put at its disposal. Most importantly, similar to the European Central Bank under the Single Supervisory Mechanism, the EBCG will be able to require Member States to take timely corrective action; in case of failure to do so, the EBCG would be empowered to intervene directly without the consent of the Member State concerned. Finally, a European Return Office, created within EBCG, will deploy European Return Intervention Teams to return illegally staying third-country nationals. The EU border guards could also enforce the mandatory and semi-automatic mechanism for redistributing asylum seekers and refugees, which the Commission suggested as part of the planned reform of the Dublin Regulation.[16] The proposed distribution key system is to be activated whenever a Member State faces a disproportionate number of asylum applications, such as more than 150 per cent of its capacity). It shall reflect the relative size, wealth and absorption capacities of Member States and shall be monitored by the EASO with the help of a computerised system. Member States refusing to accept asylum seekers shall have to pay a €250,000 'solidarity contribution' to the hosting Member State. The computerized reallocation is to depoliticize EU decisions on asylum. It would break with the core rule of the Dublin regime established in 1990 that the Member State through which asylum seekers and refugees first entered the EU have to handle their applications on behalf of all other Member States and have to accept those migrants that others forcibly return to them. If the so-called Dublin III Regulation is amended by a new regulation, national parliaments would not even have to give their consent (European Parliament/European Council, 2013). At the time of writing it is highly questionable, however, whether the Council will adopt the Commission's formal proposal for the supranational centralization of the Common Asylum System even if only a qualified majority is necessary. Slovakia and Hungary have already filed court cases against temporary reallocation quota. An automatic reallocation mechanism would fly right into the face of Hungarian Prime Minister Orbán and his referendum, where he plans to ask Hungarians whether they 'want the EU to be able, without the consent of the Parliament, to prescribe the mandatory settlement of non-Hungarian citizens into Hungary?'[17]

In sum, the migration flows have seen an even more intensified, one-sided politicization than the euro crisis where populist forces in the Member States, at times joining forces, appeal to illiberal, nationalist and exclusionary ideas of Europe. By justifying

---

[16] *EUobserver*, 4 May 2016.
[17] *EUobserver*, 24 February 2016.

national unilateralism as a response to the absence of, and to generate pressure for, a joint European approach, Germany, Austria and the V4 have so far reached exactly the opposite position or so it seems.

III. Stuck in Post-functionalist Governance: A Plea for Transnationalized Cosmopolitanism

Even those who see crisis as 'the natural ways of development for the EU' (Ágh, 2014, p. 5), acknowledge that the most recent series of crises has attained a new quality since it may challenge the very foundations of the project of European Integration. Unlike in the past, muddling through, experimenting with new modes of governance or extending the mix of supranational centralization and intergovernmental co-ordination in the shadow of supranational hierarchy do not provide the necessary escape from the EU's failure to manage the crises Europe has been facing.

I have argued that the governance crisis of the EU is not caused by the weakness of the 'Community of Europeans' (Risse, 2010) or the inability of Europeans to show enough 'solidarity among strangers' (Habermas, 2006) when it comes to redistribution. Nor is it the growing politicization of the EU and European integration *per se*. The failure to adopt and implement common European solutions to the crises is rooted in the political controversies over who should bear what costs, which are driven by populist politicians that advocate an illiberal, nationalist Europe, which is exclusionary and anti-Islam. Their growing electoral success not only impedes national governments from agreeing on workable policies at the EU level but also undermines their compliance with already adopted EU laws and agreements. The failure to come up with common European solutions further fuels euro-nationalist populism. This is the bad news. The good news is that there is a way out of this vicious circle. The lesson of the euro crisis is that trying to depoliticize EU redistributive issues and silencing public debates by isolating EU decisions from public scrutiny is not only futile but counter-productive. What the EU needs instead is not necessarily *more* transnationalized politicization either. Other Europeans are already present in national public spheres 'as both speakers and audiences' (Risse, 2014, p. 1211). They also use similar common European frames and claims across borders (Risse, 2014; *cf.* Risse, 2015a). The issue rather is that populist politicians, such as Geert Wilders, Marine Le Pen, Victor Orbán or Jarosław Kaczyński with their illiberal, nationalist ideas of Europe have dominated the transnational politicization of the EU and its crises policies. Liberal voices, which represent the opposite pole and appeal to the Europeanized national identities invoking solidarity, liberty and humanity to mobilize support for the institutionalization of redistribution at the EU level, have been far weaker, both among governments and societal actors.

National public spheres are sufficiently Europeanized to allow for transnational debates on the future of the EU and European integration (Risse, 2015a). Students of politicization have recommended focusing these debates on policy rather than constitutional and constitutive issues. Europeans should argue over what kind of policies they want from the EU, rather than over who they are, who belongs to them or how much power the EU should have (Copsey, 2015; Risse, 2015a). Substantive policy issues are also easier to square with the more traditional socioeconomic cleavages in the Member States (left–right) that are orthogonal to the cosmopolitan–nationalist cleavage (Kriesi *et al.*, 2008; Risse, 2010). However, constitutive and constitutional issues have become politicized (Grande and Kriesi, 2014; Statham and Trenz, 2014) and are here to stay. Attempts to ignore or reframe them as policy issues are not only likely to be futile but will fuel euroscepticism. Moreover, redistribution is not only about policy it is about who we are and who belongs to us. I would, therefore, argue that we need to strengthen cosmopolitanism as the opposite pole to nationalism in the polarized contestation of Europe (for a similar argument see Grande and Kriesi, 2014). The upgrading of the common European interest and the scaling up of solidarity among Europeans requires state and civil society actors that invoke liberal, inclusionary frames to mobilize support among the majority of Europeans with Europeanized identities. Inclusionary and redistributive policies require the transfer of more political authority to the EU level. However, rather than supranational centralization and supranational decision-making, EU redistributive policy-making should rely on intergovernmental coordination in not too strong a shadow of supranational hierarchy. The EU can set minimum standards and goals, which should be binding but leave the Member States sufficient discretion in exercising their political authority for economic and migration policy.[18] This governance mix has worked for policy adoption in the past – the issue is implementation and compliance, which can only be assured by more political and electoral accountability, not less. An EU-framework for redistribution requires the involvement of national parliaments since the European Parliament alone is unlikely to have sufficient democratic legitimacy to generate social acceptance of EU redistributive policy among Europeans. The EU has to start relying on the social acceptance of Europeans in the Member States to ensure compliance, rather than granting more supranational enforcement powers to the Commission, the European Court of Justice, the ECB or newly created supranational bodies, such as a European Border and Coast Guard or a European Union Agency of Asylum.

Finally, EU and national decision-makers should stop accommodating national governments and parties that appeal to illiberal, nationalist ideas of Europe as a fortress against globalization and Islam in referenda or electoral campaigns on membership, the allocation of political authority between the EU and the national level, or redistributive issues. If this means 'core Europe',[19] so be it. More likely, however, we should see more differentiated integration (Schimmelfennig and Winzen, 2014). Rather than excluding them altogether, Member States that prefer unilateralism over co-operation on and compliance with EU policies and institutions should be given the opportunity to exit parts of the EU, such as Schengen or the euro. This might render the EU more complex but it will certainly not be its ultimate demise. On the contrary, putting a price-tag on non-co-operation and non-compliance would help unite 'integrationist', 'protectionist' and 'minimalist' Member States in the 'Europeanist camp'[20] behind solidarity, liberty and humanity, which have made European integration the most successful peace project in history.

[18] For a similar argument see Nicolaidis and Watson (2016).
[19] Available online at: https://www.cducsu.de/upload/schaeublelamers94.pdf. Last accessed: 25 February 2016.
[20] See Kriesi's contribution to this volume.

References

Àgh, A. (2014) 'Decline of Democracy in East-Central Europe: The Last Decade as the Lost Decade in Democratization'. *Journal of Comparative Politics*, Vol. 7, No. 2, pp. 4–33.

Bayoumi, T. and Eichengreen, B. (1993) 'Shocking Aspects of European Monetary Unification'. In Torres, F. and Giavazzi, F. (eds) *Adjustment and Growth in the European Monetary Union* (Cambridge: Cambridge University Press), pp. 193–235.

Bickerton, C.J., Hodson, D. and Puetter, U. (2014) 'The New Intergovernmentalism: European Integration in the Post-Maastricht Era'. *JCMS*, Vol. 53, No. 4, pp. 703–22.

Bohle, D. and Greskovits, B. (2012) *Capitalist Diversity on Europe's Periphery* (Ithaca, NY: Cornell University Press).

Börzel, T.A. (2010) 'European Governance - Negotiation and Competition in the Shadow of Hierarchy'. *JCMS*, Vol. 48, No. 2, pp. 191–219.

Börzel, T.A. (2012) 'The European Union - A Unique Governance Mix?'. In Levi-Faur, D. (ed.) *Oxford Handbook of Governance* (Oxford: Oxford University Press), pp. 613–27.

Bundesministerium Für Inneres Der Republik Österreich (2016) 'Managing Migration Together: Declaration', Vienna, 24 February.

Chalmers, D., Jachtenfuchs, M. and Joerges, C. (eds) (2016a) *The End of the Eurocrats Dream. Adjusting to European Diversity* (Cambridge: Cambridge University Press).

Chalmers, D., Jachtenfuchs, M. and Joerges, C. (2016b) 'The Retransformation of Europe'. In Chalmers, D., Jachtenfuchs, M. and Joerges, C. (eds) *The End of the Eurocrats Dream. Adjusting to European Diversity* (Cambridge: Cambridge University Press), pp. 1–28.

Chang, M. (2016) 'The (Ever) Incomplete Story of Economic and Monetary Union'. *Journal of Contemporary European Research*, Vol. 12, No. 1, pp. 487–501.

Checkel, J.T. and Katzenstein, P.J. (eds) (2009) *European Identity* (Cambridge: Cambridge University Press).

Coen, D. and Héritier, A. (eds) (2006) *Refining Regulatory Regimes in Europe: The Creation and Correction of Markets* (Cheltenham: Edward Elgar).

Coen, D. and Thatcher, M. (2008) 'Network Governance and Multi-level Delegation: European Networks of Regulatory Agencies'. *Journal of Public Policy*, Vol. 28, No. 1, pp. 49–71.

Commission, P.O.T.E. and The Heads of State or Government of Albania, Bulgaria, Croatia, the Former Yugoslav Republic of Macedonia, Germany, Greece, Hungary, Romania, Serbia and Slovenia (2015) 'Leaders' Meeting on Refugee Flows along the Western Balkans Route: Leaders' Statement'. Available online at: http://ec.europa.eu/news/2015/docs/leader_statement_final.pdf'. Last accessed: 1 May 2016.

Copsey, N. (2015) *Rethinking the European Union* (Basingstoke: Palgrave).

Council of the European Union (2015a) 'Council Decision (CFSP) 2015/778 on a European Union Military Operation in the Southern Central Mediterranean (EUNAVFOR MED)', OJ L 122/31, 18 May.

Council of the European Union (2015b) 'Council Decision [...] Establishing Provisional Measures in the Area of International Protection for the Benefit of Italy and Greece', OJ L 248, 24.9.2015, p. 80–94', 2015/1601, 22 September.

De Rynk, S. (2016) 'Banking on a Union: The Politics of Changing Eurozone Banking Supervision'. *Journal of European Public Policy*, Vol. 23, No. 1, pp. 119–35.

De Wilde, P., Leupold, A. and Schmidtke, H. (2016) 'Introduction: The Differentiated Politicisation of European Governance'. *West European Politics*, Vol. 39, No. 1, pp. 3–22.

Directorate General for Developmental Cooperation of the Italian Ministry of Foreign Affairs and International Cooperation and the European Commission on Behalf of the European Union (2014) 'Agreement Establishing the European Union Regional Trust Fund in Response to the Syrian Crisis, 'The Madad Fund', and its Internal Rules'. Available online at: http://ec.europa.

eu/dgs/home-affairs/what-we-do/policies/european-agenda-migration/background-information/docs/2_factsheet_emergency_trust_fund_africa_en.pdf'. Last accessed: 1 May 2016.

Eberlein, B. and Grande, E. (2005) 'Reconstituting Political Authority in Europe: Transnational Regulatory Networks and the Informalization of Governance in the European Union'. In Grande, E. and Pauly, L.W. (eds) *Complex Sovereignty: On the Reconstitution of Political Authority in the 21st. Century* (Toronto: University of Toronto Press), pp. 146–67.

Eckert, S. (2011) 'European Regulatory Governance' In Levi-Faur, D. (ed.) *Handbook of the Politics of Regulation* (Cheltenham: Edward Elgar Publishing), pp. 513–24.

European Commission (2015a) 'Annex (4) to the Communication from the Commission to the European Parliament, the European Council and the Council Managing the Refugee Crisis: State of Play of the Implementation of the Priority Actions under the European Agenda on Migration', COM(2015) 510 final, 14 October.

European Commission (2015b) 'Annex (5) to the Communication from the Commission to the European Parliament, the European Council and the Council Managing the Refugee Crisis: State of Play of the Implementation of the Priority Actions under the European Agenda on Migration', COM(2015) 510 final, 14 October.

European Commission (2015c) 'Communication from the Commission to the European Parliament and the Council: Progress Report on the Implementation of Hotspots in Greece', COM (2015) 678 final, 15 December.

European Commission (2015d) 'Communication from the Commission to the European Parliament and the Council: Progress Report on the Implementation of the Hotspots in Italy', COM(2015) 679 final, 15 December.

European Commission (2015e) 'Draft Amending Budget No 7 to the General Budget 2015: Managing the Refugee Crisis: Immediate Budgetary Measures under the European Agenda on Migration', COM(2015) 485 final, 30 September.

European Commission (2015f) 'A European Agenda on Migration: A European Union Emergency Trust Fund for Africa'. Available online at: http://ec.europa.eu/dgs/home-affairs/what-we-do/policies/european-agenda-migration/background-information/docs/2_factsheet_emergency_trust_fund_africa_en.pdf'. Last accessed: 1 May 2016.

European Commission (2015g) 'European Commission - Fact Sheet: European Agenda on Migration: Securing Europe's External Borders', MEMO/15/6332, Strasbourg, 15 December.

European Commission (2015h) 'Managing the Refugee Crisis: EU-Turkey Joint Action Plan: Implementation Report'. Available online at: http://europa.eu/rapid/press-release_IP-16-268_en.htmhttp://europa.eu/rapid/press-release_IP-16-268_en.htm'. Last accessed: 1 May 2016.

European Commission (2015i) 'Securing Europe's External Borders: A European Border and Coast Guard'. Available online at: http://europa.eu/rapid/press-release_MEMO-15-6332_en.htm. Last accessed: 1 May 2016.

European Commission (2016a) 'Communication from the Commission to the European Parliament and the Council on the State of Play of Implementation of the Priority Actions under the European Agenda on Migration', COM(2016) 85 final.

European Commission (2016b) 'European Semester 2016: Country Reports'. Available online at: http://ec.europa.eu/news/2016/02/20160226_en.htm. Last accessed: 1 May 2016.

European Parliament/European Council (2013) 'Regulation No 604/2013 [...] Establishing the Criteria and Mechanisms for Determining the Member State Responsible for Examining an Application for International Protection Lodged in one of the Member States by a Third-country National or a Stateless Person', OJ L 180, 29.6.2013, p. 31–59', 604/2013, 26 June.

European Parliament/European Council (2014) 'Regulation (EU) No 516/2014 [...] 16 April 2014 establishing the Asylum, Migration and Integration Fund, amending Council Decision

2008/381/EC and repealing Decisions No 573/2007/EC and No 575/2007/EC of the European Parliament and of the Council and Council Decision 2007/435/EC', OJ L 150/168, 16 April.

European Parliament/European Council (2015) 'Regulation [...] establishing an EU common list of safe countries of origin for the purposes of Directive 2013/32/EU of the European Parliament and of the Council on Common Procedures for Granting and Withdrawing International Protection, and amending Directive 2013/32/EU', COM(2015) 452 final, 9 September.

Fabbrini, S. (2013) 'Intergovernmentalism and its Limits: Assessing the European Union's Answer to the Euro Crisis'. *Comparative Political Studies*, Vol. 46, No. 9, pp. 1003–29.

Fabbrini, F. (2014) 'The Euro-crisis and the Courts: Judicial Review and the Political Process in Comparative Perspective'. *Berkeley Journal of International Law*, Vol. 32, No. 1, pp. 64–123.

Fasone, C. (2013) 'European Economic Governance and Parliamentary Representation. What Place for the European Parliament?'. *European Law Journal*, Vol. 20, No. 2, pp. 164–85.

Finger, M. (2011) 'Towards an European Model of Regulatory Governance?' In Levi-Faur, D. (ed.), *Handbook on the Politics of Regulation* (Cheltenham: Edward Elgar Publishing), pp. 525–35.

Fligstein, N. (2009) 'Who Are the Europeans and How Does This Matter for Politics?'. In Checkel, J.T. and Katzenstein, P.J. (eds) *European Identity* (Cambridge: Cambridge University Press), pp. 132–66.

Follesdal, A. (2015) 'Democracy, Identity, and European Public Spheres'. In Risse, T. (ed.) *European Public Spheres: Politics is Back* (Cambridge: Cambridge University Press), pp. 247–62.

Genschel, P. and Jachtenfuchs, M. (2016a) 'Conflict-minimising Integration: How the EU Achieves Massive Integration Despite Massive Protest'. In Chalmers, D., Jachtenfuchs, M. and Joerges, C. (eds) *The End of the Eurocrats' Dream. Adjusting to European Diversity* (Cambridge: Cambridge University Press), pp. 166–89.

Genschel, P. and Jachtenfuchs, M. (2016b) 'More Integration, Less Federation: The European Integration of Core State Powers', *Journal of European Public Policy*, Vol. 23, No. 1, pp. 42--59.

George, S. and Bache, I. (2001) *Politics in the European Union* (Oxford: Oxford University Press).

Grande, E. and Kriesi, H. (2014) 'The Restructuring of Political Conflict in Europe and the Politicization of European Integration'. In Risse, T. (ed.) *European Public Spheres. Politics Is Back* (Cambridge: Cambridge University Press), pp. 190–223.

Grande, E. and Kriesi, H. (2016) 'Conclusions: The Postfunctionalists Were (Almost) Right'. In Hutter, S., Grande, E. and Kriesi, H. (eds) *Politicising Europe: Integration and Mass Politics* (Cambridge: Cambridge University Press), pp. 279–300.

Habermas, J. (2006) *The Divided West* (Cambridge: Polity Press).

Habermas, J. (2013) 'Democracy, Solidarity and the European Crisis'. *Social Europe: The Journal of the European Left*, Vol. 7, No. 2, pp. 18–25.

Harrison, S. and Bruter, M. (2015) 'Media and Identity: The Paradox of Legitimacy and the Making of European Citizens'. In Risse, T. (ed.) *European Public Spheres: Politics is Back* (Cambridge: Cambridge University), pp. 165–89.

Héritier, A. (1999) *Policy-Making and Diversity in Europe. Escape from Deadlock* (Cambridge: Cambridge University Press).

Héritier, A. and Lehmkuhl, D. (eds) (2008) 'The Shadow of Hierarchy and New Modes of Governance', *Journal of Public Policy*, Vol. 28 No. 1, pp. 1–17.

Hix, S. (2015) 'Democratizing a Macroeconomic Union in Europe'. In Cromme, O. and Hobolt, S. B. (eds) *Democratic Politics in a European Union under Stress* (Oxford: Oxford University Press), pp. 180–98.

Hodson, D. and Maher, I. (2001) 'The Open Method as a New Mode of Governance: The Case of Soft Economic Policy Co-ordination'. *JCMS*, Vol. 39, No. 4, pp. 719–46.

Hooghe, L. (ed.) (1996) *Cohesion Policy and European Integration: Building Multi-Level Governance* (Oxford: Oxford University Press).

Hooghe, L. and Marks, G. (2009) 'A Postfunctionalist Theory of European Integration: From Permissive Consensus to Constraining Dissensus'. *British Journal of Political Science*, Vol. 39, No. 1, pp. 1–23.

Howarth, D. and Quaglia, L. (2013) 'Banking Union as Holy Grail: Rebuilding the Single Market in Financial Services, Stabilizing Europe's Banks and "Completing" Economic and Monetary Union'. *JCMS*, Vol. 49, No. s1, pp. 119–41.

Joerges, C. (2016) 'Integration Through Law and the Crisis of Law in Europe's Emergency'. In Chalmers, D., Jachtenfuchs, M. and Joerges, C. (eds) *The End of the Eurocrats' Dream. Adjusting to European Diversity* (Cambridge: Cambridge University Press), pp. 299–338.

Junge, D., König, T. and Luig, B. (2015) 'Legislative Gridlock and Bureaucratic Politics in the European Union'. *British Journal of Political Science*, Vol. 45, No. 4, pp. 777–97.

König, T., Danwolf, T. and Luetgert, B. (2012) 'EU Legislative Activities and Domestic Politics'. In Brouard, S., Costa, O. and König, T. (eds) *The Europeanization of Domestic Legislatures. The Empirical Implications of Delors' Myth in Nine Countries* (New York: Springer), pp. 21–37.

Kriesi, H., Grande, E., Lachat, R., Dolezal, M., Bornschier, S. and Frey, T. (2008) *West European Politics in the Age of Globalization* (Cambridge: Cambridge University Press).

Kuhn, T. and Stoeckel, F. (2014) 'When European Integration Becomes Costly: The Euro Crisis as a Test of Public Support for European Economic Governance'. *Journal of European Public Policy*, Vol. 21, No. 4, pp. 624–41.

Lavenex, S. (2007) 'Mutual Recognition and the Monopoly of Force: Limits of the Single Market Analogy'. *Journal of European Public Policy*, Vol. 15, No. 4, pp. 762–79.

Levi-Faur, D. (1999) 'The Governance of Competition: The Interplay of Technology, Economics, and Politics in European Union Electricity and Telecom Regimes'. *Journal of Public Policy*, Vol. 19, No. 2, pp. 175–207.

Mair, P. (2007) 'Political Opposition and the European Union'. *Government and Opposition*, Vol. 42, No. 1, pp. 1–17.

Majone, G. (1994) 'The Rise of the Regulatory State in Europe'. *West European Politics*, Vol. 17, No. 3, pp. 77–101.

Majone, G. (2005) *Dilemmas of European Integration: The Ambiguities and Pitfalls of Integration by Stealth* (Oxford: Oxford University Press).

Majone, G. (2014) *Rethinking the Union of Europe Post-Crisis: Has Integration Gone Too Far?* (Cambridge: Cambridge University Press).

Molina, O. and Rhodes, M. (2008) 'The Political Economy of Adjustment in Mixed Market Economies: A Study of Spain and Italy'. In Hancké, B., Rhodes, M. and Thatcher, M. (eds) *Beyond Varieties of Capitalism: Conflict, Contradiction and Complementarities in the European Economy* (Oxford: Oxford University Press), pp. 223–52.

Nicolaidis, C. and Watson, M. (2016) 'Sharing the Eurocrats' Dream: A Democratic Approach to EMU Governance in the Post-crisis Era'. In Chalmers, D., Jachtenfuchs, M. and Joerges, C. (eds) *The End of the Eurocrats' Dream. Adjusting to European Diversity* (Cambridge: Cambridge University Press), pp. 50–77.

Nicolaidis, K. and Shaffer, G. (2005) 'Transnational Mutual Recognition Regimes: Governance without Global Government'. *Law and Contemporary Problems*, Vol. 68, No. 3–4, pp. 263–318.

Nugent, N. and Rhinard, M. (2016) 'Is the European Commission Really in Decline?'. *JCMS*. DOI:10.1111/jcms.12358.

Polyakova, A. and Fligstein, N. (2016) 'Is European Integration Causing Europe to Become More Nationalist? Evidence from the 2007–9 Financial Crisis'. *Journal of European Public Policy*, Vol. 23, No. 1, pp. 60–83.

Puetter, U. (2014) *The European Council and the Council. New Intergovernmentalism and Institutional Change* (Oxford: Oxford University Press).

Quaglia, L. (2010) *Governing Financial Services in the European Union* (London: Routledge).

Risse, T. (2010) *A Community of Europeans? Transnational Identities and Public Spheres* (Itahaca, NY: Cornell University Press).

Risse, T. (2014) 'No Demos? Identities and Public Spheres in the Euro Crisis'. *JCMS*, Vol. 52, No. 6, pp. 1207–15.

Risse, T. (2015a) 'European Public Spheres, the Politicization of EU Affairs, and Its Consequences'. In Risse, T. (ed.) *European Public Spheres. Politics Is Back* (Cambridge: Cambridge University Press), pp. 141–64.

Risse, T. (ed.) (2015b) *European Public Spheres. Politics Is Back* (Cambridge: Cambridge University Press).

Savage, J.D. and Verdun, A. (2016) 'Strengthening the European Commission's Budgetary and Economic Surveillance Capacity since Greece and the Euro Area Crisis: A Study of Five Directorates-General'. *Journal of European Public Policy*, Vol. 23, No. 1, pp. 101–18.

Scharpf, F.W. (1997) *Games Real Actors Play. Actor-Centered Institutionalism in Policy Research* (Boulder, CO: Westview Press).

Scharpf, F.W. (2009) 'Legitimacy in the Multilevel European Polity'. *European Political Science Review*, Vol. 1, No. 2, pp. 173–204.

Scharpf, F. W. (2006) 'The Joint-Decision Trap Revisited'. *JCMS*, Vol. 44, No. 4, pp. 845–64.

Scharpf, F.W. (2015) 'Political Legitimacy in a Non-optimal Currency Area'. In Cromme, O. and Hobolt, S.B. (eds) *Democratic Politics in a European Union under Stress* (Oxford: Oxford University Press), pp. 19–47.

Scharpf, F.W. (2016) 'The Costs of Non-Disintegration. The Case of EMU'. In Chalmers, D., Jachtenfuchs, M. and Joerges, C. (eds) *The End of the Eurocrats Dream. Adjusting to European Diversity* (Cambridge: Cambridge University Press), pp. 29–49.

Schimmelfennig, F. (2014) 'European Integration in the Euro Crisis. The Limits of Postfunctionalism'. *Journal of European Integration*, Vol. 36, No. 3, pp. 321–37.

Schimmelfennig, F. and Winzen, T. (2014) 'Instrumental and Constitutional Differentiation in the European Union'. *JCMS*, Vol. 52, No. 2, pp. 354–70.

Schmidt, S.K. (2007) 'Mutual Recognition as a New Mode of Governance'. *Journal of European Public Policy*, Vol. 14, No. 5, pp. 667–81.

Schmidt, V.A. (2006) *Democracy in Europe. The EU and National Polities* (Oxford: Oxford University Press).

Statham, P. and Trenz, H.-J. (2014) *The Politicization of Europe: Contesting the Constitution in the Mass Media* (London: Routledge).

Streeck, W. and Elsässer, L. (2016) 'Monetary Disunion: The Domestic Politics of Euroland'. *Journal of European Public Policy*, Vol. 23, No. 1, pp. 1–24.

Sun, J.-M. and Pelkmans, J. (1995) 'Regulatory Competition in the Single Market'. *JCMS*, Vol. 33, No. 1, pp. 67–89.

Thielemann, E.R. and El-Enany, N. (2010) 'Refugee Protection as a Collective Action Problem: Is the EU Shirking Its Responsibilities?'. *European Security*, Vol. 19, No. 2, pp. 209–29.

Tömmel, I. (2016) 'EU Governance of Governance: Political Steering in a Non-Hierarchical Multilevel System'. *Journal of Contemporary European Research*, Vol. 12, No. 1, pp. 406–23.

Van Ark, B., Chen, V., Colijn, B., Jaeger, K., Overmeer, W. and Timmer, M. (2013) *Recent Changes in Europe's Competitive Landscape and Medium-Term Perspectives: How the Sources of Demand and Supply Are Shaping Up In European Economy* (Brussels: European Commission).

Wilson, J.Q. (1980) 'The Politics of Regulation'. In Wilson, J.Q. (ed.) *The Politics of Regulation* (New York: Basic Books), pp. 357–94.

Wodak, R. (2015) *The Politics of Fear. What Right-Wing Populist Discourses Mean* (London: Sage).

Zürn, M. (2012) 'The Politicization of World Politics and Its Effects. Eight Propositions'. *European Political Science Review*, Vol. 61, No. 1, pp. 47–71.

JCMS 2016 Volume 54. Annual Review pp. 32–47　　　　　　　　　DOI: 10.1111/jcms.12406

The Politicization of European Integration

HANSPETER KRIESI
Department of Social and Political Science, European University Institute

Introduction

The European Union has had to deal with a series of crises in the past, but currently, it faces an exceptional accumulation of tensions triggered by the eurozone crisis, the refugee crisis, Islamic terrorism, the imperial aspirations of Putin and Brexit ambitions. Does the politicization of European integration increase under these conditions? And who are the possible drivers of a process of politicization of European integration?

In this contribution I argue the politicization of European integration is not only time-dependent, but also embedded in national political conflict structures which vary systematically between three European regions: the Northwest, the South and the East of Europe. In order to understand the impact of contemporary crisis conditions on the politicization of European integration, I argue we have to take into account how these crisis conditions are linked to the underlying region-specific national conflict structures. Given these different national conflict structures, and given the different types of crises experienced by the populations of the three regions, the type of politicization of European integration is likely to be very different from one region to the other.

As has been pointed out by Hooghe and Marks (2009), there is nothing inevitable about the politicization of European integration. It takes *partisan* entrepreneurs who are capable and willing to mobilize the latent structural potentials for euroscepticism to become politically and electorally relevant. If an issue is not debated in public and is not articulated by political organizations it can only be politicized to a limited extent (Hutter and Grande, 2014). Moreover, *national* politics are still the crucial arena for the politicization of European integration. As a result of the weakness of the partisan channel of representation at the European level, partisan entrepreneurs still focus on national politics and they will most likely continue to do so for quite some time to come.

Within national party competition it is the eurosceptics who have turned out to be the main drivers of the politicization of European integration (Grande and Kriesi, 2016; Hooghe and Marks, 2009), given that the pro-Europeans have done everything to depoliticize the European integration process. The repertory of the pro-Europeans' depoliticization strategies has been vast (see de Wilde and Zürn, 2012; Genschel and Jachtenfuchs, 2013; Schimmelfennig, 2014). It has included techniques such as de-emphasizing the issue of European integration in national elections (as in the 2013 German elections), sidestepping treaty changes in order to avoid referendums (as in the case of the Fiscal Compact), delegation to so-called 'non-majoritarian', technocratic supranational institutions (such as the European Central Bank (ECB), the European Court of Justice (ECJ) or the Commission), euro-compatible government formation (excluding eurosceptics from government coalitions), adopting incomplete contracts (agreements which either cover up conflicts by vague wording or defer them to later stages of the political process), and, most generally, integration by regulation (the EU as a 'regulatory state', which protects the illusion of sovereignty of the Member States). Depoliticizing the integration process has served the pro-Europeans well as long as they got away with it. In this contribution I suggest that the eurosceptics are likely to be increasingly successful in calling the bluff of the pro-Europeans, but that, depending on the part of Europe, they will be of a different ilk.

I shall be painting with a very broad brush, disregarding details in order to draw attention to what I consider to be the larger picture. Given the patchy character of pertinent empirical results, there is necessarily a considerable element of speculation. My discussion is divided into five parts. First, I present the current state of politicization of European integration. Next, I discuss the preconditions of politicization at the level of the Member States of the three regions – Northwestern (NWE), Southern (SE) and Central and Eastern Europe (CEE). I first discuss the latent conflict structures that condition the region-specific party competition before I turn to the contemporary region-specific context conditions that are likely to precipitate the mobilization of these latent structures. Due to limitations of space, I only briefly touch on institutional conditions, which does not mean that they do not have an important role to play in the full account of the politicization of European integration. In the last two sections, I draw the broader implications of the politicization of European integration and conclude.

I. The Current State of Politicization of European Integration

According to Grande and Hutter (2016, p. 7), 'politicization can be defined as an expansion of the scope of conflict within the political system'. In the literature, a consensus is emerging regarding the components of what we mean by the term of 'politicization' (de Wilde et al., 2016, p. 4). According to this consensus we should distinguish between three conceptual dimensions of politicization: issue salience (visibility), actor expansion (range) and actor polarization (intensity and direction). Fully politicized issues are politicized in all three dimensions.

The politicization of European integration has been characterized by 'a patchwork of politicizing moments' rather than a uniform trend towards ever more politicization (Hutter et al., 2016). Thus, in his study of the public debates on European integration in six NWE countries (Austria, France, Germany, the Netherlands, Switzerland and the UK) during the early 2000s, Höglinger (2016) found that the public debate on European integration intensifies during extraordinary, but predictable institutional and policy-related events at the European level (such as European summits) and the national level (such as national referendums on the issue). These events are initiated and scheduled by either the EU or national governments and public authorities who have largely succeeded so far in keeping them under control. Höglinger concludes that politicization of European integration remained limited, given the conflict-tempering effect of the multi-layered system of representation in the EU.

Hutter et al. (2016) have also analyzed the politicization of European integration in NWE, but over a longer period of time (from the 1970s up to 2012), based on three 'windows of observation': public debates on integration steps, national election campaigns and Europeanized protest events. Overall, this broader study confirms that there is 'something like politicization' (Schmitter, 1969, p. 211), but politicization has been neither systematically increasing over time, nor has it been sustained at a certain elevated level, which serves to disconfirm de Wilde and Zürn's (2012) 'authority transfer' hypothesis. Politicization is certainly not a post-Maastricht phenomenon as some have maintained (see de Wilde and Zürn, 2012; Hooghe and Marks, 2009), but has been flaring up and temporarily reaching impressive levels at specific moments in time before and after Maastricht. Moreover, politicization has been rather moderate. There has been virtually no mobilization in the streets. In the protest arena, not only has the level of politicization been consistently low, it even declined in the 2000s. Grande and Kriesi (2016) use the term 'punctuated politicization' to characterize the overall pattern of politicization, but maybe 'intermittent politicization' would be a more appropriate term.

Confirming Höglinger's results, Hutter et al. (2016) find that it is 'integration steps' which constitute the perfect occasions for the politicization of the European integration process. Unlike national elections they directly focus attention on specific aspects of European integration – either transfers of authority and changes in the institutional framework of the EU or the admission of new Member States. The so-called northern enlargement in the early 1970s, the Maastricht Treaty, the failed Constitutional Treaty and the Lisbon Treaty stand out as cases with particularly intense public debates, as do the accession debates in Austria, Sweden and Switzerland (the accession to the European Economic Space (EES) and the Bilateral Treaties). National referendums serve as catalysts of politicization in such debates, because they are not easily controlled by the authorities. Referendums provide dissenting voices with a public forum they usually lack. The risks of referendums for the public authorities are especially large in countries (such as the Netherlands or France) where they do not have much experience with such institutions.

To the institutionalized integration steps we should add the European crises which equally constitute exceptional moments of politicization. The euro crisis certainly is a case in point. However, as Kriesi and Grande (2016) show, the results are mixed with respect to the overall politicization of the debate about the euro crisis: on the one hand, this debate has been exceptionally salient and has contributed to the increased visibility of Europe in the politics of the Member States. On the other hand, the euro crisis debate was confined to national and supranational executive actors and has not accelerated the transfer of European politics into 'mass politics', at least not in the six NWE countries (Austria, France, Germany, Sweden, Switzerland and UK) in question. Rather, it has mainly taken place in the intergovernmental channel and has been dominated by supranational executive agencies and national governments. This is why it did not trigger an unprecedented level of politicization of European integration.

With respect to national elections Hutter et al. (2016) find an overall increase of politicization of the European integration process over the last four decades, but the most important result in this respect is the large variation from one country to the other. There is no uniform politicization process in the electoral arena developing at more or less the same time and with similar intensity across all countries. Instead, conflicts over the country's own EU membership, which occurred at different moments in time, spilled over into the electoral arena and led to an intense politicization of the integration process. Such conflicts have been especially intense in Britain and Switzerland. Membership conflicts concerning the accession of third countries also spilled over into national elections, as is exemplified by the conflicts over Turkey's EU membership in Austrian, German and

French elections. The country-specific differences found by this study are, however, limited by the fact that they are all located in NWE.

To appreciate the full range of country-specific variations with respect to the role of European integration in national elections, we should, of course, take into account the experience of countries from all parts of Europe. For this purpose, we can rely on Haughton's (2014) overview of the impact of the EU on roughly 60 national parliamentary elections in EU Member States during the period from May 2004 to December 2012. Reducing his ordinal impact measure to a dichotomy of 'low' and 'medium-high' impact, we observe that the bulk of these elections fall into the 'low' category (82 per cent). However, there are significant differences between the three regions: while the EU has a 'medium-high' impact in only 8 and 14 per cent of the elections, respectively in CEE and NWE countries, the corresponding share is as high as 40 per cent in SE. Moreover, it is striking that all the elections with a medium-high impact fall into the more recent 'crisis' period, not only in the South, but also in the other two parts of Europe. In SE, three Greek elections (2009, 2012I+II), as well as the Portuguese (2011), Spanish (2011) and Cypriot (2011) crisis elections are characterized by a considerable EU impact. Outside of the South, there are three recent high impact elections in NWE (Finland 2011, Ireland 2011 and the Netherlands 2012), and two in CEE (Bulgaria 2009 and Lithuania 2012).

European elections have been famously said to be secondary elections and mainly about domestic issues. In his analysis of the 1994 and 2004 European elections in Austria, France, Germany and the UK, Dolezal (2012) found, however, that the salience of European issues increased from 1994 to 2004, reaching more than 50 per cent of all the issues debated in the European Parliament (EP) election campaigns in three out of the four countries (Germany being the exception). However, the bulk of these European issues were related to constitutional matters, that is to issues for which the EP has only a limited role to play. Moreover, as Dolezal also documents, these issues mainly set the eurosceptics against the mainstream parties.

The most recent European elections have further substantiated these earlier results. While the 'Spitzenkandidaten' largely went unnoticed (Hobolt, 2015, p. 10), the context of the eurozone crisis changed the European quality of these elections and turned them into 'the most "European" electoral contests to date' (Hobolt, 2015, p. 19). The clearest indication that voters were more concerned about European issues was the surge in popularity for political parties that proposed radical reform of, or even exit from, the EU. What is most striking from Hobolt's results is that protest vote factors were secondary, while ideological factors (factors linked to euroscepticism) dominated the vote and that the impact of these factors varied across European regions. It was in Western Europe (Hobolt does not distinguish between North and South) that the ideological factors were particularly important, while in CEE the explanatory power of all of the variables turned out to be quite weak in Hobolt's study.

What distinguishes the South from the North in Western Europe is the type of eurosceptic party that proved to be successful. Table 1 presents the vote shares of left and right eurosceptic parties from the three regions in the 2014 EP elections. As we can easily see, it is the eurosceptics from the right who dominated in NWE, while the eurosceptics from the left dominated in SE. In the CEE countries, the eurosceptics from the right were also more important than those from the left – especially in Poland and in Hungary. The table presents two sets of figures – one from Hobolt (2015) and one from

Table 1: Vote Shares of Left and Right Eurosceptic Parties from the Three Regions of Europe in the 2014 EP Elections (%)

Region	Left		Right		N
	Hobolt (2015)	Hernandez and Kriesi (2016b)	Hobolt (2015)	Hernandez and Kriesi (2016b)	
NWE	5.6	4.0	17.4	14.7	11
SE	17.1	17.3	7.6	4.1	6
CEE	2.0	1.1	21.4	13.8	10
CEE (without HUN and PL)	2.5	1.4	13.2	3.6	8
Average	6.8	5.9	16.7	12.0	27

Hernandez and Kriesi (2016b). The latter figures differ from the former to the extent that they include only strongly eurosceptic parties. Restricting euroscepticism to the hard core leads to the conclusion that, with the exception of Hungary and Poland, eurosceptics hardly played any role at all in CEE countries.

These results provide strong confirmation for the point stressed by de Wilde *et al.* (2016) that politicization of European integration has not only been varying over time, but that it has also been highly differentiated across countries. In order to understand this differentiation in space, I suggest, we need to take into account the development of national conflict structures into which the politicization of European integration is embedded. Doing so requires that we take a longer-term perspective.

II. The National Political Conflict Structures

In his *Reflections on the Revolution in Europe*, Ralf Dahrendorf (1990, pp. 79–93) distinguished between three speeds of the political transition to democracy: the hour of the lawyer, the hour of the politicians and the hour of the citizens. He suggested that the hour of the lawyer, that is, the formal process of constitutional reform, takes at least six months. After the establishment of the constitution, normal politics takes over and sets in motion political and economic reforms. This is the hour of the politicians, which takes at least six years before a general sense that things are moving up is likely to spread. The third speed refers to the citizens, that is to 'the social foundations which transform the constitution and the economy from fair-weather into all-weather institutions which can withstand the storms generated within and without, and 60 years are barely enough to lay these foundations' (p. 93). I think Dahrendorf's three hours are applicable not just to the democratization of CEE, but to processes of political development more generally. In other words to understand the politicization of European integration we need to keep in mind the important transformations of the social foundations that have been giving rise to the national conflict structures in the different parts of Europe over the last 60 years. While acknowledging that the national conflict structures differ from one country to the other, I suggest it still makes sense to reduce the complexity by insisting on the respective differences between three large European regions: the Northwest, the South and the East.

In NWE two social transformations have been highly consequential for political conflict: a first set of structural transformations that were endogenous to the NWE nation-states – processes of increasing affluence, secularization, deindustrialization, tertiarization, expansion of tertiary education, feminization of the work force and occupational upgrading – together attenuated traditional cleavages of religion and class and brought about a value change – a 'silent revolution' (Inglehart, 1990). This change was driven by the expanding new middle class, or more precisely, by the socio-cultural segment of the new middle class that articulated its demands in the so-called 'new social movements' (see, for example, Kriesi, 1989). These new social movements – environmental, peace, solidarity, squatters', women's and 'rights' movements' of different kinds – stood at the origin of the rise of the New Left, of 'new politics', of the Green parties and of the transformation of the West European social-democratic parties which in the process have become middle-class parties in almost all countries of NWE (Gingrich and Häusermann, 2015; Häusermann, 2015).

Second, structural transformations that were exogenous to the West-European nation-states – processes of 'globalization', 'denationalization' (Zürn, 2001), opening up of national borders in economic, political and cultural terms (Kriesi et al., 2008, 2012) – have brought about an increasing awareness of the fragility of the sovereignty of the nation-state and of national culture more generally. European integration has been part and parcel of this 'denationalization' process (Kriesi, 2009, p. 222), but this process cannot be reduced to European integration. In addition, immigration from culturally ever more distant shores has been another important element of this overall process. Economic pressure on certain segments of the workforce (especially low-skilled workers) who have become doubly squeezed by competition from abroad (in the form of offshoring of their jobs) and at home (in the form of competition from immigrants) (Dancygier and Walter, 2015) is also part of this process. As we have argued (Kriesi et al., 2008, 2012), these processes created a heterogeneous set of 'globalization losers' who have been mobilized mainly by the radical populist right (or the New Right), which, in the process, has become the party of the working class in many West European countries (Oesch, 2013). Some of the parties of the New Right have newly emerged (such as the French Front National, the Dutch Freedom Party (PVV), or the Sweden Democrats (SD)), while others (such as the Austrian FPÖ, the Swiss SVP, or the True Finns) are actually transformed (liberal-) conservative mainstream parties that have existed for a long time.

From the point of view of the politicization of European integration, it is crucial that these social transformations, and the double wave of political mobilization they gave rise to, have been much weaker in the other two regions of Europe. In SE, Greece, Portugal and Spain remained under authoritarian regimes until the mid-1970s and the cultural revolution of the late 1960s/early 1970s simply did not take place in these countries. Accordingly, the mobilization by new social movements was comparatively weak or non-existent in SE,[1] and there was no New Left at the time. When these countries emerged from their authoritarian regimes, traditional cleavages of religion, class and region still prevailed and prevented the establishment of a New Left or a New Right comparable to those in NWE. To a certain extent the same applies to Italy even if the cultural revolution of the late 1960s had left a stronger imprint on this country. Across SE, class cleavages in particular remained stronger than in NWE because of the divided left and the competition between its two components – the (more radical) Communists and the (more moderate)

---

[1] There are comparative data for Spain in the 1980s, which show the weakness of these movements (Koopmans, 1996, pp. 38–40).

Socialists, which left little room for the autonomous mobilization by the new social movements. The New Left developed in the shadow of the 'old left' and remained weak. Accordingly, Green parties have been equally weak in SE and the socialists have assumed fewer of the characteristics of the New Left than they did in NWE.

Not just the class cleavage, but also the religious cleavage remained comparatively strong and aligned with the class antagonism: a secular and rather radical left opposed a conservative and religious right. Moreover, the Centre-Periphery cleavage also kept political importance – at least in Spain and Italy, where strong regionalist movements continued to mobilize in Catalonia and the Basque country as well as in Northern Italy. Given the legacy of authoritarian/fascist regimes, and given the fact that they have mainly been emigration countries, the radical populist right also remained weak or non-existent in SE. Where it did develop, as in the Lega Nord in Italy, it was linked to the regionalist cause. Moreover, euroscepticism, to the extent that it existed at all, was mainly located in the old Communist left (Verney, 2011).

In CEE it is less the impact of traditional cleavages than the absence of clear-cut cleavages that has characterized the political conflict structure. It has been argued that the Communist inheritance left a fragmented society and an unstructured pattern of political conflict. This thesis has been contradicted by subsequent empirical analyses which showed that CEE countries were characterized by social cleavages of ethnicity (especially in the Baltic countries), religion (especially in Poland), region and class, as well as age and education (Evans, 2006). But the multiplication of conflicts does not yet make for a clear-cut cleavage structure. Indeed, as Casal Bértoa (2014) has argued, cross-cutting cleavages constrain party system institutionalization, too. If measured against the four criteria of institutionalization that have been introduced by Mainwaring and Scully (1995), the party systems in CEE still appear to be poorly institutionalized. They have not (yet) developed stable roots in society. The concept of cleavages structuring the party system barely applies to them. They are hardly considered legitimate by the citizens of their countries, their organizations tend to be unstable and they are characterized by an extraordinarily high level of volatility (Powell and Tucker, 2013; Rohrschneider and Whitefield, 2012).

Coman's (2015) recent study suggests that the main dimension of conflict in CEE countries is, indeed, strongly connected to cultural issues. However, given the absence of the cultural revolution of the late 1960s/early 1970s in these countries and given the absence of immigration and the generally low salience of European integration after accession (Haughton, 2014), these are not the cultural issues that have come to structure the party systems in NWE. The common denominator of the cultural issues mobilizing the conservative side of the CEE electorates seems to be rather a defensive nationalism asserting itself against internal enemies (such as ethnic minorities, including Roma and Jews) and external ones (such as foreign corporations colonizing the national economy). This defensive nationalism is fuelled by the existence of contested national borders (for example, national diasporas in neighbouring countries), by the unassimilated legacy of World War II and the Communist regimes, and by 'more deep-seated vulnerabilities' (Haughton, 2014, p. 80). Given the lack of institutionalization of the party systems, parties in CEE countries have a greater latitude in the mobilization of structural conflicts (see Sitter, 2002), and the strategies of the parties on the right prove to be decisive for the mobilization of this defensive nationalism, as is exemplified by Orbán's Fidesz in Hungary (Enyedi, 2005) and Kacziński's Law and Justice (PiS) in Poland.

Figure 1: Assessment of Current National Economy (Share of Citizens Assessing the State of the National Economy as Rather/Very Good), by Region.

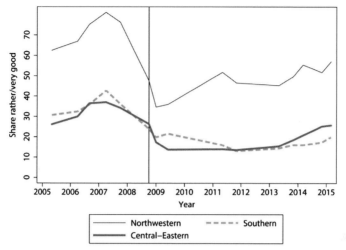

Source: Eurobarometer, on average two measures (spring and autumn) per year.
Note: The vertical line indicates the fall of Lehman Brothers in September 2008.

III. The Contemporary European Context Conditions: The Assessment of the Economic and Political Crises

The accumulation of crises in the contemporary European context is likely to precipitate the mobilization of the latent political potentials which I have sketched in the previous section. In this respect, it is important to distinguish between two types of crisis: an economic crisis and a political crisis of representation. I would like to show that the three regions of Europe are quite distinct with respect to their experience of these two types of crises. This demonstration is based on very simple aggregate indicators. For the *economic* crisis, I use an attitudinal indicator that refers to the individuals' assessment of the current situation of their national economy. Figure 1 presents the development of this indicator (the share of people who consider the situation as rather/very good) over time for the three regions of Europe. The vertical line in the figure indicates the beginning of the Great Recession in autumn 2008.

Three points become quite apparent from Figure 1. First, people's assessments of the state of the economy are generally much more optimistic in NWE than in the other two regions, where they have been equally pessimistic all along. It is well known that SE and CEE have been hit much harder by the Great Recession than NWE, but we may have been less aware of the considerable economic pessimism that already prevailed in the former regions some time before the onset of the Great Recession. Second, in all three regions the positive assessments peaked in spring 2007, before the collapse of Lehman Brothers. In the autumn 2008, the positive assessments dropped precipitously to much lower levels across the board.[2] Third, while the assessments in NWE began to recover in late 2009,

---

[2] Note that there are, unfortunately, no figures for spring 2008, which enhances the impression that the precipitous decline had already set in before the autumn of 2008. Given the much higher pre-crisis level in NWE, the drop was especially spectacular in NWE.

deep pessimism continued to characterize the overall economic sentiment in the other two regions. Only more recently have the assessments also picked up a little in CEE countries. Note, however, that even in NWE, the overall sentiments have not reached the levels of optimism that were characteristic for this region before the crisis.

For the general *political* context conditions, I rely on two aggregate attitudinal indicators. The first one refers to the overall assessment of the quality of democracy at the national level based on the widely used question 'How satisfied are you with the way democracy works in your country?' Despite its wide use among political scientists, this indicator is not uncontroversial, but for the assessment of the quality of liberal democracy in particular it provides a relatively reliable measure (Ferrin, 2016). The second indicator measures trust in the European Parliament as a proxy for the general assessment of support of the EU. Figure 2 presents the development of these two indicators over time for the three regions of Europe. The vertical lines in the two subgraphs of this figure again indicate the beginning of the Great Recession in the autumn of 2008.

The first part of Figure 2 documents the dramatic regional differences with regard to the development of assessments of the quality of democracy at the domestic level: in NWE, large majorities of the citizens have been fairly/very satisfied with the way democracy works in their country since the 1990s. The economic crisis has not changed the overall satisfaction in these countries. Democratic satisfaction has remained at the high level it had reached by the time of the fall of Lehman Brothers. By contrast the level of satisfaction has been much lower in the CEE countries since the early 1990s, hovering around one third of the citizens. The Great Recession did not change much in this respect in these countries either. There is widespread dissatisfaction among the CEE publics with the way their politics work and a deep-seated disenchantment of citizens with democratic politics. Finally, SE presents a third pattern which is distinct from both of the other regions. The assessment of the quality of democracy by the Southern Europeans proves to be more variable over time. Most importantly, however, it has dramatically decreased since the onset of the Great Recession and reached the low level of CEE countries by 2013.

The second part of Figure 2 presents the corresponding development of trust in the European Parliament (EP). As we can see from this figure, trust in the EP was higher in SE and CEE than in NWE before the crisis. As a reaction to the crisis, trust in the EP decreased in all three regions, but while the decline remained limited in NWE and CEE, it took on dramatic proportions in SE. Only towards the end of 2014, after the most recent European elections, did trust in the EP start to pick up again across Europe.

It is true that there are country-specific variations within each one of the regions – variations I cannot go into here for lack of space. The key point is that in the aftermath of the Great Recession the dramatic disenchantment with both their national politics and with European politics sets the Southern Europeans apart. They are not only very pessimistic about the state of their national economy. In the aftermath of the Great Recession, they have also become disillusioned politically with respect to both domestic and European politics. Slovenia is the only other country that is characterized by a similar pattern of precipitous double disenchantment. In SE we currently witness a combination of an economic and an acute political crisis. Northwestern Europeans, by contrast, remain satisfied with their national politics and, while they have lost some confidence in European politics, a majority of them still trusts the European institutions. And finally in CEE, people have been disenchanted with their domestic politics since long before the Great

Figure 2: Assessment of the Quality of Democracy/of the EP by Region.

a) Satisfaction with the way democracy works at the domestic level (share of fairlyand very satisfied citizens)

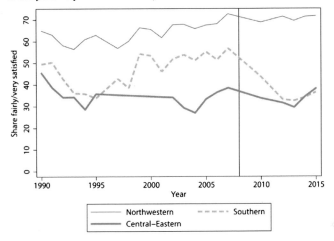

b) Trust in the European Parliament: Share of the trusting citizens(share of citizens who trust the EP)

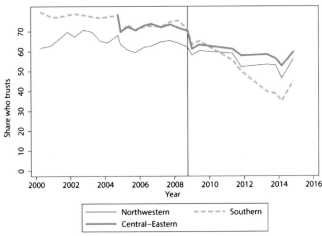

Source: Eurobarometer, on average two measures (spring and autumn) per year.
Note: The vertical line indicates the fall of Lehman Brothers in September 2008.

Recession, but a majority of them continue to trust European institutions, even if this majority has become smaller.

IV. Implications for the Politicization of European Integration

As we saw in the last section the NWE countries have rather rapidly recovered from the economic crisis and their public still supports the EU to a large, although somewhat reduced extent. Against this background, rather than a reaction to the Great Recession, the continuing rise of euroscepticism in NWE is likely to be part of a long-term rise of the New Right, which dates at least as far back as the early 1980s when the French *Front National* achieved its first electoral success. Although the recent spectacular score of this party in the 2014 EP elections constitutes its greatest electoral achievement so far, it only marks the latest step in a long-term development that is characteristic of the transformation of the national party systems in NWE in general. The series of recent breakthroughs of UKIP, the Sweden Democrats, the True Finns and the *Alternative für Deutschland* (AfD), while being spectacular in a short-term perspective, is nothing but an expression of the fact that the corresponding party systems are belatedly catching up with the general long-term trend. Particularly inhospitable institutional (UK) and structural conditions (Sweden and Finland) as well as adverse political legacies (Germany) have previously prevented the rise of such parties in these countries. According to this interpretation, their success should not be attributed to the more recent crises in the European integration process, but to the general conflict between universalism and particularism, which has been articulated by the New Left and the New Right and of which the European integration process is an important part. If this interpretation is correct, we may expect the current refugee crisis to provide additional fuel for the rise of eurosceptics in this part of Europe because it plays directly into the hands of the anti-immigration position of the parties from the New Right in NWE.

By contrast the euro crisis in combination with the national political crisis has served as a catalyst for the rise of the New Left and a specific type of euroscepticism in SE. To understand this development, it is important to keep in mind that in SE the crisis has been a combination of an economic and a political crisis that has given rise to two overlapping conflicts (an economic and a political one) with two targets (a domestic and a European one). The economic conflict has been about austerity while the political conflict has been about corruption and democracy. The main target of both conflicts has arguably been the domestic elites. The salience of European targets, by contrast, has varied from one country to the other. While European targets have been crucial in Greece, their importance has been much more limited in the other SE countries (Hutter *et al.*, 2016).[3] In all of these countries, however, the conflict with the established domestic elites drove the rise of new challengers.

In SE, the compromised historical legacy of the radical right and the extent of economic hardship have favoured new challengers from the left, that is challengers who call for national and European social solidarity. Tellingly, however, the beneficiaries on the left were not from the 'old', communist left, but from the 'new' left: Syriza in Greece, Podemos in Spain, M5S in Italy and Bloco de Esquerda in Portugal. What these parties have in common is their opposition to the established national elites. In the Spanish case, we need to add Ciudadanos, a party that is best compared to parties like D'66 in the Netherlands, left-liberals who mobilize for the renewal of politics while at the same time supporting an economically liberal programme (Rodriguez-Teruel and Barrio, 2015, p. 10). As recent electoral analyses show (Vidal-Lorda, 2016), both Podemos and Ciudadanos have mainly been chosen for their challenge to the established political elites.

---

[3] See Featherstone's contribution to this volume.

With the exception of Ciudadanos, these parties also oppose the austerity policies that have been imposed by domestic and European elites. Contrary to the principled euroscepticism of the old Communist left in SE, however, the euroscepticism of this New Left is not incompatible with EU and euro membership (see, for example, Altiparmakis, 2016). What these parties desire is a different, more social Europe that is in solidarity with the predicament of the populations in the South – a predicament for which they blame both their domestic and European elites.

Arguably, Syriza is the paradigmatic case of this New Left. It has forcefully mobilized against both domestic and European elites: Alexis Tsipras, Syriza's leader, used the phrase 'external troika – internal troika', where the three-party coalition government (ND, PASOK and DIMAR) was effectively equated with the country's emergency lenders (EC, ECB and IMF). Syriza's double goal was to overthrow two-partyism and austerity policies (Stavrakakis and Katsambekis, 2014).[4] Originally a splinter from the Greek communist party, Syriza remained in the shadow of the 'old' left for quite some time, but shed its communist legacy with the schism that led to the departure of its remaining old-left components in the run-up to the autumn 2015 elections. Typical for a party of the New Left, Syriza is 'one of the most consistent advocates of the immigrants' equal rights and their full inclusion in Greek society' (Stavrakakis and Katsambekis, 2014, p. 132). By contrast, the Italian M5S at first sight seems to fit least into the New Left category, as many of its supporters have defected from the right. But this challenger, too, has a number of features in common with the new social movements and the parties they spawned. As Biorcio (2014, p. 37) has observed, in many ways, this movement recalls the German Greens 30 years ago. In the same way as the German and other new social movements in the late 1960s and early 1970s M5S criticizes representative democracy, the established political elites (la 'casta') and the established media in the name of direct and deliberative democracy (to be practiced through the internet).

Finally, the euro crisis has not had much of an impact on CEE countries, because they were either less affected economically or recovered rather quickly and probably also because their population had a higher pain threshold (Coffey, 2013). As a matter of fact, several of these countries were happy to join the eurozone in the midst of the euro crisis (Slovakia 2009, Estonia 2011, Latvia 2014, Lithuania 2014). Politicians in these net-recipient states tend to see the EU as a 'cash cow to be milked' (Haughton and Rybář, 2009, p. 550). The domestic political crisis, by contrast, significantly influenced the more recent electoral outcomes (Hernandez and Kriesi, 2016a), confirming Haughton's (2014, p. 80) observation that '[a]nti-corruption and a general feeling that the existing political elites are incompetent is a particularly potent theme in the contemporary politics of CEE'.

However, to the extent that the EU is no longer part of the solution to the problems of its CEE Member States, but rather becomes perceived as a source of problems, euroscepticism may also increase in CEE countries. Rising euroscepticism in CEE is expected to be an expression of the defensive nationalism which is characteristic for this region. While opposition to Europe in SE is above all economically motivated in the East it is likely to be above all culturally motivated. Accordingly, and in contrast to the euro crisis, the refugee crisis is likely to fuel euroscepticism on the basis of the defensive nationalism. Thus, in tune with the general style of Hungarian party politics which emphasizes

[4] See Featherstone's contribution to this volume.

cultural issues, Orbán's Fidesz is exploiting this crisis for its own purposes in line with its earlier strategy of re-aligning the political field and re-profiling its own electorate to the right of the political spectrum (Enyedi, 2005). Similarly, Kaczińsky's PiS is exploiting this crisis with a decidedly religious bent. For PiS the refugee issue is about protecting Poland's culture, tradition and heritage from a perceived external, non-Christian threat. The refugee crisis also lends itself to the organization of cross-national co-ordinated efforts of defensive reactions: in February 2016, Hungary and Poland were joined by Slovakia and the Czech Republic, the other two partners of the so-called Visegrad group, to discuss border protection against refugees. To the extent that the defensive nationalism becomes the defining feature of the East Europeans' euroscepticism, it brings them closer to the situation in NWE, that is to a euroscepticism driven by the New Right.

Conclusion

In the tough intergovernmental bargaining processes during the euro crisis, the European governments represented their national interest as 'debtor' or 'creditor' nations whatever their partisan composition. Given the importance of intergovernmental crisis management, the public debate on the euro crisis has been dominated by supranational executive agencies and national executives. Most importantly, this debate has led to the dominant role of the German executive not only in the German debate, but also in the debate in the other countries (Kriesi and Grande, 2016), a process that has been replicated in the refugee crisis.

As a result of this development the divergence of the positions on European integration among Member States has been accentuated. However, divergence between Member States in this respect is nothing new. In our analysis of the European integration debate we have uncovered a stable configuration of four actor clusters that has been characterizing the European integration process ever since the 1970s (Maag and Kriesi, 2016). This configuration reproduces the antagonism between Europeanists and eurosceptics at the Europe-wide level, but adds considerable detail with respect to the predominant Europeanist camp.

In fact this camp turns out to be divided into (at least) three clusters based on the different views of European integration among executive actors in the multilevel governance structure. First, there are the 'integrationists' (the supranational actors and their national allies, with the German government the most important among them), who fully endorse the integration process as it has been shaping up over recent decades. They face the 'protectionists' (the French and Italian governments and their allies), who support the integrationists but are more sceptical about economic liberalization, and the neoliberal 'minimalists' (the British government and its allies), who, on the contrary, endorse market liberalization and enlargement but consistently reject any other kind of integration. The important point is that the major structuring conflicts at the European level are those between governments representing their national interests and not those opposing parties which represent the interests of social groups that cut across national borders.

The structuring of conflicts at the European level is, however, connected to the structuring of partisan conflicts at the national level given that the composition of the national governments which represent the Member States in the intergovernmental governance structures is determined by the outcome of the national elections. One of the most important findings of Hutter et al.'s (2016) study is that the two kinds of structuring conflicts – the intergovernmental conflict between different visions of European integration and the inter-partisan conflict between pro-Europeanists and eurosceptics at the domestic level – feed into each other. Gains by eurosceptics in electoral weight at the national level, therefore, will also make their influence increasingly felt at the intergovernmental level.

To the extent that it will no longer be possible to keep them out of governing coalitions, the eurosceptics will introduce national resistance into supranational governance, while the conflicts between the Member States that become visible in the intergovernmental crisis management are likely to feed back into national politics where they pitch pro-Europeans against eurosceptics. Already, eurosceptics from the populist right in NWE have become part of governing coalitions in Austria (FPÖ), Finland (True Finns), Norway (People's Party), or have supported minority centre-right governments from the outside in the Netherlands (PVV) and in Denmark (DPP). In other NWE countries the dominant governing party has had to deal with internal eurosceptic opposition, most notably the British Conservatives (divided by the 'Brexit' referendum), the German CDU-CSU (under pressure both in the euro and the refugee crisis) and the French Socialist Party (torn apart by major treaty reforms causing anxieties about a 'neoliberal' Europe). In SE eurosceptics from the populist right have been in government in Italy for quite some time (Lega Nord), while in Greece the New Left eurosceptics from Syriza have become the dominant governing party in 2015. In CEE eurosceptics like Fidesz or PiS currently dominate their governments.

Finally, to the extent that the eurosceptics increasingly become part of the governing coalitions in the different regions of Europe, they are likely to become mainstream parties themselves. They can be expected to introduce their regionally different visions of Europe into the intergovernmental process – visions reaffirming the sovereignty of the Member States in NWE and CEE contrasting with visions insisting on European-wide solidarity in SE. With the expected 'mainstreaming' of eurosceptic parties the politicization of the European integration process is likely to shift from the debate between principled support (defended by the 'old' mainstream parties) and principled opposition (defended by the 'old' eurosceptics) to the conflict concerning the kind of European Union that we Europeans wish to construct – essentially the choice between a minimalist, neoliberal union of sovereign nation-states (defended by the 'mainstreamed' New Right) and an ever closer, solidary union of an as yet still to be defined institutional architecture (defended by the 'mainstreamed' New Left).

References

Altiparmakis, A. (2016) *The Age of Hay*, unpublished manuscript (Florence: European University Institute).

Biorcio, R. (2014) 'The Reasons for the Success and Transformations of the 5 Star Movement'. *Contemporary Italian Politics*, Vol. 6, No. 1, pp. 37–53.

Casal Bértoa, F. (2014) 'Party Systems and Cleavage Structures Revisited: A Sociological Explanation of Party System Institutionalization in East Central Europe'. *Party Politics*, Vol. 20, No. 1, pp. 16–36.

Coffey, E. (2013) 'Pain Tolerance: Economic Voting in the Czech Republic'. *Electoral Studies*, Vol. 32, No. 3, pp. 432–7.

Coman, E. (2015) 'Dimensions of Political Conflict in West and East: An Application of Vote Scaling to 22 European Parliaments'. *Party Politics* (forthcoming). DOI:10.1177/1354068815593454.

Dahrendorf, R. (1990) *Reflections on the Revolution in Europe* (London: Chatto and Windus).

Dancygier, R. and Walter, S. (2015) 'Globalization, Labor Market Risks, and Class Cleavages'. In Beramendi, P., Häusermann, S., Kitschelt, H. and Kriesi, H. (eds) *The Politics of Advanced Capitalism* (Cambridge: Cambridge University Press) pp. 133–56.

de Wilde, P., Leupold, A. and Schmidtke, H. (2016) 'Introduction: the Differentiated Politicization of European Governance'. *West European Politics*, Vol. 39, No. 1, pp. 3–22.

De Wilde, P. and Zürn, M. (2012) 'Can the Politicization of European Integration be Reversed?' *JCMS*, Vol. 50, No. 51, pp. 137–53.

Dolezal, M. (2012) 'Restructuring the European Political Space: The Supply Side of European Electoral Politics'. In Kriesi, H., Grande, E., Dolezal, M., Helbling, M., Höglinger, D., Hutter, S. and Wüest, B. (eds) *Political Conflict in Western Europe* (Cambridge: Cambridge University Press) pp. 127–50.

Enyedi, Z. (2005) 'The Role of Agency in Cleavage Formation'. *European Journal of Political Research*, Vol. 44, pp. 697–720.

Evans, G. (2006) 'The Social Bases of Political Divisions in Post-Communist Eastern Europe'. *Annual Review of Sociology*, Vol. 32, pp. 245–70.

Ferrín, M. (2016) 'An Empirical Assessment of Satisfaction with Democracy'. In Ferrín, M. and Kriesi, H. (eds) *How Europeans View and Evaluate Democracy* (Oxford: Oxford University Press) pp. 283–306.

Genschel, P. and Jachtenfuchs, M. (2013) 'Alles ganz normal! Eine institutionelle Analyse der Euro-Krise'. *Zeitschrift für Internationale Beziehungen*, Vol. 20, No. 1, pp. 75–88.

Gingrich, J. and Häusermann, S. (2015) 'The Decline of the Working-class Vote, the Reconfiguration of the Welfare Support Coalition and Consequences for the Welfare State'. *Journal of European Social Policy*, Vol. 25, No. 1, pp. 50–75.

Grande, E. and Hutter, S. (2016) 'Introduction: European Integration and the Challenge of Politicization'. In Hutter, S., Grande, E. and Kriesi, H. (eds) *Politicizing Europe. Integration and Mass Politics* (Cambridge: Cambridge University Press) pp. 3–31.

Grande, E. and Kriesi, H. (2016) 'Conclusion: the Postfunctionalists were (Almost) Right'. In Hutter, S., Grande, E. and Kriesi, H. (eds) *Politicizing Europe. Integration and Mass Politics* (Cambridge: Cambridge University Press) pp. 279–300.

Haughton, T. (2014) 'Money, Margins and the Motors of Politics: the EU and the Development of Party Politics in Central and Eastern Europe'. *JCMS*, Vol. 52, No. 1, pp. 71–87.

Haughton, T. and Rybář, M. (2009) 'A Tool in the Toolbox: Assessing the Impact of EU Membership on Party Politics in Slovakia'. *Journal of Communist Studies and Transition Politics*, Vol. 25, No. 4, pp. 540–63.

Häusermann, S. (2015) *Electoral Realignment and Social Policy Positions of Social Democratic Parties*, Revised draft for the project 'Party competition and voter alignments in times of welfare state transformation', EUI Florence, 18–19 June, 2015.

Hernandez, E. and Kriesi, H. (2016a) 'The Electoral Consequences of the Financial and Economic Crisis in Europe'. *European Journal of Political Research*, Vol. 55, No. 2, pp. 203–24.

Hernandez, E. and Kriesi, H. (2016b) 'Turning your Back on the EU: The Role of Eurosceptic Parties in the 2014 European Parliament Elections'. *Electoral Studies* (forthcoming). DOI:10.1016/j.electstud.2016.04.013.

Hobolt, S.B. (2015) 'The 2014 European Parliament Elections: Divided in Unity?' *JCMS*, Vol. 53, No. s1, pp. 6–21.

Höglinger, D. (2016) *Politicizing European Integration. Struggling with the Awakening Giant* (Basingstoke: Palgrave Macmillan).

Hooghe, L. and Marks, G. (2009) 'A Postfunctionalist Theory of European Integration: From Permissive Consensus to Constraining Dissensus'. *British Journal of Political Science*, Vol. 39, No. 1, pp. 1–23.

Hutter, S., Grande, E. and Kriesi, H. (eds) (2016) *Politicizing Europe. Integration and Mass Politics* (Cambridge: Cambridge University Press).

Hutter, S. and Grande, E. (2014) 'Politicizing Europe in the National Electoral Arena: A Comparative Analysis of Five West European Countries, 1970–2010'. *JCMS*, Vol. 52, No. 5, pp. 1002–18.

Inglehart, R. (1990) *Culture Shift in Advanced Industrial Society* (Princeton, NJ: Princeton University Press).

Kriesi, H. (1989) 'New Social Movements and the New Class in the Netherlands'. *American Journal of Sociology*, Vol. 94, pp. 1078–116.

Kriesi, H. (2009) 'Rejoinder to Liesbet Hooghe and Gary Marks, "A Postfunctional Theory of European Integration: From Permissive Consensus to Constraining Dissensus"'. *British Journal of Political Science*, Vol. 39, No. 1, pp. 221–4.

Kriesi, H., Grande, E., Dolezal, M., Helbling, M., Hoeglinger, D., Hutter, S. and Wüest, B. (2012) *Political Conflict in Western Europe* (Cambridge: Cambridge University Press).

Kriesi, H., Grande, E., Lachat, R., Dolezal, M., Bornschier, S. and Frey, T. (2008) *West European Politics in the Age of Globalization* (Cambridge: Cambridge University Press).

Kriesi, H. and Grande, E. (2016) 'The Euro Crisis: a Boost to the Politicization of European Integration?' in Hutter, S., Grande, E. and Kriesi, H., *Politicizing Europe*: *Integration and Mass Politics* (Cambridge: Cambridge University Press), pp. 240–75.

Koopmans, R. (1996) 'New social movements and changes in political participation in Western Europe'. *West European Politics*, Vol. 19, No. 1, pp. 28–50.

Maag, S. and Kriesi, H. (2016) 'Politicization, Conflicts and the Structuring of the EU Political Space'. In Hutter, S., Grande, E. and Kriesi, H. (eds) *Politicizing Europe. Integration and Mass Politics* (Cambridge: Cambridge University Press) pp. 207–39.

Mainwaring, S. and Scully, T.R. (1995) 'Introduction: Party Systems in Latin America'. In S., M. and T.R., S. (eds) *Building Democratic Institutions. Party Systems in Latin America* (Palo Alto: Stanford University Press) pp. 1–34.

Oesch, D. (2013) 'The Class Basis of the Cleavage between the New Left and the Radical Right: an Analysis for Austria, Denmark, Norway and Switzerland'. In Rydgren, J. (ed.) *Class Politics and the Radical Right* (London: Routledge), pp. 31–51.

Powell, E.N. and Tucker, J.A. (2013) 'Revisiting Electoral Volatility in Post-Communist Countries: New Data, New Results and New Approaches'. *British Journal of Political Science*, Vol. 44, No. 1, pp. 123–47.

Rohrschneider, R. and Whitefield, S. (2012) *The Strain of Representation. How Parties Represent Diverse Voters in Western and Eastern Europe* (Oxford: Oxford University Press).

Schimmelfennig, F. (2014) 'European Integration in the Euro Crisis: The Limits of Post-Functionalism'. *Journal of European Integration*, Vol. 36, No. 3, pp. 321–37.

Schmitter, P.C. (1969) 'Three Neo-Functionalist Hypotheses about International Integration'. *International Organization*, Vol. 23, pp. 161–6.

Sitter, N. (2002) 'Cleavages, Party Strategy, and Party System Change in Europe, East and West'. *Perspectives on European Politics and Society*, Vol. 3, No. 3, pp. 425–51.

Stavrakakis, Y. and Katsambekis, G. (2014) 'Left-wing Populism in the European Periphery: the Case of SYRIZA'. *Journal of Political Ideologies*, Vol. 19, No. 2, pp. 119–42.

Verney, S. (2011) 'Euroscepticism in Southern Europe. A diachronic perspective'. *South European Society and Politics*, Vol. 16, No. 1, pp. 1–29.

Vidal-Lorda, G. (2016) *Challenging Business as Usual? The Rise of New Parties in Spain in Times of Economic Crisis*, unpublished manuscript (Florence: European University Institute).

Zürn, M. (2001) 'Politische Fragmentierung als Folge der gesellschaftlichen Denationalisierung?' in Loch, D. and Heitmeyer, W (eds.), *Schattenseiten der Globalisierung* (Frankfurt: Suhrkamp), pp. 111–39.

JCMS 2016 Volume 54. Annual Review pp. 48–64   DOI: 10.1111/jcms.12411

Conditionality, Democracy and Institutional Weakness: the Euro-crisis Trilemma*

KEVIN FEATHERSTONE
London School of Economics and Political Science

Introduction

The sovereign debt crises of the eurozone have raised a set of systemic challenges for the European Union (EU) that questions the credibility and legitimacy of its governance across two levels, European and domestic. The challenges are both instrumental and normative. The critical case in these respects is Greece. In 2015 it needed a third bailout, but it also launched a political confrontation with the EU following the election of a leftist-led government. The political drama made the enduring challenges even more acute. Firstly, there were (and are) questions of leadership. How could the eurozone provide leadership and lever domestic reform to keep Greece inside the euro? Was there the political will to do so, at either the European or national levels? Further, there was the institutional challenge that stems from the juxtaposition of complex and disparate leadership at the EU level with low-quality institutions for policy delivery domestically. Beyond the structural conditions there are normative questions of the terms of the rescue, but also issues of the accountability and legitimacy of the decision-making process. What can elections decide in a state under an adjustment programme? Together, these challenges pose a conundrum that is existential in nature for the EU: a trilemma in which the external leadership of reforms via conditionality confronts national democratic choice and the operational deficiencies of weak domestic institutions.

This contribution considers the three themes of the conundrum as evident in the continuing Greek debt crisis of 2015 and the implications for eurozone governance. Section I considers the literature covering IMF rescues and EU conditionality to illustrate key aspects that have made the Greek 'rescue' problematic. Section II examines the particularly intense negotiations Greece had with its eurozone partners over the course of 2015 to highlight the conflicting political interests and bargaining dynamics. Section III links these to the normative challenges of choice and legitimacy for the EU stemming from the Greek crisis. Section IV discusses the problems of institutional capacity at both the EU and the domestic levels as a structural constraint on performance. The conclusion draws these strands – the strategic, the institutional and the ideational – together and considers what lessons are apparent from this case for the understanding of the euro system. The eurozone's design and operation faced its biggest systemic shock in 2015. Evidently, Member State expulsion was now possible. In the face of a deepening debt problem, the eurozone embedded itself even more deeply into ordo-liberal austerity, the EU Commission was forced to draw serious lessons about its engagement with national government administrations and the eurozone's response to popular protest was to face it down. This leaves the single currency regime skewed and vulnerable.

*I am grateful for the assistance of Michalis Cottakis and for the comments of George Kyris and the editors of the *JCMS Annual Review*. Any errors remain mine alone.

I. Conditionality is Barely Working

With the first Greek bailout of May 2010 the EU embarked on an unprecedented programme of loan conditionality with a eurozone Member State. Given that two further bailouts have been deemed necessary, the question arises as to why the conditionality strategy has seemingly proved ineffective for Greece. By contrast, it appeared to have met with more success in Ireland, Portugal and Cyprus.

The wider literature on the performance of IMF rescues internationally, suggests a number of structural factors that are relevant to explaining the difficulties of the Greek case. More particularly support for reforms amongst key stakeholders has long been recognised as a prerequisite for success (Rodrik, 1996). In a large comparative study Ivanova et al. (2003) found that political systems with strong vested interests and high political polarization were less likely to deliver on externally-mandated reform programmes. The Greek system has traditionally displayed pronounced levels of political conflict within the party system and a 'disjointed corporatism' amongst government, business and unions, greatly reducing the scope for reform by consensus (Lavdas, 1997; Featherstone, 2005; Lijphart, 2012). The impact of the crisis was to intensify political conflict. While it is true that Greece since 2011 has experienced unprecedented (post-war) periods of coalition government, Ivanova et al. (2003) also identified multi-party governments as less likely to succeed with reforms, providing more opportunities for conflict. Pop-Eleches (2009) argued that conditionality was unlikely to work if both the government and the opposition had divergent ideological preferences from the IMF, a matter also related to the intensity and nature of the rescue task. In 2010, the reform content of Greece's rescue flatly contradicted the reflationary aspirations of the PASOK (socialist) government of George Papandreou and the stance of the main opposition, the centre-right New Democracy party, was to oppose the bailout of that year on the grounds that it was too draconian, though it was also seen as being opportunistic.

In the literature on IMF conditionality,[1] the effectiveness of reform is seen as being dependent on the number and extent of the specified reforms: the greater the conditionality, the less space there is to build reform coalitions and encourage 'ownership' by the government (Bird and Willett, 2004; Beazer and Woo, 2015). Certainly, the conditions set for Greece across its successive bailouts have grown in scope and number.[2] In parallel, though, the space for dialogue, domestic prioritization and choice and building consensus has been very limited. This, in itself, has undermined the basis for 'ownership' of the reform programme as it weakens the standing and legitimacy of the domestic leaders of reform. Moreover, the IMF experience suggests that right-wing governments will find it more difficult to implement reforms if the conditions are extensive, as this will create scope for left parties to oppose each new condition while restricting the scope for the government to compromise and compensate the losers from the reforms (Beazer and Woo, 2015). Extensive conditionality ties the hands of governments that need the most flexibility to see reforms through (Beazer and Woo, 2015). As the acceptance of the Troika reform programme by Greek governments in the 2010–14 period was sufficient for them to be seen as 'right-wing', the opposition in the form of the SYRIZA party

---

[1] I am grateful to Antonio Barroso for assistance with this literature.
[2] The Second Economic Adjustment Programme was substantially longer than the first (as were the associated review documents) and, though the third was shorter, the range of policy areas covered has continuously expanded across all three.

was provided with much opportunity to attack the extensive conditions in the programme. In parallel, the legitimacy of centre-left and centre-right leaders plummeted.

Seen in the context of the literature on IMF conditionality, the Greek case has thus displayed exceptional characteristics and this helps to explain its problematic performance. Further evidence of its exceptionalism may be gained from a more agency-centred approach that highlights the contradictory rational interests of domestic actors. With respect to EU enlargement, Schimmelfennig and Sedelmeier (2004, p. 663) developed a now classic 'external incentives model of governance' in which the domestic actors involved are assumed to be strategic utility-maximizers interested in the maximization of their own power and welfare. As such, it follows a standard 'logic of consequences' (March and Olsen, 1989) in which the EU maintains a strategy of reinforcement by reward and the hypothesis is:

> ... that a state adopts EU rules if the benefits of EU rewards exceed the domestic adoption costs. In turn, this cost–benefit balance depends on (i) the determinacy of conditions, (ii) the size and speed of rewards, (iii) the credibility of threats and promises, and (iv) the size of adoption costs. (Schimmelfennig and Sedelmeier, 2004, p. 664).

In the Greek case, the depth of the recession has created an intensity not matched in the other eurozone states involved in rescue conditionality and the stakes have been much higher.

The Schimmelfennig and Sedelmeier model was developed for a different type of case: that of states wishing to join the EU 'club', rather than the setting of conditions to remain within the eurozone. Yet, the differences are illuminating for why conditionality in the Greek case has faltered so much. For Greece, the size of the adoption costs has been frequently seen as high and impacting in the short- and medium-term. With unemployment reaching 27 per cent (and almost two thirds of those aged 24 or younger), salary cuts of up to 32 per cent for workers aged below 25 years (ELSTAT, 2015), pension reductions of between 40–50 per cent for public sector workers (European Parliament, 2015) and bankruptcies at record levels, the socio-economic environment for major structural reforms has been very difficult. Moreover, with strong political conflict over the bailouts, ministers charged with reform have incentives to protect their own positions by thwarting the implementation of reforms (Zahariades, 2013), a process partly facilitated by the 'silo'-like fragmentation of central government and the weaknesses of the Prime Minister's position (Featherstone and Papadimitriou, 2015). Since 2010, governing parties have faced major challenges in maintaining party unity: PASOK has almost disappeared as an electoral force and SYRIZA endured splits in mid-2015.

At the same time, the size and speed of the rewards for compliance have been questionable. Beyond the important immediate domestic sphere, the long-term projections for public debt have offered little incentive for short-term sacrifice: with each successive bailout, the time when Greece will return to the pre-crisis debt levels – themselves exceptionally high – has been put back well beyond 2020. Moreover, the immediate reforms have often been horizontal in nature: cutting salaries and pensions across-the-board, creating many losers and few winners. This has undermined the scope to build a stronger pro-reform domestic coalition.

Over the successive Greek bailouts, it has been evident that the creditors have felt obliged to be more precise in the determinacy of the conditions set. While, in principle, this can be regarded as conducive to conditionality compliance, the cost can be to exacerbate the sense of external imposition and the squeezing-out of a dialogue on reform with domestic allies (Featherstone, 2015). Greek public debate has, indeed, focussed on the immediate imposition and pain, to the neglect of a domestically-driven consideration of alternative models and objectives. A notable example of the over-determinacy of loan conditions for Greece came with the first Greek loan Memorandum setting a target of Greece shedding 150,000 public servant posts between 2011–15. This was not a figure developed on the basis of an assessment of staffing or skills needed; it was purely a calculation derived from the budget savings required of Greece. In a highly sensitive sector the target became almost impossible to be defended by domestic reformers. It contributed to destroying political careers and undermining support for reform agendas (Featherstone, 2015).

Having endured considerable hardship, opponents of the bailouts came to question the credibility of the threats behind non-compliance with the conditions imposed on Greece. Public opinion has overwhelmingly wished to remain inside the 'euro', but the opposition became increasingly successful in arguing that Greece's creditors would not risk 'GREXIT'. This was seen as going 'nuclear', involving mutually-assured losses, and the call was for Greek leaders to stand-up and call the bluff of Germany and the others. The path set by the eurozone was criticized as being against the interests of all, a theme endorsed by some leading international economists like Paul Krugman (2015) and Joseph Stiglitz (2015), and a Greek challenge could open-up a new European-wide political struggle. No Greek politician was more successful in these arguments than Yanis Varoufakis, an academic economist/TV star and briefly a SYRIZA frontman. He had written many years previously of actor strategies in the context of ignoring incredible threats and being prepared to gamble (for example, Hargreaves-Heap and Varoufakis, 2005). At the start of 2015, Varoufakis became Greek Finance Minister, following SYRIZA's election victory. He was to serve less than six months in office, but in this time he stunned the world by his audacity and his celebrity manner, a style that was a gift to the media. Afterwards, he was left to write his personal account of his experience (Varoufakis, 2016).

In reality, of course, the seduction was shared by a party and an electorate strongly opposed to the austerity of Greece's bailout terms. SYRIZA's election campaign (with its slogan 'Hope is coming; Greece goes forward; Europe is changing' offered the promise of ending austerity while still staying in the euro. To television interviewers querying whether the party had a fall-back position, SYRIZA leaders emphasized that Greece's eurozone partners would back down.[3] The electorate seemed persuaded. In the last week before the election, a GAP opinion poll found 56 per cent of Greeks believing that, if it came to a confrontation between Angela Merkel and Alexis Tsipras, the former would concede. After his election victory on 25 January, Alexis Tsipras as the new Prime Minister, declared an 'end to the vicious cycle of austerity'.[4]

By 2015, the loan conditionality had seemingly come unstuck in Greece. The lenses of IMF and EU enlargement conditionality highlight the key differences of the intervention in Greece: the uncertainty of reward and threat; the intense political conflict and a lack of ownership; the use of rather crass targets; and the severity of the recession. That said, the

---

[3] *Star Channel*, 13 January 2015.
[4] *Kathimerini*, 26 January 2015.

bailout was not without some achievement: the Greek economy finished 2014 out of recession, albeit with a fragile growth path.[5]

II. Varoufakis' Game of 'Chicken' with Europe

The 'game of chicken' that Varoufakis initiated with Greece's euro partners in 2015 was without parallel in EU politics with the stakes high for both sides.[6] Moreover, collectively the players in Greece had almost no experience of public office; their ambition, however, was grand-scale. In elaborating how the game played out, a number of important characteristics become evident: the importance of the time constraint; the predictability of the eurozone's response; the precariousness of Greece's finances and the government's attempts to find cash; the isolation of the Greek government at the EU level; the lack of trust underlying the bargaining; the real threat of expulsion; and a clear defeat for Athens.

The first factor was time. The previous New Democracy-led government of Prime Minister Antonis Samaras had left matters unresolved until after an election it feared it might lose. It had not satisfied the conditions for the last tranche of loan funding (totalling €7.2 billion) under the second bailout and the agreement was due to expire by the end of February 2016. The new government had to face the tough reality. One week before this deadline, the Eurogroup agreed to extend financial support to Greece for a further four months to allow the earlier conditions to be met by Greece and on the basis that the country would continue to honour all its debts, continue with the previously agreed reforms and not take any unilateral measures, while the extension period could be used to negotiate a further programme of support. The agreement did foresee Greece having a lower primary budget surplus target for 2015 (than 3 per cent), which would provide some scope for fiscal easing. But, it also moved the bank recapitalization funds for Greece to the EFSF (European financial stability fund) beyond the reach of the new Greek government. Overall, the terms of the extension were widely seen as a defeat for the SYRIZA-led coalition, as it had not secured any of its main election demands.

A few days later, the Greek government submitted its first list of reforms it would implement in order to satisfy the completion of the second bailout. On 24 February, the Eurogroup accepted these as a 'valid starting-point' for an agreement that would be necessary by the end of April. However, subsequent iterations of these reform proposals were repeatedly rejected by the Eurogroup as insufficient. The contentious issues involved further pension cuts, increases in VAT rates, debt-restructuring, increased flexibility in the Greek labour market and the setting of a lower budget surplus for 2015.

The Greek government's attempts to win allies within the eurozone came to nought. Its failure was fundamentally due to the wide divergence in policy stance and conflicting interests. This was already clear well before SYRIZA took power and it raised questions as to how it believed it would be able to change the terms of engagement with the eurozone. As Tsebelis (2015, p. 3) has commented, '[t]he Greek leadership did not understand that the negotiating deck was stacked in the EU's favour and wasted time learning the

---

[5] See Benczes and Szent-Iványi's contribution to this volume.
[6] On developments in eurozone governance in 2015 see Hodson's contribution to this volume; more generally, see Copsey (2015).

obvious'. Much of the eurozone's response was path-dependent behaviour. Rather than the crisis creating a critical juncture for policy change, it invested more deeply in the original ordo-liberal paradigm, as I have argued previously (Featherstone, 2012). The orthodoxy maintained a straitjacket and credibility risked no flexibility.

Moreover, these factors were soon overlaid by unprecedented levels of mistrust of the Greek government – indeed, disdain for its stance and its behaviour – from its eurozone partners. Varoufakis' personal relations with his German counterpart, Wolfgang Schäuble, were quickly antagonistic – with the former saying 'We didn't even agree to disagree', after an early meeting in February. Even before SYRIZA took office, Schäuble (2016) had warned Tsipras he could not both remain in the eurozone and reject the agreed bailout programme. There was also the sense that Greek leaders were behaving improperly. Varoufakis upset Pier Carlo Padoan, the Italian Finance Minister, by declaring on TV in Rome that the Italian debt was also 'unsustainable'.[7] In June, Tsipras commented that the IMF had 'criminal responsibility' for the damage to the Greek economy.[8] For her part, IMF Chief, Christine Lagarde, lamented the slow progress of the creditors' negotiations with Greece and said there was an urgent need for dialogue 'with adults in the room'.[9] Commission President, Jean-Claude Juncker, who began with one of the more consensual approaches, effectively accused Tsipras of lying to the Greek Parliament at the end of June in his account of the negotiations. The Greek Prime Minister had presented the eurozone's latest offer as one of 'take it-or leave it', but according to Juncker, Tsipras knew 'perfectly well that was not the case'.[10] The Commission President said Tsipras had to 'observe some minimum rules' of behaviour. Jeroen Dijsselbloem, President of the Eurogroup, was repeatedly exasperated with Varoufakis' tactics. When he left office, Varoufakis observed 'I shall wear the creditors' loathing with pride'. In April, Tsipras went to see Putin in a crude attempt to suggest an alternative ally for Greece, but Moscow offered little. Diplomatically, Greece had shown abject failure.

Throughout, Greece remained isolated: one against eighteen. Given its policy stance, the scope for it to build a counter-coalition to Germany was limited. Recent French governments have had a much weaker voice in the eurozone than at its Maastricht birth (Dyson and Featherstone, 1999). Michel Sapin only made muted noises in Greece's support. Later, Varoufakis would also conclude that Greece's success would have been the 'greatest nightmare' for Portugal, Spain, Italy and Ireland.[11] But, it is more arguable that there was room for a less harsh deal than that eventually obtained. Clearly, Greece lacked credibility and commitment on the terms being proposed. A lack of trust probably reinforced the attractiveness of 'GREXIT' and undoubtedly placed the option more firmly on the table, with secret contingency plans in Berlin and elsewhere being updated.[12]

---

[7] *The Guardian*, 2 February 2015.
[8] *The Daily Telegraph*, 16 June 2015.
[9] *The Guardian*, 18 June 2015.
[10] *The Guardian*, 7 July 2015.
[11] *New Statesman*, 13 July 2015.
[12] Indeed, well after the third bailout was agreed, mistrust and low credibility were a continuing problem as evident from the leaking of a private telephone conversation between IMF officials – a matter that led to angry exchanges between the IMF's Christine Lagarde and Tsipras (*Financial Times*, 3 April 2016).

The slowness of the negotiations increased the eurozone's exasperation with Athens.[13] Greece rejected both an exit from the eurozone and the imposition of 'rescue' terms that it saw as repeating past failures. By April, the Greek government was running out of money. It compelled pension funds, state corporations, regional and local authorities and universities to transfer cash reserves to sustain its operational needs.[14] Adding to the pressure, the IMF refused a delay in Greece's debt repayments – something that no developed economy had previously requested. With a poor atmosphere and a sustained impasse, Tsipras made changes to the Greek negotiating team. Varoufakis was moved aside and Euclides Tsakalotos, a deputy minister of international financial relations, was placed centre-stage as the co-ordinator. Tsakalotos was much closer to Tsipras and had a far more consensual manner.

Greece's situation became increasingly precarious. At the start of May it managed to make a debt repayment of €200 million to the IMF and then another later of €750 million, but only with money held at the IMF itself. By the end of May, Greece was warning that it might be forced to default on €1.6 billion debt repayment due in June claiming it had to prioritize the payment of wages and pensions at home. Indeed, Athens informed the IMF that it would delay its repayments till the end of the month.

With the expiration of the bailout extension approaching at the end of the month, the rest of the eurozone offered to extend it by a further five months (though with no extra funding). This was rejected by Athens on 26 June as too draconian. Instead, Alexis Tsipras in the early hours of the morning announced a referendum on the most recent proposal made by the eurozone side. His government would advocate a 'no' vote in the referendum to what he described as 'blackmail' and 'humiliation'. Greece's partners viewed this as breaking-off the negotiations that were ongoing; they had expected a further counter-proposal from Athens. The creditors refused a one-week extension beyond the referendum date. Thus the second bailout programme, and the funds earmarked from it, expired. Athens had not received any funding since the previous August. This intensified Greece's budget predicament and it decided to default, as it had already signalled, on an IMF loan of €1.5 billion at the end of June. The ECB also froze its emergency funding of Greece's banks, leading to Greece having to introduce capital controls to stop money leaving the banking system. Foreign transactions were severely limited and the banks were shut (for three weeks). The Athens stock market was also closed. The government took emergency steps: delaying paying its private contractors and ordering public utilities to transfer their reserves to the central bank.

The referendum was a very hurried affair taking place just a week after it had been announced. The question in the referendum was neither clear nor, perhaps, even valid, as several EU leaders, including Commission Vice-President Valdis Dombrovskis and Christine Lagarde pointed out.[15] Greece's highest administrative court also queried the legitimacy of the referendum and the question's validity.[16] The text of the question was long and opaque. The text it referred to was mostly not in Greek. More particularly, the proposal had already been withdrawn by Greece's partners. But politics overrode the actual text and the government saw it as a pro-/anti-austerity issue. Crucially, it stressed

[13] *Kathimerini*, 23 April 2015.
[14] *Kathimerini*, 23 April 2015.
[15] *Die Welt*, 2 July 2015; *BBC News*, 28 June 2015.
[16] *The Guardian*, 3 July 2015.

that this was not an 'in–out' choice over the euro – though both Merkel and Hollande declared that a 'no' vote would, indeed, be a vote for exit. On 5 July, 61.3 per cent voted 'no' on a turnout of 62.5 per cent. SYRIZA trumpeted it as a popular rejection of the austerity imposed by the eurozone.

Yet, a week later the government was obliged to accept terms that, in many respects, were even more punitive than before. Indeed, the deal was worse than that which had been floated at the time of the Samaras government the previous autumn. Greece's eurozone partners, led by the Merkel government, were intent on reaffirming the policy frame that she must follow – 'rules are rules', as Schäuble had it (2016) – and to exorcise any impression that SYRIZA's irresponsibility had produced rewards.

In the days after the Greek referendum, the onus was on the Greek government to submit fresh proposals. Two days later, Varoufakis resigned as Greece's Finance Minister and Tsakalotos replaced him, seemingly easing relations with the rest of the 18. But in the air of scepticism and uncertainty, Schäuble's office the following Friday circulated an email to eurozone partners that stipulated that in the absence of an acceptable submission from Athens over the weekend then by Monday, 'Greece should be offered swift negotiations on a time-out from the eurozone' of some five years' duration.[17] Further, Greece should be obliged to transfer assets worth €50 billion, a quarter of its national wealth, into a trust fund located in Luxembourg. The assets would be sold-off gradually and the proceeds used to pay-off the Greek debt. It was modelled on the privatization scheme for East German property after 1989. The German move was sharp and threatening. In any event, Tsipras had presented proposals to the Greek Parliament that evening that were very similar to those just rejected in the referendum and had obtained the overwhelming support of MPs for them. Though the next day both the EU Commission and the ECB declared the Greek submission as a good starting-point, they proved not enough – both the Finnish and Slovak finance ministers pressed at the start of the negotiations in the afternoon for Greece's expulsion from the eurozone.[18]

The finance ministers' negotiations became increasingly bitter and inconclusive. Jeroen Dijesselbloem, as Chair of the Eurogroup, circulated a paper on Sunday morning that retained the option of Greece's exit. A full European Council had been scheduled for late Sunday – again, a signal that the agenda would be how to deal with Greece's departure – but Donald Tusk, the Council President, decided to restrict it to eurozone heads. By late Sunday the negotiations were focussed on Tsipras, Merkel, Hollande and Tusk – who often had separate meetings - leaving the rest idly standing-by. In the early hours of Monday 13 July, Tsipras battled for his redlines: no state assets transferred to an overseas trust fund; no IMF involvement; and no rolling-back of SYRIZA's recent reforms. Between 4 am and 7 am, the same 'inner group' reconvened to struggle over a compromise: Greek state assets would be transferred to a fund based in Greece (not Luxembourg) and €12.5 billion of the total of €50 billion would be available for 'investment'. The compromise had been crafted by Dutch Prime Minister, Mark Rutte, and his Portuguese counterpart, Pedro Passos Coelho.[19] Instead of the 'Troika', four institutions (the IMF, the EU Commission, the ECB and the European Stability Mechanism) would oversee the new bailout. Some of SYRIZA's reforms would remain, though

[17] See the account in *The Guardian*, 22 October 2015.
[18] *The Guardian*, 22 October 2015.
[19] *The Guardian*, 22 October 2015

there would be new, tougher cutbacks. It was envisaged that the new bailout could provide up to €86 billion in loans for Greece over three years.

Formal negotiations – the 'Memorandum of Understanding' – on the detail of the programme were concluded in mid-August. The first loan payment to Greece of €23 billion (including €10 billion reserved for bank recapitalizations) was made on 20 August. By the end of the year, the recapitalization of the Greek banks had been completed at a much lower cost than expected. However, at the same time, the creditors' representatives were again seeing the Athens government as dragging its feet on the adoption of '13 prior actions'.[20] The first review of whether Greece had met the terms of the new bailout stretched well into 2016 – emulating the pattern of the Tsipras government's predecessors – with pension reforms and budget 'black-holes' again the points of contestation.

Politically, Alexis Tsipras continued to out-manoeuvre his domestic opponents. The snap election called for 20 September 2015 secured his position in the face of the left-wing of his party splitting-away. Tsipras was re-elected and the results closely mirrored those of the previous January, with SYRIZA only slightly losing support (at just over 35 per cent) and reforming its coalition with the Independent Greeks party. Survey evidence suggested that while two-thirds of voters rated the government's economic performance as 'bad' or 'very bad', most accepted the party's narrative of having tried and having stood up for Greece.[21] During the campaign, Tsipras had told Alpha TV that, 'I feel comfortable giving people a reason to judge me for all those things I accomplished and those I didn't.'[22] He said he fought as hard as he could to defend Greece's interests in talks with its lenders. 'The No to a bad deal, I turned it into a Yes to a deal which has problems, but provides potential', he said.

The Tsipras Government thus finished 2015 with a deal that had kept Greece in the eurozone for the present, but one that appeared worse than might have been available a year earlier and over which it would continue to delay and haggle. Moreover, a new debt crisis could not be ruled out.

III. The EU's Normative Challenge

Jyrki Katainen, EU Commission Vice-President, responded to the election of the SYRIZA government in Athens and the challenge to Greece's bailout terms with a much-quoted remark that, '[w]e don't change our policy according to elections.'[23] It signalled the tension between EU-level agreements signed by governments and the exercise of choice and accountability in national political systems. There are inherent difficulties in the two-level system of governance within the EU where an electoral challenge is more readily expressed within domestic institutional confines, leaving the supranational level to appear imperious and unaccountable.

During 2015, Greece voted in two parliamentary elections (25 January and 20 September) and one national referendum (5 July). Each returned decisive victories for the anti-austerity political forces. Individually and collectively, however, they produced no retreat from austerity – indeed, the impact was quite the reverse. The normative question for the EU

[20] *Kathimerini*, 2 December 2015.
[21] *Kathimerini*, 16 October 2015.
[22] *EU Observer*, 27 August 2015.
[23] *EU Observer*, 29 January 2015.

polity provoked by Greece in 2015 was, thus, what is the purpose and legitimacy of popular ballots for a state under an externally-agreed adjustment programme? When, and under which conditions, can an electorate mandate a change of policy course?

For in the two-level, multi-state EU polity there are cross-cutting dimensions of accountability and legitimacy. The electorates of donor-states have equal normative rights to be heard and have impact as the voters of 'bailed-out' systems. Thus, the rights of voters in Munich have to be counter-balanced with those in Athens. Would a default by Greece – by definition breaking an international agreement – contravene the rights of donor electorates to have their interests (and money) safeguarded? The conflict is between two moralities: that of the duty in a Union to show solidarity and that of the moral hazard: individual states should not 'free-ride' and ignore their obligations.

For some in Greece in 2015, the response was to argue that their 'human rights' were being infringed by the EU–IMF bailouts. The colourful SYRIZA President of the Greek Parliament, Zoe Konstantopoulou, a human rights lawyer, established 'The Truth Committee on Public Debt' on 4 April, seemingly emulating the Truth and Reconciliation Commission of post-apartheid South Africa. Critics dismissed the venture as a political gimmick and dismissed its work. The task of the Truth Committee was to investigate 'the creation and the increase of public debt, the way and reasons for which debt was contracted, and the impact that the conditionalities attached to the loans have had on the economy and the population' [sic] (Truth Committee, 2015, p. 1). Lest there be any doubt about its assessment of justice, its mandate was 'to formulate arguments and options concerning the cancellation of the debt' (2015, p. 1).[24] No allowance was made in the Committee's report for any of the social and economic rights to be dependent on the prevailing market conditions. Rather, Greece had a right to the unilateral repudiation of the debt due to the absence of good faith, the violation of domestic laws, the precedence of human rights over other contractual obligations, the coercion in the debt restructuring, debt suspension on grounds of state necessity, and, ultimately, the right to unilateral sovereign insolvency (2015, pp. 58–62; see also Salomon, 2015). The work of the Committee was brought to a halt by the calling of the September elections and Zoe Konstantopoulou resigning from SYRIZA and joining the new Popular Unity party, led by Panagiotis Lafazanis. Later, however, Alexis Tsipras, announced a fresh parliamentary investigation in March 2016 into the debts owed by Greek political parties in an entanglement (*diaploki*) of financial links with banks and media tycoons which was seen as an attack on the previous governments of New Democracy and PASOK.

These conflicts of rights – between a nation rejecting an overpowering debt-burden and an EU system protecting collective rules – added to the conflicts over solidarity and moral hazard, responsibility and accountability in a two-level system of governance. One side or the other might be criticised for indulging in populist blameshift or opportunism, but the conundrum is systemic and was brought to the fore by SYRIZA in 2015. Certainly, Tsipras' activation of blameshift – resonating with a cultural tradition of victimhood – created a cultural resistance to reform for the sake of the bailout.

Another normative dimension of the debt crisis has been the 'ever closer union' between the rules and provisions of euro-governance and the economic paradigm of ordo-liberalism

---

[24] This author was called to appear before the Truth Committee, but the calling of fresh elections terminated its proceedings.

58

and austerity. Successive reforms of eurozone governance during the crisis, culminating in the EU's 'Fiscal Compact' signed in 2012, have displayed a 'lock-in' to the ideational frame of 'sound money, sound finances', going further than that established at Maastricht (Featherstone, 2012). The original treaty had itself been given a narrow normative base that overrode the disparate policy traditions of modern Europe (Dyson and Featherstone, 1999, p. 796). It stressed the importance of monetary policy and market forces for supply-side flexibility. From a neo-Keynesian perspective, the Maastricht design had major cognitive gaps: it was liable to a politics of deflation, promoting regulation rather than facilitating (re-)distributive governance, and undermining a sense of solidarity. With the eruption of the debt crisis and its asymmetric shocks, the predisposition was to punish errant behaviour and to shift the blame to mistakes made at the domestic level. The Treaty on Stability, Coordination and Governance in the Economic and Monetary Union (TSCG) entrenched the existing rules on deficits and debt more deeply. Article 3(ii) committed Member States to put into their national laws or constitutions that such provisions be an obligation and that a 'correction mechanism' for deviations be established; Article 4 made it a requirement that national debt be kept within 60 per cent of GDP; and, Article 8(ii) allowed for one government to challenge the fiscal position of another before the Court and the latter could impose a lump sum payment or fine (Featherstone, 2012). This represented the near-Constitutionalization at the European level of supply-side economics and of ordo-liberalism (Bellamy and Weale, 2015). As a result, the ideational frame and images of 'Europe' were being defined by austerity, provoking new political cleavages and popular backlashes.

Indeed, the SYRIZA-led government in Athens fanned the protests against the economic paradigm. It expressed support for workers striking against the measures it had implemented on behalf of the 'Troika'. More fundamentally, Tsipras declared 'I was blackmailed, there were no good options and I chose the least bad'. Thus, '[t]he government does not believe in these measures (and).... We will do our best to protect people from measures we do not believe in but are forced to implement'. Varoufakis, despite voting for the bailout, said the package would 'go down in history as the greatest disaster of macroeconomic management ever.'[25] Their scepticism was shared by the IMF (and a number of international economists) who assessed Greece's new public debt levels to be unsustainable, a crucial condition preventing the Fund's participation in a rescue. The normative choices that underlay the third bailout for Greece placed 'Europe' on one side of an increasingly heated debate; indeed, to some, the measures appeared so punitive that they belied an intention to force Greece out of the eurozone.

The Greek crisis in 2015 had thus challenged the eurozone's normative underpinnings like never before. It had posed fundamental questions of when elections matter, of the rights of voters across donor and recipient states, of the moral balance between monetary order and socio-economic rights and of the tying of 'Europe' to 'rescue' via austerity. The creation of the euro regime had neglected the wider issues of governance by endeavouring to keep it as a largely technocratic project without disturbing the norms of national systems of accountability, choice and legitimacy. The Greek crisis exposed these limitations and gave rise to contrary answers at the popular level, risking elites appearing as imperious. A further governance taboo was of the ability of the eurozone to manage policies via its current institutional structures and on the basis of low-quality domestic institutions.

[25] *BBC News*, 18 July 2015; *The Independent*, 18 July 2015.

IV. The Two-level Problem of Institutional Capacity: European and National Governance

Studies of IMF rescues have long recognized the importance of institutional capacity: the quality of the government administration correlates positively with reform delivery (Steinwand and Stone, 2008). In the Greek case, a rapid sequence of three bailouts poses questions of how the rescue strategy – and its instruments – was structured. The EU was reluctant to enter into the first Greek bailout in 2010 as it was unprecedented and it challenged the basic ordo-liberal precepts of the Maastricht agreement. The Treaty explicitly barred a bailout of a Member State government (Article 125). It made no provision for the expulsion of an errant state, its policy coordination and 'excessive deficit procedure' proved weak and it failed to provide EU institutions with sufficient investigatory powers to guard against unreliable reporting of national statistics and 'moral hazard' risks more generally. This was a dangerous cocktail: a number of economists had already foreseen that the disciplinary rules were 'unenforceable' (Buiter *et al.*, 1993). The provisions not only delayed the first bailout, they undoubtedly increased the costs of the rescue.

The eurozone had to invent a governance structure for the first Greek bailout. In doing so it built on the post-2008 experience of the EU in rescuing three non-eurozone countries (Romania, Hungary and Latvia) that had encountered major debt problems. All three had been provided with both IMF and EU aid, the latter under Article 119 (of the Treaty establishing the EC), a provision for states not part of the Economic and Monetary Union (EMU). The Latvian case had produced a shift. Previously, the EU and the IMF had coordinated their respective loan programmes, but from 2009 they conducted joint review missions (Lütz and Kranke, 2010). Moreover, the difficulties of Latvia were interpreted as stemming from a failure to follow EU rules. Similarly, Rogers (2012, p. 175) argues that the involvement of the IMF in the eurozone's rescue of Greece enabled the blame for the Greek debt crisis to be placed on Athens, rather than design faults with the euro regime itself. Some EU governments – led by Germany – insisted on the IMF's involvement in the Greek bailout to lend the programme credibility not least with restless voters at home. A 'Troika' mechanism was created, to be headed by the IMF's Poul Thomsen, to represent the lead institutions of the European Commission, the European Central Bank and the IMF. This was to undertake periodic review missions to Athens to gauge the government's progress in implementing the reforms required by the loan's conditionality (as elaborated in the 'Memorandum of Understanding' between Greece and other eurozone governments). Far more than in the other cases the EU had dealt with, Thomsen became a highly controversial figure – the 'fall-guy' for the tough austerity measures that provoked the Greek opposition – and the Troika set-up an office in Athens and regularly inspected government ministries to probe their actions. Yet at different stages of the Greek bailout, it was the IMF that had shown a move away from the 'Washington consensus'-type austerity measures, to a softer stance, and the EU that 'very actively promoted orthodox measures in return for loans' (Lütz and Kranke, 2010). Repeatedly, the IMF questioned whether Greece's debt would be sustainable after the bailout and in 2013 it admitted that the Greek programmes had underestimated the multiplier effects of austerity (IMF, 2013). While the EU been more disparate in its voices, it has also been pulled along by the tougher stance of the chief paymaster, Germany, and its allies.

The successive bailouts of Greece have been consistent in their implicit blaming of past governments for running-up high levels of public debt. Thus the terms of the loans

60

must not only be corrective of the debt, but also of the behaviour that led to it – a lesson in ordo-liberal thinking. Penalties are for (past) mistakes, to defend retrospectively against moral hazard and to assuage donor-country voters that they were not 'being taken for a ride'. They gave little acknowledgement to how far Greece's lack of adjustment to the eurozone was a result of a domestic institutional incapacity to deliver reforms (Börzel et al., 2010).

The bailouts required Greece to undertake a Herculean-task. In dire circumstances, Greece implemented one of the largest fiscal consolidation programmes in history, with measures amounting to over 30 per cent of GDP (Tsakloglou, 2015). According to the OECD's indicator of 'reform responsiveness' to its own three priority areas (labour market productivity, product markets and growth-friendly tax reforms) across the 2011–14 period Greece scored higher (0.81) than any of the other bailout states and the eurozone average (0.47) (OECD, 2014). Similarly, the 'Adjustment Progress Indicator' commissioned by Berenberg Bank and the Lisbon Council also scored Greece consistently the eurozone's highest performer for the same five-year period for external adjustment, fiscal adjustment and the change in real unit labour costs (EuroPlus Monitor, 2014).

But the state institutions themselves remain very problematic agents of policy reform and implementation. The Bertelsmann Stiftung 'Sustainable Governance Index', measuring institutional quality, has repeatedly placed Greece the lowest of all OECD countries (Bertelsmann Stiftung, 2015). Indeed, the problems of public administration in Greece are well-established. It has a deeply-embedded administrative tradition displaying the influence of the Napoleonic model (hierarchical, centralist) with a stress on procedural regulation rather than innovation (Spanou, 2008) and has suffered from being low-skilled and low-tech. The institutional weaknesses affecting reform are linked to wider socio-cultural conditions. State institutions have grown amidst a politics of clientelism and corruption. Low levels of trust create a classic collective action problem inhibiting reform and sustaining something of a 'social trap' (Rothstein, 2005). With the Troika finding 'a state machine deficient in its ability to deliver targeted measures on a set of priorities and according to an agreed schedule, solutions were found in horizontal cuts in public expenditure (salaries, pensions, jobs, etc.) that further recalibrated the pay-offs for political actors (Featherstone, 2015). There were deeper ideational and cultural clashes with the Troika agenda: 'This is an administrative setting that struggles to self-reflect, that has not prioritized norms of service delivery and of evaluation' (Featherstone, 2012).

The EU has struggled with an agenda of enhancing administrative capacity at the domestic level. In 2011, it established the EU Taskforce for Greece to help improve its operation and its processing of EU funding. This taskforce was to be replicated in the case of the bailout of Cyprus. In parallel, bilateral technical assistance was provided to Greece by France, Germany, the Netherlands and other EU states, alongside the OECD. The Taskforce was disbanded in June 2015. In its place, the Commission created a new Structural Reform Service within the Secretariat-General (under Valdis Dombrovskis) to assist Member States in implementing administrative and structural reforms. The current Europe 2020 programme refers to cooperation in improving national public administrations and this agenda is included in the EU's half-yearly reviews of economic performance for each eurozone Member State, but the process is of 'soft coordination'. This is clearly an area of much political sensitivity across national governments as it impinges on matters of sovereignty and admissions of failure.

In the context of the instrumentation to lever domestic reform, Greece has been the critical case – an unprecedented challenge for the EU, posing a number of important strategic and operational questions. In February 2014, the European Parliament's Committee on Economic and Monetary Affairs (2014, p. 17) released a lengthy report on the 'Role and Operations of the Troika with Regard to the Euro Area Programme Countries' (Greece, Ireland, Portugal and Cyprus). It criticized the potential for a conflict of interest on the part of the EU Commission between its traditional obligations and its role within the Troika. Similarly, it was concerned 'that the Troika is made up of three independent institutions with an uneven distribution of responsibility between them, coupled with differing mandates, as well as negotiation and decision-making structures with different levels of accountability, [that] has resulted in a lack of appropriate scrutiny and democratic accountability of the Troika as a whole' (2014, pp. 17–18). The transition to four institutions (the Troika plus representatives of the European Stability Mechanism) in the 2015 bailout has not erased such concerns.

An assessment of the Commission's Taskforce for Greece (TFGR) by the European Court of Auditors in 2015 similarly highlighted the shortcomings of the initiative (ECA, 2015). It had been set up very rapidly, without a full analysis of other options and without a dedicated budget. It had no single comprehensive strategic document for the delivery of TA [technical assistance] or for deciding between competing priorities, despite the TFGR's mandate to identify and coordinate the TA. In the absence of such a document, the TFGR worked with the Greek authorities 'on demand' and based on the programme's conditionality (2015, p. 7). Moreover, 'it did not systematically monitor either the way the Greek authorities followed up recommendations or the broader impacts of TA, although it would be useful for TA planning' (2015, p. 8). In addition, there was a process problem: the Taskforce expended a lot of its time on coordination with a large number of Member States, international organizations and EU bodies.

There was much for the Commission to learn from the experience of both the Troika and the Taskforce. Strategically, its multiple roles became confused and its performance ('output legitimacy') appeared tied to debates over the severity of the austerity measures, with periodic controversies over whether reforms had met their targets or not. Operationally, the Commission's intervention highlighted the fundamental problem of how to lever reform in a domestic setting of low quality public administration and high political conflict. As the EU's chief operational agent, its effectiveness was undermined by concerns as to its lack of preparedness and planning, as well as its difficulties of coordination and feedback monitoring. Its task was daunting: to fill a vacuum at the EU level and to overcome the barriers to entry in Athens. Across the EU's two levels of governance, there were systemic issues of institutional capability and legitimacy – paralleling those found in central Europe (Haughton, 2011).

Conclusion

The Greek political drama of 2015 confronted fundamental precepts of eurozone governance, highlighting issues of the effectiveness of external leverage over reform, the normative content to European obligations, the implications for democracy and accountability and institutional vulnerabilities in policy delivery. Together these constituted a systemic shock and confronted established norms and assumptions. At one level, by the end of the year, a normality had been restored. Greece had been forced to accept a more stringent rescue and the eurozone remained largely as it was the previous January. 'Bamboo'-like, the euro-system had been stretched but not broken.

Yet 2015 prompted a reflection and a need for lesson-drawing. The immediate reviews concerned the institutional mechanics of the Troika and Taskforce deployment. More generally, these linked to the tentative EU agenda on building-up administrative capacity across Member States and the role that the Commission and EU aid might play. This is surely an agenda that will need to progress in the future as the Commission's own consultations suggest.

Strategically, Varoufakis' game of chicken showed both the resolve of the eurozone to stick with the existing policy paradigm on rescue via austerity and the conditions under which it would countenance a Member State exit. Despite SYRIZA's expectations to the contrary, the eurozone responded in a fundamentally path-dependent fashion. Germany's imprint on policy was barely less at the end than at the start of the year. This indicated the continuing weakness of an alternative policy coalition, reflected in Athens uniting the rest against itself. Also, the threat of expulsion became real, even if the reward for compliance looked ever more questionable.

In parallel, however, the normative base of the eurozone looked rather more exclusive. Ideationally, Europe was hitched to ordo-liberal regulation. Two elections and a referendum in Greece had confirmed Jyrki Katainen's comment, cited above: policy did not change as a result of any of the three voting rounds. Indeed, Greece suffered worse than before, in many respects. At the same time the rights of voters in donor states made the normative position contested.

The implications of this case for eurozone governance are clear. It struggles with a conundrum, only more so: how to combine choice (democracy), compliance (conditionality) and capability (institutional quality) in an economy that is in crisis? As such the eurozone faces unresolved systemic questions that make it skewed and vulnerable. How far can it allow a diversity of national economic policies, responsive to differing domestic preferences and needs? Is its insistence on an 'ordo-liberal' inspired conditionality commensurate with an heterogeneous Europe? How can it best intervene to overcome domestic institutional capacities to facilitate policy delivery? These questions arise from the existing diversity of the eurozone: they are not uniquely relevant to Greece, but in 2015 Athens exposed them like no other state had done before. The (non-)resolution of these questions will determine the future unity, credibility and legitimacy of the eurozone.

References

Beazer, Q. and Woo, B. (2015) 'IMF Conditionality, Government Partisanship, and the Progress of Economic Reforms'. *American Journal of Political Science*, Vol. 60, No. 2, pp. 304–21.

Bellamy, R. and Weale, A. (2015) 'Political Legitimacy and European Monetary Union: Contracts, Constitutionalism and the Normative Logic of Two-Level Games'. *Journal of European Public Policy*, Vol. 22, No. 2, pp. 257–74.

Bertelsmann Stiftung (2015) *Sustainable Governance Indicators 2015* (Berlin: Bertelsmann Stiftung).

Bird, G. and Willett, T. (2004) 'IMF Conditionality, Implementation and the New Political Economy of Ownership'. *Comparative Economic Studies*, Vol. 46, No. 3, pp. 423–50.

Boerzel, T. and Risse, T. (2010) 'Governance without a State: Can it Work?'. *Regulation and Governance*, Vol. 4, No. 2, pp. 113–34.

Buiter, W., Corsetti, G. and Roubini, N. (1993) 'Excessive Deficits: Sense and Nonsense in the Treaty of Maastricht'. *Rivista di Politica Economica*, Vol. 1, No. 1, pp. 3–82.

Copsey, N. (2015) *Rethinking the European Union* (London: Palgrave).

Dyson, K. and Featherstone, K. (1999) *The Road to Maastricht: Negotiating Economic and Monetary Union* (Oxford: Oxford University Press).

ELSTAT (2015) (Greek Statistical Authority) *Labour Force Survey* (Athens: ELSTAT).

European Court of Auditors (2015) *Special Report No. 19* (Luxembourg: European Court of Auditors). Rapporteur: Cvikl, M.

European Parliament (2014) *Committee on Economic and Monetary Affairs Reports* (Brussels: European Parliament). Rapporteur : Karas, O.

European Parliament (2015) *DG for Internal Policies Greece Reports* (Brussels: European Parliament). Rapporteur: Tinios, P.

Euro Plus Monitor Spring Update (2014) (Brussels: Lisbon Council and Berenberg Bank).

Featherstone, K. (2005) *Politics and Policy in Greece: The Challenge of Modernisation* (London: Routledge).

Featherstone, K. (2012) 'Le Choc de la Nouvelle? Maastricht, Déjà Vu and EMU Reform', LEQS Paper No. 52.

Featherstone, K. (2015) 'External Conditionality and the debt crisis: the "Troika" and public administration reform in Greece'. *Journal of European Public Policy*, Vol. 22, No. 3, pp. 295–314.

Featherstone, K. and Papadimitriou, D. (2015) *Prime Ministers in Greece: The Paradox of Power* (Oxford: Oxford University Press).

Hargreaves-Heap, S. and Varoufakis, Y. (2005) *Game Theory: A Critical Text* (London: Routledge).

Haughton, T. (ed.) (2011) *Party Politics in Central and Eastern Europe: Does EU Membership Matter?* (London: Routledge).

International Monetary Fund (2013) *Country Report 13/156.* (Washington, DC: International Monetary Fund). Rapporteur: Gordon, J.

Krugman, P. (2015) 'Greece on the brink'. *The New York Times*, 20 April.

Ivanova, A., Mayer, W., Mourmouras, A. and Anayiotos, G. (2003) 'What Determines the Implementation of IMF-Supported Programs?' IMF Working Paper No. 3.

Lavdas, K. (1997) *The Europeanization of Greece: Interest Politics and the Crises of Integration* (London: Palgrave Macmillan).

Lijphart, A. (2012) *Patterns of Democracy* (2nd edition) (New Haven: Yale University Press).

Lütz, S and Kranke, M. (2010) 'The European Rescue of the Washington Consensus? EU and IMF Lending to Central and Eastern European Countries' LEQS Paper No. 22.

March, J. and Olsen, J. (1989) *Rediscovering Institutions: The Organizational Basis of Politics* (New York: Free Press).

OECD (2014) *Going for Growth: Annual Report* (Paris: Organisation for Economic Cooperation and Development).

Pop-Eleches, G. (2009) 'Public Goods of Political Pandering: Evidence from IMF Programmes in Latin America and Eastern Europe'. *International Studies Quarterly*, Vol. 53, No. 1, pp. 787–816.

Rodrik, D. (1996) 'Understanding Economic Policy eformx'. *Journal of Economic Literature*, Vol. 34, No. 1, pp. 9–14.

Rogers, C. (2012) *The IMF and European Economies* (London: Palgrave Macmillan).

Rothstein, B. (2005) *Social Traps and the Problem of Trust* (Cambridge: Cambridge University Press).

Schimmelfennig, F. and Sedelmeier, U. (2004) 'Governance by Conditionality: EU Rule Transfer to the Candidate Countries of Central and Eastern Europe'. *Journal of European Public Policy*, Vol. 11, No. 4, pp. 661–79.

Salomon, M. (2015) 'Of Austerity, Human Rights and International Institutions'. *European Law Journal*, Vol. 21, No. 4, pp. 521–45.

Schäuble, W. (2016) 'Managing Europe – What is Germany's Responsibility?' Presentation at the German Symposium, LSE, 3 March.

Spanou, C. (2008) 'State Reform in Greece: Responding to Old and New Challenges'. *International Journal of Public Sector Management*, Vol. 21, No. 2, pp. 150–73.

Steinwand, M. and Stone, R. (2008) 'The International Monetary Fund: The Review of the Recent Evidence'. *The Review of International Organisations*, Vol. 3, No. 2, pp. 123–49.

Stiglitz, J. (2015) 'A Greek Morality Tale: Why We Need a Debt Restructuring Framework'. *The Guardian*, 4 February.

Truth Committee (2015) *Truth Committee on Public Debt: Preliminary Report* (Athens: Hellenic Parliament).

Tsakloglou, P. (2015) 'Restructuring the Greek Economy 2010–2014', Presentation at the European Institute, LSE, 12 March.

Tsebelis, G. (2015) 'Lessons from the Greek Crisis'. *Journal of European Public Policy*, Vol. 23, No. 1, pp. 25–41.

Varoufakis, Y. (2016) *And the Weak Suffer What they Must?* (London: The Bodley Head).

Zahariades, N. (2013) 'Leading Reform amidst Transboundary Crises: Lessons from Greece'. *Public Administration*, Vol. 91, No. 3, pp. 648–62.

JCMS 2016 Volume 54. Annual Review pp. 65–82   DOI: 10.1111/jcms.12436

Beelines, Bypasses and Blind Alleys: Theory and the Study of the European Union

TIM HAUGHTON
University of Birmingham

Introduction

Whilst the European Union has been beset by economic, political and existential crises in recent years, if our yardstick is the number of articles and books produced, the same cannot be said for the academic study of the EU. Indeed, the scholarly industry of analyzing and seeking to explain what Jacques Delors once dubbed the 'Unidentified Political Object' is in rude health.[1] If crisis is good copy for journalists, crisis and complexity are often helpful ingredients for scholarly enquiry and provoke interest from publishers and journals.

A sizeable slice of recent literature on the EU has sought to offer new theories, new theoretical contributions or contributions to theory building. But to what extent have they improved our knowledge and understanding? After reflecting on the broader challenges associated with attempts to theorize and theory's role in the study of the EU, this contribution seeks to make four main arguments. First, four new theoretical routes are identified: alternative, adaptation, synthesis and explaining disintegration. Each of these adds something to our understanding of the European Union and, as the great scholar of European politics Stanley Hoffmann (1959) argued, help fulfil the purpose of theory: to pose better questions.

Second, building on some of the insights of the new theories it argues that given the complexities of the current crises (Copsey, 2015; Phinnemore, 2015) and the broader processes of European integration, differentiated integration and disintegration, the study of the EU would benefit from the adoption of more combinatorial approaches and greater use of interdisciplinary and transdisciplinary approaches.

Third, I argue there is a tendency to presentism, to focus on the current crises, but the real merit of close analysis of developments is usually in placing developments in the broader historical context of integration. Painting on a wider historical canvas offers an opportunity to observe the short- and long-term dynamics of integration.

Fourth, it calls for a historical and empirical turn. Whilst recognizing that there is to some extent an implicit theoretical choice in any empirical study (Rosamond, 2006), it suggests that there is a danger of what Hoffmann (1977, p. 57) dubbed 'the rage for

*Countless colleagues have offered constructive criticism. I am particularly grateful to Anthony Arnull, Lorenzo Cladi, Nathaniel Copsey, Josefin Graef, Dermot Hodson, George Kyris, Julian Pänke, Willie Paterson, Nicole Scicluna and Mark Webber for comments on various iterations of this contribution.
[1] See Delors (1985).

premature theorizing'. Before we can explain *why* something happened (or not) we need to know *what* happened. We need a firm foundation of facts and more empirical studies to help avoid the risk of a 'tendency towards *compulsive and mindless theorizing*' [emphasis in the original] (Hirschman, 1970, p. 229). As scholars of the EU our interests do not lie in calculating how many angels can dance on the head of a pin, but rather how the EU works (or does not) and when, why, how and in what form integration (or disintegration) occurs. At the heart of these questions are empirical puzzles requiring empirical study.

The purpose of this contribution is not to 'critique' any one theoretical framework, question its ontological and epistemological assumptions and suggest that a particular framework is inherently 'right' or superior to the rest. Rather, my purpose is to assess the contribution these new approaches can make to bringing us closer to understanding what Puchala (1971) famously depicted as the 'elephant', highlight what needs to be done, and to ask what role theory plays and what role it should play in the study of the European Union.

I. Theory and scholarship

There are two major challenges made against theory. Firstly, the search for, and refinement of, theory drives scholars away from policy-relevant 'useful' work. Secondly, theory hinders rather than helps scholarship, or at least it encourages scholarship to drive down what turn out to be blind alleys rather than short cuts. The worst aspect of this second tendency is akin to the driver who slavishly follows his/her GPS convinced it *must* be right rather than looking around to see if the directions make sense. Although I have much sympathy with those who bemoan ivory tower 'scholasticism' (Mead, 2010), the primary purpose of this contribution is not to engage in a debate about the dreaded 'impact' agenda particularly well-known to those who work in British academia. Rather, in light of recent scholarship, my purpose is more to consider the second question.

Casting her eye over the state of academic life Jane Austen might remark today that it is a truth universally acknowledged that a scholar in search of academic fame, fortune or just a job is a need of his or her own theory. Thanks to the incentive structures of academia, scholars are often quick to theorize or claim their work contributes in some (significant) way to theory. Indeed, two of the great weaknesses of modern academia are the stronger incentives for individual achievement rather than collective knowledge and the vaulted position of theory *vis-à-vis* empirical work.

Theory offers scholars frameworks for understanding, opportunities to find meaning in a morass of data and a beeline to an explanation for a set of phenomena. In a trenchant defence of the importance of theory, Mearsheimer and Walt (2013, pp. 431–432) argue that theories 'identify how independent, intervening, and dependent variables fit together' and '[m]ost importantly, a theory *explains* why a particular hypothesis should be true, by identifying the causal mechanisms that produce the expected outcome(s)' [emphasis in the original]. 'Well developed theories', they assert, are 'falsifiable and offer non-trivial explanations [which] yield unambiguous predictions'. They maintain that '[a] single article that advances a new theory or makes sense of a body of disparate findings will be more valuable than dozens of empirical studies with short shelf-lives' (Mearsheimer and Walt, 2013, p. 448).

Their defence of theory raises numerous questions. I shall return to the value of theory *vis-à-vis* empirical studies below, but for now focus on three themes. First, all theories are implicitly or explicitly built on ontological and epistemological positions. For some, any enquiry a scholar undertakes is imbued with these stances which cannot be removed like a sweater, but rather are more akin to a scholar's skin (Furlong and Marsh, 2002). These positions frame scholars' thinking and identify appropriate questions to pose. To buy into a particular theory in this thinking, therefore, requires not just an acceptance, but an adoption of the same epistemological and ontological positions. Whilst respecting the position of the purists, I would suggest the logical extension of that argument is a scholarly cacophony in which everyone talks past everyone else or else silence in which no-one interacts because there is no agreement on the fundamentals. Blending and the type of combinatorial approaches I discuss below have distinct dangers, but the payoffs of explanation outweigh the costs of a lack of purity.

Second, although Wittgenstein bemoaned that 'we are bewitched into thinking that if we lack a scientific theory of something, we lack any understanding of it' (Monk, 1999) almost all scholars (in the social sciences) agree that theory is foundational to study. At that point views diverge markedly. For many who would classify themselves as constructivists, for instance, 'theory is a guide to empirical exploration, a means of reflecting more or less abstractly upon complex processes' (Hay, 2002, p. 47); a view which sits less comfortably with a description of theory as a 'causal argument of universal, transhistorical validity and nomothetic quality, which can be tested through the falsification of a series of hypotheses' (Diez and Wiener, 2009, p. 3). The broader, abstract understanding of theory has its merits, but ultimately in both the natural and social sciences and in significant slices of the humanities, the key questions are causal. Why is it like that? What caused that? Why did it not turn out differently? If theory has *any* role in scholarship it is to advance our understanding of causality. Even the more abstract constructivist theorizing is ultimately seeking to contribute answers to why questions.

Third, although in the minds of some the discovery of causal mechanisms leads on to prediction, the very notion of predictability sits uncomfortably with 'those whose philo-sophical worldview tells them that the political world is so complex and indeterminate that it is not amenable to prediction' (Hay, 2002, p. 37). Even those like Waltz (1990, p. 29), whose *Weltanschauung* is similar to Mearsheimer and Walt, argue that prediction does not have to be part of theory, noting that 'theories of evolution predict nothing in particular'. Predictability can be helpful and is integral to the attempts to explain European *dis*integration, but it is not a necessary component of any theory.

II. The uses and limitations of theory in the study of the EU

There has been hitherto no shortage of theorizing on the European Union. Each of the major theories has offered a substantial contribution to our understanding of the motors and locus of power in the process of European integration. Nonetheless, a number of challenges face anyone seeking to theorize the EU.

The first challenge, what can be dubbed the Number 1 problem, is the uniqueness of European integration. Neofunctionalists sought to develop theories of regional integration based on the post-war pooling of sovereignty (see, for example, Haas, 1958), but most theoretical activity focused on European integration has tended to respond to the challenge 'of what is this an instance?' (Rosenau and Durfee, 1995), by focusing on the case in hand and just making the occasional reference to wider lessons and the possibility of theoretical travel. Can – or indeed should – we focus just on the theoretical analysis of a single case? There is a real danger that a theory applied to one case becomes 'little more than a sophisticated description of that one case' (Rosamond, 2000, p. 69). Nonetheless, variations over time and in different policy fields offer traction from any theory of European integration, albeit one with more limited traction than the grand theories of politics or international relations.

This criticism segways into a second challenge laid down by Hix (1994, 1996) who not only argued that just as we have no theory of American or German politics there could not be a theory of the EU, but also that neofunctionalist and intergovernmentalist accounts largely conducted by international relations scholars were asking the wrong questions. For Hix, the study of the EU required an embrace of the toolkit of comparative politics. I would wholeheartedly agree that comparative politics can bring – and indeed has brought (see, for example, Jachtenfuchs, 2001) – considerable insights into the workings of the EU system, but does that mean we should abandon EU integration theory altogether?

Even accepting that there is merit in a theory focused on EU integration, poses the dependent variable problem: what exactly *is* European integration (Haas, 1971; Rosamond, 2000)? If there have been disagreements between scholars over this fundamental question (Diez and Wiener, 2009) one might ask what hope is there for meaningful dialogue between different theoretical traditions let alone for developing a more cogent theory? Nonetheless, at the heart of most understandings of integration is the pooling of sovereignty, that is, the responsibility for certain decisions rests at a supranational level. Through political, economic and legal analysis of the degree of delegation and the extent of pooling it is possible to produce measures of the variety and depth of integration across a large number of policy areas (see, for example, Börzel, 2005).

I would suggest there is still merit in integration theory, which explains the pace, degree and variable nature of integration, stagnation and disintegration. In their different ways each of the four routes discussed below highlights the merits of integration theory. Adaptation and combinatorial approaches provide an explanation for the amount and form of the pooling of sovereignty, alternative theories encourage us to look in different ways and places, and disintegration theorists indicate reasons why the integration project may unravel. The four routes outlined below offer new directions for research which enhance our understanding although none *per se* is fully satisfactory and they all provoke deeper questions and concerns.

III. Four routes towards a better understanding of the EU and european integration

Recent developments in the study of the European Union have spurred scholars to travel down four theoretical routes: alternative, adaptation, synthesis and explaining disintegration. In order to unlock the puzzles of European integration, alternative approaches use different disciplines and non-mainstream paths, adaptation accounts amend and refine existing frameworks and synthesis scholarship seeks to blend and combine different approaches. I begin though with attempts to explain not integration, but rather disintegration.

Explaining disintegration: why the only way isn't necessarily up

Now appears a particularly 'appropriate' time to consider both integration and disintegration (Schimmelfennig, 2015, p. 723). Indeed, by the time this contribution is published, one of the major Member States may – or may not – have voted to leave the European Union. But it was not so much the threat of Brexit or even the existential challenge to the EU posed by the migration/refugee crisis, but rather the eurozone crisis, which fuelled an explosion of literature seeking to examine European *dis*integration, (see, for example, Vollard, 2014; Webber, 2014).

The great merit of the burgeoning disintegration scholarship – which encompasses scholars of very different backgrounds and persuasions with both positive and normative agendas – is to remind us that integration can go in both directions. Any theory of integration worth its salt should be able to explain the speed, extent, variations *and* direction of integration. Whilst the emphasis on alternative directions of travel in disintegration accounts is to be welcomed, we would be wise, however, not to overemphasize their novelty. Neofunctionalists, for instance, did consider the conditions for disintegration: not just spillover, but spillback (Haas, 1967; Schmitter, 1969).

Alternative: discipline and deviance

Alternative, or non-mainstream, theories have been present in scholarship for many years (see, for example, Cafruny and Ryner, 2003; Cocks, 1980; Strange and Worth, 2012), but much like the disintegration scholarship it has been the economic woes afflicting the eurozone and the general malaise surrounding European integration in recent times which has fuelled a new wave of interest in alternative theories, especially – but not exclusively – from scholars from critical theory/Marxist traditions (Manners and Whitman, 2016).

Mainstream and critical theorists, however, have often talked about each other with barely concealed disdain or more frequently just talked past each other. Much of this stems from perceived irreconcilable ontologies and *Weltanschauungen*, but also from muddying or insuperable mixing (take your pick) of normative and positive positions. Radical left approaches offer at times astute analysis of the role of capital and capitalism. The crisis in the banking sector, for instance, played a significant role in precipitating the eurozone crisis. Moreover, examining where a large slice of the bailout funds went and the general thrust of policies designed to tackle the eurozone's predicament underline that the response to the post-2008 economic crisis 'fundamentally subordinated social concerns to market imperatives' (Macartney, 2013, p. 8). Indeed, it is difficult to understand the current crisis without appreciating that it is inextricably linked to the structures of power, the replication of those structures in capitalist systems and the power of international capital. For non-Marxists it is worth remembering that whilst his predictions and broader historicism may be highly questionable, Trier's most famous son's analysis of the workings of 19th century capitalism was insightful. But that does not mean we have to swallow hook, line and sinker a Marxist approach. At the very least we need to recognize the leaders and finance ministers sitting around the European Council and Eurogroup tables were not just the pawns of international capital.

The need to embrace alternative insights also extends beyond disciplinary boundaries. Hitherto political scientists have been at the forefront of theorizing European integration.

This dominance has offered disciplinary rigour, but also disciplinary constraints (Rosamond, 2007, p. 233). Given the increasing specialization of modern academia where it is hard enough to keep up with the literature in whatever specific sub-sub-sub-discipline most of us work in, it is perhaps no surprise that scholars grappling to explain European integration have not embraced the perspectives of other disciplines as much as they should. As Jones and Torres (2015, p. 714) noted, 'it is a harsh reality that in a world indexed by Google and narrated by Twitter, the barriers to entry in any disciplinary conversation are large'.

Scholars of the EU have been better than most political scientists in recognizing the need to integrate the insights of other disciplines. Not only has the study of law and legal institutions enriched the scholarship of integration (see Alter, 2009; Sandholtz and Stone Sweet, 1998; Scicluna, 2014), for example, but it is clearly integral to cogent explanation. The European Court of Justice may not be the behemoth portrayed by eurosceptic politicians and journalists, but thanks to both landmark cases such as *Cassis de Dijon* and day-to-day rulings it has played – and continues to play – an important role in European integration. More engagement with different disciplinary perspectives, especially history as I argue below, is needed in order for us to better understand Puchala's elephant.

Adaptation

Recognizing the limitations of the standard theories of neofunctionalism and intergovernmentalism (both the original and the liberal variants), Christopher Bickerton, Dermot Hodson and Uwe Puetter (2015a, 2015b) have adapted the long-standing tenants of the intergovernmental school and developed 'new intergovernmentalism'. At the heart of their study is what they label the 'integration paradox': since the passing of the Treaty on European Union, whilst the basic constitutional features of the EU have remained stable, EU activity has expanded to an unprecedented degree. Member States, they argue, 'pursue more integration but stubbornly resist further supranationalism' (Bickerton *et al.*, 2015a, p. 705).

Much *has* changed since the early 1990s. Bickerton et al. (2015a, p. 705) maintain there has been a proliferation of *de novo* bodies such as the European External Action Service, the European Food Safety Agency, the EU Agency for Fundamental Rights and the European Banking Authority 'that often enjoy considerable autonomy by way of executive or legislative power and have a degree of control over their own resources'. For the new intergovernmental thesis the key here is that these new bodies fulfil functions that were not delegated to the Commission and tend to contain mechanisms for Member State representation. More broadly, and indicative of the centrality of Member States to the process of European integration, the European Council, as Puetter (2014, p. 68) argues, has become the 'new centre of political gravity'.

Frank Schimmelfennig (2015, p. 724), however, challenged the empirical basis of the new intergovernmentalism thesis, maintaining that the *de novo* bodies 'display a wide variation of intergovernmental and supranational features, the Commission and European Parliament have gained powers since the early 1990s and in the post-Maastricht era the "Ordinary Legislative Procedure" (i.e., the most advanced form of the Community method) is indeed, the "ordinary" decision-making logic and procedure' (p. 725).

Moreover, other studies have questioned whether the Commission has been so peripheral in recent times (Nugent and Rhinard, 2016).[2]

Highlighting the argument I make about presentism below, the most telling criticism of new intergovernmentalism, however, lies in the temporal division. Although we can make a distinction between a pre-Maastricht era which was mostly about markets and a post-Maastricht era where non-market policies became more prominent in European integration, to see Maastricht as a watershed 'overlooks the extent to which it codified and built on existing integration dynamics within and around the then European Communities' (Phinnemore, 2015, p. 72). Indeed, Schimmelfennig (2015, p. 726) points out that European Political Cooperation (1970), the Monetary Committee (1958), the 'snake in the tunnel' (1972), the European Monetary System (1979), the TREVI anti-terrorist intergovernmental network (1975), the beginnings of regional policy (1975) and the Schengen Agreement (1985) were 'all dominated by intensifying intergovernmental policy co-ordination both within and outside the Treaty framework'.

Whilst we may challenge the 'new' and question new intergovernmentalism's 'blanket characterization of EU integration' (Bulmer, 2015, p. 294), Bickerton *et al.* (2015a, 2015b) make a strong and persuasive case for an intergovernmentalist framework. They enrich intergovernmental accounts in two ways. Firstly, although Andrew Moravcsik's (1998) liberal intergovernmentalism offered a detailed discussion of national preference formation largely in terms of the economic preferences Member States brought to the treaty negotiation tables, the crisis period in particular has highlighted the 'unstable set of relationships between domestic constituencies, member state governments, and EU policies and institutions' (Bickerton *et al.*, 2015b p. 22). These relationships need to be understood much better, in particular the vulnerabilities, which shape states' decisions to pool sovereignty (Haughton 2010; Keohane, 1982). With some notable exceptions (for example, Lucarelli, 2015; Paterson, 2011), studies of individual Member States have remained largely the preserve of textbooks (for example, Bulmer and Lequesne, 2013). Yet without detailed, empirically grounded studies of Member States, theorizing on the European Union has weak foundations.

The second insight concerns public opinion. In their post-functional theory of European integration, Liesbet Hooghe and Gary Marks (2009, p. 5) observed since the early 1990s a shift in public opinion from 'permissive consensus' to 'constraining dissensus'. Bickerton *et al.* challenge the post-functionalist expectation that a more politicized public would 'shrink […] the scope of agreement' (Bickerton *et al.*, 2015b, p. 26). Indeed, the raft of measures agreed upon by the Member States in recent years to combat the eurozone crisis (EFSF, ESM, Six-Pack, Two-Pack, Fiscal Compact etc.) suggests any 'constraint' exerted by public opinion has been limited.[3] Moreover, Bickerton *et al.* argue that the gap between governments and peoples has created an unprecedented opportunity for expanding the activities of the EU, but has also been a powerful constraint on the manner in which integration has taken place.

Public opinion, however, does matter. At times decision-making has been characterized by insulation and separation, but popular will has played a role. Indeed, it is difficult to

---

[2]See also Dinan's contribution to this volume.
[3]See Hodson's contributions to this and previous issues of the *Annual Review.*

understand the stances taken by Angela Merkel and David Cameron around the European Council table without considering the role played by public opinion. In Germany, the 'politics of timing and the timing of politics' has mattered to Merkel (Jacoby, 2015) and in the past few years it has felt as though the Farage-fuelled eurosceptic public opinion in the UK has been the tail wagging the dog in British policy and practice in Brussels. We should not underestimate the political antennae of those sitting round the key decision-making bodies in the EU representing Member States. Critics might point to the disregard of Greek public opinion expressed during two elections and a referendum during the course of 2015,[4] but whilst some individuals may have been driven by plans and ideology, we would be unwise to ignore domestic political opinion in other Member States. Public opinion does matter for politicians as it will ultimately determine how long they stay in their seats. As Jean-Claude Juncker once famously remarked, 'We all know what to do, we just don't know how to get re-elected afterwards'.[5]

The eurozone crisis, the possibility of Brexit and perhaps most especially the migration/refugee crisis have ensured a high level of politicization of the EU (Risse, 2015). Any satisfactory theory of European integration needs to integrate public opinion and political linkage into the equation in a robust and systematic manner highlighting when they do and do not matter. As Hanspeter Kriesi argues in this volume, politicization is not simply a post-Maastricht phenomenon. Indeed, rather than Maastricht marking a watershed it may be better to refer to 'intermittent politicization'. Moreover, politicization has not only varied over time, but is highly differentiated across countries. This argument underlines the need for more bottom-up empirically grounded studies rather than examinations of top-down Europeanization.

Combinatorial

Whereas Bickerton et al. have sought to identify and elaborate a new general theory of integration, when confronted with the challenge of explaining the post-2008 crisis period of the EU or the development of integration in non socio-economic areas over a longer period of time, other scholars have sought instead to build new theoretical models and insights in a combinatorial, eclectic or synthetic manner (see, for example, Jones et al., 2016; Leuffen et al., 2013), drawing explicitly or implicitly on calls for combination and to transcend the theoretical divides over 'isms' (see, for example, Jupille et al., 2003; Lake, 2011; Saurugger, 2014; Verdun, 2002).

Jones et al. (2016), for instance, combine intergovernmentalism with neofunctionalism in their explanation for the incremental, step-by-step response of the EU to the daunting economic and financial challenges of the eurozone crisis. Intergovernmental bargaining, they argue, leads to incompleteness because it forces states with diverse preferences to settle on lowest common denominator solutions. Incompleteness then unleashes forces that lead to crisis and Member States respond yet again by agreeing to lowest common denominator solutions. In their schema, the EU 'fails forward': 'again and again responding to the failures of incremental reforms by taking new steps to expand the scope

[4]See Featherstone's contribution to this volume.
[5]*The Economist*, 15 March 2007.

and intensity of integration' (Jones *et al.*, 2016, p. 1012). But such an intergovernmental account by itself could indicate two different directions of travel. What pushes the states towards solutions involving more integration are the 'forces of neofunctional spillover and supranational activism' (Jones *et al.*, 2016, p. 1015).

A different way of conceiving European integration using a combinatorial approach has been offered by Dirk Leuffen, Berthhold Rittberger and Frank Schmimmelfennig (2013). They set out to explain variation in the integration process, both in horizontal (the 'territorial extension of the EU's policy regimes') and vertical (capturing the 'depth or centralization of supranational decision-making in different policy areas') terms (Leuffen *et al.*, 2013, p. 245).

Identifying differentiation *per se* is nothing new (see, for example, Kölliker, 2006; Stubb, 1996), but 'differentiation has increased rather than diminished in the course of European integration' (Leuffen *et al.*, 2013, p. 26) and is worthy of explanation. Although Leuffen *et al.* agree on the importance of intergovernmentalism, in contrast to Jones *et al.*'s, (2016, p. 1015) emphasis on neofunctionalism's ability to explain the 'gradual patterns of change over time', they suggest an intergovernmental baseline model which is affected by both institutional path-dependencies at the supranational level stressed by historical institutionalists (Pierson, 1996) and identity politics at the domestic level (Hooghe and Marks, 2009).

To be convincing as an overall theoretical framework for explaining integration, any combinatorial approach cannot just be a pick and mix theory which suggests X matters here, but Y matters there. It has to confront the challenge of whether the components can be combined in a meaningful and coherent manner. Ontological and epistemological purists might suggest different positions are 'unalloyable', but combination is 'possible' (Jupille, 2006, p. 213). Indeed, in a prize-winning book Frank Schimmelfennig (2003), for instance, blended constructivist and realist ideas effectively into the most cogent explanation of the eastern enlargement of the EU.

Even if we navigate the ontological and epistemological hurdle, however, there are further challenges. For some, theoretical approaches such as neo-functionalism are a 'package deal' (Alter, 2009, p. 14). But on closer inspection some of the major theoretical traditions are not a million miles apart. If we examine the major (supranational and liberal intergovernmental) accounts of what drove the internal market programme of the late 1980s, putting aside '[d]ifferences in emphasis', 'the ingredients of both explanations are very similar' (Schimmelfennig, 2010, p. 40). Moreover, several conditions of integration (interdependence, convergence of preferences and politicization) 'are stipulated explicitly or accepted implicitly by intergovernmentalism, supranationalism and constructivism' (Leuffen *et al.*, 2013, p. 260). In other words, the challenge is not so much whether combination is possible, but how to construct a cogent combinatorial framework. Integral to that task are questions related to empirical foundations and the manner in which we undertake research.

IV. Extending and enhancing the road to a better understanding

The four routes sketched out above provide promising avenues of understanding, but I suggest theoretical work on EU integration needs to go further in three ways.

The parts, the sum and the whole

Although it contains only a passing reference, Leuffen *et al.*'s *Differentiated Integra-tion* (2013), can be seen as illustrative of what Rudra Sil and Peter Katzenstein (2010) have labelled 'analytical eclecticism'. Taking inspiration from Hirschman's (1970) argument that paradigms can be a 'hindrance to understanding' and drawing on a number of examples of scholarships that have combined different approaches, Sil and Katzenstein make a strong and persuasive case for a combinatorial approach. They argue that '[s]implifications based on a single theoretical lens involve trade-offs, and can produce enduring blind spots unless accompanied by complementary, countervailing efforts to "recomplexify" problems' (Sil and Katzenstein, 2010, p. 9). The word 'eclecticism' may be synonymous with 'indiscriminate' and 'ragtag' (Bennett, 2013, p. 461), but Sil and Katzenstein's purpose is to emphasize taking the best from a variety of different approaches, methods or styles. They see analytical eclecticism's value-added as 'a more open-ended analysis that can incorporate the in-sights of different paradigm-bound theories' (Sil and Katzenstein, 2010, p. 20).

Sil and Katzenstein are not suggesting that combinatorial approaches are necessarily suitable in all cases. Narrow questions can be – and perhaps are best – addressed within single paradigms, but for what they see as 'open-ended' and real world problems of inter-national politics, Sil and Katzenstein argue there is a need to examine them in all their complexity and breadth. So far, beyond studies in European security and foreign policy (Cladi and Locatelli, 2016; Pohl and van Willigen, 2015) there has been little explicit use of analytical eclectic approaches in studies of the EU, but the evolving EU elephant seems a highly appropriate specimen to examine using analytical eclecticism. Indeed, it is striking not just that Jabko (2006) and Schimmelfennig's (2003) work are referenced as examples of the kind of approach Sil and Katzenstein advocate, but also that *Analytical Eclecticism* is dedicated to three scholars who made major contributions to the study of European integration: Ernest Haas, Karl Deutsch and Stanley Hoffmann.

Changing realities, changing theories: the problem of presentism

For obvious reasons political science tends to have a bias towards the present. New theoretical frameworks have tended to emerge out of a feeling the existing ones do not explain the present (for example, Egan *et al.*, 2010; Hoffmann, 1966; Hooghe and Marks, 2009) and the multiple crises besetting the EU have understandably prompted scholars to search for new explanations. Crisis periods often feel new and distinct. If they really are so new and distinct, requiring new theorizing, then we open ourselves up to the accusation that rather than just limiting ourselves to n = 1 we restrict ourselves to n = only a fraction of 1. Any truly convincing theory of European integration would be able to explain, for example, the lack of any integration after World War I, the decision to pool sovereignty after World War II, the subsequent speed, nature and variety of integration and ultimately any disintegration. The ability of the work of Haas (1958), Hoffmann (1966) and Moravcsik (1998) to address at least most of these questions is part of the reason for their enduring appeal. Of course one strand of theorizing on the EU, historical institutionalism, *has* stressed the role of historical decisions in shaping the course of European integration, particularly in terms of identifying the stickiness of institutions and 'critical junctures'

(Pierson, 1996; Verdun, 2015) and it is no surprise that combinatorial approaches have embraced historical institutionalism (for example, Leuffen *et al.*, 2013).

Indeed, in seeking to understand the current crisis we would be wise to think in more historical terms. Braudel highlighted how the focus on the present of *'l'histoire evenmentielle'* flaring up in the night like a 'firework display of phosphorescent fireflies' and briefly illuminating the landscape around it might catch our eyes, but it can detract attention away from understanding 'the slower trajectories of change and the enduring continuities' (Braudel, 1980, pp. 10, 26; Tosh, 2008, p. 43).

Moreover, a deeper understanding of historical developments can help explain the crises and the responses of Member States. The Central and East European states' response to the flow of refugees is intimately linked to historical issues of weaker statehood and comparatively limited experience of migration during communist times (Haughton, 2016), the Brexit referendum of 2016 has striking parallels with the previous UK referendum of 1975, and Germany's stance and actions in the eurozone crisis cannot be understood without reference to the experience of unification a quarter of a century previously (Newman, 2015).[6]

This is not to suggest the present and the current crises are somehow carbon copies of past developments, but rather to stress the need to be more cognizant of longer-term historical developments. Jones *et al.*'s (2016) theorizing which offers a distinction between short-term intergovernmentalist dynamics and a much longer-term neofunctional logic, for instance, offers a helpful way of incorporating historical insights.

Who, Where, What, When ... and Why?

Scholars who have taken us down the alternative, adaptation, combination and disintegration routes have shed light on actors and processes and have provoked thinking about the speed, nature, motors, brakes and direction of European integration. Nevertheless, there is a more fundamental question to pose about advancement in knowledge: does theory help or hinder the search for understanding? Theories – as all adherents of them stress – offer fast-tracks and short-cuts, allowing us to speed along bypassing seemingly unimportant detail and getting us quickly to explanations. Yet do we know enough in order to theorize? The precursors of a satisfactory answer to a 'why?' question are answers to the questions of who, where, what and when? Even Waltz (1990, p. 23), who offers a trenchant defence of theory, argues that we cannot ask how does X work or does it all hang together unless one has some clear idea of what the 'thing' or the 'it' might be.

The pace of change in the eurozone and the EU over the past few years has been striking. A plethora of measures, agreements and actions have ensured the single currency has survived and possibly with it the entire EU. The crisis, though, is not over. Until the eurozone crisis is behind us there are difficulties in thinking about causes and consequences, let alone the contribution of those events to the wider theoretical agenda. Indeed, it is striking that not only have many of the best accounts to explain the state of the EU largely eschewed theory (Copsey, 2015; Schmidt, 2009; Tsoukalis, 2011),[7] but probably

---

[6]It is worth remembering that Wolfgang Schäuble was a major player in the negotiations for German unification and the eurozone crisis (Novotná, 2015).

[7]See also Börzel's contribution to this volume.

the two most insightful accounts of the eurozone crisis published so far have either sidestepped the theories of European integration (Marsh, 2010) or refrained from discussing the grand theories of integration until the penultimate chapter (Matthijs and Blyth, 2015). I am not suggesting that we should avoid all theorizing, but rather be more cautious of theorizing an on-going process.

Moreover, the rush to theorize is having a potentially deleterious impact on our scholarship. Inspired in part by developments in US legal scholarship the main direction of travel in legal studies of the EU over the past few decades has been away from doctrinal research involving article by article commentary and annotation and a close reading of texts towards more contextual and political analysis (Arnull, 2008, 2010). Whilst the greater interdisciplinarity of that shift was very much to be welcomed, the contextual work is only possible 'because other writers have conducted the necessary doctrinal analysis' (Arnull, 2008, p. 426). If too many scholars abandon analysis based on a close reading of the texts, there is a danger that contextual work will be based on insecure foundations. We can draw a parallel here with trends in the study of comparative politics. Robust and convincing large 'n' studies are frequently built on the insights of country experts. Without those who know the detail about specific cases, there is the danger of number-crunchers confusing what is 'measurable' with what is 'meaningful' (Copsey, 2015, p. 209). Indeed, it is striking that some of the most significant theoretical contributions to political science have grown out of detailed empirical scholarship of a single case (for example, Putnam, 1993).

These two arguments underline the need for scholars not just to have greater knowledge of the twists and turns of more recent events, but also to have a solid historical grounding of developments. Yet despite the obvious linkages between history and political science, it is striking how little dialogue there is between the two disciplines. History is not just about descriptive detail, but can provide much of the flesh for political scientists helping to turn their arguments from lightweight to heavyweight.

Nevertheless, we need to ask a more fundamental question about how we use theory. To claim that theory might distract, or worse distort, scholarship provokes numerous objections. If we simply seek an empirical route might we just end up with a mindless collection of data? The European Union is not the most scintillating object of study at the best of times, but if we all become bean counters then we may end up trading interesting ideas for dull as ditchwater detail. Moreover, Rosamond (2006, p. 450) rightly reminds us, 'the selection of particular events or phenomena in the EU's history is in and of itself a theoretical choice'. Perhaps the greater risk, however, lies in theoretical cherry picking, i.e. choosing assumptions that will generate the kinds of results the investigator wants to find (Pfleiderer, 2014). Instead of offering us a beeline to an explanation, theory may send us down a blind alley.

My purpose here is not to suggest that theory has no role (it does), but rather to argue we should be careful not to fetishize theory. Moreover, a specific theory should not be the starting point, guiding light and the end point of research activity. Instead of starting with a theory, generating a research question and undertaking empirical research to test theoretical expectations, we would be better off with deeper empirical studies unencumbered by specific theories as we generate and clarify the puzzles and only at a later stage testing and refining theories. Such studies would move at a slower pace, along empirical side roads rather than theoretical super-highways. They may not yield much ultimate insight – but then neither do unsatisfactory theories – but they will generate raw material which can be used for wider reflections. It is striking that Hooghe and Marks (2009) acknowledged that one of the major stimuli for their post-functional theory of European integration was the mass of data generated by the Chapel Hill expert surveys which simply aimed at mapping party politics in the Member States. Moreover, Kassim *et al.*'s (2013) extensive survey of Commission officials' background and beliefs provides the basis for more robust theorizing. Neither Marks and Hooghe nor Kassim *et al.* embarked on their data collection viewing European integration through a specific theoretical lens, but as Donald Trump might put it, 'to figure out what the hell is going on'.

Stanley Hoffmann (1959, p. 358) warned us nearly six decades ago that '[c]ollecting facts is not enough; it is not helpful to gather answers when no questions have been asked first'. Few would disagree, but how do we generate those questions? Put simply, we can be driven by paradigms or puzzles. Whilst there is merit in paradigm-driven research agendas if we want to test specific theories, grappling with the open-ended questions of European integration is far better suited to puzzle-driven research. Not only can starting from empirical questions be a more engaging way to teach (Edkins and Zehfuss, 2014), but it will ultimately take us to better destinations.

Conclusion: the long and winding road

We should welcome the recent contributions of scholars who have forwarded alternative, adaptation, synthesis and disintegration frameworks for understanding European integration. Disintegration scholars remind us the direction of travel is not always forwards, whereas synthesis scholars underline that combining different approaches is not only possible, but necessary to grasp 'the multifaceted and hybrid nature of European integration' (Egan *et al.*, 2010, p. 2). As Hoffmann (1959, p. 372) warned many years ago, '[e]xcessive emphasis on one perspective produces optical illusions'. Adaptation scholars question whether the same frameworks can be used in different time periods and the alternative theories highlight that at the heart of an integration process which has markets and states requires an understanding of the functioning of capitalism and more broadly they remind us that a single disciplinary toolkit is not enough.

Genuine interdisciplinary and transdisciplinary approaches are much harder to construct and co-ordinate, but given the collective acquired wisdom they can contain, they have a much better chance of grasping the elephant in its entirety. In particular, any attempt to explain integration needs to be built on a solid historical basis. Arguably the most telling critiques of the theories of integration have come from historians (see Lieshout *et al.*, 2004; Milward, 1992). Moreover, our response to theories not seeking to explain the present is often to generate new theories, but these should also provoke us to look again more carefully at the empirical bases in previous periods. Present periods may be exceptions rather than the rule.

The *JCMS Annual Review* of 2015 is an appropriate place to reflect on the role of theory in the study of the European Union not just due to the significant scholarly activity of recent times, but also given Stanley Hoffmann's sad death in September 2015 and his lifetime contribution to the study of European politics and society. This is not to suggest Hoffmann was a ground-breaking theorist. Indeed, his elegantly written articles highlighted the role and motivations of obstinate states, adding a necessary note of caution to our use of theories rather than outlining a systematic theory of intergovernmentalism.

Theories are neither panaceas nor silver bullets. At best they can offer us a speedy and direct route to understanding, but we need to be cautious. '[W]e have to proceed methodically and gradually', conscious that 'the weakness of many theories comes from their attempt to skip several stages' (Hoffmann, 1959, p. 370). Robust theorizing needs not only to take adequate cognizance of the existing corpus, avoiding the dumping of existing theories just because they do not explain the present predicament, but also it needs to be grounded in thorough and detailed empirical knowledge. If well constructed theories will help us pose better questions, uncover new and potentially promising paths of discovery, and ensure the long and winding road to understanding is at least a little shorter.

References

Alter, K.J. (2009) *The European Court's Political Power: Selected Essays* (Oxford and New York: Oxford University Press).

Arnull, A. (2008) 'The Americanization of EU Law Scholarship'. In Arnull, A., Eeckhout, P. and Tridimas, T. (eds) *Continuity and Change in EU Law: Essays in Honour of Sir Francis Jacobs* (Oxford: Oxford University Press), pp. 415–31.

Arnull, A. (2010) 'European Union Law: A Tale of Microscopes and Telescopes'. In Egan, M., Nugent, N. and Paterson, W.E. (eds) *Research Agenda in EU Studies Stalking the Elephant* (Basingstoke and New York: Palgrave), pp. 168–88.

Bennett, A. (2013) 'The mother of all isms: Causal mechanisms and structured pluralism in International Relations theory'. *European Journal of International Relations*, Vol. 19, No. 3, pp. 459–81.

Bickerton, C.J., Hodson, D. and Puetter, U. (2015a) 'The New Intergovernmentalism: European Integration in the Post-Maastricht Era'. *JCMS*, Vol. 53, No. 4, pp. 703–22.

Bickerton, C.J., Hodson, D. and Puetter, U. (2015b) 'The New Intergovernmentalism and the Study of European Integration'. In Bickerton, C.J., Hodson, D. and Puetter, U. (eds) *The New Intergovernmentalism: States and Supranational Actors in the Post Maastricht Period* (Oxford: Oxford University Press), pp. 1–48.

Börzel, T. (2005) 'Mind the Gap! European Integration between Level and Scope'. *Journal of European Public Policy*, Vol. 12, No. 2, pp. 217–36.

Braudel, F. (1980) *On History,* translated by Sarah Matthews (London: Weidenfield & Nicolson).

Bulmer, S. (2015) 'Understanding the New Intergovernmentalism: Pre- and Post-Maastricht Studies'. In Bickerton, C., Hodson, D. and Puetter, U. (eds) *The New Intergovernmentalism: States and Supranational Actors in the Post Maastricht Period* (Oxford: Oxford University Press), 289–303.

Bulmer, S. and Lequesne, C. (eds) (2013) *The Member States of the European Union* (2nd edition) (Oxford: Oxford University Press).

Cafruny, A.W. and Ryner, M. (eds) (2003) *A Ruined Fortress? Neoliberal Hegemony and Transformation in Europe* (Lanham, MD: Rowman & Littlefield).

Cladi, L. and Locatelli, A. (eds) (2016) *International Relations Theory and European Security: We Thought We Knew* (London and New York: Routledge).

Cocks, P. (1980) 'Towards a Marxist Theory of European Integration'. *International Organization*, Vol. 34, No. 1, pp. 1–40.

Copsey, N. (2015) *Rethinking the European Union* (London: Palgrave).

Delors, J. (1985) Speech by Jacques Delors, Luxembourg, 9 September 1985. Available online at: <<http://www.cvce.eu/obj/speech_by_jacques_delors_luxembourg_9_september_1985-en-423d6913-b4e2-4395-9157-fe70b3ca8521.html>>. Last accessed: 23 April 2016.

Diez, T. and Wiener, A. (2009) 'Introducing the Mosaic of Integration Theory'. In Wiener, A. and Diez, T. (eds) *European Integration Theory* (2nd edition) (Oxford: Oxford University Press), pp. 1–22.

Edkins, J. and Zehfuss, M. (2014) *Global Politics: A New Introduction* (2nd edition) (London and New York: Routledge).

Egan, M., Nugent, N. and Paterson, W.E. (2010) 'Introduction: Researching the European Union'. In Egan, M., Nugent, N. and Paterson, W.E. (eds) *Research Agenda in EU Studies Stalking the Elephant* (Basingstoke and New York: Palgrave), pp. 1–13.

Furlong, P. and Marsh, D. (2002) 'A Skin Not A Sweater: Ontology and Epistemology in Political Science'. In Marsh, D. and Stoker, G. (eds) *Theory and Methods in Political Science* (Basingstoke: Palgrave Macmillan), pp. 17–41.

Haas, E. (1958) *The Uniting of Europe: Political, Social, and Economic Forces, 1950–1957* (Palo Alto: Stanford University Press).

Haas, E.B. (1967) 'The "Uniting of Europe" and the "Uniting of Latin America"'. *JCMS*, Vol. 5, No. 4, pp. 315–43.

Haas, E. (1971) 'The Study of Regional Integration: Reflections on the Joy and Anguish of Pretheorizing'. In Lindberg, L.N. and Scheingold, S.A. (eds) *European Integration: Theory and Research (Cambridge* (MA: Harvard University Press).

Haughton, T. (2010) 'Zranitelnost, povstupní kocovina a role předsednictví: Formováni národních preferencí nových členských států EU'. *Mezinárodní vztahy*, Vol. 45, No. 4, pp. 11–28.

Haughton, T. (2016 forthcoming) 'Central and Eastern Europe: The Sacrifices of Solidarity, the Discomforts of Diversity and the Vexations of Vulnerabilities'. In Dinan, D., Nugent, N. and Paterson, W.E. (eds) *The European Union in Crisis* (London: Palgrave Macmillan).

Hay, C. (2002) *Political Analysis: A Critical Introduction* (Basingstoke and New York: Palgrave).

Hirschman, A.O. (1970) 'The Search for Paradigms as a Hindrance to Understanding'. *World Politics*, Vol. 22, No. 3, pp. 329–43.

Hix, S. (1994) ''The Study of the European Community: The Challenge to Comparative Politics'. *West European Politics*, Vol. 17, No. 1, pp. 1–30.

Hix, S. (1996) 'CP, IR and the EU! A Rejoinder to Hurrell and Menon'. *West European Politics*, Vol. 19, No. 4, pp. 802–4.

Hoffmann, S. (1959) 'International Relations: The Long Road to Theory'. *World Politics*, Vol. 11, No. 3, pp. 346–77.

Hoffmann, S. (1966) 'Obstinate or Obsolete? The Fate of the Nation-State and the Case of Western Europe'. *Daedalus*, Vol. 95, No. 3, pp. 862–915.

Hoffmann, S. (1977) 'An American Social Science: International Relations'. *Daedalus*, Vol. 106, No. 3, pp. 41–60.

Hooghe, L. and Marks, G. (2009) 'A Postfunctionalist Theory of European Integration: From Permissive Consensus to Constraining Dissensus'. *British Journal of Political Science*, Vol. 39, No. 1, pp. 1–23.

Jabko, N. (2006) *Playing the Market: A Political Strategy for Uniting Europe, 1985–2005* (Ithaca, NY: Cornell University Press).

Jachtenfuchs, M. (2001) 'The Governance Approach to European Integration'. *JCMS*, Vol. 39, No. 2, pp. 245–64.

Jacoby, W. (2015) 'Europe's New German Problem: The Timing of Politics and the Politics of Timing'. In Matthijs, M. and Blyth, M. (eds) *The Future of the Euro* (Oxford and New York: Oxford University Press), pp. 187–209.

Jones, E. and Torres, F. (2015) 'An "Economics" Window on an Interdisciplinary Crisis'. *Journal of European Integration*, Vol. 37, No. 7, pp. 713–22.

Jones, E., Kelemen, R.D. and Meunier, S. (2016) 'Failing Forward? The Euro Crisis and the Incomplete Nature of European Integration'. *Comparative Political Studies*, Vol. 49, No. 7, pp. 1010–34.

Jupille, J. (2006) 'Knowing Europe: Metatheory and Methodology in European Studies'. In Cini, M. and Bourne, A. (eds) *Palgrave Advances in European Union Studies* (Basingstoke: Palgrave Macmillan), pp. 209–32.

Jupille, J., Caporaso, J.A. and Checkel, J.T. (2003) 'Integrating Institutions: Rationalism, Constructivism and the Study of the European Union'. *Comparative Political Studies*, Vol. 36 Nos. 1–2, pp. 7–40.

Kassim, H., Peterson, J., Bauer, M.W., Connolly, S., Dehousse, R., Hooghe, L. and Thompson, A. (2013) *The European Commission of the Twenty First Century* (Oxford: Oxford University Press).

Keohane, R.O. (1982) 'The Demand for International Regimes'. *International Organization*, Vol. 36, pp. 325–55.

Kölliker, A. (2006) *Flexibility and European Unifications: the Logic of Differentiated Integration* (Lanham: Rowman & Littlefield).

Lake, D.A. (2011) 'Why "isms" are Evil: Theory, Epistemology and Academic Sects as Impediments to Understanding and Progress'. *International Studies Quarterly*, Vol. 55, pp. 465–80.

Lieshout, R.H., Segers, M.L.L. and van der Vleuten, A.M. (2004) 'De Gaulle, Moravcsik and The Choice for Europe: Soft Sources, Weak Evidence'. *Journal of Cold War Studies*, Vol. 6, No. 4, pp. 89–139.

Leuffen, D., Rittberger, B. and Schimmelfennig, F. (2013) *Differentiated Integration: Explaining Variation in the European Union* (Basingstoke: Palgrave).

Lucarelli, S. (2015) 'Italy and the EU: From True Love to Disenchantment'. *JCMS*, Vol. 53, No. s1, pp. 40–60.

Macartney, H. (2013) *The Debt Crisis and European Democratic Legitimacy* (Basingstoke: Palgrave Macmillan).

Manners, I. and Whitman, R. (2016) 'Another Theory is Possible: Dissident Voices in Theorising Europe'. *JCMS*, Vol. 54, No. 1, pp. 3–18.

Marsh, D. (2010) *The Euro: The Politics of the New Global Currency* (New Haven and London: Yale University Press).

Matthijs, M. and Blyth, M. (eds) (2015) *The Future of the Euro* (Oxford and New York: Oxford University Press).

Mead, L.M. (2010) 'Scholasticism in Political Science'. *Perspectives on Politics*, Vol. 8, No. 2, pp. 453–64.

Mearsheimer, J. and Walt, S. (2013) 'Leaving Theory Behind: Why Simplistic Hypothesis Testing is Bad for International Relations'. *European Journal of International Relations*, Vol. 19, No. 3, pp. 427–57.

Milward, A.S. (1992) *The European Rescue of the Nation State* (London: Routledge).

Monk, R. (1999) 'Wittgenstein's Forgotten Lesson', *Prospect*, 20 July.

Moravcsik, A. (1998) *The Choice for Europe: Social Purpose and State Power from Messina to Maastricht* (Ithaca, NY: Cornell University Press).

Newman, A. (2015) 'Germany's Euro Experience and the Long Shadow of Reunification'. In Matthijs, M. and Blyth, M. (eds) *The Future of the Euro* (Oxford and New York: Oxford University Press), pp. 117–35.

Novotná, T. (2015) *How Germany Unified and the EU Enlarged: Negotiating the Accession through Transplantation and Adaptation* (London: Palgrave Macmillan).

Nugent, N. and Rhinard, M. (2016) 'Is the European Commission Really in Decline?' *JCMS*. DOI:10.1111/jcms.12358.

Paterson, W.E. (2011) 'The Reluctant Hegemon? Germany Moves Centre Stage in the European Union'. *JCMS*, Vol. 49, No. s1, pp. 57–75.

Pfleiderer, P. (2014) 'Chameleons: the Misuse of Theoretical Models in Finance and Economics', Stanford Graduate School of Business Working Paper no. 3020, Available online at: <<https://www.gsb.stanford.edu/faculty-research/working-papers/chameleons-misuse-theo-retical-models-finance-economics>>.

Phinnemore, D. (2015) 'Crisis-Ridden, Battered and Bruised: Time to Give Up on the EU?' *JCMS*, Vol. 53, No. s1, pp. 61–74.

Pierson, P. (1996) 'The Path to European Integration: A Historical Institutionalist Analysis'. *Comparative Political Studies*, Vol. 29, No. 2, pp. 123–63.

Pohl, B. and van Willigen, N. (2015) 'Analytical Eclecticism and EU Foreign Policy (In)action'. *Global Society*, Vol. 29, No. 2, pp. 175–98.

Puchala, D. (1971) 'Of Blind Men, Elephants and International Integration'. *JCMS*, Vol. 10, No. 3, pp. 267–84.

Puetter, U. (2014) *The European Council and the Council: New Intergovernmentalism and Institutional Change* (Oxford: Oxford University Press).

Putnam, R.D. (1993) *Making Democracy Work: Civic Traditions in Modern Italy* (Princeton, NJ: Princeton University Press).

Risse, T. (ed.) (2015) *European Public Spheres: Politics is Back* (Cambridge: Cambridge University Press).

Rosamond, B. (2000) *Theories of European Integration* (Basingstoke and New York: Palgrave).

Rosamond, B. (2006) 'The Future of European Studies: Integration Theory, EU Studies and Social Science'. In Eilstrup-Sangiovanni, M. (ed.) *Debates on European Integration: A Reader* (Basingstoke and New York: Palgrave Macmillan), pp. 448–60.

Rosamond, B. (2007) 'European Integration and the Social Science of EU Studies: The Disciplinary Politics of a Subfield'. *International Affairs*, Vol. 83, No. 1, pp. 231–52.

Rosenau, J.N. and Durfee, M. (1995) *Thinking Theory Thoroughly: Coherent Approaches in an Incoherent World* (Boulder, CO: Westview).

Sandholtz, W. and Stone Sweet, A. (eds) (1998) *European Integration and Supranational Governance* (Oxford: Oxford University Press).

Saurugger, S. (2014) *Theoretical Approaches to European Integration* (Basingstoke and New York: Palgrave Macmillan).

Scicluna, N. (2014) *European Union Constitutionalism in Crisis* (London: Routledge).

Schimmelfennig, D. (2003) *The EU, NATO and the Integration of Europe: Rules and Rhetoric* (Cambridge: Cambridge University Press).

Schimmelfennig, F. (2010) 'Integration Theory'. In Egan, M., Nugent, N. and Paterson, W.E. (eds) *Research Agenda in EU Studies Stalking the Elephant* (Basingstoke and New York: Palgrave), pp. 37–59.

Schimmelfennig, F. (2015) 'What's the News in "New Intergovernmentalism"? A Critique of Bickerton, Hodson and Puetter'. *JCMS*, Vol. 53, No. 4, pp. 723–30.

Schmidt, V. (2009) 'Re-envisioning the European Union: Identity, Democracy, Economy'. *JCMS*, Vol. 47, No. s1, pp. 17–42.

Schmitter, P.C. (1969) 'Three Neo-Functional Hypotheses about International Integration'. *International Organization*, Vol. 23, No. 1, pp. 161–6.

Sil, R. and Katzenstein, P. (2010) *Beyond Paradigms. Analytical Eclecticism in the Study of World Politics* (Basingstoke and New York: Palgrave MacMillan).

Strange, G. and Worth, O. (eds) (2012) *European Regionalism and the Left* (Manchester and New York: Manchester University Press).

Stubb, A. (1996) 'A Categorization of Differentiated Integration'. *JCMS*, Vol. 34, No. 2, pp. 283–95.

Tosh, J. (2008) *Why History Matters* (Basingstoke and New York: Palgrave).

Tsoukalis, L. (2011) 'The JCMS Annual Review Lecture: The Shattering of Illusions – And What Next?' *JCMS*, Vol. 49, No. s1, pp. 19–44.

Verdun, A. (2002) 'Merging Neofunctionalism and Intergovernmentalism: Lessons from EMU'. In Verdun, A. (ed.) *The Euro: European Integration Theory and Economic and Monetary Union* (Lanham, Boulder, New York and Oxford: Rowman & Littlefield), pp. 9–28.

Verdun, A. (2015) 'A Historical Institutionalist Explanation of the EU's Responses to the Euro Area Financial Crisis'. *Journal of European Public Policy*, Vol. 22, No. 2, pp. 219–37.

Vollaard, H. (2014) 'Explaining European Disintegration'. *JCMS*, Vol. 52, No. 5, pp. 1142–59.

Waltz, K.N. (1990) 'Realist Thought and Neorealist Theory'. *Journal of International Affairs*, Vol. 44, No. 1, pp. 21–37.

Webber, D. (2014) 'How Likely is it that the European Union will Disintegrate? A Critical Analysis of Competing Theoretical Perspectives'. *European Journal of International Relations*, Vol. 20, No. 2, pp. 341–65.

JCMS 2016 Volume 54. Annual Review pp. 83–90   DOI: 10.1111/jcms.12428

The 2015 Latvian Presidency of the Council of the European Union*

DAUNIS AUERS and TOMS ROSTOKS
University of Latvia

Introduction

The lasting legacy of Latvia's first presidency of the Council of the European Union in the first half of 2015 is neither political, economic nor diplomatic. Rather it is an iconic building – the Latvian National Library, a glassy, jagged structure perched by the Daugava river that runs through the heart of the capital city Riga – that was first sketched by Latvian-American architect Gunārs Birkerts in 1989 and broadly debated for two decades before work finally began on construction in 2008 (Wright, 2014). However, at the end of that same year Latvia sank into a deep recession that saw the economy shed 24 per cent of GDP in less than two years. Government spending was cut and construction work on the library plodded on until the immediate requirements of the upcoming presidency saw the building rapidly finished just months before the presidency kicked off.[1] The library hosted almost all of the different high (and low) level meetings of the presidency, including Jean-Claude Juncker's bizarre greeting of European leaders – with his now infamous, albeit prescient, 'here comes the dictator' greeting to Hungary's Victor Orbán – in May 2015.[2]

The frantic completion of the National Library indicated the seriousness of purpose with which Latvia undertook the middle presidency in a troika comprising Italy, Latvia and Luxembourg.[3] This was Latvia's first Council Presidency and public officials saw it as both a challenge and an opportunity. The challenge was to prepare Latvia's relatively small, inexperienced and youthful civil service to live up to the high standards typically expected from a successful presidency. These six months were also seen as an opportunity to (a) explain the EU to a largely disinterested Latvian public, (b) revise the negative public image of the bureaucracy, and (c) promote Latvia's international profile. Thus, Latvia's presidency-related priorities were balanced between different interests both domestic (to raise EU awareness and improve the image of the public service) and international (to advance salient EU policies and advertise Latvia).

Latvia used the presidency to position itself as a 'good European' – an 'honest broker' – and adopted a Brussels-based presidency framework. Latvia's permanent representation tripled from 62 officials to 185 in the first half of 2015 (Juhansone, 2014). This Brussels-based approach reflects weak domestic policy-making capacity – Latvia's political parties are the smallest in Europe in terms of membership, typically have short lives and are

---

* We are grateful to the *JCMS Annual Review* editors, Nathaniel Copsey and Tim Haughton, for their advice and comments.
[1] It is rumoured that Latvia had no choice but to complete the building. No other building in Riga was big enough to host the enormous round table for meetings that travels from country to country along with the presidency.
[2] *Euronews*, 22 May 2015.
[3] On the Italian presidency see Carbone (2015), on Luxembourg's presidency see Högenauer in this volume.

pragmatic rather than ideological – as much as a strategic choice. Weak policy-formulation capabilities has meant that Latvia has often had no clear national position on European policies that do not directly affect Latvia's security or economic interests. As a result, Latvia's public officials have often relied on European institutions to develop policy and are resultantly well-versed in deep cooperation with the Brussels institutions. Moreover, the lack of clearly formulated national interests in a number of policy areas – including two of the three main policy blocs (competitive Europe and digital Europe) – left Latvia better equipped to be a genuine 'honest broker'.

This contribution first discusses the domestic and international contexts that framed the presidency. It then considers Latvia's policy priorities and achievements. Finally, the conclusion evaluates the presidency as a whole.

I. Domestic and International Contexts

Latvia's EU presidency was framed by domestic, European and global contexts. In domestic terms, Latvia's deep economic recession between 2008 and 2010 made the expense of hosting the presidency a hotly debated issue. Government officials argued that holding the rotating EU presidency was one of the key elements of EU membership. Others, however, questioned the wisdom of spending scarce post-recession government resources on such intangible results. Even the then President, Andris Bērziņš, declared that he believed the EU presidency to be 'an unnecessary waste of money… No-one has been able to explain any real or logical benefits to Latvia' (Vīksne, 2013).

Nevertheless, this kind of criticism was relatively rare in government circles. Indeed, preparations for the presidency began early and the Latvian Foreign Minister's annual report in 2011 had a separate section on the presidency that spelled out the key preparatory elements, particularly the creation of a separate secretariat for coordinating the presidency (Ministry of Foreign Affairs, 2011). This was established in February 2012. As with other first-time presidencies, Latvia intensively trained civil servants in EU-relevant skills and knowledge. Programme participants initially assessed their competence on EU affairs at an average of 4.8 (on a ten-point scale) with the self-assessment rising to 7.3 by the end of the course (Ministry of Foreign Affairs, 2015).

These well-laid plans had the potential to be derailed by Latvia's October 2014 parliamentary elections that were scheduled just months before the presidency was to begin. However, the three broadly pro-European governing parties maintained a parliamentary majority and agreed to continue in a coalition led by Laimdota Straujuma, who had held the post of Prime Minister since January 2014. More importantly, perhaps, other key political figures such as Foreign Minister Edgars Rinkēvičs and Chairman of the Parliamentary Foreign Affairs Committee Ojārs Kalniņš also stayed in office. The Foreign Minister had recommended creating a special 'Minister of Europe' post to deal with the strain of the presidency, but the cabinet rejected the idea, largely because of the added expense. Zanda Kalniņa-Lukaševica, who had served as the Chair of the Parliament's European Committee in the previous parliament, was appointed the Parliamentary Secretary of the Foreign Ministry after the election – a *de facto* junior minister post. However, this was an unusual example of coalition discord on the presidency. Conflict was rare largely because the major political parties had, similarly to the Slovenian presidency, signed a pact in December 2013 agreeing to not use the presidency to settle domestic grievances

(Latvijas Republikas 11 Saeima; Kajnč, 2009). Nevertheless, in the final weeks of the presidency there were persistent rumours that Prime Minister Straujuma would be forced from office as soon as the presidency baton was passed on to Luxembourg. Although it did not happen immediately, the Prime Minister was indeed pushed out of office in December 2015. This indicates that the political agreement to suspend conflict during the presidency may well have had a stabilizing effect on the coalition.

At the European level, the presidency was framed by the 2014 European Parliament elections and the following change of leadership in both the European legislature and the European Commission that assumed office in November 2014, as well as Donald Tusk taking up office as the President of the European Council on 1 December 2014. Thus the Latvian presidency came at the beginning of the leadership cycle which meant that the Commission and Parliament's own policy priorities were also at the initial phase of the policy-making process. Moreover, President Jean-Claude Juncker had stated that his Commission would be "'big on big things and small on small things", which translated into a very thin work programme for 2015' (Lezi and Blockmans, 2015). As a result, the European institutions actually had a limited impact on Latvia's presidency agenda.

The broader international context was framed by the military conflict in Ukraine and the gradual acceleration of Europe's migrant crisis over the first half of 2015. The former posed a threat to security in Europe – particularly felt in Latvia, which shares a border with Russia – while the latter threatened European cohesion and solidarity. However, neither crises had a major effect on Latvia's presidency. The conflict in Ukraine faded after the signing of the Minsk agreement on 11 February 2015 while the refugee crisis reached its apex in the second half of 2015 during Luxembourg's presidency. Thus international issues did not hijack the agenda in the first half of 2015.

As a result, the domestic, European and international environment was largely favourable. Latvia had a stable and experienced pro-European government at the political helm, the new European Commission and European Parliament were broadly in step with Latvia's agenda and there were no major international crises to distract attention. As a result, it is no surprise that Latvia was broadly successful in pushing forward its modest agenda.

II. Presidency Priorities and Achievements

Initial preparations for the presidency began in 2012 with the first round of public discussion on potential priorities. A total of 13 public discussions aimed at formulating the presidency's policy priorities were held over the course of the year with a second follow-up round of public discussions held in late 2013 (Skujiņa, 2015). In terms of substance, the discussions did not have a decisive influence on the final shape of the presidency's priorities. However, the public debates did serve two important functions. First, they put the presidency on the media agenda and thus started the process of informing and shaping public opinion. Second, the discussions involved most relevant actors in government, the NGO sector, academia and business in the discussion of the priorities and mobilized them in preparation for the first half of 2015.

However, the domestic discourse was just one part of the priority formulation process. From the very beginning it was assumed that Latvia's priorities should both reflect the long-term priorities of the EU and that the presidency should be flexible in adjusting to whatever issues were suddenly thrown on the EU decision-making agenda (that is, fire-fighting). Thus the Latvian priorities had to be synchronized with the defined priorities of the incoming European Commission. Although Jean-Claude Juncker assumed office as President of the European Commission in November 2014, his nomination in June 2014 had allowed for plenty of time for co-ordination of Latvia's priorities with those of the Commission. Latvia also synchronized its presidency priorities with the other two countries of the troika: Italy and Luxembourg.

The troika agreed on financial stability and growth, employment, the digital agenda and the strengthening of the EU's global role as the major presidency priorities. The main objective of the troika was 'to fully overcome the economic and financial crisis, strengthen the Union's capacity to deliver more jobs and to seize digital opportunities, to safeguard fundamental rights and to fully play its role in a fast changing world' (Council of the European Union, 2014, p. 9). Naturally, niftier titles were adopted: Competitive Europe, Digital Europe and Engaged Europe.[4]

Competitive Europe

The Competitive Europe pillar was driven by two influences: the incoming European Commission's Juncker Plan for increasing investment and Latvia's long-term push for establishing an Energy Union to strengthen energy independence from Russia by diversifying energy production and constructing greater energy links between EU states.

The European Commission's Investment Plan aimed to boost investment in the European economies – investment had remained at low levels since the economic crisis across the Union – through the European Fund for Strategic Investments, jointly established with the European Investment Bank. Put simply, the plan aimed to muster private financing for strategic investment. The Latvian presidency swiftly guided the plan through the European legislative process, reaching a provisional agreement with the European Parliament at the end of May with the Council adopting the regulation at the end of June. The speed with which the legislation was adopted indicates the widespread support for the initiative among the Member States.

The second key issue was establishing the Energy Union. For Latvia, this was a far greater priority than the Investment Plan, particularly after the Russian annexation of Crimea in 2014 further raised security concerns. A move to strengthen the Energy Union was thus seen as a key dimension of strengthening Latvia's own security (70 per cent of Latvia's energy needs are met by gas – and in 2014, 100 per cent of Latvia's gas was imported from Russia), although it also has great salience for the Union, which imports more than half of its energy needs from third countries. This priority had several dimensions, including linking the Baltic states' energy infrastructure with that of Northern and Central/Western Europe, as well as diversifying supply into the Union and developing energy efficiency (with a view to cutting the need for energy imports). A high-level conference in Riga on 4 February formally launched the Energy Union process and while no major agreement was reached or signed during the Latvian presidency, Latvian officials made a big push to ensure that energy issues would remain on the EU agenda well into the future.

---

[4] These natty titles were formulated by the staff at the Permanent Representation of Latvia to the European Union in Brussels.

Digital Europe

Latvia focused on the telecoms dimension of the broader digital strategy and this is the area where the presidency saw perhaps the most concrete results, albeit only sealed in the last weeks, days and even hours of the presidency. The Council and the European Parliament agreed to three deals right at the end of the Latvian presidency. First, on 15 June, after three years of negotiation, the Council reached agreement on the Data Protection Regulation that focuses on the security of individuals in the digital world. Second, on 29 June an agreement was reached on the Network and Information Security Standards Directive that tackles cyber threats. Third, a similarly dramatic, last minute deal (struck on 30 June, just hours before the presidency ended) was reached on roaming charges, with Latvia managing to persuade both the Council and the Parliament to compromise on a starting date of June 2017 for the new legislation – the Council had pushed for 2018 and the Parliament for 2016.

Engaged Europe

As with energy security, Latvia had a clear set of policy positions in the foreign policy and security dimension. The geostrategic environment in Europe had changed dramatically since the annexation of Crimea and the outbreak of fighting in Ukraine. However, after the initial outpouring of sympathy, Latvia's Western partners had grown increasingly wary about the seeming inability of Ukraine and other Eastern Partnership frontrunners to achieve meaningful reform. There was also concern that a stronger Eastern Partnership might provoke an even more hostile reaction on the part of Russia. Thus Latvia's main aim eventually became a straightforward preservation of what had been achieved since the initiation of the Eastern Partnership in 2009 rather than an ambitious step forward. In short, Latvia was running to stand still. While the Eastern Partnership Riga summit in May 2015 was initially seen as the centrepiece of the presidency, its centrality was eventually played down as it gradually became clear that the summit would not be marked by any great agreement.

Despite these unfavourable conditions, Latvia arguably managed to achieve meaningful progress on the Eastern Partnership during the presidency. Diplomats mounted a major effort to reach out to all of the involved parties before the summit. This involved not only extensive contacts with EU partners and the six Eastern Partnership countries, but also reaching out to Russia. Although Latvia most likely did not manage to convince Russia that the Eastern Partnership policy was not aimed against Russia's interests, the presidency did manage to avoid some of the more unpleasant aspects of Lithuania's EU presidency such as Russia's attempt to curb Lithuania's foreign policy activism by imposing direct economic sanctions. The most visible sign of the success of Latvia's diplomatic efforts was, in the words of Juris Poikans, Latvia's former ambassador at large for the Eastern Partnership, 'the highest representation ever seen in the Eastern Partnership Summit since its inception in 2009' (Poikāns, 2016, p. 36). In terms of substance, the Riga summit furthered the differentiation among the Eastern Partnership countries making it increasingly possible for different partners to choose different depths and intensities of relations with the EU. Taking into account the deteriorating security environment in Eastern Europe and its impact on Latvia's security, the Riga summit also took major steps in the further normalization of relations between Belarus and the EU.

Fire-Fighting

In contrast to neighbouring Lithuania, whose first six-month presidency of the EU in 2014 saw Russia's annexation of Crimea and separatist fighting in Eastern Ukraine (Vilpišauskas, 2014), Latvia faced no great Europe-wide crises. The Latvian presidency responded to the *Charlie Hebdo* shootings in January by calling an informal Justice and Home Affairs Council at the end of January and adopting the Riga statement on counter-terrorism. The migrant crisis was still in its early stages in the first half of 2015, although it worked its way up the agenda with every passing month.[5] This was recognized in a 20 April joint meeting of European Interior and Foreign Ministers and then later in a June Justice and Home Affairs Council when a first effort to create national quotas for the relocation of asylum-seekers from Italy and Greece floundered and was rejected (only to reappear on the agenda of the Luxembourgian presidency in the second half of 2015). However, these were modest crises in comparison to what came before, and after, Latvia's six-month presidency.

III. Conclusions

The introduction argued that the presidency was an opportunity to (a) explain the EU to the domestic audience, (b) revise the negative public image of the bureaucracy, and (c) promote Latvia's international profile. The presidency was largely successful in achieving these ambitions. First, as to the government's ability to explain the EU to the domestic audience, the results were mixed. A public opinion survey from April 2015 revealed that 81 per cent of respondents were aware that Latvia was holding the EU Council Presidency (DnB Nord, 2015). However, respondents' views on the EU had not markedly changed. Public opinion survey results from August 2015 revealed that the EU was regarded favourably by 63 per cent of respondents, a result identical to survey data from July 2014 (SKDS, 2015). Also, the public did not correlate the presidency with increased influence within the Union – 73 per cent of respondents of the DnB Nord survey were of the opinion that Latvia has little to no influence on EU decision-making. Second, the presidency has undoubtedly had a positive impact on Latvia's public service although it remains to be seen how many of the now well-trained and experienced civil servants will pursue long-term careers in public service rather than opting for the private sector or international careers. It also had a positive economic impact estimated at €64.5 million (albeit with direct costs of €45 million and indirect costs of around €37 million[6]) (KPMG Baltics, 2014). Third, in terms of Latvia's international profile, the Foreign Ministry recorded that 142 different television channels produced 5,710 TV reports on the presidency and that 800 journalists from over 40 countries visited Latvia for presidency events (Ministry of Foreign Affairs, 2015). There was a determined effort to position 'Riga' as a part of European history – hence the 'Riga Process on the Energy Union', 'Riga declaration on e-inclusion', 'Joint Riga declaration of the Eastern Partnership Summit', 'Riga declaration on remotely piloted aircraft (drones)' and so on. However, none of these efforts are likely to 'stick' in the public consciousness like Schengen, Maastricht or the Bologna process

---

[5] See Monar's contribution to this volume.
[6] The costs are broadly similar to the €62 million direct spending by neighbouring Lithuania on its 2014 presidency (Vilpišauskas, 2014).

because no major landmark deal was struck during the Latvian presidency (although the bizarre greetings to leaders made by Juncker at the start of the Eastern Partnership Summit at the Latvian National Library will likely remain long in the memory).

In terms of policy impact, the Latvian presidency was certainly effective in advancing the EU policy agenda. The Latvian presidency is proof that even a small country holding the presidency for the first time can advance the EU policy agenda if it acts as an honest broker and is not distracted by 'fire-fighting'. Thus, Latvia secured an agreement on both the European Fund for Strategic Investments (EFSI) and the Energy Union Framework Strategy. Latvia brokered a deal on ending mobile phone roaming charges and safeguarding open internet access in the last days of the presidency. Significant advances were made in moving forward the Digital Single Market (DSM), and two further rounds of talks on the Transatlantic Trade and Investment Partnership (TTIP) with the US were held. Latvia also managed to avoid neighbouring Lithuania's misstep of overseeing a major political disappointment such as the failure to sign the Association Agreement with Ukraine at the Eastern Partnership summit during Lithuania's presidency in November 2013 (Vilpišauskas, 2014).

The 'success' of presidencies can be difficult to evaluate because domestic and international expectations and impressions of the six months can differ (Manners, 2003, 2013). Nevertheless, Quaglia and Moxon-Browne (2006) offer an evaluation of four key presidency roles – business manager, mediator, political leader and internal/external representation – as objective measures of the success of a presidency. Latvia performed well in terms of the first two criteria, largely because they are administrative and technocratic in nature. However, Latvia was less successful in terms of the political leadership and representation dimensions that require more of a political investment. Latvia's major policy priority was the external 'engaged Europe' dimension, but the Riga Summit saw only incremental progress with the Eastern Partnership. Broadly speaking, Latvia successfully *managed* the agenda of the presidency, but was rather less successful in *setting* and *influencing* the agenda. However, this is likely to have met both the internal and external expectations of one of the smaller, poorer EU states taking the presidency for the first time.

As a result, the Latvian presidency can be judged a modest success. While it may have lacked the drama of Lithuania's presidency or the urgent crises of Luxembourg's six months, the presidency saw steady technocratic movement towards several of the EU's long-term goals and ambitions. Latvia will benefit from an upgrading of the public service's skills and experience. Roll on the next presidency in 2029.

References

Carbone, M. (2015) 'Beyond the Telemachus Complex: Courses, Discourses and the 2014 Italian Presidency of the Council of the European Union'. *JCMS*, Vol. 53, No. s1, pp. 83–92.

Council of the European Union (2014) 'Programme of the Council Activities prepared by the Future Italian, Latvian and Luxembourg Presidencies', 10948/1/14 REV 1, 17 June 2014. Available online at: http://register.consilium.europa.eu/doc/srv?l=EN&f=ST%2010948%202014%20REV%201.

DnB Nord (2015) *Latvijas prezidentūra ES Padomē* (Latvia's EU Council Presidency) DnB Latvia's Barometer No. 80. Available online at: https://www.dnb.lv/sites/default/files/dnb_latvian_barometer/documents/2015/dnb-latvijas-barometrs-petijums-nr80.pdf.

Juhansone, I. (2014) 'Latvia is Ready to Take Charge', *The Parliament Magazine*. Available online at: https://www.theparliamentmagazine.eu/articles/opinion/latvia-ready-take-charge.

Kajnč, S. (2009) 'The Slovenian Presidency: Meeting Symbolic and Substantive Challenges'. *JCMS*, Vol. 47, No. s1, pp. 89–98.

KPMG Baltics (2014) 'Assessment of the Impact of the Latvian Presidency of the Council of the European Union on the Latvian Economy' (Riga: KPMG). Available online at: http://www.es2015.lv/images/Prezidenturas_izvertejums.pdf.

Latvijas Republikas 11. Saimā pārstāvēto politisko partiju, politisko partiju apvienību un pie frakcijām nepiederošo deputātu vienošanās par Latvijas Prezidentūras Eiropas Savienības Padomē 2015. Gada pirmajā pusē sagatavošanu un īstenošanu (Agreement Between Political Parties on EU Presidency). (19.12.2013) Parliamentary Dimension of Latvia's EU Council Presidency: http://www.parleu2015.lv/files/partiju_vienosanas.pdf

Lezi, G. and Blockmans, S. (2015) 'Latvia's EU Presidency: Less is More', *CEPS Commentary*, 3 July 2015. Available online at: https://www.ceps.eu/system/files/Latvian_Presidency.pdf.

Manners, I. (2003) 'The British Presidency of 1998: New Labour, New Tone?'. In Elgström, O. (ed.) *European Union Council Presidencies: A Comparative Analysis* (London: Routledge) pp. 87–103.

Manners, I. (2013) 'The 2012 Danish Presidency of the EU: Bridging Exclusion'. *JCMS*, Vol. 51, No. s1, pp. 70–9.

Ministry of Foreign Affairs (2011) 'Ārlietu ministra ziņojums par valsts ārpolitiku un Eiropas Savienības jautājumiem' [Foreign Minister's Report on Foreign Policy and EU Affairs]. Available online at: http://www.mfa.gov.lv/data/file/Arpolitika/zinojums.pdf.

Ministry of Foreign Affairs (2015) 'Results of the Latvian Presidency of the Council of the European Union'. Available online at: https://eu2015.lv/images/news/EU2015LV_results_en.pdf.

Poikāns, J. (2016) 'The Eastern Partnership – Latvia's Contribution'. In Sprūds, A. and Bruge, I. (eds) *Latvian Foreign and Security Policy Yearbook 2016* (Riga: Latvian Institute of International Affairs) pp. 87–103.

Quaglia, L. and Moxon-Browne, E. (2006) 'What Makes a Good EU Presidency? Italy and Ireland Compared'. *JCMS*, Vol. 44, No. 2, pp. 349–68.

SKDS (2015) 'Latvijas iedzīvotāju vērtējumi Eiropas Savienībai'. ASV un Krievijai. SKDS data, pp. 2014–5.

Skujiņa, I. (2015) 'Latvijas prezidentūra Eiropas Savienības Padomē', *Latvijas Intereses Eiropas Savienībā*, No. 3, pp. 7–12.

Vīksne, I. (2013) 'Bērziņš Apšauba Latvijas ES Prezidentūras Lietderību'. *NRA*, Vol. 6, p. 1.

Vilpišauskas, R. (2014) ''Lithuania's EU Council Presidency: Negotiating Finances, Dealing with Geopolitics''. *JCMS*, Vol. 52, No. s1, pp. 99–108.

Wright, H. (2014) 'Motown to Mountain: Gunnar Birkerts' New National Library of Latvia. *Design Curial*. Available online at: http://www.designcurial.com/news/motown-to-mountain-4346260/.

JCMS 2016 Volume 54. Annual Review pp. 91–100   DOI: 10.1111/jcms.12410

Luxembourg's EU Council Presidency: Adapting Routines to New Circumstances

ANNA-LENA HÖGENAUER
University of Luxembourg

Introduction

Luxembourg took over the rotating presidency of the Council of the European Union on 1 July 2015 in a climate of internal and external crisis. The budgetary situation in Greece had worsened to the point where Greece's ability to remain in the eurozone (and the EU) was at stake. At the same time, a bank-run forced Greece's banks to temporarily close. Moreover, the refugee crisis reached a climax in 2015 and tensions between EU Member States about the handling of the situation and the distribution of refugees made a common approach difficult even in the face of humanitarian disaster. Furthermore, the Ukraine crisis simmered on. In addition, a terrorist attack in Paris brought internal security issues to the fore. Finally, following British Prime Minister David Cameron's promise of a referendum on whether Britain should remain in the European Union, the EU had to start a phase of renegotiation of certain policies and processes to allow Cameron to avoid Brexit.

The organization of this EU presidency fell to one of the smallest – but most experienced – Member States of the European Union. It was Luxembourg's 12th rotating presidency, which meant that many officials and some ministers had experienced at least one if not more previous presidencies. In addition, the institutional context of this presidency had also changed quite dramatically since the 11th Luxembourgish presidency in 2005 thanks to the Lisbon Treaty and the creation of the trio presidencies.

If one adopts Vandecasteele and Bossuyt's (2014) criteria for the performance of presidencies, the prospects for Luxembourg were mixed. In their review of the literature on the presidencies of the Council of the European Union, Vandecasteele and Bossuyt (2014, p. 241) identify conditions for presidency performance that fall into three categories: external context, national conditions and issue-specific characteristics. A favourable environment is seen as facilitating success, but external crises can also offer opportunities for leadership. By contrast Kietz (2007) underlines the extent to which external crises and highly sensitive dossiers challenge the ability of presidencies to reach compromise. In terms of national conditions, three appear key: good preparation, Brussels-based presidencies where the Permanent Representation has some leeway in the negotiations and a good reputation (which includes expertise and experience). Being a small state like Luxembourg can be advantageous, *if* it goes hand-in-hand with better communication within the ministries and a willingness to act as an honest broker, rather than defender of national interests (Vandecasteele and Bossuyt, 2004, pp. 241–242). But, as evidenced by Warntjen's (2007) analysis of the impact of presidencies on environmental policy-making, neither small nor large states can be said to have a systematic advantage. Quaglia and Moxon-Browne (2006) also emphasize the importance of 'intangible' factors like expertise, credibility and a pro-European attitude of the government holding the presidency based on their comparison of the Irish and Italian presidencies of 2003 and 2004.

The effect of issue-specific characteristics is more disputed, but it seems that qualified majority voting (QMV) makes it easier for the presidency to succeed in reaching an agreement and to shape that agreement (Tallberg, 2004; Warntjen, 2007). Also, diverse interests among actors may make it easier for the presidency to shape a compromise that reflects (some of) its own interests, but only if the disagreements are not too strong. Intense disagreements lower the chances of success (Vandecasteele and Bossuyt, 2014, p. 243).

In the light of these arguments, this contribution analyses how the difficult external context of the Luxembourgish presidency affected it in the context of the Lisbon Treaty, and to what extent the presidency could create the conditions for success. For this purpose, it will first review the context, resources and style of the presidency, before reviewing its priorities and achievements.[1]

I. Managing the Presidency in a Changed Context

The Lisbon Treaty

The Lisbon Treaty of 2009 introduced three important changes from the point of view of the rotating presidency. It created a new permanent president of the European Council, the High Representative – supported by the European External Action Service – became the chair of the Foreign Affairs Council and the Trio Presidency was modified. The first two changes in some way facilitated the work of the rotating presidency, as it reduced its workload and thus the resource requirements of presidencies.[2]

Luxembourg adapted quite well to the changed circumstances. It accepted that the big priorities are now set by the European Council and the Commission and that the Council of the European Union has become the legislative arm of the European Council. There was no competition between the permanent President of the European Council, Donald Tusk, and the Luxembourgish presidency of the Council of the European Union.[3] In the same way, Luxembourg accepted that the presidency had lost influence over the EU's foreign policy. Instead of trying to develop priorities in this area – as some of the preceding presidencies had done – it mainly focused on supporting the High Representative.[4]

The emergence of key European posts reduced the pressure on the presidency in some areas. European Council President, Donald Tusk, for example, played a particularly important role in the negotiations with the United Kingdom on the reform of the EU as these negotiations fell clearly under the competence of the Heads of State or Government. Tusk insisted that David Cameron present his demands in written form and Cameron duly obliged (Cameron, 2015). In the same vein, the Greek crisis affected the presidency less than one might expect. Most of the emergency meetings were organized at the Eurogroup

---

[1] In addition to an analysis of relevant documents and news coverage, this contribution is based on interviews with an official of the Council of the European Union and seven officials from different Luxembourgish ministries and the Permanent Representation of Luxembourg.
[2] Interview with a member of the Luxembourgish Permanent Representation in Brussels, 24 February 2016.
[3] Interview with a Council official for Transport, Telecommunications, Energy, Brussels, 15 February 2016.
[4] Interview with an official of the Ministère des Affaires étrangères, Luxembourg, 25 February 2016.

level and were thus chaired by the Eurogroup President, Jeroen Dijsselbloem. Some meetings took place at the level of Heads of State or Government and were thus chaired by Donald Tusk and only a few took place in the form of the Ecofin Council under Luxembourgish leadership. The presidency was mostly affected by certain issues spilling over into other dossiers (for example, budget negotiations) and by the general increase in workload for European finance ministries.[5]

However, other crises affected the presidency. Both the refugee crisis and debates about security in the aftermath of the terrorist attacks in Paris required the organization of a number of informal or extraordinary councils by the presidency.

In comparison, the modification of the Trio of rotating presidencies had little effect on the actual functioning of the rotating presidencies. Whereas formerly each presidency was supposed to cooperate with the preceding and the following presidency, the Trio now consists of a team of three countries that are supposed to coordinate their three presidencies over an 18-month period. In reality, interviewees felt that the Trio had little impact on the Luxembourgish presidency (and presidencies in general) (see also Warntjen, 2013). While officials appreciated the importance of drawing up a collective strategy, the strategy of the Trio was regarded as the least important influence on the priorities of the Luxembourgish presidency.[6] Changes in the composition of the European Commission and the European Parliament meant that political preferences had shifted and the Trio strategy was no longer up-to-date.

In practice, the Luxembourgish presidency – which was the last in the Trio with Italy and Latvia[7] – mainly cooperated with the preceding and following presidencies. In fact, cooperation with both Latvia and the Netherlands was very good. In the negotiations on the Juncker Plan, for example, Latvia allowed the Luxembourgish team to attend all trialogues with the European Parliament and the Commission as it was clear that this would spill over to the Luxembourgish presidency.[8] On the railway package, the Luxembourgers and the Dutch worked together almost like a double presidency, as it was clear that the negotiations would continue during the Dutch presidency.[9] The smooth transition between the Luxembourg and Dutch trios was helped by extensive experience of cooperation, for example, as part of the Benelux Union.

Resources

The Luxembourgish Presidency was relatively well-resourced in the context of the eurozone crisis. The budget for the Presidency in 2015 was €71 million (Ministère des Affaires étrangères, 2015). From a Luxembourgish perspective, these allocations were not overly generous. The guideline had been to keep the budget within the same margins as the budget of the presidency of 2005 plus inflation.[10] Even though Luxembourg weathered the eurozone crisis comparatively well and could largely avoid painful budgetary cuts, approaches to public spending had become more cautious. On the other hand, the workload had become lighter now that the Foreign Affairs Council and the European

---

[5] Interview with two officials of the Ministère des finances, Luxembourg, 31 March 2016.
[6] Interview with an official of the Ministère des Affaires étrangères, Luxembourg, 25 February 2016.
[7] On the Italian presidency see Carbone (2015); on the Latvian presidency see Auers and Rostoks in this volume.
[8] Interview with two officials of the Ministère des finances, Luxembourg, 31 March 2016.
[9] Interview with a Council official for Transport, Telecommunications, Energy, Brussels, 15 February 2016.
[10] Interview with two officials, Ministère des Affaires étrangères, Luxembourg, 21 March 2016.

Council are no longer chaired by the rotating presidency.[11] On the whole the budget was relatively generous compared to that of other countries for which data are available: Lithuania's budget was around €62 million in 2013, Ireland's around €45 million in 2013 (half of what was spent during its presidency in 2004) and Spain's around €55 million in 2010 (Heywood, 2011; Laffan, 2014; Vilpišauskas, 2014). Only Poland adopted a generous budget of around €100 million (Pomorska and Vanhoonacker, 2012).

Style

As in the past, the Luxembourgish Presidency was organized as a Brussels-based presidency. The Permanent Representation in Brussels had enough leeway to run the negotiations relatively independently, as it was felt that this approach facilitates fast and effective negotiations. In addition, the heads of the permanent representation and of COREPER I and II and many Luxembourgish officials benefitted from the experience of previous presidencies. The Permanent Representation was helped by a generous allocation of temporary support staff and delegated civil servants (189 temporary support staff were hired in total), and the staff working on migration was further increased during the presidency when it became clear that the dossier would be more prominent than expected.[12]

The presidency was seen to be European and consensual in its approach. Luxembourg had no big national agenda and was praised for allowing the 'natural compromise' to emerge (for example, in the case of the fourth railway package).[13] In this context, it is also interesting to note that the presidency did not regard the fact that Commission President Jean-Claude Juncker had been Prime Minister of Luxembourg from 1995–2013 as particularly important. The consensus among interviewees is that Juncker acted in line with the premise that Commissioners are not supposed to feel attached to a particular Member State and that his long experience as Luxembourgish Prime Minister only mattered in so far as it facilitated communication with the presidency.

In general, the presidency was perceived to be pragmatic and focused on compromise-building in line with the national culture of compromise (see also Hearl, 2006). In part this is also due to the fact that smaller states tend to be more aware of their relative weight in the Council, although there is a marked difference between the Belgian or Luxembourgish approach and the Latvian approach, which saw the presidency as an opportunity for a small state to have influence.[14] Part of this pragmatism was also the adoption of a concise list or priorities (see below) that reflected the shift of competences to the High Representative and the Permanent President of the European Council. It was felt that Luxembourg could afford to be pragmatic, given its good reputation and long and positive track-records with presidencies.[15]

Finally, the presidency benefitted from the multilingualism of Luxembourgish officials, who generally speak French, German and English. In addition, they rotate less often than officials in other Member States and thus benefit from longer-term expertise in their area. The smaller size of the administration means that people know each other

[11] Interview with two officials, Ministère des Affaires étrangères, Luxembourg, 21 March 2016.
[12] Interview with a member of the Luxembourgish Permanent Representation in Brussels, 24 February 2016. Interview with an official of the Ministère des Affaires étrangères, Luxembourg, 25 February 2016.
[13] Interview with a Council official for Transport, Telecommunications, Energy, Brussels, 15 February 2016.
[14] Interview with a Council official for Transport, Telecommunications, Energy, Brussels, 15 February 2016.
[15] Interview with an official of the Ministère des Affaires étrangères, Luxembourg, 25 February 2016.

better and that trust is easier to establish (Hearl, 2006). Moreover, they have also a more horizontal view of policies as the small size of the administration means that people often work on several dossiers.[16]

II. Priorities and Progress

The preparations of the presidency in terms of content were delayed until late 2014 by the election of the European Parliament in 2014 and the subsequent nomination of a new European Commission. These political developments meant that the views of several important European institutions were changing, which influenced in turn what goals the Council Presidency could realistically achieve.[17] In the end, the priorities took into account the stated priorities of the European Council (2014), the policy orientations of the Juncker Commission, the annual work programme of the Commission and – to a lesser extent – the work programme of the Trio (Luxembourgish Presidency, 2015a).

In line with the pragmatic style of the presidency, the priorities were summarized in a relatively short document of 33 pages, the shortest in the last six presidencies. The aim was to have a realistic and feasible programme. A common thread was concerns with a more competitive but also a more social Europe as well as with a shift to a more modern, green economy (Luxembourgish Presidency, 2015a).

Stimulating Investment to Boost Growth and Employment

In the context of the eurozone crisis, high unemployment and low growth was one of the key priorities of the presidency. An important element was the support for the Investment Plan for Europe by reducing barriers to investment and improving regulation.[18] In addition, the presidency achieved progress in several dossiers related to capital markets union, for example, by reaching political agreement on a proposal to relaunch the simple, transparent and standardized securitisation in just nine weeks (Renman and Russack, 2016).[19]

Another important achievement was the introduction of a new working method in the Competitiveness Council: the 'competitiveness check-up'. Under this new procedure, the beginning of Competitiveness Council meetings will be dedicated to an assessment of competitiveness based on certain indicators. In addition, the Competitiveness Council should broaden its debates by also considering issues that fall into the domain of other formations (for example, social affairs, environment or transport), but that could have an impact on competitiveness (Competitiveness Council, 2015; Luxembourgish Presidency, 2015b).

Finally, a major success of the Luxembourgish presidency were the negotiations of the EU's annual budget where the presidency managed to reach a unanimous agreement within the timeframe. This was the first time since the start of the financial crisis in 2008 that the Council agreed unanimously on the budget.[20]

---

[16] Interview with an official of the Ministère des Affaires étrangères, Luxembourg, 25 February 2016.
[17] Interview with an official of the Ministère des Affaires étrangères, Luxembourg, 25 February 2016.
[18] Interview with two officials of the Ministère des finances, Luxembourg, 31 March 2016.
[19] See Quaglia *et al's* contribution to this volume.
[20] See Quaglia *et al's* contribution to this volume.

Deepening the European Union's Social Dimension

The presidency aimed to encourage progress towards a Europe with a 'Triple A social rating' by boosting social investment. In this context, one non-legislative goal was to encourage (or even force) debate on the social dimension of the eurozone. This aim was difficult and even controversial, as the eurozone crisis had brought different approaches to the social dimension to the fore. In addition to discussions in the employment, social policy, health and consumer affairs (EPSCO) council, the presidency held a tripartite social summit in October 2015. It also organized the first ever informal Council of the Ministers for Employment and Social Affairs of the eurozone countries to discuss the social dimension of EMU. In this case, the government went against its culture of consensus and deliberately organized the meeting knowing that it would be contentious.[21] While several council decisions and conclusions were adopted during the presidency, for example the decision on guidelines for employment policies in the Member States, it is questionable whether EU policies became noticeably more social in substance.

Managing Migration, Combining Freedom, Security and Justice

Luxembourg was firmly committed to a European solution to the migration crisis and to an approach that respects established European values and the rule of law. The presidency managed to broker a number of difficult agreements, such as the conclusions of the Justice and Home Affairs (JHA) Council on the relocation of 160,000 people and the resettlement of 22,504 people in July and September 2015. In addition, the Council agreed in October to earmark almost half a billion euro of additional funding for the management of the migration crisis in the EU budget, allowing for the creation of 120 new positions in the relevant EU agencies. The Council also adopted conclusions on a new returns and readmission policy and prepared the ground for the EU–Turkey agreement on refugees during a summit in November. At the same time, the migration crisis actually illustrated both views on the impact of external crises on presidencies (Vandecasteele and Bossuyt, 2014). On the one hand, it offered the presidency the opportunity to play a stronger agenda-shaping role than in 'ordinary' legislative business. At the same time, the intensity of disagreement among Member States made it extremely difficult to reach decisions (Luxembourgish Presidency, 2015c). Despite the extensive efforts of Foreign Minister Jean Asselborn, it was not possible to reach consensus. The decision of the Council on quotas was thus the first decision in this policy area to be taken by qualified majority vote rather than unanimity since the Treaty of Lisbon.[22] It was a radical decision, but the presidency felt that consensus was out of reach. The fact that several Member States that 'lost' the vote brought a case before the European Court of Justice (ECJ) further illustrates the intensity of the debate.[23] The corresponding foot-dragging at the implementation stage reduced the effectiveness of the policy.

In the aftermath of the terrorist attacks in Paris concerns about security increased. The presidency held an extraordinary JHA Council meeting to discuss the coordination of responses to terrorism and improved cooperation between Member States.[24] The

---

[21] Interview with an official of the Ministère des Affaires étrangères, Luxembourg, 25 February 2016.
[22] BBC News, 22 September 2015, http://www.bbc.com/news/world-europe-34329825.
[23] Interview with an official of the Ministère des Affaires étrangères, Luxembourg, 19 April 2016.
[24] On developments in the field of Justice and Home Affairs see Monar's contribution to this volume.

presidency managed to broker a compromise between Member States and between the Council and the Parliament on the European passenger name record, a dossier that had been blocked for years with disagreements on data protection.[25] Similarly, the presidency reached an informal agreement with the European Parliament in trialogue on the Data Protection Package (Renman and Russack, 2016).

Revitalising the Single Market by Focusing on its Digital Dimension

An important success in this dimension was the advancing of the two most sensitive elements in the fourth railway package.[26] The aim of the Commission was to liberalize passenger transport service and to strengthen railway infrastructure governance by separating railway and infrastructure companies. The final compromise in the Council was a more functional separation rather than a clear division of the two types of companies. In addition, countries can still directly allocate the contract to a company subject to certain conditions. This compromise is seen to be the 'logical compromise', but also a fragile compromise as positions on liberalization diverge.[27] Similarly, in the case of the Council Conclusions on Energy Governance, thorough preparation allowed the presidency to broker an agreement on a completely new file in a very short time. It was an important dossier for Luxembourg as the administrative burden of reporting on different aspects of energy at different intervals is particularly difficult to manage for small Member States (Council, 2015).[28]

The successful climate talks at the 21st Conference of Parties at the United Nations Framework Convention on Climate Change (COP21) in Paris were another important milestone although France and the Commission also played a major part in their negotiation. In this case, the Luxembourgish presidency played a role in the coordination of a common position within the European Union whereas France and the Commission then took the lead in the actual COP21 negotiations.

Placing European Competitiveness in a Global and Transparent Framework

This important pillar included both discussion about the future direction of EMU, and various tax-related policies. As the latter concerned mainly the prevention of tax evasion within Europe and in a global context, this was a salient dossier for Luxembourg, which had come to be seen as a tax haven for multi-national corporations following the Luxleaks affair.[29]

The presidency nevertheless made important progress. It rapidly reached a political agreement on the directive on cross-border tax ruling. In addition, the presidency finalized work on the OECD Base Erosion and Profit Shifting Initiative (Luxembourgish Presidency, 2016).

[25] Interview with an official of the Ministère des Affaires étrangères, Luxembourg, 19 April 2016.
[26] http://ec.europa.eu/transport/modes/rail/packages/2013_en.htm
[27] Interview with a Council official for Transport, Telecommunications, Energy, Brussels, 15 February 2016.
[28] Interview with a member of the Luxembourgish Permanent Representation in Brussels, 24 February 2016. Interview with a Council official for Transport, Telecommunications, Energy, Brussels, 15 February 2016.
[29] *Deutschlandfunk*, 24 July 2015, http://www.deutschlandfunk.de/luxemburg-vor-dem-eu-ratsvorsitz-griechenland-und-andere.724.de.html?dram:article_id=324007.

The presidency was also marked by progress on trade agreements. In the case of the Transatlantic Trade and Investment Partnership with the US, the Luxembourgish presidency promoted demands by civil society to create reading rooms to give national parliamentarians access to the relevant documents.

Promoting Sustainable Development

This pillar, which overlaps with the fourth pillar, was salient as it gained global attention in two major conferences, the Special Summit on Sustainable Development in New York in September 2015 and COP21 in Paris in December 2015 (see above).

Internally, the reform of the emissions trading scheme (ETS) was a key issue. The market stability reserve was adopted in September as a first step towards the reform of the ETS. In addition, the first policy debate on the reform of the ETS was held during the environment council in October.

The presidency also tackled various questions of sustainability in the context of agricultural and fisheries policy. It was able to broker an agreement on the 2016 fishing quotas for certain fish stocks in December with a view to integrating sustainability into this policy area.

Strengthening the European Union's Presence on the Global Stage

This was the least ambitious pillar of the presidency's programme as it was deemed to fall largely under the remit of the High Representative of the European Union and the European External Action Service. However, the presidency organized the 12th Asia–European foreign ministers' meeting, which brought together 53 delegations. It also encouraged an active enlargement policy and was pleased that a particularly high number of chapters were opened during accession negotiations.[30] New chapters were opened for negotiation with Turkey and Montenegro and accession negotiations with Serbia began.

Perceptions of the Presidency

On the whole, despite the crises that affected the European Union, the Luxembourgish presidency itself was generally seen positively by politicians and the media.[31] The plenary debate in the European Parliament on the 'bilan de la présidence' was overwhelmingly positive. Criticism came mostly from the extreme right on migration, from the left on the need for even more social measures and there was still some criticism on Luxembourg's past policy on corporate taxation (European Parliament, 2016).

The presidency did well on its legislative programme, concluding 34 legislative files under the ordinary legislative procedure (Luxembourgish Presidency, 2016). This number is low compared to other presidencies, but it is the result of a deliberate reduction in new legislation on the part of the European Commission under Barroso and Juncker.[32] The Luxembourgish presidency also managed to negotiate a new interinstitutional agreement to facilitate better law-making in the European Union (Renman and Russack, 2016).

---

[30] Interview with an official of the Ministère des Affaires étrangères, Luxembourg, 19 April 2016.
[31] *France Inter*, 1 January 2016; *Le Quotidien*, 19 December 2015.
[32] Interview with a Council official for Transport, Telecommunications, Energy, Brussels, 15 February 2016.

Conclusion

Overall, despite the context of crisis, the presidency successfully concluded or advanced a range of important dossiers – at times quite rapidly. Part of the explanation is that the presidency had adopted a realistic programme to begin with. In addition, the presidency managed to create many of the conditions for success outlined by Vandecasteele and Bossuyt (2014). As far as national conditions are concerned, it benefited from a high level of experience and a culture of consensus, but also from a climate of trust between different Luxembourgish actors. This allowed it to become a truly Brussels-based presidency that focused on being an honest broker. Also, while it could only fix its priorities comparatively late, it was well prepared on its priorities. At the same time, unexpected shifts in the agenda or the nature of policy problems, such as the sudden prominence of the eastern route for refugees, clearly made it difficult for all actors to forge compromises.

In terms of crises, the presidency was to some extent shielded by the provisions of the Lisbon Treaty. Both the migration crisis and the terrorist attacks in Paris, however, left their mark on the presidency. The early decisions in the migration crisis, in particular, were an achievement, but also controversial. This example also illustrates the importance of being able to take decisions with qualified majority voting. At the same time, it is now obvious that Member States are reluctant to accept being outvoted in a policy area that touches what is perceived to be fundamental national interests.

References

Cameron, D. (2015) 'A New Settlement for the United Kingdom in a Reformed European Union', Letter to Donald Tusk on 10 November 2015. Available online at: http://www.consilium.europa.eu/en/policies/uk/2016-uk-settlement-process-timeline/.

Carbone, M. (2015) 'Beyond the Telemachus Complex: Courses, Discourses and the 2014 Italian Presidency of the Council of the European Union'. *JCMS*, Vol. 53, No. s1, pp. 83–92.

Competitiveness Council (2015) Outcome of the Council Meeting, *Presse* 12578/15, 1 October.

European Council (2014) 'Conclusions 26/27 June: Strategic Agenda for the Union in Times of Change'. Available online at: http://www.consilium.europa.eu/en/european-council/role-setting-eu-political-agenda/.

European Parliament (2016) 'Bilan de la présidence luxembourgeoise (débat)', plenary debate, 19 January. Available online at : http://www.europarl.europa.eu/sides/getDoc.do?pubRef=-//EP//TEXT+CRE+20160119+ITEM-003+DOC+XML+V0//FR&language=FR.

Hearl, D. (2006) 'The Luxembourg Presidency: Size Isn't Everything'. *JCMS*, Vol. 44, No. s1, pp. 51–5.

Heywood, P. (2011) 'Spain's EU Presidency: Ambitions beyond Capacity?' *JCMS*, Vol. 49, No. s1, pp. 77–89.

Kietz, D. (2007) 'Funktionen, Handlungsbedingungen und Stellschrauben der Präsidentschaft im System des EU-Ministerrats'. In Kietz, D. and Perthes, V. (eds.), *Handlungsspielräume einer EU-Ratspräsidentschaft. Eine Funktionsanalyse des deutschen Vorsitzes im ersten Halbjahr 2007* (Berlin: SWP Studie).

Laffan, B. (2014) 'In the Shadow of Austerity: Ireland's Seventh Presidency of the European Union'. *JCMS*, Vol. 52, No. s1, pp. 90–8.

Luxembourgish Presidency (2015a) 'A Union for the Citizens: Priorities of the Luxembourg Presidency', (Luxembourg: Information and Press Service of the Luxembourg Government). Available online at: http://www.eu2015lu.eu/en/la-presidence/a-propos-presidence/programme-et-priorites/.

Luxembourgish Presidency (2015b), 'Informal meeting in Luxembourg of Ministers for Competitiveness within the EU', 20–21 July. Available online at: http://www.eu2015lu.eu/en/actualites/communiques/2015/07/info-comp-annonce/.

Luxembourgish Presidency (2015c) 'Première réunion informelle des ministres de l'Emploi de la zone euro – Le renforcement de la dimension sociale dans l'UEM au centre des discussions', 5 October. Available online at: http://www.eu2015lu.eu/fr/actualites/articles-actualite/2015/10/05-info-epsco-eurozone/index.html.

Luxembourgish Presidency (2016) 'Report on the Achievements of the Luxembourg Presidency' (Luxembourg: Information and Press Service of the Luxembourg Government).

Ministère des Affaires étrangères (2015) 'Réponse de Monsieur le Ministre des Affaires étrangères et européennes à la question parlementaire N'SyO déposée par les honorables Députés Messieurs Justin Turpel et Serge Urbany (Groupe parlementaire Déi Lénk)', Chambre des Députés, 27 February.

Pomorska, K. and Vanhoonacker, S. (2012) 'Poland in the Driving Seat: A Mature Presidency in Turbulent Times'. *JCMS*, Vol. 50, No. s1, pp. 76–84.

Quaglia, L. and Moxon-Browne, E. (2006) 'What Makes a Good EU Presidency? Italy and Ireland Compared'. *JCMS*, Vol. 44, No. 2, pp. 349–68.

Renman, V. and Russack, S. (2016) 'Balancing Priorities and Emergency Measures: Luxembourg's Council Presidency', *CEPS*, EPIN Commentary No 30. 15 January.

Tallberg, J. (2004) 'The Power of the Presidency: Brokerage, Efficiency and Distribution in EU Negotiations'. *JCMS*, Vol. 42, No. 5, pp. 999–1022.

Vandecasteele, B. and Bossuyt, F. (2014) 'Assessing EU Council Presidencies: (Conditions for) Success and Influence'. *Comparative European Politics*, Vol. 12, No. 2, pp. 233–47.

Vilpišauskas, R. (2014) 'Lithuania's EU Council Presidency: Negotiating Finances, Dealing with Geopolitics'. *JCMS*, Vol. 52, No. s1, pp. 99–108.

Warntjen, A. (2007) 'Steering the Union. The Impact of the EU Presidency on Legislative Activity in the Council.' *JCMS*, Vol. 45, No. 5, pp. 1135–1157.

Warntjen, A. (2013) 'The Elusive Goal of Continuity? Legislative Decision-Making and the Council Presidency before and after Lisbon'. *West European Politics*, Vol. 36, No. 6, pp. 1239–55.

JCMS 2016 Volume 54. Annual Review pp. 101–116   DOI: 10.1111/jcms.12427

Governance and Institutions: A More Political Commission

DESMOND DINAN
George Mason University

Introduction

In November 2014, based on the new *Spitzenkandidaten* procedure, Jean-Claude Juncker became President of the European Commission (Dinan, 2015; Peñalver Garcia and Priestley, 2015). Speaking to Members of the European Parliament (MEPs) before the vote to approve the new college, in October 2014, Juncker said that he hoped to lead a different kind of Commission – what he called 'a more political Commission' – at a time of grave crisis in the European Union (Juncker, 2014).

The advent of the Juncker Commission coincided with a debate among EU scholars about the Commission's overall importance. For some time, scholars have noted the relative decline of the Commission *vis-à-vis* the Council of the EU, the European Parliament, and, especially since the onset of the euro crisis, the European Council. A number of factors account for the 'the constant murmur about the Commission being in decline' (Bauer and Becker, 2016, p. 101). These include diminishing support for the traditional Community method of EU policy-making; concern about weak democratic legitimacy in the EU; and the impact of the Lisbon Treaty, which came into effect in December 2009. Advocates of 'new intergovernmentalism' claim that, since the Maastricht Treaty of 1992, intergovernmentalism rather than supranationalism has been the driving force of European integration, with the European Council institutionally in the ascendant. The Commission is still an important player, but is constrained by new political and inter-institutional dynamics (Bickerton *et al.*, 2014).

While not challenging new intergovernmentalism head on, Nugent and Rhinard (2016) dispute the idea that the Commission is in decline. They do so by looking at three traditional areas of Commission activity: agenda setting, legislative decision-making and policy implementation. Although inevitably the Commission's involvement in these activities has changed over time, the Commission has not necessarily been diminished as a result. On the contrary, according to Nugent and Rhinard, the Commission's position may even have been strengthened in certain respects, not least because of the euro crisis.

Contributions to the *JCMS Annual Review* provide snapshots of EU institutional, policy and other developments during a particular calendar year. This year's contribution on governance and institutions focuses on the Commission. It is not possible, on the basis of such a snapshot, to contribute significantly to the Commission declinism debate. Nevertheless, a number of developments concerning the Commission in 2015 are noteworthy. Without doubt, the Commission sought to shape the EU's policy agenda. The role of the President was especially noteworthy. At the same time, the number of legislative proposals continued to fall, though this was largely because of a strategic decision intended, paradoxically, to strengthen the Commission politically. The Commission remained fully engaged in policy implementation.

The snapshot nevertheless shows something which is absent from the declinism debate, but which may be significant for the Commission's future. It has to do with what appears to be the Commission's increasing deference to the European Parliament (EP), which is particularly noticeable in the close relationship between Juncker and EP President Martin Schulz, who was himself a candidate for Commission President in 2014. The changing dynamics of Commission–EP relations goes well beyond personal connections, however, and is rooted in the procedure by which the EP forced the hand of the European Council in 2014 to nominate as Commission President the candidate whose political party won the most votes in the EP elections.

I. State of the Union

On 9 September 2015, Juncker delivered the first State of the Union address of his presidency at a plenary session of the EP in Strasbourg. The annual State of the Union and ensuing debate is a relatively recent development. It originated in the 2010 EP-Commission Framework Agreement, which the two institutions negotiated in light of the Lisbon Treaty (*Official Journal*, 2010). The address is part of a carefully choreographed series of events contributing to the annual political and legislative programming of the EU.

The idea of a State of the Union address has an obvious appeal for both institutions. For the EP, it represents 'an exercise of political accountability' on the part of the Commission to the Parliament. For the Commission, it is an opportunity for the President to appear presidential. The clear parallel with the US President's annual State of the Union address to a joint session of Congress is not lost on either the Commission or the EP (EPRS, 2015a). Though not as noteworthy as the US President's State of the Union, the Commission President's State of the Union is nonetheless a major event in the political life of the EU. Juncker's inaugural speech was particularly significant because, as he reminded his audience, he was 'the first President of the Commission whose nomination and election is the direct result of the outcome of the European Parliament elections in May 2014. Having campaigned as a lead candidate … in the run up to the elections, I had the opportunity to be a more political President' (Juncker, 2015a).

The Commission President has always had a political persona, in keeping with the Commission's responsibilities. As Juncker noted, his 'political role is foreseen by the Treaties, by means of which the Member States made the Commission the promoter of the general interest of the Union'. Indeed, the EP-Commission Agreement frequently uses the word 'political' to describe the role of the Commission and its President. The very first article specifies that the purpose of the Agreement is, *inter alia*, 'to strengthen the political responsibility … of the Commission' (*Official Journal*, 2010).

By wanting to be 'a more political President', Juncker raised an obvious question: more political than whom? Some Commission Presidents have been highly political. Walter Hallstein (1958–67) and Jacques Delors (1985–93) spring to mind. Hallstein's approach contributed to a major constitutional crisis in 1965–66; Delors' contributed to the acceleration of European integration in the late 1980s. Subsequent Commission Presidents have inevitably compared themselves or been compared to Delors. Most likely, however, Juncker was alluding to José Manuel Barroso, his immediate predecessor.

Having observed that the Commission's political role derived from the Treaties, in an implicit reproach of Barroso, Juncker complained that 'the crisis years have diminished this understanding' (Juncker, 2015a). Certainly, there was widespread media criticism of Barroso for not having been more assertive during the euro crisis, which overshadowed his second term (2010–14). Many EU politicians, especially in the EP, had criticized Barroso for being too deferential to national leaders, notably those of France and Germany. As leader of the Socialist Group in the EP in 2010, Schulz had denounced Barroso for conceding too much to 'a Franco–German directorate' (S&D, 2010). Juncker himself indirectly censured Barroso when he asserted that, unlike his predecessor, he would not leave unfair criticism from national capitals go unanswered, and that he was 'not a guy who trembles before Prime Ministers'.[1]

Regardless of Barroso's perceived political weakness, a comparison between Barroso's four State of the Union speeches (2010–13) and Juncker's 2015 State of the Union speech (there was no speech during the 2014 EP elections year) suggests many similarities between the two Commission Presidents, and no lack of political ambition on Barroso's part. In general, all five speeches are hortatory; outline key issues confronting the EU; advocate the use of the Community method where practicable; promise political leadership; and praise the EP (Barroso, 2010, 2011, 2012, 2013; Juncker, 2015a).

Despite these similarities, there were marked differences as well. Juncker built on the *Spitzenkandidaten* precedent, as a result of which he became President, to stake a claim 'to lead a political Commission. A *very* political Commission. … because I believe the immense challenges Europe is currently facing – both internally and externally – leave us no choice but to address them from a very political perspective, in a very political manner and having the political consequences of our decisions very much in mind. Recent events have confirmed the urgent need for such a political approach in the European Union' (Juncker, 2015a).

But what did being 'more political' really mean, and how would Juncker go about it? The tone and content of his speech contained some clues, notably a marked assertiveness towards national governments and a willingness to make bold proposals with respect to the euro and migration crises. In another respect Juncker's speech was different as well. Whereas in his speeches Barroso paid due deference to the EP, Juncker was gushing in his praise for the Parliament and especially for its President. Not surprisingly, the tone and content of the follow-on debates were correspondingly different. Although individual MEPs criticized Juncker, his speech was generally received with far more enthusiasm in the EP than were any of Barroso's speeches.

II. Being More Political

Juncker believed that he had the potential to be more political not only because of the greater legitimacy bestowed upon him by the *Spitzenkandidaten* procedure, but also because of the quality of his Commissioners, the reorganization of his College, and the centralization of his authority within the Secretariat-General.

---

[1] *EurActiv*, 5 November 2014.

The Commission is proud of the fact that it 'consists of political heavy-weights including nine former Prime Ministers or Deputy Prime Ministers, 19 former Ministers, seven
returning Commissioners and eight former [MEPs], all with solid economic and finance
background, and for some of them with extensive foreign relations experience' (European
Commission, 2014a). Juncker takes credit for having chosen 'politicians who have a past
and a future … So as to give the Commission a political dimension it did not have before'
(Juncker, 2015b). In fact, Juncker had relatively little say in the nomination of Commission candidates by the national governments. He was undoubtedly fortunate to have had
such a capable crop, though the desirability of Commission appointments may have as
much to do with prestige and pay as with political ambition.

But Juncker and Frans Timmermans, his First Vice-President (VP), were responsible
for an important organizational innovation in the Commission: the formation of 'project
teams', each led by one of the seven VPs. The legal requirement of one Commissioner
per Member State compromised the efficiency of the College. As Commissioners are
nominally equal, the potential for decision-making sclerosis was real. Managing a
College of 28 Commissioners had been a burden for Barroso. In an influential op-ed in
November 2013, Timmermans, then Foreign Minister of The Netherlands, had argued
that 'the EU needs to follow the logic of the treaty and create a … reformed commission
with a president and vice-presidents heading a limited number of policy clusters. The
vice-presidents would have the sole authority to initiate legislation. This would restore
the commission's focus and strengthen its clout'.[2] Having been selected as Juncker's
First VP, Timmermans put this idea into practice.

The project teams, covering key policy areas and clusters, have undoubtedly improved the functioning of the College. Teams have not always worked smoothly, with
occasional reports of clashes between strong-willed commissioners, sometimes accentuated by political differences. The Foreign Affairs and Security Policy team, under VP
Federica Mogherini, reportedly works extremely well, and may represent 'one of the –
if not the – most developed form of cluster cooperation in the Juncker Commission …
[injecting] much-needed political pragmatism into the way the Commission contributes
to EU external action' (Blockmans and Russack, 2015).

The project teams are the most visible aspect of Commission reorganization as a means
of improving efficiency and providing greater political heft. Beneath the level of the
College, Juncker and Timmermans have bolstered the size and authority of the Secretariat-General with a view to coordinating more closely the work of the Commission's
numerous Directorates-General and Services. Catherine Day, Secretary-General until
her retirement in September 2015, and Alexander Italianer, her successor, together with
Martin Selmayr, Juncker's powerful Chief of Staff, spearheaded the strengthening of
the Secretariat-General. Apart from losing senior members to the Secretariat-General,
most of the Directorates-General and Services have not been directly affected by organizational change since Juncker became President, though all feel a greater centralization of
power within the institution. Some Commissioners even complain about not being
adequately consulted, let alone fully informed, about decisions taken by a handful of
powerful people, notably Juncker, Timmermans, Selmayr and Italianer.[3]

[2] *Financial Times*, 14 November 2013.
[3] *Politico*, 8 November 2015.

Better Regulation

The quest for better regulation is a leitmotif of the Juncker Commission. Yet the Commission has struggled for years to reduce the quantity and improve the quality of its legislative work. In December 2012, the Commission launched the regulatory fitness and performance programme (REFIT), which it uses to screen the entire stock of existing legislation and legislative proposals in order to identify burdensome and inconsistent measures, and take corrective action. This includes new initiatives to simplify existing legislation and reduce regulatory overload, proposals to repeal outdated or redundant legislation, and the withdrawal of proposals with little chance of adoption (European Commission, 2016).

The fact that better regulation became the responsibility of the First VP highlights the importance of this issue for the Juncker Commission. Though seemingly arcane, better regulation is highly political. Because it suffers from chronic economic underperformance, the EU's credibility and viability depend to a great extent on its ability to provide a framework for economic growth and job creation, especially in the aftermath of the great recession and in the shadow of the euro crisis. Moreover, euroscepticism thrives on allegations of over-regulation in the EU. This was especially the case in the UK in 2015 in the heated atmosphere of the intensifying Brexit debate. Apart from the importance of better regulation for substantive policy reasons, the political salience of the issues was unusually high during the Juncker Commission's first year.

The Commission's 2015 Work Programme, adopted in December 2014, reflected Timmermans' preoccupation with better regulation, as did a Commission Communication in May 2015 on the subject (European Commission, 2014b; European Commission 2015a). The Work Programme was notable, among other things, for the paucity of legislative proposals (only 23) to be introduced in the coming year and the relatively large number of proposals (over 80) to be modified or withdrawn. These included measures under the rubric of REFIT, as well as a withdrawal of proposals based on the principle of 'political discontinuity'. This principle, enshrined in the 2010 EP–Commission Agreement, states that 'The Commission shall proceed with a review of all pending proposals at the beginning of the new Commission's term of office, in order to politically confirm or withdraw them, taking due account of the view expressed by Parliament' (*Official Journal*, 2010). It is the EU's equivalent of the principle of 'legislative discontinuity', which exists in many Member States, whereby pending proposals cease to be valid at the end of a legislative term (EPRS, 2015b).

Despite widespread agreement at EU and national levels that better regulation is a good thing, the Juncker's Commission's approach was not without controversy. The Commission was already in a legal battle with the Council over the Commission's right to withdraw proposals, which the Commission saw as the flip side of its exclusive right of legislative initiative. At issue was the Council's claim that the Commission had no right to withdraw proposals that were being actively considered by the co-legislators (Council and the EP), and had been changed in a way that the Commission disliked (the Court ruled in favour of the Commission) (EPRS, 2015c).

The controversy over the Juncker Commission's better regulation agenda had more to do with a deep attachment in the EP, in certain parts of the Commission, and among interest groups and non-governmental organizations, to a steady stream of EU legislative proposals, around which a large Brussels policy industry had developed. Timmermans acknowledged as much at the time of the Better Regulation Communication: 'In principle everybody agrees that we should be big on big things and small on small things, but then, as soon as you start defining what the big things are … you get a political debate because what is big for one political party is small for another political party'.[4] The better regulation initiative alarmed environmental organisations, trade unions and consumer groups, which called on the Commission not to drop legislative proposals for gender and environmental legislation.[5]

Within the Commission, Timmermans' aggressive approach upset the Directorates-General that traditionally generate the lion's share of proposals and whose identity is bound up with legislative output. It also fuelled complaints about excessive centralization and control. Timmermans was aware of the challenge that he faced in 'arguably one of the best public administrations in the world. … But I have told … the DGs [Directors General] … it's very simple: this organisation is going to change. … If you think by sabotaging or blocking or stopping the change we advocate that things will stay the same you're absolutely wrong … We need to be able to answer not yesterday's challenges but tomorrow's challenges. To do that we need to work differently, and that's what this Commission proposes'.[6]

Included in the Commission's Communication was a call for a new Commission–Council–EP Interinstitutional Agreement (IIA) to replace the 2003 IIA on Better Law-Making (European Commission, 2015a). This was intended to update the original Agreement, especially in view of the many procedural changes brought about by the Lisbon Treaty, and to highlight the Commission's political commitment to better regulation. Negotiations for the new IIA began on 25 June 2015. They were very much an inside Brussels affair. Although better regulation was politically consequential, the subject did not attract considerably media coverage. In any case, the negotiations were completely overshadowed by much more important developments affecting the EU, notably the euro and migration crises.

The negotiations were far from fraught, but generated some tension over what the Council and the EP saw as a Commission effort to recalculate the legislative equation in its favour by strengthening the pre-proposal stage and limiting the number of amendments that the co-legislators could introduce in subsequent stages. At issue was the role and composition of a 'REFIT platform', intended to conduct an ongoing dialogue with Member States and stakeholders on improving EU legislation, and whether the Council and EP would be obliged to conduct their own impact assessments before submitting 'substantive amendments' to draft legislation. Timmermans unsettled the co-legislators by establishing a new Regulatory Scrutiny Board in July 2015 to replace the existing Impact Assessment Board (European Commission, 2015b). Business groups generally welcomed the Commission's draft IIA and the Regulatory Scrutiny Board; other lobbyists claimed that these initiatives were potentially detrimental to social and environmental interests.

---

[4] *Financial Times*, 19 May 2015.
[5] *EurActiv*, 18 May 2015.
[6] *Financial Times*, 19 May 2015.

By its nature, regulation is complex, especially at the supranational level. Simplification is a political imperative but a huge procedural challenge. Transparency, a requirement of good governance, often comes at the cost of efficiency: it may improve the legitimacy but not necessarily the speed or quality of regulatory decisions. The new IIA, finalized on 8 December 2015, though still subject to EP approval, represented a compromise on the part of all three institutions and, overall, an improvement of the inherently complicated EU law-making process (EPRS, 2015d). Nevertheless the impact of any such agreement would not be immediately apparent.

Other Political Initiatives

Progress on regulatory improvement in 2015, culminating in the new IIA on Better Law-Making, was a significant political achievement for the Commission, and especially for Timmermans. Juncker supported the better regulation agenda, but was more interested in initiatives that were self-evidently political and that attracted substantial media and public attention. For Juncker, being 'more political' appeared to mean staking out bold positions on pressing issues, often in contradistinction to those of the Member States. In doing so, Juncker liked to operate as a traditional national politician, which he had been for much of his career, notably as Prime Minister of Luxembourg for nearly two decades. He revelled in being back in the European Council, in delivering major speeches, and in giving lengthy media interviews. He also liked to operate behind the scenes, making deals and brokering agreements.

Migration, one of the most pressing problems facing the EU in 2015, was an area in which Juncker wanted to make an impression. On 13 May, the Commission adopted a 'European Agenda on Migration' (European Commission, 2015c). On 27 May, it announced a number of implementing measures, including a proposal for a Council Decision to relocate 40,000 migrants from Italy and Greece throughout the EU, something that national governments, especially in Eastern Europe, fiercely resisted (European Commission, 2015d).[7] In his State of the Union, Juncker bluntly reminded Member States that 'not a single person in need of protection has been relocated yet', which was 'simply not good enough'. He then raised the stakes by calling on Member States to adopt a new Commission proposal 'on the emergency relocation of altogether 160,000 refugees' (Juncker, 2015a). The Council duly decided – not unanimously, as the Commission had wanted, but by a majority vote – to establish 'a temporary and exceptional relocation mechanism' for a mere 40,000 migrants, few of whom were relocated by the end of 2015 (Council, 2015).

Reviewing these and subsequent initiatives, in a speech to the EP on 16 December, Juncker justified the Commission's activism: 'The Commission is not the government of the European Union, but when the situation requires so, when there are threats to our system, we have to take our responsibility … for the system as a whole. … Under my leadership we will do everything possible to protect what we have built ... [and] to defend everything that Schengen represents'. Then he took national governments to task: 'Progress is still too slow … Member States need to do more, and they need to do it quickly' (Juncker, 2015c). In November, in an effort to pressure governments, the

[7] See Monar's contribution to this volume.

Commission launched an online 'state of play' scorecard on the commitments and actions taken by Member States to implement the measures agreed under the Agenda on Migration (European Commission, 2015e).

Juncker's confrontational approach risked antagonizing some national leaders, though not always the same ones at any particular time. Given Germany's influence in the EU and key role in the migration crisis, Chancellor Angela Merkel was the leader whose opinion mattered most. By being more political, Juncker had to be seen to be standing up to Merkel without provoking her unduly, especially in view of the sensitivity of the migration crisis in Germany. Merkel welcomed Juncker's efforts to reduce pressure on Germany by relocating refugees throughout the EU, and his involvement later in 2015 in efforts to outsource to Turkey management of the influx of migrants into the EU. But she chafed at his apparent self-aggrandizement and his constant harping on the Commission's centrality in the EU system.

In responding to the migration crisis, Juncker did not behave inappropriately as Commission President, but he acted in a markedly assertive manner. Timmermans alluded to this when he told the *Financial Times*: 'This is a very political decision [the launch the Communication on Migration] … We've taken our responsibility…. this is being political. Avoiding confrontation and not taking your responsibility – making an analysis and avoiding drawing the obvious conclusion from that analysis – that's not being very courageous. It's not being political'.[8]

Economic and Monetary Union (EMU) was another area in which the Juncker Commission was self-consciously political. This was apparent in particular with respect to the monitoring of national budgets, and the negotiation and implementation of financial assistance for Greece. In the case of national finances, as Juncker told the EP in December 2015, 'decisions on budgetary priorities, the balance between revenues and expenditures, the level of taxation, the performance of public administrations and social systems, are all political decisions which require a political Commission' (Juncker, 2015d). What that meant had become apparent in January 2015, when the Commission issued a Communication on flexible implementation of the stability and growth pact (European Commission, 2015f). Subsequently, instead of sanctioning France and Italy for continuing to exceed the EU-mandated budget deficit of 3 per cent of GDP, the Commission recommended giving both countries an additional two years to bring their finances into line, on the basis of their respective economic reform plans. The context of the decision was growing opposition to austerity, which was fuelling the rise of anti-EU parties. Despite warnings from Germany and other hardline countries about the danger of deviating from austerity, in March 2015 the Council concurred in the Commission's recommendation.[9]

The Commission's leniency marked a sea change from the previous Commission's orthodoxy. Juncker's preference was 'not to dictate what [countries] have to do', but to let them 'propose themselves what they intend to do … If you are president of the commission …you have to listen to countries. You have to understand what is happening in different countries'.[10] Pierre Moscovici, the Commissioner for Economic and Financial Affairs, who happens to be French, justified the decision not to sanction France and Italy

---

[8] *Financial Times*, 19 May 2015.
[9] *Financial Times*, 10 March 2015.
[10] *Financial Times*, 27 November 2014.

on the grounds that the Commission's aim was to encourage deep reform and not apply penalties 'willy-nilly'. While fines remained an option, 'penalties are a failure' both for the country sanctioned and the body imposing the fine'. Then he chanted the mantra: 'This is a political commission'.[11]

On the question of conditionality for assistance to Greece, Juncker also deviated from the orthodoxy of the Barroso Commission. Accordingly, he launched a study of the social impact of the adjustment measures taken in Greece since the outbreak of the crisis, and urged the troika of creditors (the Commission, the European Central Bank and the International Monetary Fund) to show some leeway in implementing the assistance programme there (Juncker, 2015b).[12] In contrast to the strict position that he had taken as President of the Eurogroup (the forum for finance ministers of the Eurozone countries) during the early phase of the euro crisis, as Commission President Juncker became the voice of moderation. At the height of the crisis in summer 2015, Juncker argued fiercely in favour of keeping Greece in the eurozone and tried to shield Greece against the might of the creditor countries.

Yet Juncker's patience was sorely tested by the political inexperience – or machinations – of Alexis Tsipras, the new Greek Prime Minister, and Yanis Varoufakis, his overbearing Finance Minister. In February 2015, during a series of tense Eurogroup meetings, Varoufakis claimed that the EU has agreed to favourable terms for an extension of the second bailout, on the basis of a phone call between Juncker and Tsipras and a discussion between Moscovici and Varoufakis. Jeroen Dijsselbloem, President of the Eurogroup, disavowed the putative agreement, which the Eurogroup had not endorsed. This was an implicit rebuke not only of the Greeks, but also of the Commission.[13]

Perhaps chastened by his experience in February 2015, Juncker was more cautious in his dealings with the Greek government when the crisis escalated four months later. In June 2015, Juncker rebuked Tsipras for highly critical remarks about the Commission that Tsipras had made in the Greek parliament.[14] Nevertheless Juncker continued to cast himself as a protector of Greece and as an indefatigable defender of the integrity of the eurozone. Even so, during the height of the crisis later in the summer, Juncker was not included in the small group (the German Chancellor, French President, Greek Prime Minister and the European Council President) that met on the sideline of the euro summit to find a way out of the Greek impasse.[15]

Juncker's best-known contribution to alleviating the euro crisis was his stewardship of the Five Presidents' Report on strengthening EMU.[16] This was a follow-up to the 2012 Four Presidents' Report, *Towards a Genuine Economic and Monetary Union*, which the European Council President had spearheaded (Van Rompuy, 2012). (The other presidents were of the European Central Bank and the Eurogroup in 2012; plus the President of the European Parliament in 2015). The reason why the European Commission President rather than the European Council President directed the 2015 report was personal more than institutional: Juncker was far more familiar with EMU than was European Council

---

[11] *Financial Times*, 25 February 2015.
[12] On conditionality, Greece and the Eurozone crisis, see Featherstone's contribution to this volume.
[13] *Financial Times*, 1 March 2015.
[14] *Financial Times*, 7 June 2015.
[15] *Financial Times*, July 6 2015.
[16] See Hodson's contribution to this volume.

President Donald Tusk, who was not from a eurozone country and was happy to cede primacy on this issue (by contrast Herman van Rompuy, Tusk's predecessor, had been thoroughly familiar with EMU). Tusk was nevertheless more central than Juncker in dealing with the euro crisis in 2015, given Tusk's institutional position as President of the European Council, the EU's crisis-management body.

The European Council had called for a new report at its meeting in October 2014, though some countries, notably Germany, were doubtful about the feasibility of additional steps to strengthen EMU (EPC, 2014). Juncker's well-known preference for fiscal federalism and other far-reaching reforms to buttress monetary union bothered the Germans because of the political sensitivity of such proposals in a country suffering from acute crisis fatigue, and where concerned citizens were prone to bring cases before the Constitutional Court. The EU had already taken several sweeping measures to shore-up EMU, such as the Fiscal Compact, enhanced economic surveillance, and the European Stability Mechanism.[17] But it was natural for governments to do only as much as necessary, as late as possible, to cede further sovereignty on economic policy-making, especially at a time of rampant euroscepticism.

Juncker presented the Five Presidents' Report to the European Council in June 2015 (Juncker, 2015e). As expected, it went farther in its recommendations than many national leaders found acceptable. The battle ground over the following months centred on banking union, one of the most important parts of the still incomplete EMU edifice. The Commission seemed determined to press ahead with plans for a eurozone-wide deposit insurance scheme. Wolfgang Schäuble, Germany's Finance Minister, denounced this and other Commission proposals. Apart from resenting what he saw as Commission overreach, what bothered Schäuble was that German taxpayers could end up paying most of the cost of depositor bailouts at a time when banks were still vulnerable to shocks.[18]

Juncker relished the clash between Germany and the Commission over the proposed deposit insurance scheme. In this case the Commission appeared to be doing the right thing, attempting to shore up EMU with the strong support of the European Central Bank. The Commission was being political in an irreproachable way, whereas Germany was being political in a self-interested way. Juncker knew that the Commission would not prevail in the face of concerted German opposition, but he also knew that standing up to Germany would do him no harm.

Juncker launched numerous other initiatives, in keeping with the 2014 Political Guidelines. One of the best known was an investment plan, which bore his name, to raise €315 billion over five years for infrastructure and other economic development projects throughout the EU. Other key initiatives called for 'A Connected Digital Single Market' and 'A Resilient Energy Union' (European Commission, 2014b). There was no doubt about the Juncker Commission's busyness in 2015, though its effectiveness was debatable. The Juncker plan, in particular, seemed over-ambitious (Martin, 2015). Not surprisingly, it had failed to deliver as much as promised by the end of 2015 (Gros, 2015).

Nevertheless Juncker was living up to his promise of being more political by raising the Commission's profile, taking bold initiatives, and occasionally confronting national governments on sensitive policy issues. One of the most interesting of Juncker's

[17] See Hodson's contribution to this and previous *Annual Reviews*.
[18] *Frankfurter Allgemeine Zeitung*, 29 July 2015.

initiatives was not mentioned in his 2014 political guidelines or in the Commission's 2015 Work Programme, though he had spoken about it during the EP elections campaign. That was his call, in a newspaper interview in March 2015, for an EU army, which would 'help us to develop a common foreign and security policy, and to fulfill Europe's responsibilities in the world'.[19] The dream of an EU army – a nightmare for eurosceptics – goes back to the days of the failed European Defence Community in the 1950s and has been a hallowed aspiration of Euro-federalists ever since. By airing the idea as Commission President, albeit informally, Juncker demonstrated his audacity as a political agenda setter.

III. Commission–Parliament Relations

The success of the *Spitzenkandidaten* procedure – the fact that the candidate representing the party that received the most votes in the EP elections became Commission President, despite considerable controversy – inevitably generated speculation about parliamentarianism in the EU (Fabbrini, 2015). Having acquired greater budgetary, legislative and oversight responsibilities, might the EP not become a 'real' parliament by electing the government as well? Such thoughts indicate an unrealistic comparison between the EU system and national political systems. The Commission is accountable to the EP, its members are approved by the EP and its President is elected by the EP. But the Commission is not a government that stands or falls on the basis of having to maintain the support of a majority of MEPs. Nevertheless the EP revelled in the patina of parliamentarianism in the aftermath of the 2014 elections (Dinan, 2014). Juncker paid due homage to parliamentarianism in the EU, but also saw the outcome as an opportunity to strengthen presidentialism in the Commission. The juxtaposition of parliamentarianism and presidentialism in the shadow of the *Spitzenkandidaten* procedure was somewhat ironic, and demonstrated the plasticity of the EU system of governance.

Even if the events of 2014 did not move the EU in the direction of a parliamentary system, they moved the Commission – or at least Juncker – towards a more compliant relationship with the EP. In the political guidelines that he presented to the EP, Juncker promised that he would animate the 'special partnership' between the two institutions 'with new life' (Juncker, 2014). Politicians are practiced at buttering up their audience. What followed in Juncker's case was an effusive encomium to the EP: 'You stood up for democracy, and you were right to do so. A Parliament which upholds democracy is performing a noble task and does not deserve to be subjected to bitter, unjustified criticism or to have its motives unfairly challenged'. Thinking that perhaps he might have gone too far, Juncker told MEPs that, despite hoping to 'be elected by your assembly', he would not be 'at your beck and call; I'm not going to be the European Parliament's lackey'. However, MEPs should not 'doubt for one moment my willingness to remove a Commissioner who no longer benefits from your trust, or my willingness to take action, in principle by way of a legislative proposal, when you call on me to do so' (Juncker, 2014).

Being a more political Commission, which Juncker stressed in every address to the EP, seemed to mean being highly sensitive to the interests of the Parliament and its President. In the 2014 elections, Juncker had been the candidate of the European People's Party

---

[19] *Die Welt*, 8 March 2015.

(EPP); Schulz of the Party of European Socialists (PES). In the new Parliament, the EPP and the Socialists and Democrats (S&D) – the political group of the PES – agreed to form a 'grand coalition' to support Commission initiatives. ALDE, the Liberal group, threw in its lot with the grand coalition, but Guy Verhofstadt, the Liberal leader, was excluded from the Juncker–Schulz duumvirate.

The use of the term 'grand coalition' gave credence to the idea of emerging parliamentarianism in the EU. Yet the fractiousness of political groups in the EP, in comparison to the cohesion of governing parties or coalitions in most national parliaments, illustrated the extent to which the EP was a case apart. It is revealing that the EP failed to agree, in January 2015, on a joint resolution on the Commission's Work Programme. Whereas the EPP was willing to vote for the Programme in its entirety, S&D members were too dissatisfied with aspects of the Commission's better regulation agenda for the political group to do so.[20] Failure to pass a resolution was a mild embarrassment for the EP and a symbolic setback for the grand coalition. Although individual members of the EPP and the S&D continued to resist the party line on particular Commission proposals, the idea of the grand coalition persisted throughout 2015.

The dissatisfaction of some MEPs with the Commission was not necessarily based on ideology or political affiliation, but had to do as well with their EP Committee membership. Just as some Commission Directorates-General, used to a heavy legislative workload, were suspicious of Timmermans' approach to better regulation, so too were the corresponding EP Committees. Like the Commission, Timmermans remarked in May 2015, the Parliament needed 'to understand that legislation is not the answer to every problem and that there are problems that we need to tackle … without creating new legislation. … we're talking about not just a change in policies, [but] about changing the culture of major European institutions'.[21]

Regardless of the misgivings of many MEPs, the relationship between Juncker and Schulz grew unusually close in 2015. Professional ambition may partly explain this. In order to win a second term as Commission President (if that is what he wanted), it made sense for Juncker to play up parliamentarianism and cultivate the support of the EP. Schulz was already in an unprecedented second term as EP President, a post that ordinarily rotated between the EPP and S&D halfway through a parliamentary mandate, based on an informal agreement between the two groups. Schulz had managed to be re-elected President in July 2014 in return for offering Juncker and the EPP the support of a grand coalition. Already in 2015, Schulz hinted at wanting to win a third term so that he could oversee the grand coalition during the remainder of Juncker's (first) term as Commission President (2014–19). As a leading EPP politician, Juncker could help Schulz with that.

Whatever the motive, Juncker's apparent devotion to Schulz seemed to symbolize the Commission's relationship with the EP. Two examples stand out. First, it was thanks to Juncker that what would have been a second Four Presidents' Report on EMU became the Five Presidents' Report. Juncker elaborated on this in his State of the Union: 'It was self-evident for me to include President Schulz in this important work. After all, the Parliament is the heart of democracy at [the] EU level … The [EP] is and must remain the Parliament of the euro area. … I am therefore glad that for the first time, we have

---

[20] *Parliament Magazine*, 15 January 2015.
[21] *Financial Times*, 19 May 2015.

written not a 'Four Presidents' Report', but a 'Five Presidents' Report" (Juncker, 2015a). Second, in a joint press conference on 15 October 2015, Schulz and Juncker announced that in future they would confer before every meeting of the European Council to try to align their positions. Schulz explained 'that this decision [was] based on inclusive cooperation between the two institutions [which] share the joint project of strengthening the community method for the functioning of the EU' (EPRS, 2015e).

There were media reports in 2015 that Juncker and Schulz, together with Timmermans from the Commission, EPP leader Manfred Weber and S&D leader Gianni Pittella, were meeting regularly for dinner, in an informal group called the 'G5', in order to oil the wheels of the grand coalition. Such intimate meetings among supposed rivals are hardly unusual in politics. However, the idea of a 'G5' raised concerns in Brussels about possible backroom deals and an unhealthy coziness between the Commission and the EP.[22]

It is difficult to know how useful the grand coalition was in 2015. There were several spats between the Commission and the EP – more precisely between some Commissioners and some MEPs – during the year, but there were no battles on institutional or policy matters. The willingness of the EPP and S&D to cooperate closely may have helped to move certain Commission initiatives along, but it is hard to say if the outcome would have been different had the grand coalition not existed. By contrast, a frequently cited example of the utility of the grand coalition reflected poorly on all concerned. That was the alleged complicity of Schulz, Weber and Pittella in quashing an effort in the EP, supported by some EPP and S&D members as well as by many other MEPs, to hold Juncker to account for the LuxLeaks affair (the allegation that Luxembourg had facilitated tax avoidance by multinationals while Juncker was Prime Minister there). After Juncker survived a no-confidence vote in November 2014, Schulz, Weber and Pittella reportedly tried to prevent the EP from setting up a committee of inquiry into the matter and then succeeded in neutering the committee's work. The way that Juncker and his EP allies handled LuxLeaks contrasted sharply with the Commission's initiative in 2015 to crackdown on corporate tax evasion throughout the EU.[23]

Conclusion

There was a widespread perception in 2014 among politicians, officials and commentators that the Commission was losing ground in Brussels. The Barroso Commission appeared to have run out of steam, which may have been inevitable at the end of two terms in office (2005–14). Even if the Commission had gained new responsibilities as a result of measures taken to strengthen economic governance and implement financial assistance programmes, the euro crisis had constrained the space in which the Commission operates and limited the political prominence of its president, who was not a principal (voting) member of the all-important European Council. Barroso was unable to offset this weakness by developing a close political connection with the European Council's leading members, the French President and the German Chancellor.

Juncker had much keener political instincts than Barroso. He had the additional advantage of having become president on the back of the *Spitzenkandidaten* procedure, which

---

[22] *Politico*, 18 June 2015.
[23] *EurActiv*, 17 September 2015; *Spiegel Online International*, 6 November 2015.

allowed him to claim a stronger democratic mandate. He forged a close alliance personally with Schulz and institutionally between the Commission and the Parliament. Juncker
sought to boost the Commission's standing by assuming a high political profile, taking
robust policy initiatives, and securing the support of a grand coalition in the EP. He also
networked with national leaders in and around the European Council, but was not particularly close to the French and German leaders.

As Commission President Juncker was energetic and engaged, but how effective was
he? Did his first full year in office signal an improvement in the Commission's fortunes,
even if the academic argument about Commission declinism was overblown? Despite being 'more political', it is difficult to claim that the Juncker Commission was substantially
more influential at the end of 2015 than the Barroso Commission had been at the end of its
mandate. Nor was it likely that Juncker could become a transforming leader (Tömmel,
2013). Most of Juncker's major initiatives were worthy but not particularly fruitful. It is
easier to set the agenda by adopting communications and issuing declarations than to
achieve concrete results. Making speeches is not the same as making a material difference. Cozying up to Schulz and aligning the Commission closely with the Parliament
were not necessarily in the institution's best interest.

In one important respect, however, the Juncker Commission made a strong impression.
That had to do with better regulation, which was Timmermans' bailiwick. An experienced
politician who already knew Brussels inside-out, Timmermans was a highly effective
First VP. Indeed, the tale of the Commission in 2015 is the tale of two Commission
leaders: Juncker and Timmermans. Whereas Juncker was showy and self-consciously political, Timmermans was solid and hard working. Arguably Timmermans would have
been the ideal President for the Commission in 2015. The true test of the
Spitzenkandidaten procedure in 2019 will not be simply whether the largest vote winner
in the EP elections once again becomes Commission President, but whether the big political
parties will nominate the right people for the job – people of the calibre of Timmermans.

References

Barroso, J. M. (2010) 'State of the Union 2010', Strasbourg, 7 September. Available online at:
    http://europa.eu/rapid/press-release_SPEECH-10-411_en.htm
Barroso, J. M. (2011) 'State of the Union Address 2011', Strasbourg, 28 September. Available
    online at: http://europa.eu/rapid/press-release_SPEECH-11-607_en.htm
Barroso, J. M. (2012) 'State of the Union 2012 Address', Strasbourg, 12 September. Available
    online at: http://europa.eu/rapid/press-release_SPEECH-12-596_en.htm.
Barroso, J. M. (2013) 'State of the Union Address 2013', Strasbourg, 11 September. Available
    online at: http://europa.eu/rapid/press-release_SPEECH-13-684_en.htm
Bauer, M.W. and Becker, S. (2016) 'Absolute Gains are Still Gains: Why the European Commission is
    a Winner of the Crisis, and Unexpectedly So. A rejoinder to Eugénia da Conceição-Heldt'. *Journal
    of European Integration*, Vol. 38, No. 1, pp. 101–6.
Bickerton, C.J., Hodson, D. and Puetter, U. (2014) 'The New Intergovernmentalism: European
    Integration in the Post-Maastricht Era'. *JCMS*, Vol. 53, No. 4, pp. 703–22.
Blockmans, S. and Russack, S. (2015) 'The Commissioners' Group on External Action', CEPS
    Special Report, December. Available online at: https://www.ceps.eu/system/files/SR125%
    20SB%20and%20SR%20Commissioners%20Group%20on%20External%20Action_0.pdf

Council (2015) 'Relocation of 40,000 Refugees in Greece and Italy Agreed by Council', 14 September. Available online at: http://www.consilium.europa.eu/en/press/press-releases/2015/09/14-jha-relocation-refugees/

Dinan, D. (2014) 'Governance and Institutions: The Unrelenting Rise of the European Parliament'. *JCMS*, Vol. 52, No. s1, pp. 109–24.

Dinan, D. (2015) 'Governance and Institutions: The Year of the *Spitzenkandidaten*'. *JCMS*, Vol. 53, No. s1, pp. 93–107.

EPC (2014) 'Low Key But Not Low Impact: The Results of the ERU's 'Transition' Summit,' Brussels, 27 October. Available online at: http://www.epc.eu/documents/uploads/pub_4935_post-summit_analysis_-_27_october_2014.pdf

EPRS (2015a) 'The State of the Union Debate in the European Parliament', Brussels, 3 September. Available online at: http://www.europarl.europa.eu/thinktank/en/document.html?reference=-EPRS_BRI(2015)565909

EPRS (2015b) 'European Commission's 2015 Work Programme', Brussels, January. Available online at: http://www.europarl.europa.eu/EPRS/EPRS-Briefing-545732-Commissions-2015-work-programme-FINAL.pdf

EPRS (2015c) 'The European Commission's Right to Withdraw a Legislative Proposal', April. Available online at: http://www.europarl.europa.eu/RegData/etudes/ATAG/2015/554204/EPRS_ATA(2015)554204_EN.pdf

EPRS (2015d). 'Interinstitutional Agreement on Better Law-Making', 3 March. Available online at: http://www.europarl.europa.eu/RegData/etudes/ATAG/2016/579061/EPRS_ATA(2016)579061_EN.pdf

EPRS (2015e). 'Outcome of the European Council of 15 October 2015', 20 October. Available online at: http://www.europarl.europa.eu/RegData/etudes/BRIE/2015/558796/EPRS_BRI%282015%29558796_EN.pdf

European Commission (2014a) 'First College meeting of the Juncker Commission', 5 November. Available online at: http://ec.europa.eu/news/2014/11/20141105_en.htm

European Commission (2014b) 'Commission Work Programme 2015—A New Start', COM (2014)910 final, Strasbourg, 16 December. Available online at: http://ec.europa.eu/atwork/pdf/cwp_2015_en.pdf

European Commission (2015a) 'Better Regulation for Better Results—An EU Agenda', COM (2015)215 final, Strasbourg, 17 May. Available online at: http://ec.europa.eu/transparency/regdoc/rep/1/2015/EN/1-2015-215-EN-F1-1.PDF

European Commission (2015b) 'Better Regulation, Regulatory Scrutiny Board'. Available online at: http://ec.europa.eu/smart-regulation/impact/iab/iab_en.htm

European Commission (2015c) 'A European Agenda on Migration', COM (2015)20 final, Brussels, 27 May. Available online at: http://ec.europa.eu/lietuva/documents/power_pointai/communication_on_the_european_agenda_on_migration_en.pdf

European Commission (2015d) 'First Measures under the European Agenda on Migration', Brussels, 27 May. Available online at: http://europa.eu/rapid/press-release_MEMO-15-5038_en.htm

European Commission (2015e) 'State of Play: Measures to Address the Refugee Crisis', Brussels, 4 November. Available online at: http://europa.eu/rapid/press-release_IP-15-5958_en.htm

European Commission (2015f) ' Making the Best Use of the Flexibility within the Existing Rules of the Stability and Growth Pact', COM (2015)012 final. Available online at: http://eur-lex.europa.eu/legal-content/EN/TXT/?uri=CELEX%3A52015DC0012

European Commission (2016) 'Better Regulation: REFIT'. Available online at: http://ec.europa.eu/smart-regulation/refit/index_en.htm

Fabbrini, S. (2015) 'The European Union and the Puzzle of Parliamentary Government'. *Journal of European Integration*, Vol. 37, No. 5, pp. 571–86.

Gros, D. (2015) 'The Juncker Plan: From €21 to €315 billion, through smoke and mirrors', *CEPS Commentary*, 27 November. Available online at: https://www.ceps.eu/system/files/CEPS% 20Commentary%20The%20Juncker%20Plan%20D%20Gros.pdf

Juncker, J. C. (2014) 'A New Start for Europe: Political Guidelines', 15 July. Available online at: http://ec.europa.eu/priorities/sites/beta-political/files/juncker-political-guidelines_en.pdf

Juncker, J. C. (2015a) 'State of the Union 2015: Time for Honesty, Unity and Solidarity', Strasbourg, 9 September. Available online at: http://europa.eu/rapid/press-release_SPEECH-15-5614_en.htm

Juncker, J. C. (2015b) 'Commission after One Year', Speech to the Economic and Social Committee, 28 October. Available online at: http://europa.eu/rapid/press-release_SPEECH-15-5946_en.htm

Juncker, J. C. (2015c) 'Preparation of the European Council meeting of 17-18 December 2015', Speech to EP before the December 2015 European Council, 16 December. Available online at: http://europa.eu/rapid/press-release_SPEECH-15-6346_en.htm

Juncker, J. C. (2015d) 'Speech by President Juncker at the European Parliament Plenary session on the Economic and Monetary Union', Speech to the EP on EMU, 15 December. Available online at: http://europa.eu/rapid/press-release_SPEECH-15-6328_en.htm

Juncker, J. C. (2015e) 'Completing Europe's Economic and Monetary Union', Brussels, 22 June. Available online at: https://ec.europa.eu/priorities/sites/beta-political/files/5-presidents-report_en.pdf

Martin, M. (2015) 'Why Juncker's Investment Plan Is A Good Try But Not Enough'. *Social Europe Journal*, Vol. 8, No. 2, pp. 22–4.

Nugent, N. and Rhinard, M. (2016) 'Is the European Commission *Really* in Decline?' *JCMS*, (forthcoming). DOI:10.1111/jcms.12358.

Official Journal of the European Union (2010) 'Interinstitutional Agreements: Framework Agreement on Relations between the European Parliament and the European Commission', L 304/47, Luxembourg, 20 November. Available online at: http://eur-lex.europa.eu/ LexUriServ/LexUriServ.do?uri=OJ:L:2010:304:0047:0062:EN:PDF

Peñalver Garcia, N. and Priestley, J. (2015) *The Making of a European President* (London: Palgrave).

S&D (2010) 'Schulz attacks Barroso over State of the European Union', 7 September. Available online at: http://www.socialistsanddemocrats.eu/newsroom/schulz-attacks-barroso-over-state-european-union

Tömmel, I. (2013) 'The Presidents of the European Commission: Transactional or Transforming Leaders'. *JCMS*, Vol. 51, No. 4, pp. 789–805.

Van Rompuy, H. (2012) 'Towards a Genuine Economic and Monetary Union', Brussels, 5 December. Available online at: http://www.consilium.europa.eu/uedocs/cms_Data/docs/ pressdata/en/ec/134069.pdf

JCMS 2016 Volume 54. Annual Review pp. 117–133   DOI: 10.1111/jcms.12412

Eurozone Crisis Management, Citizenship Rights and the Global Reach of EU Data Protection Law: EU Legal Developments in 2015

THOMAS HORSLEY
Liverpool Law School

Introduction

2015 was another productive year for the EU judiciary. Collectively, the Court of Justice and General Court delivered a total of 954 judgments on a diverse range of substantive topics.[1] The year began with an urgent preliminary ruling on the allocation of jurisdiction in intra-EU matrimonial disputes.[2] It ended in late December, with a nod to upcoming seasonal festivities, with a judgment scrutinizing the Scottish Government's plans to introduce minimum unit pricing for alcoholic drinks.[3]

The past year was also marked by important changes at the Luxembourg Court. In October 2015, Koen Lenaerts (a Belgian) was elected President of the Court, replacing Vassilios Skouris, who served three full terms as President (the maximum tenure).[4] Antonio Tizzano (an Italian) was also elected Vice-President. He replaced Koen Lenaerts who had occupied that role since its establishment in 2012. At the end of 2015, and in a separate development, the Member States also reached agreement on significant institutional reforms to the size and shape of the Court. The Member States' approach to reform essentially sees 'more Court' as the response to the problems of workload and the need to ensure the delivery of judgements within reasonable time – as mandated by Article 47 of the Charter of Fundamental Rights (EUCFR).[5] The agreed reforms entered into force on Christmas Day and provide, first and foremost, for a progressive increase in the number of judges at the General Court.[6] By 2019, that Court, which functions principally at first instance, will be staffed by an additional 21 judges.

Following past practice, this contribution surveys a selection of the key legal developments in EU integration in 2015. As in previous years the spotlight is placed on the work of the Court's upper tier, the Grand Chamber. In 2015 the Grand Chamber delivered 41 judgments across the full spectrum of EU institutional, political and

---

[1] Statistics from InfoCuria. Available online at: http://curia.europa.eu/juris/recherche.jsf?language=en. Last accessed: 10 March 2016.
[2] *Bradbrooke v Anna Aleksandrowicz* (Case C-498/14 PPU) ECLI:EU:C:2015:3.
[3] *Scotch Whisky Association and Others v Lord Advocate and Advocate General for Scotland* (Case C-333/14) ECLI:EU:C:2015:845.
[4] The President and Vice-President of the Court are elected from and by its judges by secret ballot for a renewable term of three years. See Article 253(3) TFEU and Article 8 of the Rules of Procedure of The Court of Justice [2012] OJ L 265/1.
[5] See Recital No. 2 of Regulation (EU, Euratom) 2015/2422 of the European Parliament and of the Council of 16 December 2015 amending Protocol No. 3 on the Statute of the Court of Justice of the European Union [2015] OJ L341/14.
[6] Articles 1 and 2 of Regulation (EU, Euratom) 2015/2422, note 4.

economic activity. Amongst other things, it ruled on the Council's competence to adopt measures authorizing the signature and provisional application of mixed international agreements[7]; the Commission's competence to withdraw legislative proposals[8]; the application of EU equality law in the context of disputes over the physical positioning of consumer electricity meters[9]; and the compatibility with EU law of Swedish legislation exempting public postal services and stamps from VAT payments.[10]

For reasons of scope this contribution focuses on exploring three of the highlights from last year's jurisprudence. Section I begins by considering the Grand Chamber's most anticipated decision of 2015: *Gauweiler*.[11] In that judgment, the Court upheld the validity of one of the EU's key eurozone crisis management tools: the European Central Bank's programme of outright monetary transfers. Section II then turns to consider two important cases in the area of EU citizenship each of which make further contributions to the changing nature of that evolving legal status. Finally, section III reflects on recent judicial developments in the field of EU data protection, following on from the landmark judgements in *Digital Rights Ireland* and *Google Spain* considered in last year's review.[12]

I. Case C-62/14 Gauweiler and others

On the 16 June 2015, the Grand Chamber of the Court delivered its verdict on the validity of the European Central Bank's (ECB) programme of 'Outright Monetary Transfers' (OMTs). Its *Gauweiler* decision is without doubt the single most important judgment of the year. The Court's broad approval of the OMT programme offers financial markets further reassurance that the ECB has the necessary instruments at its disposal to ensure the stability of the euro and tackle future sovereign debt crises within the eurozone. Nevertheless, the survival of the ECB's OMT programme is not yet guaranteed. The German Federal Constitutional Court (BVerfG), which requested its first ever preliminary reference from the Court of Justice, expressed serious doubts about the validity of the OMT programme. Moreover, and most crucially, it also challenged the Court of Justice's competence to have the final say on the matter. Its reply to the Grand Chamber's decision is expected later in 2016.

This section begins with a brief review of the OMT programme and summary of the Court's principal conclusions in *Gauweiler* on its compatibility with the EU Treaty framework (see also Borger, 2016; Craig and Markakis, 2016; Hinarejos, 2015). It then highlights the significance of the decision with respect to the relationship between the Court of Justice and the German Federal Constitutional Court as constitutional actors in EU integration.

---

[7] *Commission v Parliament and Council* (Case C-28/12) ECLI:EU:C:2015:282.
[8] *Council v Commission* (Case C-409/13) ECLI:EU:C:2015:217.
[9] *CHEZ Razpredelenie Bulgaria AD v Komisia za zashtita ot diskriminatsia* (Case C-83/14) ECLI:EU:C:2015:480.
[10] *Commission v Sweden* (Case C-114/14) ECLI:EU:C:2015:249.
[11] *Gauweiler and Others v Deutscher Bundestag* (Case C-62/14) ECLI:EU:C:2015:400.
[12] *Digital Rights Ireland and Seitlinger and others* (Joined Cases C-293/12 and C-594/12) ECLI:EU:C:2014:238 and *Google Spain SL and Google Inc.* (Case C-131/12) ECLI:EU:C:2014:317.

Outright monetary transfers

The OMT programme is a central tool in the ECB's response to the eurozone sovereign debt crisis.[13] Its creation injected substance into Mario Draghi's announcement in the midst of the recent crisis that 'the ECB is ready to do whatever it takes to preserve the euro.'[14] Briefly summarized, the OMT programme provides for the ECB to purchase – in unlimited quantities – sovereign bonds on secondary markets at critical junctures as a means to prevent (eurozone) Member State governments risking default. Under the terms of the OMT programme, which was announced by the ECB in 2012 by press release, the purchase of sovereign bonds on secondary markets is also subject to specific conditions. These technical features relate, *inter alia*, to conditionality, coverage, creditor treatment and transparency.

In the proceedings giving rise to the preliminary reference, the applicant, a German politician, and adjoining parties argued that the ECB's OMT programme was invalid as a matter of EU law. Two specific objections were raised in that regard. First, it was argued that, by establishing the OMT programme, the ECB had exceeded its strict mandate under the Treaty framework to manage *monetary*, not economic policy within the eurozone. Secondly, the applicants argued that the programme also infringed Article 123(1) TFEU. That provision prohibits the ECB and Member State central banks from granting overdraft or any other credit facilitates to public authorities and bodies of the Union and/or the Member States and, further, from purchasing their debt instruments directly from them.

Is the ECB's OMT programme compatible with the treaties?

The BVerfG made no secret of the fact that it had serious doubts about the compatibility of the OMT programme with the EU Treaty framework. In its view, unless strictly construed by the Court of Justice,[15] the programme displayed all the hallmarks of an '*ultra vires*' act:

> 'Subject to the interpretation by the Court of Justice of the European Union, the Federal Constitutional Court considers the OMT Decision incompatible with Article 119 and Article 127 sec. 1 and 2 TFEU and Article 17 et seq. of the ESCB Statute because it exceeds the mandate of the European Central Bank that is regulated in these provisions and encroaches upon the responsibility of the Member States for economic policy. It also appears to be incompatible with the prohibition of monetary financing of the budget enshrined in Article 123 TFEU.'[16]

The Grand Chamber upheld the validity of the OMT programme, subject to conditions. First, with respect to the ECB's mandate, the Court concluded that the OMT programme was an instrument of monetary policy and, therefore, within the competences of the ECB.[17] This finding was central to the Court's decision to uphold the validity of the

---

[13] On eurozone governance, see the contributions by Hodson to this and previous issues of the *JCMS Annual Review*.
[14] Speech by Mario Draghi, President of the European Central Bank at the Global Investment Conference in London 26 July 2012. Available online at: https://www.ecb.europa.eu/press/key/date/2012/html/sp120726.en.html. Last accessed: 10 March 2016.
[15] See here BVerfG, Order of 14 January 2014–2 BvR 2728/13 at para. 100.
[16] *Ibid.*, at para. 55.
[17] At paras 46–65.

OMT programme. Under the Treaty framework, the EU enjoys exclusive competence for monetary policy within the eurozone; by contrast, economic policy remains principally a matter for individual Member State governments.

The Grand Chamber determined the character of the OMT programme with reference to the primary objective of EU monetary policy: the maintenance of price stability. As it noted with reference to its earlier decision in *Pringle*, the EU Treaty framework does not offer a precise definition of monetary policy, but instead simply outlines the objectives of that policy and the instruments that may be used to achieve those objectives.[18] In short, the Court concluded that the OMT programme's focus on safeguarding 'an appropriate monetary policy transmission and the singleness of the monetary policy' served the goal of maintaining price stability and was therefore an instrument of EU monetary policy.[19] The fact that the programme was also liable to impact *indirectly* on aspects of *economic* policy within the eurozone – again, an area of primary Member State responsibility – did not undermine that finding. On that point, the Court was clear in its reply to the BVerfG: 'a monetary policy measure cannot be treated as equivalent to an economic policy measure merely because it may have indirect effects on the stability of the euro area'.[20]

The Grand Chamber also rejected challenges to specific technical aspects of the OMT programme. Most significantly perhaps, the Court sanctioned the *conditionality* requirements built into the ECB programme. Under the terms of the OMT programme, recipient Member State governments are required to comply fully with an EU macroeconomic adjustment programme: the European Financial Stability Facility (EFSF) or European Stability Mechanism (ESM). On the one hand, the Court accepted that bond-buying on secondary markets could be regarded as a component of *economic* policy when undertaken by the ESM.[21] On the other hand, however, it concluded that the position was different with respect to the purchase of bonds by the ECB under the terms of the OMT programme.[22] According to the Court, the latter activity is undertaken independently of macroeconomic adjustment programmes and strictly on the basis of objectives particular to monetary policy.[23]

On the second issue, compliance with Article 123 TFEU, the Grand Chamber was particularly sensitive to the applicants' (and BVerfG's) concerns regarding the programme's validity. Both maintained that empowering the ECB to engage in sovereign bond buying on secondary markets through the OMT programme effectively circumvented the prohibition on *direct* bond purchases in Article 123 TFEU.[24] The Court of Justice recognised fully the risks at play in its appraisal of the programme's validity against that provision. In particular, it acknowledged that the central aim of Article 123 TFEU was to ensure that Member States follow sound budgetary policies. They should not allow the monetary financing of public deficits or privileged access by public authorities to the financial markets to lead to excessively high levels of debt or excessive Member State deficits.[25] Accordingly, the Court concluded that the validity of the OMT programme was

---

[18] At para. 42. See here also *Pringle* (Case C-370/12) ECLI:EU:C:2012:756 at para. 53 to which the Court referred.
[19] At paras 46–50.
[20] At para. 52.
[21] At para. 63.
[22] At para. 64.
[23] *Ibid.*
[24] At para. 6.
[25] At paras 94–100.

conditional on the existence of sufficiently robust safeguards to protect against unlawful monetary financing.[26]

In the final analysis, the Court of Justice took the view that the OMT programme was compatible with Article 123 TFEU. On its assessment, the ECB's programme was not, in practice, liable to have an effect equivalent to the direct purchase of government bonds. The Grand Chamber's assessment on that point relied, in particular, on additional explanations provided to the Court by the ECB.[27] The Court was satisfied by the ECB's assurances, contained within a draft decision and draft guidelines, that the primary market for sovereign bonds would not be distorted by the OMT programme. For example, the ECB indicated that the purchase of bonds on the secondary market (including details on timing and quantity) would not be announced in advance.[28] Likewise, the ECB committed to ensuring a minimum period is observed between the issue of debts by Member States on the primary market and their purchase by that institution on the secondary market.[29]

The court of justice and the BVerfG: strained relations?

Gauweiler is significant not simply for its verdict on the validity of the OMT programme as a key instrument of eurozone crisis management. It also highlights broader constitutional issues, in particular, the tension between the Court of Justice and the BVerfG with respect to the ultimate power to determine the limits of EU integration. A review of the Grand Chamber's judgment would not be complete without brief mention of this critical feature. Briefly summarized, since the 1970s, the BVerfG has asserted its competence to have the final say on the application of EU law within Germany – mandating the suspension of direct effect and primacy with respect to specific EU measures within that State where necessary (see, for example, Mollers, 2011; Payandeh, 2011). The substance of the BVerfG's *'ultra vires'* review has, of course, evolved over time, but is now essentially focussed on two things. In short, the BVerfG essentially reserves the right – in exceptional circumstances – to examine whether acts of European institutions and agencies (1) comply with the limits on EU integration set out in the EU Treaties, and/or (2) affect areas of national constitutional identity, which cannot be transferred to the Union as a matter of German constitutional law.[30]

The applicants in *Gauweiler* objected to the OMT programme before the BVerfG with reference to both aspects of the above legal framework (the *'ultra vires'* and 'constitutional identity' reviews, respectively). Unsurprisingly, the Court of Justice did not respond on questions of German constitutional identity (2). That is a matter for the BVerfG alone. The Court of Justice's competence is strictly limited to scrutinizing the validity of the OMT programme for compliance with the EU Treaties.

All eyes are now on the German Court. Has the Court of Justice done enough in its decision to address the BVerfG's clearly articulated concerns with respect to the validity of the OMT programme as a matter of EU law? Politically, the German Court is likely to face a strong pull towards compliance, not least given the success of the OMT programme

---

[26] At para. 102.
[27] At paras 105–106.
[28] At para. 106.
[29] *Ibid.*
[30] See, for example, BVerfG, Order of 14 January 2014–2 BvR 2728/13 at para. 22 and the case law of the *Bundesverfassungsgericht* cited therein.

in reassuring markets that appropriate instruments are now in place to protect the single currency from future shocks. Nonetheless, aspects of the Grand Chamber's reasoning in *Gauweiler* have the potential to trigger a new level of institutional conflict between the two courts.

In particular, the Court of Justice arguably crossed a number of apparent 'red lines' drawn by the BVerfG in its own assessment of the OMT programme in light of the Treaty framework.[31] For instance, the Grand Chamber adopted different positions on the requirement for quantitative limits on ECB bond buying and the level of creditor protection – key benchmarks identified by the BVerfG in its own assessment of the validity of the OMT programme.[32] At the same time, however, the Grand Chamber arguably engaged sufficiently robustly with several of the BVerfG's other fundamental concerns regarding, for example, the need to ensure that ECB bond buying did not undermine the conditionality of the EU's macroeconomic adjustment mechanisms. Likewise, the Court of Justice was also clearly sensitive to the German's Court arguments that the legality of the OMT programme depended on its supportive nature as regards economic policy.

For its part, the Grand Chamber expressly reminded the BVerfG that Member State courts are bound to comply with its conclusions on the interpretation and validity of EU law.[33] The BVerfG's response is expected during 2016.[34] Oral proceedings opened on 16 February 2016. However, at the time of writing, no date has been fixed for the delivery of the Court's decision.

II. EU citizenship rights

2015 was another notable year for developments in EU citizenship rights. Two key cases stand out in that respect: *Alimanovic* and *Delvigne*.[35] The first decision provides further evidence of the Court's recent turn to the framework of secondary Union law as a means to circumscribe the rights of EU citizenship (see also Nic Shuibhne, 2015). The continuation of that turn will no doubt appeal to (certain) Member State governments with growing concerns about the impact of EU citizenship rights on, *inter alia*, social welfare systems and national immigration law. Conversely, the Grand Chamber's judgment in *Delvigne* (on prisoner voting rights) indicates clearly that there is still scope for judicial dynamism in the development of EU citizenship rights, including in sensitive political areas such as electoral rights.

Case C-67/14 Alimanovic v. Jobcenter Berlin Neukölln

In *Alimanovic* the Grand Chamber was requested to determine whether EU law precludes Member States from denying EU citizens who qualify as workseekers under EU law access to non-contributory social welfare benefits. The case arrived at the Court by way of preliminary reference from Germany. The applicant, Ms. Alimanovic, and her three children are all Swedish nationals who had sought to contest the decision by a German

---

[31] For details, see BVerfG, Order of 14 January 2014–2 BvR 2728/13 at para. 100.
[32] See *Gauweiler* at paras 88 and 126, respectively.
[33] At para. 16.
[34] http://www.bundesverfassungsgericht.de/EN/Verfahren/Jahresvorausschau/vs_2016/vorausschau_2016_node.html. Last accessed: 10 March 2016.
[35] *Alimanovic* (Case C-67/14) ECLI:EU:C:2015:597 and *Delvigne* (Case C-650/13) ECLI:EU:C:2015:648, respectively.

employment agency to refuse them payment of a non-contributory subsistence allowance for the long-term unemployed (Arbeitslosengeld II). At the material time, neither Ms. Alimanovic nor her eldest daughter was engaged in economic activity in Germany. Both had only limited records of past temporary employment in that state.

The Grand Chamber concluded that EU law did not preclude Member States from restricting access to social welfare systems in such circumstances. Whilst it acknowledged that Ms. Alimanovic and her eldest daughter could claim *residence rights* under secondary EU law on the basis of their status as workseekers, the Court held that that status did *not* give rise to the right to equal treatment with respect to non-contributory social welfare benefits.[36] On the contrary, pursuant to Article 24(1) of Directive 2004/38 EC, Member States are not obliged to extend entitlements to social assistance to EU citizens who reside within the host State on the basis of their status as workseekers. As the Grand Chamber surmised:

> 'Although... Ms. Alimanovic and her daughter Sonia may rely on [Article 14(4)(b) of Directive 2004/38 EC] to establish a right of residence ... which entitles them to equal treatment with the nationals of the host Member State so far as access to social assistance is concerned, it must nevertheless be observed that, in such a case, the host Member State may rely on the derogation in Article 24(2) of that Directive in order not to grant that citizen the social assistance sought.'[37]

Alimanovic further underscores the Grand Chamber's recent shift in approach to defining the scope of EU citizenship rights. Following its judgment in *Dano*, considered in last year's review, the Grand Chamber in *Alimanovic* considered the scope of EU citizens' rights to residence and equal treatment exclusively through the lens of *secondary* EU law, namely Directive 2004/38 EC.[38] As before in *Dano*, there was no mention of *primary* Union law (Articles 20 and 21 TFEU) as the ultimate source of EU citizens' rights of residence and equal treatment – once a staple feature of the Court's citizenship case law. Likewise, in *Alimanovic*, the Court of Justice again dropped its reference to EU citizenship as 'destined to be the fundamental status of nationals of the Member States.'[39] For many years, express appeals to both the Treaty framework and its normative view on the trajectory of EU citizenship had, on key occasions, furnished the Court with powerful tools to review (and expand) the limits on EU citizenship rights contained within secondary Union law, including Article 24 of Directive 2004/38 EC on equal treatment.[40] That period of dynamism feels increasingly distant, entirely eclipsed by the (now) apparently exhaustive framework of secondary Union law.

Under the new settlement, Directive 2004/38 EC is fast becoming the touchstone that is used, first, to establish EU citizens' rights of residence in host Member States and, secondly, where such rights exist, to determine entitlement to equal treatment with respect, in particular, to social assistance. Indeed, as the Grand Chamber makes explicit in *Alimanovic*:

---

[36] At paras 57–58.
[37] At para. 57.
[38] *Dano* (Case C-333/13) EU:C:2014:2358.
[39] *Grzelczyk* (C-184/99) EU:C:2001:458.
[40] See, for example, *Baumbast and R* (C-413/99) EU:C:2002:493, *Grzelczyk* (C-184/99) EU:C:2001:458, *Collins* (Case C-138/02) ECLI:EU:C:2004:172 and *Vatsouras and Koupatantze* (Joined Cases C-22/08 and C-23/08) ECLI:EU:C:2009:344.

'A Union citizen can [now] claim equal treatment with nationals of the host Member State under Article 24(1) of Directive 2004/38 EC only if his residence in the territory of the host Member State complies with the conditions of Directive 2004/38 EC.'[41]

Alimanovic also makes a further, key concession to Member States with concerns about the impact of EU citizenship rights on national welfare systems. In short, the Court makes it clear that Member States are not required to conduct assessments of EU citizens' individual circumstances prior to rejecting social assistance claims under Article 24(2) of Directive 2004/38 EC.[42] In other words, Member States may, without restriction, refuse to grant social assistance to EU citizens who reside in the host State as workseekers *solely* on the basis of Article 24(2) of Directive 2004/38 EC.[43]

This is a subtle, but significant development. The Court of Justice had previously emphasized that Member States were obliged to take into consideration the individual situation of the EU citizen concerned in connection with the assessment of his or her social assistance claim. Thus, in *Brey*, it ruled that Member States may not automatically preclude EU citizens who are not economically active from receiving particular social security benefits without *first* conducting an overall assessment of the specific burden that awarding that benefit to the EU citizen concerned would place on the national social assistance system *as a whole*.[44] Following *Alimanovic* – as recently confirmed in *García-Nieto* – it would appear that the obligation to consider individual circumstances with respect to social assistance claims is restricted to the situation of economically inactive citizens who reside in the host Member State *beyond* the initial three month period and *other than* as workseekers by virtue of Article 14(4)(b) of Directive 2004/38 EC.[45]

Overall, the Court of Justice thus appears in its recent case law to be working towards establishing a legal framework that effectively insulates Member State social security systems from claims made by specific (and typically very vulnerable) categories of non-economically active EU citizens. Those affected include EU citizens such as Ms. Alimanovic and her daughter, who reside in host States as workseekers under Article 14(4)(b) of Directive 2004/38 EC. It also encompasses the situation of individuals such as Mr. Peña Cuevas in *García-Nieto*, who reside in host Member States as economically inactive EU citizens under Article 6(1) of Directive 2004/38 EC. That provision grants all EU nationals the right to reside in Member States of which they are not nationals for a period of up to three months, subject to the requirement that they do not become an 'unreasonable burden' on the host Member State.

Reviewing Article 24(2) of Directive 2004/38 EC, the Grand Chamber in *Alimanovic* was satisfied that the interests of the above categories of non-economically active EU citizens had been sufficiently taken into account by the EU legislature within the general scheme of the directive.[46] Furthermore, and in a powerful reversal of perspective, the Court of Justice went so far as to state that the application of the Article 24(2) derogation without scope for individual adjustment actually *promoted* the interests of individual EU citizens. In particular, the Court observed that the existence of that provision in its pure

[41] At para. 49.
[42] At para. 59.
[43] At para. 58.
[44] *Brey* (Case C-140/12) EU:C:2013:565, at paras 64, 69 and 78.
[45] *Alimanovic* at para. 58 and *García-Nieto* (Case C-299/14) ECLI:EU:C:2016:114 at paras 46–48.
[46] At para. 60.

form offered EU citizens 'a level of legal certainty and transparency' with respect to the availability of social assistance within particular host States.[47] The contrast with the Court's dynamic, inclusive approach to the development of EU citizenship rights in years gone by could not be more striking.

Case C-650/13 Delvigne

In recent years, the issue of prisoner voting rights has grabbed headlines across Europe. This attention follows from a series of important judgments of the European Court of Human Rights (ECtHR) and national decisions on the legality of Member State restrictions on prisoners' electoral rights.[48] In *Delvigne*, the Grand Chamber was afforded its first opportunity to express its position on the topic as a matter of EU law (see also Kornezov, 2016; Shaw, 2016). Specifically, the Luxembourg Court was requested to determine whether Arts. 39 and 47 of the EU Charter (EUCFR) preclude Member States from denying their nationals the right to vote in elections to the European Parliament in cases where the individuals concerned were convicted and imprisoned for serious criminal offences.

The applicant in *Delvigne* was a French national who had been convicted in France for murder in 1988 and imprisoned for a period of 12 years. At the time of sentencing, French law imposed an automatic restriction on the applicant's voting rights by way of ancillary penalty for the duration of his sentence. In 1994, the legal framework governing prisoner voting rights was reformed prospectively, but leaving the applicant's penalty in place.

Mr. Delvigne sought judicial review of a decision by the French authorities to remove his name from the electoral role. In summary, he argued that the French legislation on prisoner voting rights was contrary to Article 39 of the EU Charter. In particular, that provision guarantees EU citizens the right, *inter alia*, to vote in elections to the European Parliament in the Member State in which he/she resides under the same conditions as nationals of that State (Article 39(1) EUCFR).[49] It also provides that Members of the European Parliament shall be elected by universal suffrage in a free and secret ballot (Article 39(2) EUCFR). Furthermore, Mr. Delvigne also maintained that the French State's decision in 1994 to amend the criminal code only prospectively, leaving his own voting ban in place, was incompatible with Article 47 of the EU Charter. The final sentence of that provision states that 'if, subsequent to the commission of a criminal offence, the law provides for a lighter penalty, that penalty shall be applicable.'

The first question for the Grand Chamber was jurisdictional: did the applicant's situation fall within the scope of EU law? Several intervening Member State governments argued that it did not, pointing to the apparent absence of any connection between the contested national legislation and provisions of EU law.[50] The Grand Chamber confirmed its jurisdiction to reply to the request for a preliminary ruling. It recalled that, pursuant to Article 51(1) EUCFR, the Charter binds Member States only to the extent that

---

[47] At para. 61. See also *García-Nieto* (Case C-299/14) ECLI:EU:C:2016:114 at para. 49.

[48] See, for example, *Hirst v United Kingdom* (No. 2) (2005) 42 EHRR 894, *Scoppola v Italy* (No. 3) (2012) 56 EHRR 633 and *R (Chester) v Secretary of State for Justice*; *R (McGeogh) v The Lord President of the Council and Another (Scotland)* (2013) UKSC 63.

[49] Article 39(1) also guarantees the same category of beneficiaries the right to stand as candidates in elections to the European Parliament – a matter not at issue in the main proceedings.

[50] At para. 24.

© 2016 The Authors JCMS: Journal of Common Market Studies published by University Association for Contemporary European Studies and John Wiley & Sons Ltd

they are 'implementing EU law.'[51] In line with its *Fransson* judgment, the Court linked the concept of implementation in that provision to the determination of whether the applicant's legal situation fell 'within the scope of Union law.'[52] The Grand Chamber was clear that it did. It ruled that, when exercising their competence to determine the procedure for elections to the European Parliament, Member States are implementing obligations under Article 14(3) TEU and Article 1(3) of the 1976 Act on European Parliament elections annexed to Council Decision 76/787 EEC.[53]

On the second issue – whether or not the contested French legislation was compatible with Article 39 of the EU Charter – the Grand Chamber drew an important distinction. On the one hand, the Court ruled Article 39(1) EUCFR was inapplicable to the main proceedings. According to the Court, that provision guarantees EU citizens the right to vote in elections to the European Parliament in Member States of which they are not nationals.[54] On the other hand, and crucially for the applicant, the Grand Chamber concluded that Article 39(2) EUCFR guaranteed *all EU citizens* – including Mr. Delvigne – the right to vote in European Parliament elections, *including in the Member State of which they are nationals.*[55] Moreover, the Court ruled that national legislation depriving EU citizens of the right to vote in such circumstances represents a limitation of their electoral rights under Article 39(2) EUCFR, requiring justification.[56]

The Grand Chamber's interpretation of Article 39(2) EUCFR represents a significant development in the electoral rights of EU citizens. Previously, the Court had alluded to the existence of a freestanding right to vote in elections to the European Parliament for all EU citizens. In *Spain v United Kingdom*, for instance, the Grand Chamber had remarked *obiter dictum* that Article 19(2) EC (now Article 22(2) TFEU) 'implies that nationals of a Member State have the right to vote and to stand as a candidate *in their own country.*'[57] However, in that earlier judgment, the Court opted not to develop that point further. Instead, in a dispute over the UK's extension of voting rights to citizens of Gibraltar, the Grand Chamber ruled instead that Member States retained competence to determine the franchise for European Parliament elections, subject to compliance with EU law.[58] In practice, for Member States, the requirement to comply with EU law in that regard translated into an obligation not to discriminate, without objective discrimination, between different categories of national citizen when determining eligibility to vote in elections to the European Parliament.[59]

The Court's approach in *Delvigne* places its case law on the right of EU citizens to participate in elections to the European Parliament, in the Member State of which they are nationals, on a much stronger constitutional footing. The Grand Chamber could arguably have reached the very same result on the strength of its existing case law: the contested French legislation introduced a difference in treatment between Member State nationals, which, following *Eman and Sevinger*, required objective justification.

---

[51] At para. 25.
[52] *Ibid. Fransson* (Case C-617/10) ECLI:EU:C:2013:105.
[53] At paras 29–33.
[54] At para. 43.
[55] At para. 44.
[56] At para. 45.
[57] *Spain v United Kingdom* (Case C145/04) ECLI:EU:C:2006:543 at para. 76 (emphasis added).
[58] At para. 78.
[59] See here esp. *Eman and Sevinger* (Case C-300/04) ECLI:EU:C:2006:545 at para. 61.

However, the Court elected to be bolder. Its chosen approach establishes a right of EU citizens to vote in elections to the European Parliament in the Member State of which they are nationals as a fundamental right, protected by Article 39(2) of the EU Charter. In effect, Article 39(2) EUCFR is cast, within the scope of Union law, as the direct counterpart to Article 3 of Protocol No. 1 of the ECHR. The latter provision provides the basis of the right to vote as a fundamental right under the European Convention. In parallel to Article 39(2) of the EU Charter, that provision provides that:

> 'The High Contracting Parties undertake to hold free elections at reasonable intervals by secret ballots, under conditions that will ensure the free expression of the people in the choice of the legislature.'

Regrettably for Mr. Delvigne, and persons in comparable situations across Europe, what the Court gave with one hand it took back with the other. In the final analysis, the Grand Chamber concluded that the contested French restrictions on prisoner voting rights were compatible with the EU Charter.[60] As the Court noted, Article 52(1) EUCFR permits limitations to Article 39(2) EUCFR insofar as these meet specific conditions. In summary, the Charter requires that all derogations are provided for by law, respect the essence of rights and, in accordance with the principle of proportionality, are necessary and genuinely meet objectives of a general interest recognized by the EU or protect the rights and freedoms of others.[61] In *Delvigne*, the Court of Justice ruled that these requirements were satisfied with regard to the French restrictions on prisoner voting rights at issue in the main proceedings.

The Grand Chamber's assessment of the criteria for derogation is notably deferential to Member State autonomy. Unsurprising perhaps in light of the acutely sensitive nature of prisoner voting rights. A bold Court treads carefully. The Court of Justice essentially satisfied itself with the finding that French law provided the possibility for the applicant to apply to have his electoral rights reinstated.[62] Its assessment of Member States' rights to impose restrictions on prisoner voting rights is otherwise rather 'light touch,' particularly on the issue of the proportionality of any such restrictions.

The same applies *mutatis mutandis* with respect to the Court's appraisal of the French legal framework in light of Article 49 of the EU Charter (the applicant's second ground of review). As noted above, the final sentence of that provision states that 'if, subsequent to the commission of a criminal offence, the law provides for a lighter penalty, that penalty shall be applicable'. The Court roundly rejected Mr. Delvigne's efforts to invoke that provision as a means to challenge the prospective nature of the French Government's reforms to prisoner voting rights.[63] Yet, strikingly, the Grand Chamber did not really say why.[64] In line with its review of the French legislation against Article 39(2) EUCFR, the Court appeared satisfied with a parallel issue, namely that French law provided the possibility for the applicant to apply to have his electoral rights reinstated. The applicant's argument based on Article 49 EUCFR was admittedly a rather weak one. Nonetheless, a determined Court might have been expected to scrutinize it more rigorously.

---

[60] At paras 46–58.
[61] At para. 46.
[62] At paras 47–52.
[63] At paras 53–57.
[64] See here esp. para. 56.

However, without doubt, the standout feature of the Court's justification assessment is the absence of any reference to the Strasbourg Court's jurisprudence on the right to vote. This is particularly remarkable given the Court's decision effectively to read Article 39(2) EUCFR as a direct counterpart to Article 3 of Protocol No. 1 of the ECHR in Union law. Indeed, that move arguably establishes a positive *obligation* on the Court's part to engage with the Strasbourg Court's detailed case law on electoral rights. Article 53(3) EUCFR provides:

> 'In so far as this Charter contains rights which correspond to rights guaranteed by the Convention on the Protection of Human Rights and Fundamental Freedoms, the meaning and scope of those rights shall be the same as those laid down by the said Convention. This provision shall not prevent Union law providing more extensive protection.'

It is therefore unfortunate that the Grand Chamber opted, on this occasion, not to reflect expressly on the ECtHRs' case law. The latter Court's jurisprudence is now a *necessary* source of enrichment in the development of the Court of Justice's own case law on the legitimacy of Member State restrictions on the right to vote in elections to the European Parliament. Furthermore, as Article 53(3) EUCFR makes clear, the Strasbourg Court's jurisprudence on the restrictions on electoral rights should be viewed as setting *minimum* standards for rights protection in Union law. In *Delvigne*, discussion of the Strasbourg case law is to be found only in the Opinion of the Advocate General (Cruz Villalón).[65]

III. The global reach of EU data protection law

This final Section considers further key developments in EU data protection law. Last year's review examined two landmark cases in the field: *Digital Rights Ireland* and *Google Spain*. In both judgments, the Grand Chamber robustly defended EU citizens' fundamental rights to privacy and data protection guaranteed by Articles 7 and 8 of the EU Charter.

In 2015, the Grand Chamber was invited in *Schrems* to review another aspect of EU data protection law: the legal framework governing the transfer of EU citizens' personal data to *third countries* – specifically to the United States. Its decision to strike down the central EU instrument regulating data transfers between the Member States and the US – Decision 2000/520 (the so-called 'Safe Habour' agreement) – should not surprise those well versed in its recent data protection case law.[66] The Grand Chamber's judgment, though carefully constructed, closely follows its basic approach to the scrutiny of EU measures regulating transfers and processing of EU citizens' personal data *within* the European Union. This will not disappoint the Commission or European Parliament. Nevertheless, the Court's ruling has precipitated political challenges, not least the immediate requirement to renegotiate arrangements for EU/US data transfers that are fully compliant with EU law.

---

[65] At paras 108–124.
[66] Commission Decision pursuant to Directive 95/46/EC of the European Parliament and of the Council on the adequacy of the protection provided by the safe harbour privacy principles and related frequently asked questions issued by the US Department of Commerce – notified under document number (2000) OJ L215/7.

The EU legal framework on EU/US data transfers

Directive 95/46 EEC – the EU's principal, if now rather dated, instrument on data protection – governs transfers of personal data between Member States and third countries.[67] In summary, Article 25(1) of that Directive permits the transfer of EU citizens' personal data to third countries for processing only where the receiving State guarantees an 'adequate level of protection.' Notably, Directive 95/46 EEC does not further define what constitutes adequate protection. However, Article 25(1) offers some additional guidance. That provision states that the level of protection afforded to EU citizens in third countries is to be assessed:

> 'in light of all the circumstances surrounding a data transfer operation or set of data transfer operations; particular consideration shall be given to the nature of the data, the purposes and duration of the proposed processing operation or operations, the country of origin and country of final destination, the rules of law, both general and sectoral, in force in the third country in question and the professional rules and security measures which are complied with in that country.'

The Commission is empowered to determine by decision that specific third countries satisfy the 'adequacy' requirement in Article 25(1) of Directive 95/46 EEC.[68] The adoption of any such decision may follow as the result of successful negotiations between the Commission and individual third states in cases where the Commission or the Member States have expressed serious doubts about the adequacy of protection in third countries.[69]

In July 2000, the Commission adopted Decision 2000/520 with respect to transfers of personal data between the Member States and the United States.[70] That decision incorporated a set of privacy principles agreed with the United States government and known as the 'Safe Harbour Privacy Principles' (SHPPs). On the strength of those principles, and the accompanying guidance on their implementation issued by the US Department of Commerce, Decision 2000/520 provided the basis for the lawful transfer of EU citizens' personal data to the US for processing. In essence, the SHPPs established a voluntary system of self-certification for US undertakings in receipt of personal data from the European Union. That system was largely declaratory and commitment based, with a degree of public oversight and limited provision for individual redress. Crucially, it applied only to private undertakings and was also subject to a (US) national security exemption.

Enter Herr Schrems

The applicant in *Schrems* was an Austrian law student with concerns about the protection of his personal data following the exposure by Edward Snowden of the US Government's mass surveillance activities.[71] As a Facebook user, some of his personal

---

[67] Directive 95/46/EC of the Parliament and Council on the protection of individuals with regard to the processing of personal data and on the free movement of such data [1995] OJ L281/31.
[68] Art 25(6).
[69] Arts 25(4) and (5).
[70] Commission Decision [2000] OJ L215/7, note 66 above.
[71] Schrems (case C-362/14) ECLI:EU:C:2015:650. The Commission and European Parliament had also expressed concerns at the level of protection under the existing arrangements. See paras 11–25.

data was stored on the company's servers located in Ireland and, further, subject to transfer to the US for processing. In short, Mr. Schrems argued that the current legal framework governing the transfer and processing of data between Member States and the United States – under Decision 2000/520 – was incompatible with EU law and Articles 7 and 8 of the EU Charter in particular. As the 'Snowden files' had dramatically exposed, that framework did very little at all to protect EU citizens' personal data from routine and large-scale access by US intelligence agencies. Indeed, all of the US undertakings involved in the US Government's flagship PRISM intelligence gathering programme had self-certified with the SHPPs incorporated by Decision 2000/520.

In its preliminary reference to the Court of Justice, the referring Irish Court sought clarification on two points. The first was procedural: did the existence of Decision 2000/520 preclude Member State authorities – and the Irish Data Protection Commissioner in particular – from investigating complaints with respect to the 'adequacy' of EU citizens' protection? The Grand Chamber ruled that it did not. According to the Court, the supervisory authorities of the Member States remained competent to examine complaints that the laws and practices in force in third countries such as the United States do not ensure an adequate level of protection for EU citizens.[72] At the same time, the Court recalled that, in line with established principles, it retained exclusive competence to rule definitively on the validity of EU acts.[73] Thus, where doubts are raised as to the validity of EU data protection instruments in the course of Member State investigations, these must be put to the Court of Justice for resolution by way of preliminary reference.

The second question in *Schrems* addressed the validity of Decision 2000/520. As the referring Court recognized, this issue was the real focus of the applicant's concerns. Did that Decision, and the SHPPs it incorporated, comply with Article 25 of Directive 95/46, interpreted in light of Arts 7 and 8 of the EU Charter?

In its reply to the Irish High Court, the Grand Chamber ruled that Decision 2000/520 was contrary to EU law. Interestingly, the Court based its decision on a specific technicality, namely the absence of an explicit reference in Decision 2000/520 to the fact that US law actually 'ensures' an adequate level of protection with respect to EU citizens' personal data.[74] For the Court, the omission of such a reference was itself sufficient to seal the Decision's fate as a matter of EU law. Yet, in substance, the Court's ruling goes much further. It presents a robust critique of the existing SHPPs.[75] Moreover, looking ahead, the Grand Chamber also offers the Commission detailed guidance for the (re) negotiation of a legal framework for EU/US data transfers that complies with Article 25 of Directive 95/46 and Arts 7 and 8 EUCFR. To a greater extent that guidance represents a direct transposition of core aspects of the Court's earlier jurisprudence on data protection with regard to *intra-EU* transfers and processing.

[72] At paras 64–66.
[73] At para. 65.
[74] At paras 97–98.
[75] At paras 79–95.

Out with the old and in with the new

The Grand Chamber identified a number of key deficiencies in its review of the validity of Decision 2000/520. First, the Court noted that that instrument provided for the suspension of the SHPPs contained therein 'to the extent necessary to meet [US] national security, public interest, or law enforcement requirements.'[76] Secondly, it drew attention to the fact that those principles did not enjoy primacy over conflicting provisions of US law.[77] Thirdly, and perhaps most crucially, the Grand Chamber observed that the SHPPs did not bind US public authorities.[78] Finally, the Court noted that, with respect to the latter authorities' activities, EU citizens enjoyed no rights to administrative or judicial redress in the US.[79]

Taken together, the Court of Justice accepted that Decision 2000/520 provided the perfect regulatory conditions for precisely the type of public surveillance activities that Mr. Schrems feared possible. In short, it enabled:

> 'United States authorities ... to access the personal data [of EU citizens] transferred from the Member States to the United States and process it in a way incompatible, in particular, with the purposes for which it was transferred, beyond what was strictly necessary and proportionate to the protection of national security.'[80]

The Grand Chamber was in no doubt that granting US public authorities access to EU citizens' personal data on such terms was incompatible with the right to privacy protected by Article 7 of the EU Charter.[81]

The Court's decision to strike down Decision 2000/520 left a critical regulatory gap with respect to lawful transfers of EU citizens' personal data between the Member States and the US. That gap required immediate political attention: around 4,000 US undertakings relied on the SHPPs as the legal basis to secure access to (and process) EU citizens' personal data. At the time of writing, the Commission is working with key stakeholders to revise the terms of the SHPPs. On 2 February 2016, the Commission announced that it had reached agreement with the United States on a new legal framework to manage EU/US data flows.[82] The draft legal texts of that agreement – designated in its revised form the 'EU-US Data Shield' – were published on 29 February 2016.[83]

The new agreement purports to address directly the principal concerns exposed by the Court of Justice in *Schrems*. In that decision, the Grand Chamber set clear – and strict – legal parameters for political renegotiation. To comply with Article 25 of Directive 95/46 and Articles 7 and 8 EUCFR, the replacement instruments must offer EU citizens a level of protection with regard to EU/US data transfers that is 'essentially equivalent' to that

---

[76] At para. 84.
[77] At para. 86.
[78] At para. 82.
[79] At para. 89.
[80] At para. 90.
[81] See esp. para. 94.
[82] EU Commission and United States agree on new framework for transatlantic data flows: EU-US Privacy Shield, *Commission Press Release* IP/16/216.
[83] EU Commission and United States agree on new framework for transatlantic data flows: EU-US Privacy Shield, *Commission Press Release* IP/16/433.
[84] At para. 74.

guaranteed within the European Union.[84] Accordingly, in line with its ruling on intra-EU data transfers in *Digital Rights Ireland*:

> 'EU legislation involving interference with the fundamental rights guaranteed by Article 7 and 8 of the Charter must … lay down clear and precise rules governing the scope and application of [the interference] and imposing minimum safeguards, so that the persons whose personal data is concerned have sufficient guarantees enabling their data to be effectively protected against the risk of abuse and against any unlawful access and use of that data.'[85]

The EU-US Data Shield arrangements seek to meet the standards of protection mandated by the Court through the introduction of new guarantees and assurances.[86] These include, for instance, new safeguards governing access by US public authorities to EU citizens' personal data for the purposes of national security. Access to such data is also made subject to clear limitations, safeguards and oversight mechanisms. Furthermore, and for the first time, EU citizens are to have access to redress mechanisms through an independent ombudsman within the US Department of State. In addition, the new EU-US Data Shield agreement will also enhance EU citizens' rights *vis-à-vis* private undertakings. The revised agreement introduces, for example, stricter rules on commercial transfers and processing EU citizens' personal data and also establishes new mechanisms to bolster the enforcement of individual rights within the United States.

It remains to be seen whether EU and US authorities have done enough to satisfy the terms of the Court's ruling in *Schrems*. The Court of Justice will likely be presented with an opportunity to scrutinise the finalized EU-US Data Shield in the near future. Enter another Herr Schrems.

Concluding remarks

2015 was another significant year for EU legal developments. It was also a year of institutional change at the Luxembourg Court with key personnel changes and agreement reached on important reforms to the size and shape of the General Court. This contribution has surveyed a selection of headline judgments from the Court's upper tier, the Grand Chamber. The chosen decisions span a range of critical issues: eurozone crisis management (*Gauweiler*); EU citizenship rights (*Almanovic* on entitlements to social assistance; *Delvigne* on EU electoral rights); and, finally, the global reach of EU Data Protection law (*Schrems*). In each area of activity, we see – once again – the centrality of law and judicial adjudication in determining the direction – and boundaries – of EU integration on full display. Crucially, the jurisprudence also illuminates the non-linear character of judicial developments. The Court of Justice does not expand the outer limits of EU law (and the rights of EU citizens in particular) at every available opportunity – as is often assumed. On the contrary, decisions such as *Almanovic* remind us that, at times, the Court not only stands still, but is even prepared to revisit fundamental aspects its own jurisprudence in order to adopt more restrictive approaches to determining the boundaries

---

[85] At para. 91.
[86] For details, see the Commission's Draft Implementing Decision pursuant to Directive 95/46/EC of the European Parliament and of the Council on the adequacy of the protection provided by the EU-US Privacy Shield. Available online at: http://ec.europa.eu/justice/data-protection/files/privacy-shield-adequacy-decision_en.pdf. Last accessed: 10 March 2016.

of EU law. Legal developments in the year ahead will no doubt be marked by the continuation of these established trends.

References

Borger, V. (2016) 'Outright Monetary Transactions and the Stability Mandate of the ECB: Gauweiler'. *Common Market Law Review*, Vol. 53, No. 1, pp. 139–96.

Craig, P. and Markakis, M. (2016) 'Gauweiler and the Legality of Outright Monetary Transactions'. *European Law Review*, Vol. 41, No. 1, pp. 4–24.

Hinarejos, A. (2015) 'Gauweiler and the Outright Monetary Transactions Programme: The Mandate of the European Central Bank and the Changing Nature of Economic and Monetary Union'. *European Constitutional Law Review*, Vol. 11, No. 3, pp. 563–76.

Kornezov, A. (2016) 'The Right to Vote and an EU Fundamental Right and the Expanding Scope of Application of the EU Charter of Fundamental Rights'. *Cambridge Law Journal*, Vol. 75, No. 1, pp. 24–7.

Mollers, C. (2011) 'German Federal Constitutional Court: Constitutional *Ultra Vires* Review of European Acts Only Under Exceptional Circumstances'. *European Constitutional Law Review*, Vol. 7, No. 1, pp. 161–7.

Nic Shuibhne, N. (2015) 'Limits Rising, Duties Ascending: The Changing Legal Shape of Union Citizenship'. *Common Market Law Review*, Vol. 52, No. 4, pp. 889–938.

Payandeh, M. (2011) 'Constitutional Review of EU Law after *Honeywell*: Contextualizing the Relationship between the German Constitutional Court and the EU Court of Justice'. *Common Market Law Review*, Vol. 48, No. 1, pp. 9–38.

Shaw, J. (2016) 'Prisoner Voting: Now a Matter of EU Law', *EU Law Analysis* (online blog). Available online at: http://eulawanalysis.blogspot.co.uk/2015/10/prisoner-voting-now-matter-of-eu-law.html. Last accessed: 10 February 2016.

JCMS 2016 Volume 54. Annual Review pp. 134–149   DOI: 10.1111/jcms.12409

Justice and Home Affairs

JÖRG MONAR
College of Europe

Introduction

In its 16 years of existence the Union's 'area of freedom, security and justice' (AFSJ) has surely not seen a more challenging one than 2015. The year started with the unprecedented *Charlie Hebdo* terrorist attack in Paris on freedom of expression and ended with many questions about the effectiveness of EU counter-terrorism co-operation in the aftermath of the vicious assaults which in November left 130 people dead who had been enjoying an unusually mild autumn evening in Paris, attacks which also justified the steadily increasing concerns about 'foreign fighters' trained by the self-proclaimed 'Islamic State' returning to Europe. Running almost in parallel with the enhanced terrorist challenges, the very foundations of the AFSJ – the openness of the EU's internal borders within the Schengen context – came under threat because of a massive surge of refugees and migrants, mainly from Syria, which created serious domestic problems in the primary target country Germany, and led to the temporary reintroduction of controls at some Schengen borders and caused serious divisions in the EU Council. The combined pressures of the refugee crisis and terrorist challenges accounted for an unprecedented number of nine meetings of the Justice and Home Affairs (JHA) Council, a rather exceptional Joint Council meeting of the Home Affairs Ministers and the Foreign Ministers in April and an informal meeting of the JHA Ministers in July. Progress was made with adoption of several legal instruments, including in the civil law field, but at the end of the year there was still considerable uncertainty about the effectiveness and implementation of measures taken in response to both the refugee and terrorism challenges.

Developments in Individual Policy Areas

Asylum and Migration

From spring onwards, the deteriorating security situation and living conditions in the EU's wider neighbourhood, especially in Syria, Iraq and Afghanistan, in combination with the perception of the EU's relative openness led to unprecedented numbers of third-country nationals seeking shelter and a better life in the EU. After the numbers steadily climbed during the spring with hundreds of lives lost in the Mediterranean in April, the second half of the year saw the streams of human misery and hope reach magnitudes not seen in Europe since the end of World War II. For the latter half of the year Frontex reported 803,056 illegal border crossings via the Eastern Mediterranean route into the EU and – mostly as a follow-on of the former – 696,529 via the Western Balkans route. In the fourth quarter the increase on the Eastern Mediterranean route reached an unprecedented 3,015 per cent of the level in the same period the year before (Frontex, 2016a and author's own calculations). By the end of the year the total number of first time asylum applications in the EU had nearly doubled to 1,255,600 (Eurostat, 2016). The situation was made worse by an equally unprecedented asymmetry in the pressure on the destination Member States, with Germany alone having attracted a total of 1.1 million refugees by the end of the year (Bundesministerium des Innern, 2016).

The refugees' overwhelming choice of Germany as a destination country, which led both to acrimonious domestic political debates within Germany and the German government's strong insistence on the need for a European solution, not only indicated the refugees' well informed focus on a destination with relatively open doors and better living conditions than that on offer in the EU border and/or transit countries, but was also surely encouraged by German Chancellor Angela Merkel's much publicized assertion on 31 August of 'Wir schaffen das' ('We will manage') with regard to the evolving crisis (Bundesregierung, 2015).

Although the situation in Germany dominated headlines (and part of the Union's agenda) it should be noted that there were other Member States whose apparently more attractive reception conditions forced them to cope with even heavier pressures in terms of asylum applications than Germany. Whereas Germany had to deal with 'only' 5,411 applications per million inhabitants (a total of 441,800), it was Hungary which topped this list in relative terms with 17,435 per million inhabitants (a total of 174,435) followed by Sweden with 16,016 per million inhabitants (a total of 156,110) and Austria with 9,970 per million inhabitants (a total of 85,505) (Eurostat, 2016). However, having already applied for asylum elsewhere in the EU many of the refugees subsequently moved on to Germany and Sweden, for the reason – as aptly described in a *New York Times* report of 5 September looking at the large numbers of refugees moving on from Hungary – that 'they want to live in a truly developed land of opportunity', an aspiration for a better life which made the EU's 2015 'refugee crisis' partly undistinguishable from an immigration crisis.

The EU could, for once, not be accused of having woken up late to the challenge. Already on 23 April the European Council had agreed a special meeting in response to the worsening situation in the Mediterranean on a number of strategic objectives to strengthen the EU's presence at sea, to fight the traffickers, to prevent illegal migration flows and to reinforce internal responsibility and solidarity, the latter in particular through a voluntary internal resettlement scheme for refugees (European Council, 2015a). Partly because of prompting by the European Council the European Commission was – at least conceptually – well prepared for the rapidly escalating refugee emergency as it had adopted on 13 May a 'European Agenda on Migration' which proposed both a number of immediate actions and medium-term objectives to address the Union's refugee and migration challenges (European Commission, 2015a). The immediate action agenda included a legislative proposal to activate the emergency scheme for the temporary protection of displaced persons in the event of a massive inflow under Article 78(3) TFEU on the basis of fixed relocation percentages between the Member States. These percentages took into account the population size, GDP, asylum applications received between 2010 and 2014, and the unemployment rate of each Member State. In addition, the recommendations for an EU-wide resettlement scheme for 20,000 refugees based on the same distribution key, a funding package for the financing of such a scheme of

€50 million, emergency funding of €60 million for Member States under particular
pressure, the tripling of the allocation for the Triton and Poseidon maritime surveillance
operations and immediate support to a possible Common Security and Defence Policy
(CSDP) mission on smuggling migrants were also factored into the calculations.

The more medium-term objectives were regrouped around four 'pillars' comprising (1)
the reduction of incentives for irregular migration, (2) improved external border management, (3) a 'stronger' common asylum policy and (4) a 'new' policy on legal migration
(European Commission, 2015a). While this 'Agenda' was at least partially innovative
in its aim of a mandatory resettlement scheme for refugees and more solidarity measures,
its 'stronger' asylum policy consisted mainly of improved implementation of existing instruments and principles and a 'new' legal migration policy of familiar themes such as
more skill-selective labour immigration, visa facilitation and improved integration which
had in the past made only limited progress in a Council dominated by national migration
sensitivities and labour market considerations as well as EU interferences with national
competences.

Rather noteworthy, however, was that the 'Agenda on Migration' was presented on
13 May at a press conference not only by Commission Vice-President Frans
Timmermans and the Commissioner for Migration, Home Affairs and Citizenship
Dimitris Avramopoulos but also – the first time for a migration policy document – by
the High Representative and Commission Vice-President Federica Mogherini, a fact
which underlined the Commission's desire to arrive at a better linking of EU internal
and external instruments. This aim had clearly also been pursued by the Council when
holding a rather exceptional joint meeting of the foreign affairs and interior ministers in
Luxembourg on 20 April, but in its results this meeting had not gone beyond a rather
general affirmation of the need to step up the fight against organised crime and traffickers involved in irregular migration, to increase efforts to save the lives of refugees
at sea and a fair sharing of responsibilities in resettlement projects (Council of the European Union, 2015a).

The Commission's significant political investment in the new 'European Agenda on
Migration' failed, however, to achieve an immediate breakthrough in the Council. At
the Justice and Home Affairs (JHA) Council meeting on 15–16 June little progress was
made as some Member States were clearly reluctant to accept any mandatory relocation,
emphasizing the need 'to strike the right balance between solidarity and responsibility'
(Council of the European Union, 2015b). The matter was then brought to the table of
the 25–26 June European Council which agreed amidst the background of the already
rapidly increasing pressure on the external borders on the 'temporary and exceptional relocation' of 40,000 refugees over two years from the frontline Member States Italy and
Greece to other Member States (European Council, 2015b). This figure was double the
initial Commission target and came on top of an agreement to proceed with a target of
resettling 20,000 refugees via voluntary schemes. The European Council 'Resolution',
however, was far from entirely consensual as Denmark and the United Kingdom – using
their 'opt-out' rights under the Treaties – decided not to participate in the measure.
Moreover, Austria and Hungary, not having any 'opt-out' rights, but already under heavy
domestic political pressure, refused to indicate the number of refugees they were willing
to take. This contributed to the total number of refugees to be relocated 'as a first step'
of 32,256, falling well short of the 40,000 target. The JHA Council of 20 July saw

Austria, Denmark and the UK committing to participation in the voluntary resettlement schemes – which by then had reached a pledged total of 22,504 refugees – but not to the mandatory relocation scheme the formal decision on which was postponed to September after consultation of the Parliament (Council of the European Union, 2015c).

Over the summer the situation became more critical as projections for total refugee numbers before the end of the year now started to exceed 1 million. Germany, which on 21 August had unilaterally suspended the application of the Dublin Regulation allowing it to return refugees to first countries of entry into the EU for all refugees from Syria (Bundesamt für Migration und Flüchtlinge, 2015), pushed hard for other Member States to show solidarity. In response, the Luxembourg Presidency convened on 14 September an extraordinary JHA Council meeting to deal with the escalating crisis.[1] With the European Parliament having in the meantime been consulted, the ministers were able to adopt the formal decision to relocate the previously agreed 40,000 refugees (Council of the European Union, 2015d), but this was bordering on the purely symbolic given the streams of refugees now entering the Union. A Commission proposal to increase the number of refugees to be relocated to other Member States according to a complex mathematical formula by 120,000 was met by staunch resistance from the Visegrad countries (the Czech Republic, Hungary, Poland and Slovakia), which preferred border protection measures in combination with measures in favour of refugees within the external crisis regions. The Luxembourg Minister of Foreign and European Affairs Jean Asselborn convened another JHA Council for 22 September. After a heated debate with a majority of Member States in favour of the Commission proposal Asselborn put it to a vote which resulted – mainly thanks to Poland lifting its initial objections – in its adoption by qualified majority against the votes of the Czech Republic, Hungary, Romania and Slovakia, with Finland abstaining (Council of the European Union, 2015e).

While the 22 September Council Decision covered new ground both by establishing an unprecedented mandatory relocation system with substantial financial EU support (€6,000 per relocated refugee) and forcing it through by a vote in the Council – an unprecedented step in the JHA domain – it could, at best, be regarded as a Pyrrhic victory for the Member States. Covering only 160,000 refugees in a year when over 1.25 million asylum applications were made, the two Council Decisions of 14 and 22 September were clearly already inadequate at the time of their adoption. Moreover, they gave Member States two years of time for the implementation of their obligations, with the predictable result that most governments – faced with little domestic enthusiasm to accept increased refugee numbers – delayed effective action as much as possible. By 11 December only 54 asylum-seekers had been relocated from Greece and 130 from Italy (Carrera et al., 2015, p. 6). In a sense even more problematic were the political costs. For the first time since the 2004 enlargement a relatively clear 'East–West' split emerged in the Union with Central and Eastern European 'new' Member States being mostly opposed to the relocation mechanism, a split further enhanced when the new Polish Prime Minister Beata Szydło of the national-conservative Law and Justice (PiS) party announced on 23 November that Poland would stop accepting refugees under the relocation scheme because of security concerns following the November terrorist

---

[1] On the Luxembourg presidency see Högenauer's contribution to this volume.

attacks in Paris.[2] Hungary's Prime Minister Viktor Orbán had accused his German counterpart Angela Merkel of 'moral imperialism' over the refugee issue in September[3] and had organized a bus service to transport refugees who had arrived in Hungary more quickly towards Austria and Germany. Following a parliamentary vote on 3 December his government filed an action for annulment against the 22 September Council Decision on relocation on grounds of lack of an appropriate legal base and procedural irregularities (Court of Justice of the European Union, 2016a). One day earlier the Slovak Republic had also lodged an action for annulment on the grounds of an infringement of the principles of institutional balance and representative democracy as well as procedural irregularities (Court of Justice of the European Union, 2016b), making that Council Decision the most Member State contested JHA measure ever.

But the fall-out of the refugee crisis was not limited to the contested relocation system. After Germany had re-introduced temporary border controls at its border with Austria on 13 September to at least allow for the proper registration of the arriving refugees, Austria followed with a focus on controls towards Slovenia on 16 September, Slovenia with regard to borders with Hungary on 17 September, Hungary, after having completed a fence at the borders with Croatia and Serbia, towards Slovenia on 17 October, Sweden for all borders on 12 November and Norway (an associated Schengen member) also for all borders on 26 November (European Commission, 2016a). At the end of the year, with Denmark also appearing likely to reintroduce controls and France having done so after the Paris terror attacks of 13 November the entire Schengen open internal border system appeared increasingly at risk, giving some substance to Jean Asselborn's dramatic warning of 9 November that the Union could 'break apart' under the impact of the crisis.[4] Hardly less serious were the effects of the crisis on the domestic political settings in some Member States. In Germany the Eurosceptic right-wing *Alternative für Deutschland* climbed in opinion polls ahead of the next regional elections in Germany and the Federal Crime Office reported more than four times as many criminal acts against refugee installations than the year before (924 against 199).[5] Eurosceptic and anti-immigration parties including the French *Front National*, the *Dutch Partij voor de Vrijheid* and the UK Independence Party[6] all tried to make the most of the Union's refugee and migration predicament, reducing further many EU governments' willingness to volunteer for the transfer of refugees from other Member States.

While much political attention was focused on the contested relocation decisions, EU action was not limited to those decisions. In order to ensure a better control and management of the refugee flows and to facilitate relocation, the European Council approved in June the Commission's proposal to establish 'hotspots' with specifically trained personnel and dedicated facilities in frontline Member States – primarily Greece and Italy – to ensure the screening, identification and fingerprinting of third-country nationals arriving irregularly at EU external borders. Aimed at channelling those arriving either into the national asylum system, or an EU relocation, or a return, the 'hotspot' approach looked like a promising instrument to bring some order into the at times rather chaotic situation

---

[2] *Deutsche Welle*, 23 November 2015.
[3] *Deutsche Welle*, 23 September 2015.
[4] *Politico*, 9 November 2015.
[5] *Tagesschau.de*, 13 January 2016.
[6] See Kriesi's contribution on political parties in this volume.

in the main entry areas of the refugees. Yet in spite of EU funding and the deployment of experts from both Frontex and the European Asylum Support Office (EASO) national authorities struggled to put the necessary infrastructure in place. At the end of the year only one out of five hotspot areas identified in Greece (Lesbos) and only two out of six hotspot areas in Italy (Lampedusa and Trapani) had become operational, a delay which did not help with implementation of the relocation targets (European Commission, 2016c)

With many more refugees potentially eligible for at least temporary protection more attention was given to the (old) issue of returning those not eligible. On 8 October the Council endorsed a Commission-proposed Action Plan on Return (European Commission, 2015b) and the Return Handbook (European Commission, 2015c) aimed at facilitating and accelerating the return of third-country nationals having entered or staying in the EU irregularly, asking the Commission at the same time to identify any obstacles to the effective application of the 2009 EU Return Directive in view of potential additional legislative action (Council of the European Union, 2015f). In its proposal the Commission had underlined that less than 40 per cent of the migrants ordered to leave the EU in 2014 had done so, and the approved Action Plan placed an almost equal emphasis on enhancing voluntary return (through additional funding and more use of re-integration projects) as on the strengthening of forced return (through better information sharing between national authorities, the creation of national contact points on the withdrawal of residence permits and potential legislative action on the compulsory introduction of entry bans and returns decisions into the Schengen Information System).

In order to increase the possibilities of return the Commission proposed on 9 September a substantial Action Plan on Return Regulation amending the recast 2013 Asylum Procedures Directive and establishing a common EU list of safe countries of origin including Albania, Bosnia-Herzegovina, the Former Yugoslav Republic of Macedonia (FYROM), Kosovo, Montenegro, Serbia and Turkey (European Commission, 2015d). The proposal responded to the Member States' growing interest in a harmonised approach to safe countries of origin especially with regard to the Western Balkans given that Albania and Kosovo alone accounted for more than 10 per cent of the EU's asylum applications during the year. Predictably this initiative met strong objections from the UNHCR and NGOs, with the European Council on Refugees and Exiles, for instance, arguing that it seriously undermined fundamental rights standards by excluding the possibility for individual asylum applicants or NGOs to challenge the designation of individual countries as 'safe' on human rights grounds. In addition, concerns were raised that it would distract national asylum authorities away from the core focus of international refugee law on the assessment of persecution risks on an *individual* basis in line with Article 3 of the 1951 Refugee Convention and instead focus on general assessments of the situation in the country of origin of the applicant. The assumed 'safety' of some of the countries on the proposed list provided some ground for questioning in light of the fact that Member States continued to grant international protection to applicants from those countries, with applications from Turkey, in particular, resulting in protection decisions at the relatively high rate of 28.1 per cent and 29.3 per cent in the 32 EU and Schengen Associated States during the first and second quarter of 2015 (European Council on Refugees and Exiles, 2015).

Efforts were also made to substantially reinforce return and reception co-operation with transit countries, in particular Turkey, through which most of the Afghan and Syrian refugees were reaching the EU, and the Western Balkan countries on the 'Balkan route' which a large number of the refugees were taking after having transited through Greece. A High-Level Conference on the Eastern Mediterranean-Western Balkans Route on 8 October involving representatives from all potential return third-countries (Council of the European Union, 2015g) and an EU-Turkey Joint Action Plan agreed on 15 October providing for commitments on both sides with a strong emphasis on EU financial assistance and readmission on the Turkish side (European Commission, 2015e) were aimed at ensuring an improvement of reception conditions with EU financial assistance and fundamental rights guarantees in the respective transit countries in view of the enhanced return policy objectives. A meeting on 25 October in Brussels of heads of government from Austria, Bulgaria, Croatia, Germany, Greece, Hungary, Romania and Slovenia with those of Albania, Serbia and Macedonia which was also attended by the President of the European Council, Parliament and Commission (European Commission, 2015g) served the same objectives, but with a stronger regional focus. The Joint-Action Plan with Turkey, which included a jointly EU and Member State funded €3 billion 'refugee facility' for Turkey, was activated at a bilateral summit on 29 November (European Commission, 2016b). Yet its full implementation and the willingness and capacity of Turkey, which was already hosting more than 2 million refugees, to accept returned refugees from the EU and to fulfil its intended role to stem the flows especially from Syria towards Greece and further into the EU were still partly in the balance at the end of the year. Many Member States were divided over the extent to which Turkish demands for more financial support, visa facilitation and the acceleration of membership negotiations in return for Turkish help with the refugee challenges should be met. The fact that Turkey emerged, with strong backing by a German government known to be not very supportive of Turkish membership, as the EU's primary external partner in tackling the crisis had its own problematic dimension at a time when the 'significant backsliding' of Turkey in the areas of freedom of expression and freedom of assembly – as noted in the Commission's November progress report on Turkey as a candidate country (European Commission, 2015h) – was becoming more and more obvious under the authoritarian leadership of President Recep Erdoğan.

With most of the measures taken or discussed in response to the refugee crisis requiring at least some funding the financial dimension acquired considerable importance. From May onwards the Commission successively proposed amendments first to the 2015 and then also to the draft 2016 EU budgets to deal with the financial challenges of the crisis, which were largely approved by Parliament and Council, partly under accelerated procedures. By the end of the year total payments and commitments for the budget years 2015 and 2016, according to the Commission, had reached €10.1 billion, of which €3.9 billion were earmarked for internal EU measures, including financial support for the relocation of refugees within the EU, emergency funding for Greece and the build-up of reception facilities, and €6.2. billion for external measures, including humanitarian aid (€2.1 billion), the EU Emergency Trust Fund for Africa (€1.8 billion), the facility for refugees in Turkey (€1.0 billion), the EU Trust Fund for Syria (€0.5 billion) and funding for the return of refugees and displaced persons (€0.28 billion). While this total was clearly substantial relative to the size of the EU budget, the short-term effects of the funding in relieving pressure on the most affected Member States were less obvious, with only €335 million of the internal funding being made available for emergency assistance and the substantial external humanitarian aid and Trust funding being unlikely to relieve pressure on the Member States rapidly. Part of what was presented as 'the EU budget for the refugee crisis' also included expenditure categories such as support for security and border controls (€280 million) as well as counter-terrorism (€100 million) outside of the EU which again indicated the (usual) close nexus between EU asylum and migration policy objectives on the one hand and security objectives on the other (European Commission, 2016d).

Border Management

The refugee crisis, inevitably, cast a large shadow over both the internal and the external management of EU borders, with the Paris terrorist attacks adding to the Schengen system's troubles. On the internal side the already mentioned re-introduction of temporary border controls by six Schengen EU Member States (and Norway) until the end of the year led the Commission to warn that the Schengen system had 'been shaken to its core' and that the reintroduction of internal border controls on a sustained basis within the EU would entail huge economic, political and social costs for the EU and the individual Member States, generating immediate direct costs for the EU economy in a range between €5 and €18 billion annually (European Commission, 2016a). While the open Schengen space was disrupted by the reintroduction of internal controls in response to the refugee movements, the latter also had an impact on the borders between the United Kingdom as a Schengen opt-out and France. In response to several thousands of mainly Syrian and African refugees trying to reach the UK via Calais and attempts to board lorries by force British Prime Minister David Cameron announced on 24 June, on top of providing £12 million (around €17 million) for border management and refugee reception on the French side, the UK would also deploy additional police officers to Calais.[7] This was followed by the signing on 20 August of an agreement to step-up Franco–British border co-operation including a joint 'command and control centre' to be established at Calais and the investment of additional United Kingdom resources in making the perimeter of the Eurotunnel railhead secure through a combination of high quality fencing, CCTV and infrared detection technology (Ministère de l'Intérieur, 2015). The total absence of any EU dimension in this bilateral deal indicated once more the extent to which Member States continue to regard border management as an entirely national affair in spite of its EU-wide common challenges.

The Schengen members took the decision to re-introduce internal border controls unilaterally on the basis of the Schengen Borders Code provision for emergency situations requiring immediate action (Article 25), which allows for reintroduced controls for a period of up to two months. As the situation did not improve significantly, the controls were subsequently prolonged on the basis of Articles 23 and 24 of the Code, which allows for reintroduced controls at internal borders for a period of up to six months. In a discussion paper of 1 December evaluating the situation in view of that month's JHA Council meeting, the Luxembourg Presidency not only noted that there had not been sufficient prior consultation with neighbouring Member States before the re-introduction of controls, severely hindering the neighbours' possibility to prepare themselves for changes in migratory routes, but also that – given the huge increase of irregular border crossings because of 'serious deficiencies in external border controls' – the Council should consider inviting the Commission to present a proposal under Article 26 of the Schengen Borders Code

---

[7] *Reuters*, 24 June 2015.

for a Council Recommendation for a Member State to reintroduce controls at internal borders (Council of the European Union, 2015h). Although for diplomatic reasons it was not mentioned in the paper, the proposal was clearly targeted at Greece, which had largely applied what was later termed by the European Council as a 'wave-through approach' (European Council, 2016) at its external borders with regard to the arriving refugees. If Article 26 had been activated, it could have led to a temporary suspension of Greece's participation in the Schengen zone. The perspective of a forced temporary exclusion of this Member State from the Schengen zone following only a few months after an (aborted) similar perspective regarding its eurozone membership naturally led to some strong political reactions, and the issue was not discussed further at the December JHA Council.[8] However, at the end of the year the option of an activation of Article 26 with regard to Greece was clearly looming in the background with the Commission being expected to take it up in one way or another in its next report on the functioning of the Schengen system.

The management – or rather non-management – of Greek external borders was indeed the single biggest issue on the external side of EU border management throughout the year. Frontex reported for 2015 a total of 885,386 illegal border crossings into the EU via the Eastern Mediterranean route, with a peak of 216,000 in October alone. The vast majority of the third-country nationals using this route entered the EU via Greek islands, with Lesbos serving as the primary entry door and most of the refugees/migrants continuing their journey north towards the Greek border with the Former Yugoslav Republic of Macedonia (Frontex, 2016b). With the shortages of capacity and organizational problems of the Greek border authorities well-known from the past – and made partially worse by debt-crisis linked austerity measures – there was mounting pressure on the Greek government from the summer onwards to accept EU assistance including the deployment of registration and border guard officers from other Member States. For domestic political reasons, however, the Greek government delayed a request for border assistance, and eventually only did so on 3 December when its suspension from the Schengen system (see above) seemed a real possibility. This resulted not only in more emergency financial assistance but also an plan with Frontex for a new operation at the Greek border with the former Yugoslav Republic of Macedonia to assist with the registration of migrants as well as the deployment of a Rapid Border Intervention Team operation to provide immediate border guard support at the Greek external border in the Aegean islands. On 28 December Frontex initiated the deployment of around 300 officers and 15 vessels to the Greek islands, with more personnel and vessels planned for 2016 (Frontex, 2015).

The Mediterranean sea borders remained at the forefront of EU external borders action, both for migration control and refugee/migrant rescue operations. The Frontex Joint Operation 'Triton' in the Central Mediterranean was tripled in size and resulted in the rescuing of 155,000 people; Joint Operation 'Poseidon' in the Eastern Mediterranean came not far behind with 107,000 people rescued. At the same time the Frontex Mediterranean operations were also an important part of EU efforts to tackle the smuggling and trafficking of migrants with over 900 suspected smugglers being apprehended during the year (European Commission, 2016e). How much people smuggling had become part of the external border risks of the EU was made clear by a Frontex estimate that people smugglers earned €4 billion during 2015 from helping migrants to reach and cross EU external

---

[8] On Greece's turbulent year see Featherstone's contribution to this volume.

borders, with parts of the 'business' being organised well enough for Syrians, for instance, to be well informed via social media during the preparations for their trips about smuggling fees and therefore even being able to negotiate lower prices (Frontex, 2016c).

The Commission used the increased pressure on external borders and the all too obvious shortfalls of EU border management to propose on 15 December a Regulation for the setting-up of a European Border and Coast Guard. While the title suggested a move towards an integrated common border and coast guard the content of the proposal was slightly more modest – and politically realistic – in that it was aimed at bringing together a European Border and Coast Guard Agency built from Frontex and the Member States' authorities responsible for border management, with the latter continuing to exercise the day-to-day management of external borders. Yet the proposal did not lack ambition, providing *inter alia* for enhanced action possibilities of the Agency which would be able to draw on at least 1,500 experts capable of being deployed in under three days, to acquire for the first time border control and surveillance equipment itself, to assess the operational capacity, technical equipment and resources of Member States to face challenges at their external borders and – a politically sensitive step ahead – require Member States to take measures to address the situation within a set time-limit in case of identified vulnerabilities. The Commission also proposed that in a case of persisting deficiencies or where a Member State is under significant migratory pressure putting in peril the Schengen area and national action is not forthcoming or not enough, it would be able to adopt an implementing decision determining that the situation at a particular section of the external borders requires urgent action at the European level. This would then allow the Agency to step in and deploy European Border and Coast Guard Teams to ensure that action is taken on the ground even when a Member State is unable or unwilling to take the necessary measures (European Commission, 2015h). While the 110 page long Commission proposal was clearly based on lessons drawn from recent EU border control and surveillance emergencies and failures, some Member States were unenthusiastic about the extent of the new powers given to the Agency and Commission with regard to national border management failures. In its meeting on 18 December the European Council only agreed to instruct the Council to 'rapidly examine' the proposal (European Council, 2015c).

Internal Security Co-operation

The assault by Islamist terrorists on the offices of the French satirical weekly newspaper *Charlie Hebdo* on 7 January and related attacks in the Ile-de-France region, which claimed 17 lives, were widely seen both as an attack on the European fundamental value of freedom of expression and a powerful reminder of the threat posed by home grown Islamist terrorism (the *Charlie Hebdo* attackers had been French citizens born to Algerian immigrants). After having received proposals from both the EU Counter-Terrorism Coordinator and the Commission on 29 January, the ministers of interior and justice adopted at their informal meeting in Riga on 29 and 30 a 'Riga Joint Statement'. The statement stressed, *inter alia*, the need to address the risks of radicalisation – with a strong focus on counter-measures regarding the internet – not only at the EU but also the national and local levels, to reinforce information exchange and data-matching mechanisms by making better use of the Europol Focal Point Travellers (which regroups data on foreign terrorist fighters, FTF), the Europol Dumas working group on FTF, the Schengen

Information System II (SIS II) and the European Criminal Records Information System (ECRIS), to consider targeted checks at external borders and to speed up the adoption of the Passenger Name Record (PNR) directive (Council of the European Union, 2015i). The main orientations of the Riga Statement having been approved by the heads of state or government at their informal meeting on 12 February, the JHA Council on 12–13 March mandated Europol to establish an EU Internal Referral Unit (EU IRU) on internet content promoting terrorism or violent extremism and agreed to implement systematic checks on documents and persons based on a risk assessment at external borders (Council of the European Union, 2015j). While the Europol Referral Unit became operational on 1 July, with Europol also set to establish a new European Counter Terrorist Centre (ECTC) for investigative information-sharing by 1 January 2016, it needed the pressure generated by the Paris terrorist attacks of 13 November for the Council to decide on 20 November to 'implement immediately' the necessary systematic and coordinated checks at external borders, including on individuals enjoying the right of free movement, and to upgrade the Schengen Member States' border control systems (electronic connection to the relevant Interpol databases at all external border crossing points and automatic screening of travel documents) by March 2016. After repeated warnings by the EU's Counter-terrorism Co-ordinator Gilles de Kerchove about the insufficient use and implementation of data storage and exchange mechanisms, the Council also decided on that occasion that Member States would have to ensure that national authorities systematically enter data on suspected foreign terrorist fighters into the SIS II, carry out awareness raising and training on the use of the SIS, define a common approach to the use of the SIS II data relating to foreign fighters and speed up full implementation and effective use of the *acquis* in terms of interconnection and consultation of national databases on DNA, fingerprints and vehicle registration (Council of the European Union, 2015k).

The shock generated by the heinous Paris attacks accelerated the forging of a compromise between the Council and the European Parliament on the proposed directive on the use of PNR data for the prevention, detection, investigation and prosecution of terrorist offences and serious crime. The Commission had originally proposed the directive in February 2011, but negotiations between the Council and the Parliament, in whose ranks there were major concerns over proportionality and data protection, had failed to make substantial progress until the Paris terrorist attacks added urgency to the issue.

On 2 December, Parliament and Council negotiators agreed on a draft compromise according to which air carriers will be obliged to provide national authorities with the PNR data for flights entering or departing from the EU, allowing Member States, but not obliging them, to collect PNR data concerning selected intra-EU flights. Each Member State will be required to set up a so-called Passenger Information Unit (PIU), which will receive the PNR data from the air carriers. The compromise text also defined the purposes for which PNR data can be processed in the context of law enforcement (pre-arrival assessment of passengers against pre-determined risk criteria or in order to identify specific persons; the use in specific investigations/prosecutions; input in the development of risk assessment criteria) and data storage conditions (data will initially be stored for six months, after which they will be 'masked out', i.e. depersonalized by the removal of personal data such as name and address, and stored for another period of four and a half years). In the negotiations with the Council, the European Parliament was successful not just in insisting the start of the mask-out period begins after six months instead of two years, but also on an obligation for national PIUs to appoint a data protection officer responsible for monitoring the processing of PNR data and implementing the related safeguards, enhanced powers for the national supervisory authority as regards the checking of the lawfulness of the data processing and the granting of access to the full PNR data was to be set only under very strict and limited conditions after the initial retention period (European Parliament, 2015). With both the Council having approved the compromise on 4 December and the Parliament's Civil Liberties Committee on 14 December this controversial piece of (mainly) anti-terrorism legislation appeared finally on the way towards adoption in early 2016.

The EU was able to move a bit faster in the fight against terrorist financing by the adoption on 20 May of its fourth Directive (EU 2015/849) on the prevention of the use of the financial system for the purposes of money laundering or terrorist financing. The new Directive, *inter alia*, lowers the cash payment threshold to which monitoring and reporting rules are applicable from €15,000 to €10,000, obliges Member States to set up central registers of information on beneficial ownership of companies accessible to competent authorities, financial intelligence units and banks, the inclusion of tax crimes and proceeds from gambling activities, an extensive range of new rules on mandatory risk assessments by the European Commission, Member States and the 'obliged entities' (banks and other) as well as enhanced rules on sanctions which establish a maximum pecuniary sanction of at least 200 per cent of the amount of the benefit derived from a breach or a minimum of €1 million, with higher punitive sanctions (at least €5 million or 10 per cent of turnover) being possible if credit or financial institutions are concerned (European Parliament/Council of the European Union, 2015a).

While the number of EU counter-terrorism meetings and initiatives reached levels not seen since the 2004 Madrid and 2005 London attacks, it again became clear that the main challenge for the EU was not the absence of counter-terrorism mechanisms and instruments – of which plenty had already been agreed upon after previous terrorist emergencies – but their effective use and implementation. In his progress report of 30 November on action taken since February 2015, de Kerchove stressed that the fact that some of the perpetrators of the Paris attacks had travelled undetected to and from Syria which demonstrated that the measures taken to strengthen external border controls were not sufficient and efforts were needed to increase the amount of FTF entered into the SIS II and to check the SIS II and Interpol databases systematically at external borders. He also noted, amongst many other shortfalls, that despite the 'Common Risk Indicators' now used by most Member States, there were still too many gaps in the checks of persons using the intra-EU right to free movement, and that only 14 of the 28 Member States had by then connected their counter terrorism authorities to the Secure Information Exchange Network Application (SIENA) hosted by Europol, a key enabling platform for counter-terrorist information exchange (Council of the European Union, 2015l).

Given both the slow decision-making and the implementation deficits in the counter-terrorism field the 'Renewed European Union Internal Security Strategy 2015–2020' adopted by the JHA Council on 16 June after a 2014 Commission proposal, several rounds of negotiations and numerous Member State contributions appeared rather like a mantra recital of fairly obvious priorities – with 'tackling and preventing terrorism' on top followed by the fight against serious and organised crime in second position and the fight against cybercrime in third – and well-known good intentions – such as 'linking the European Union internal and external security', 'improving information exchange and accessibility', 'strengthening operational co-operation' and 'enhancing prevention and investigation of criminal acts'. A 'Strategy' full of such worthy but vague objectives left the fate of EU internal security co-operation as before fully in the hands of the Member States. As if to reinforce the point, the approved text made due reference to 'national security' remaining 'the sole responsibility of each Member State according to Article 4(2) TFEU' (Council of the European Union, 2015m). Just a few months later the 13 November Paris attacks with the strong Belgian and Syrian connections of the perpetrators showed again the extent to which the concepts of 'national security' and 'national responsibility' were falling short of today's major EU internal security challenges.

Judicial Co-operation

While most of the political attention in the JHA domain was focused on the response to the refugee and migration crisis as well as the terrorist threat, the EU was able to make some progress in the field of judicial co-operation in civil matters through the adoption of two new legal instruments.

On 20 May the European Parliament adopted, on the basis of a first reading agreement with the Council, Regulation 2015/848 amending Council Regulation 1346/2000 on insolvency proceedings. The new Regulation contains provisions improving the coordination of insolvency proceedings in respect of the same debtor, extends the original regulation's scope to proceedings aimed at giving the debtor a second chance, strengthens the transparency and accessibility of the proceedings by obliging Member States to provide for insolvency registers and, by providing for the interconnection of national registers, allows for a better management of multiple insolvency proceedings related to groups of companies and reinforces the legal certainty and clarity of the jurisdictional framework (European Parliament/Council of the European Union, 2015b). By adding thus both to the effectiveness and transparency of cross-border insolvency proceedings the regulation adds to the proper functioning of the internal market, reducing incentives for parties to transfer assets or judicial proceedings from one Member State to another in order to obtain a more favourable legal position to the detriment of creditors ('forum shopping').

Also of importance to the functioning of the internal market was the adoption on 16 December by the European Parliament of Regulation (EU) 2015/2421 amending Regulation (EC) No. 861/2007 establishing a European Small Claims Procedure and Regulation (EC) No. 1896/2006 creating a European order for payment procedure. The new Regulation increases the scope of the European Small Claims Procedure (ESCP), which allows for the enforcement of decisions in any of the Member States without the need to go through the complicated process of formal mutual recognition of judgments, on claims from €2,000 to €5,000, puts electronic service of documents on an equal footing with a postal service and enhances use of remote means of communication (video conference or teleconference) for the purpose of conducting the hearings and taking of evidence (European Parliament/Council of the European Union 2015c). With these and a number of other minor changes the amending regulation can be expected to make the European Small Claims Procedure, which can be regarded as one of the success stories of EU civil law co-operation, an even faster and cheaper instrument for the enforcement of consumer rights as well as for cross-border debt recovery by small and medium sized enterprises.

In the criminal justice field, negotiations on the establishment of the European Public Prosecutor's Office (EPPO), aimed at enhancing the combatting of crimes against the EU's financial interests, continued to progress slowly. However, the December JHA Council was able to approve a Presidency compromise text (Council of the European Union 2015n) on a number of issues relating to the competence and exercise of the competence of the EPPO as well as on the initiation and conduct of investigations which slightly increased the chances of an adoption of the EPPO regulation during 2016.

Conclusions

Looking at the EU's AFSJ during this year of crises, one is reminded of the biblical 'you have been weighed and found wanting' writing on the wall during King Belshazzar's feast according to chapter 5 of the Book of Daniel. Under the pressure of an unprecedented number of refugees the Union's 'common policy' on asylum and 'common migration policy' (according to Articles 78(1) and 79(1) TFEU) revealed themselves as having not gone beyond a thin layer of EU minimal legislation and token solidarity mechanisms providing a fragile and fragmentary cloth barely hiding the persisting diversity of the still essentially national asylum and immigration policies and systems. Perhaps predictably, Member States quickly fell back on old habits of national crisis reactions largely regardless of the implications for EU cohesion and other Member States. The result endangered the functioning and potentially even the survival of the Schengen open internal border system and forged a disastrous public image for the Union. The EU's performance in response to the two series of major terrorist attacks in Paris was hardly more convincing, showing that the problem at the EU level was not the absence of effective instruments and mechanisms, but slow decision-making and poor implementation by the Member States.

At the end of the year a whole range of new decisions had been adopted on both challenges which had found the EU 'weighed and wanting', including some rather innovative ones such as the mandatory refugee relocation mechanism, but unresolved implementation questions and political disagreements especially over the response to the refugee and migrant emergency did not augur well for a better future for the AFSJ. The 2015 'crisis' of the AFSJ showed – as in the case of economic and monetary union – the risks and fallacy of the Member States launching a major European political and constitutional project without vesting the Union with the necessary powers and instruments to make it work and succeed.

References

Bundesamt für Migration und Flüchtlinge (2015) 'Verfahrensregelung zur Aussetzung des Dublinverfahrens für syrische Staatsangehörige', Az. 411 – 93605/Syrien/2015, Nürnberg, 21 August.

Bundesministerium des Innern (2016) 'Pressemitteilung: 2015: Mehr Asylanträge in Deutschland als jemals zuvor', Bonn, 6 January.

Bundesregierung (2015) 'Sommerpressekonferenz von Bundeskanzlerin Merkel', Berlin, 31 August.

Carrera, S., Blockmans, S., Gros, D. and Guild, E. (2015) 'The EU's Response to the Refugee Crisis. Taking Stock and Setting Policy Priorities'. In *CEPS Essay 20* (Brussels: Centre for European Policy Studies).

Council of the European Union (2015a) 'Outcome of the Council Meeting, 3385th Council Meeting, Foreign Affairs and Home Affairs', 8146/15, 20 April.

Council of the European Union (2015b) 'Outcome of the Council Meeting, 3396th Council Meeting, Justice and Home Affairs', 9951/15, 16 June.

Council of the European Union (2015c) 'Outcome of the Council Meeting, 3405th Council Meeting, Justice and Home Affairs', 11097/15, 20 July.

Council of the European Union (2015d) 'Council Decision (EU) 2015/1523 of 14 September 2015 Establishing Provisional Measures in the Area of International Protection for the Benefit of Italy and of Greece', OJ L 239, 15 September.

Council of the European Union (2015e) 'Council Decision (EU) 2015/1601 of 22 September 2015 Establishing Provisional Measures in the Area of International Protection for the Benefit of Italy and Greece', OJ L 248, 24 September.

Council of the European Union (2015f) 'Council Conclusions on the Future of the Return Policy', 12856/15, 8 October.

Council of the European Union (2015g) 'High-level Conference on the Eastern Mediterranean/Western Balkan Route – Declaration', 12876/15, 9 October.

Council of the European Union (2015h) 'Integrity of the Schengen Area', 14300/15, 1 December.

Council of the European Union (2015i) 'Informal meeting of the Justice and Home Affairs Ministers in Riga on 29 and 30 January 2015', 5855/15, 2 February.

Council of the European Union (2015j) 'Outcome of the Council Meeting, 3376th Council meeting, Justice and Home Affairs', 7178/15, 13 March.

Council of the European Union (2015k) 'Conclusions of the Council of the EU and the Member States meeting within the Council on Counter-Terrorism (20 November 2015)', 14406/15, 20 November.

Council of the European Union (2015l) 'EU Counter-terrorism Coordinator: Report: State of play on implementation of the statement of the Members', 14734/15, 30 November.

Council of the European Union (2015m) 'Council Conclusions on the Renewed European Union Internal Security Strategy 2015-2020', 9798/15, 10 June.

Council of the European Union (2015n) 'Proposal for a Regulation on the establishment of the European Public Prosecutor's Office - Partial general approach', 14718/15, 30 November.

Court of Justice of the European Union (2016a) 'Action brought on 3 December 2015 – Hungary v Council of the European Union (Case C-647/15)', OJ C 38, 1 February.

Court of Justice of the European Union (2016b) 'Action brought on 2 December 2015 – Slovak Republic v Council of the European Union (Case C-643/15)', OJ C 38, 1 February.

European Commission (2015a) 'Communication [...] A European Agenda on Migration', COM (2015) 240, 13 May.

European Commission (2015b) 'Communication [...] EU Action Plan on Return', COM(2015) 453, 9 September.

European Commission (2015c) 'Commission Recommendation [...] Establishing a Common 'Return Handbook' to be used by Member States' Competent Authorities when Carrying Out Related Tasks', C(2015) 6250, 1 October.

European Commission (2015d) 'Proposal for a Regulation [...] Establishing an EU Common List of Safe Countries of Origin for the Purposes of Directive 2013/32/EU of the European Parliament and of the Council on Common Procedures for Granting and Withdrawing International Protection, and amending Directive 2013/32/EU, COM(2015) 452, 9 September.

European Commission (2015e) 'EU-Turkey Joint Action Plan', MEMO15/5860, 15 October.

European Commission (2015f) 'Meeting on the Western Balkans Migration Route: Leaders Agree on 17-Point Plan of Action', Press release IP/15/5904, 25 October.

European Commission (2015g) 'Turkey 2015 Report', SWD(2015) 216, 10 November.

European Commission (2015h) 'Regulation [...] on the European Border and Coast Guard and repealing Regulation (EC) No 2007/2004, Regulation (EC) No 863/2007 and Council Decision 2005/267/EC', COM(2015) 671, 15 December.

European Commission (2016a) 'Communication [....] Back to Schengen – A Roadmap', COM (2016) 120, 4 March.

European Commission (2016b) 'EU-Turkey Joint Action Plan – Implementation Report', COM (2016) 85 Annex 1, 10 February.

European Commission (2016c) 'Refugee Crisis: Commission Reviews 2015 Actions and Sets 2016 Priorities', Press Release IP/16/65, 13 January.

European Commission (2016d) 'EU Budget for the Refugee Crisis', DG Home Affairs and Migration, 10 February.

European Commission (2016e) 'Communication [...] on the State of Play of Implementation of the Priority Actions under the European Agenda on Migration', COM(2016) 85, 10 February.

European Council (2015a) 'Special meeting of the European Council, 23 April 2015' – Statement', 23 April.

European Council (2015b) 'European Council meeting (25 and 26 June 2015) – Conclusions' EUCO 22/15, 26 June.

European Council (2015c) 'European Council meeting (17 and 18 December) – Conclusions', EUCO 18/15, 18 December.

European Council (2016) 'European Council meeting (18 and 19 February 2016) – Conclusion' EUCO 1/16, 19 February.

European Council on Refugees and Exiles (2015) 'ECRE Comments on the Proposal for a Regulation of the European Parliament and of the Council establishing an EU common list of safe countries of origin and amending the recast Asylum Procedures Directive (COM(2015) 452)', October.

European Parliament (2015) 'EU Passenger Name Record (PNR) Proposal: An Overview', *European Parliament News*, 20150123BKG12902, 14 December.

European Parliament/Council of the European Union (2015a) 'Directive (EU) 2015/849 [...] of 20 May 2015 on the Prevention of the Use of the Financial System for the Purposes of Money Laundering or Terrorist Financing, amending Regulation (EU) No. 648/2012 of the European Parliament and of the Council, and Repealing Directive 2005/60/EC of the European Parliament and of the Council and Commission Directive 2006/70/EC', OJ L 141, 5 June.

European Parliament/Council of the European Union (2015b) 'Regulation (EU) 2015/848 [...] of 20 May 2015 on Insolvency Proceedings', OJ L 141, 5 June.

European Parliament/Council of the European Union (2015c) 'Regulation (EU) 2015/2421 [...] of 16 December amending Regulation (EC) No 861/2007 Establishing a European Small Claims Procedure and Regulation (EC) No 1896/2006 Creating a European Order for Payment Procedure', OJ L 341, 24 December.

Eurostat (2016) 'Record Number of Over 1.2 Million First Time Asylum Seekers Registered in 2015', News Release 44/2016, 4 March.

Frontex (2015) 'Frontex Launches Rapid Operational Assistance in Greece', 29 December, Warsaw.

Frontex (2016a) 'FRAN Quarterly. Quarter 4. October--December 2015', Warsaw.

Frontex (2016b) 'Trends and Routes: Eastern Mediterranean Route', Warsaw.

Frontex (2016c) 'Profiting from Misery – How Smugglers Bring People to Europe', 18 February, Warsaw.

Ministère de l'Intérieur (2015) 'Managing Migratory Flows in Calais: Joint Ministerial Declaration on UK/French Co-operation', Calais, 20 August.

JCMS 2016 Volume 54. Annual Review pp. 150–166   DOI: 10.1111/jcms.12408

Eurozone Governance: From the Greek Drama of 2015 to the Five Presidents' Report

DERMOT HODSON
Birkbeck College, University of London

Introduction

Greece's membership of the eurozone has long been problematic but these problems came to a head in 2015 with an astonishing standoff between a newly-elected Greek government led by Alexis Tsipras and a coalition of fiscal hawks headed by German Finance Minister Wolfgang Schäuble. This standoff escalated in July after Tsipras called a referendum on the terms of stalled negotiations with the European Union (EU) and International Monetary Fund (IMF) and Schäuble tabled the idea of Greek exit from the eurozone. Grexit appeared to be a matter of hours away before the heads of state or government brokered a short-run solution of sorts. This deal, which paved the way for €85 billion in additional loans, had brutal conditions attached. It ended the Greek drama of 2015 but neither resolved the contradictions surrounding Greece's membership of the eurozone nor secured the fate of economic and monetary union (EMU) more generally. Over the course of the year, the eurozone also grappled with other challenges, including slow economic growth, deflationary pressures driven by low oil prices, the implementation of recent reforms to eurozone governance and the prospects for economic, fiscal, financial and political union set out in the Five Presidents' Report. The overarching theme of 2015 was that eurozone governance faced profound problems of legitimacy that policy-makers appeared more adept at aggravating than alleviating.

This contribution takes stock of these and other developments in eurozone governance in 2015. Section I gives an update on the euro crisis, focusing on the eurozone's standoff with Syriza. Section II looks at the economic outlook in 2015 and the factors driving the eurozone's tentative economic recovery.[1] Section III explores key developments in eurozone monetary policy, including the European Central Bank's (ECB) new programme of quantitative easing. Section IV focuses on the first full year of the single supervisory mechanism (SSM) and the launch of the single resolution board (SRB). Section V turns to economic policy co-ordination and reviews the Commission's efforts to promote a more flexible interpretation of the stability and growth pact. Section VI takes stock of the Five Presidents' Report and Section VII addresses external representation and the IMF's complex and evolving relationship with the eurozone.

I. The Euro Crisis in 2015: The Syriza Standoff

Last year's review ended with the fall of Antonis Samaras' New Democracy-led coalition and the rise of Alexis Tsipras' radical left-wing Syriza, which formed a government with

---

[1] On developments in the European economy as a whole, see Benczes and Szent-Ivanyi's contribution to this volume.

Figure 1: Bond Yields for Selected Eurozone Members, 2007–15.

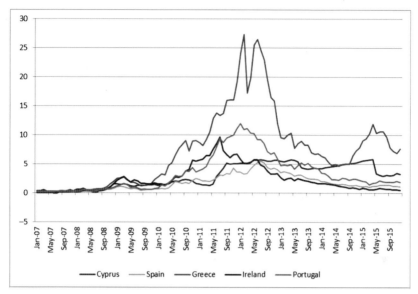

Source: ECB Statistical Warehouse.
Note: 10 Year Government Benchmark Bond Yields Relative to Germany.

the populist, right-wing Independent Greeks in January 2015 (Hodson, 2015a). From mid-2014, financial markets had started to price in the perceived risks from Syriza, which in its Thessaloniki Programme in late 2014 called for a radical revision to the terms of EU and IMF loans. The interest rate on long-term Greek debt continued to rise in early 2015 while remaining remarkably low in other peripheral eurozone economies (see Figure 1). This indicates that this act of Greece's fiscal tragedy was written in Athens, even if the overall play had many authors at home and abroad. It came as little surprise that Greek voters turned to an anti-austerity party after six years in which mainstream politicians presided over plummeting real incomes, exceptionally high unemployment and eye-watering levels of debt that have barely been stabilized.[2]

It would be wrong to see Syriza as a single-issue party born of the euro crisis; it traces its origins to the pro-European wing of the Greek Communist Party, which split in the late 1960s to form Synaspismos before forming a Coalition of the Radical Left in 2004 (Mac Fhearraigh, 2012). Syriza remains an essentially pro-European party, albeit one with strong anti-globalization credentials. This tension was apparent in Alexis Tsipras' promise on the day of his election victory to make 'the *troika* a thing of the past for our common European framework', the *troika* serving as code here for the IMF and the IMF serving in turn as a cypher for globalization.[3]

Tension between the new Greek government and its eurozone partners was evident from the beginning. Greece's new Finance Minister Yanis Varoufakis, a motorcycling Marxist with a black leather trench coat and an aversion to neckties, was by far the most

[2] See also Featherstone's contribution to this volume.
[3] *Euronews*, 26 January 2015.

unorthodox member of the Eurogroup in its 18 year history. Things got off to a bad start when Eurogroup President Jeroen Dijsselbloem cut short a joint press conference with Varoufakis in January at which the former was overheard telling the latter: 'You have just killed the troika' (Mason, 2015). Varoufakis was charismatic and, although he received a warm reception from French Finance Minister Michel Sapin in Paris in early February, the same could not be said of the Greek Finance Minister's subsequent visit to Berlin. At a joint press conference between Varoufakis and Schäuble, the latter declared that the two had 'agreed to disagree', strong language from a member of the usually consensus-seeking Eurogroup. In the opening stages of what would become some of the most turbulent few months in the history of the eurozone, the Greek government's principal achievement was to convince other eurozone members to drop references to the *troika* in favour of the more generic term 'the Institutions' (see, for example, Eurogroup, 2015).

Discussions over diplomatic rhetoric gave way to harsher political realities in late February, when Greece was offered, and agreed to, a four month extension to its existing loan agreement with the EU and IMF. In negotiations with the Eurogroup, Varoufakis had initially sought a six-month extension, talks on a new Contract for Recovery and Growth and 'possible further debt measures', in other words a diluted version of the Thessaloniki Programme.[4] In the end, Eurogroup partners insisted on four months of funding in exchange for much the same reform commitments as the Samaras administration had envisaged. Talks on what to do after these loans expired began immediately.

Varoufakis proved evasive about implanting the reforms he had reluctantly agreed to in February and EU and IMF officials were kept at arm's length from the Ministry of Finance in Athens. The result was that negotiations over future financial support from international creditors stalled and the Greek government started to run short of cash. In June Greece failed to make a scheduled loan repayment to the IMF, the first country to do so since Zimbabwe.

Since Syriza's election victory, Greek depositors had begun to withdraw their savings from Greek banks, which became increasingly dependent on short-term financing from the ECB. In February 2015, the ECB restricted Greece's access to such financing via its ordinary monetary policy operations, citing concerns over the country's commitment to international creditors. This left Greece reliant on emergency liquidity assistance (ELA) from the ECB, which increased from €50 billion in February to €90 billion in June. This move put pressure on Greece not only because ELA carries a higher interest rate compared to ordinary monetary policy operations but also because this emergency financing is reviewed by the ECB Governing Council on a biweekly basis.

By the end of June talks between the Greek government and the EU and IMF had broken down and Alexis Tsipras took the extraordinary decision to call a referendum on 5 July over the terms of these now defunct negotiations. The ECB's refusal at this time to increase emergency liquidity support to Greek banks left the Greek government with little choice but to shut down the country's banks and impose capital controls to prevent citizens from transferring large sums of money abroad. In the week running up to the referendum cash withdrawals from ATMs were limited to €60 per day. Pension payments continued but Greeks travelling abroad were unable to use credit cards and parents were allowed to make payments to children studying abroad only with special permission from Greek authorities.

---

[4] See *Reuters*, 19 February 2015.

Why Alexis Tsipras called this referendum when he did is a puzzle for political scientists. As Robert Putnam (1988) argued there can be advantages in a two-level game of tying hands through more stringent ratification rules, where such stringency encourages international partners to offer concessions that they would not otherwise have done. But, as Peter Evans (1993) notes, whatever the theoretical advantages of doing otherwise, heads of state or government typically prefer to negotiate on the international stage with as much room for manoeuvre back home as possible.

The reasons for calling this vote can be debated but the result of Greece's referendum was rarely in doubt. Framed as a vote against austerity, 61 per cent of Greek voters rejected the terms that had been offered by the EU and IMF, leading to mass demonstrations on the streets of Athens in which the people made clear their preference for policy-makers to choose a new path. Not for the first time eurozone leaders chose to carry on regardless. Tsipras' response to the referendum was conciliatory rather than defiant; he immediately replaced Yanis Varoufakis, who by now was isolated in the Eurogroup and unpopular at home, with the more emollient Euclid Tsakalotos as Finance Minister. Several rounds of inconclusive discussion between Tsakalotos and the Eurogroup concluded in July 2015 with Wolfgang Schäuble's insistence that the heads of state or government consider offering Greece a 'timeout' from the eurozone for at least five years in return for debt restructuring. From a two-level game perspective, the timeout proposal chimed with the tendency of negotiating partners to walk away from the table when a head of state or government ties their hands too tightly at home (Putnam, 1988). And yet, this explanation is difficult to square with the fact that Germany, as Greece's largest creditor and the largest economy in the eurozone, had a great deal to lose from Grexit. An alternative explanation is that Schäuble was, as Michel Sapin put it, seeking to 'entertain the gallery'. The German Finance Minister's tough approach to negotiations won plaudits with the German public, who were split on whether Greece should remain a member of the eurozone (see Cullen, 2015) and shaped by economic reforms taken in response to unification (Newman, 2015). From a European perspective, Schäuble's particular vision of European integration may have played a role here too, based, as it is, on the idea of closer co-operation among a hard core of European countries with similar economic and political philosophies (see Ghironi, 2015).

A meeting of the Euro Summit on 16 July succeeded in reaching an agreement where the Eurogroup had failed but only after 17 hours of fraught negotiations. As morning broke, with the chances of Grexit increasing by the hour, European Council President Donald Tusk reportedly told Merkel and Tsipras: 'I'm sorry, there is no way you are leaving this room' (Chassany et al., 2015). Thanks to Tusk, or perhaps more plausibly, the realization of just how costly Grexit would be to all countries concerned, a deal was struck a few hours later. This paved the way for a third round of loans from the EU and IMF and hence Greece's continued membership of the eurozone. In exchange, the Greek government signed up to a detailed and draconian set of reforms, which ranged from cutting pension entitlements to the liberalization of milk production and bakeries. Perhaps the most controversial element of this package – and the one which almost saw Tsipras walk out – involved the creation of a new privatization fund managed by Greek authorities and supervised by EU institutions with the authority to sell €50 billion in state assets to repay loans to European creditors.

It is hard to underestimate just how much damage this deal did in the short-term to the EU's fragile legitimacy. Rarely has the EU drawn such public ire, with the hashtag #thisisacoup trending on Twitter as negotiations at the July summit unfolded. As usual, the heads of state or government demonstrated their ability to reach a deal during moments of duress but rarely have they done so with such open disregard for the democratic wishes of a Member State. That said, the Greek crisis is a test of multiple democracies and eurozone members were understandably reluctant to commit taxpayers money abroad without economic assurances and appropriate forms of political accountability.

The deal struck between Greece and its eurozone partners was brutal but it provided breathing space for political leaders on both sides. For Tsipras, it brought an opportunity to stand up to EU partners but without severing external sources of financing. For Germany, Greece's creditor in chief, it ensured that EU conditionality and the unwritten rules of EU diplomacy were enforced, but without breaking up the euro. At the time of writing (April 2016) – and 2015 shows that European political realities can shift suddenly – the deal had stuck. In August, Tsipras secured parliamentary approval for some of the reforms sought by EU partners under the terms of a new €85 billion loan package before resigning. His re-election victory a month later came at the cost of a reduced parliamentary majority but his party was also shorn of those members most willing to countenance Greek exit from the eurozone.

Although the short-term political situation was stabilized, deep contradictions remain over Greece's long-term position in the eurozone. In 2016, Greece's debt-to-GDP ratio could breach 200 per cent of GDP – double what it was at the beginning of the global financial crisis. As such, a further round of debt restructuring now seems unavoidable. This will be politically difficult since most of this debt is now in the hands of governments, the EU institutions and the IMF, which will be reluctant to take a loss on outstanding loans while extending further credit. The July 2015 deal left room for 'additional measures … aim[ed] at ensuring that [Greece's] gross financing needs remain at a sustainable level' (Euro Summit, 2015). Such measures hinge on the successful completion of a review of Greece's reform efforts, now expected to take place in February 2016.

Even with further debt relief, Greece will struggle to solve its fiscal problems in the absence of growth and inflation; the outlook for both economic indicators is bleak. Having returned to growth in 2014, Greece's political standoff with EU partners pushed it back into recession in 2015. More worrying still for Greece is the outlook for inflation. Inflation would help to reduce the real value of Greek debt, but the country found itself facing a persistent fall in price levels in 2015 for the third consecutive year. In the absence of policy alternatives, the temptation remains for Greece to exit the euro, however costly such a move would be for the Greek economy and the rest of the eurozone.

II. The Economic Outlook: Recovering but not Recovered

In *One Market, One Money*, a classic study on the expected costs and benefits of EMU, the European Commission saw economic growth, price stability, sound public finances and the ability to absorb economic shocks as major advantages of the single currency (Emerson, 1992). Ten years after the euro's launch in January 1999, the European Commission (2008) could plausibly claim that the single currency was advancing these aims. A very different assessment is warranted as the euro enters the second half of its second decade. Since the euro crisis began in 2009, the single currency has experienced an extraordinary degree of economic, financial and fiscal instability as Member States have struggled to adjust to the global financial shock of 2007–08. Having entered a recession twice between 2008 and 2013, the eurozone experienced a slow and unconvincing recovery in 2014 (Hodson, 2015a). Real gross domestic product (GDP) in the eurozone increased by 1.6 per cent in 2015, an improvement on the 0.8 per cent growth rate recorded in 2014 if not exactly a cause for celebration. The United States, in comparison, saw real GDP rise by around 2.5 per cent for the second successive year.

The eurozone economy was buoyed in 2015 by a recovery in domestic demand. The contribution of public consumption, investment and, above all, private consumption to real GDP growth was higher in 2015 than was the case in 2014. Historically low oil prices and interest rates and a looser fiscal policy helped here as did falling levels of unemployment (see below). The European migration crisis had a positive macroeconomic effect on the eurozone by putting upward pressure on public expenditure (Aiyar *et al.*, 2016) and the effects are likely to be greater still as those who are granted asylum enter the labour market (European Commission, 2016, p. 36). Turning to external demand, eurozone exports to the rest of the world increased in 2015, aided, in part, by a marked depreciation of the euro relative to the currencies of key trading partners. Be that as it may, the contribution of exports to real GDP growth was entirely cancelled out by a rise in imports to the eurozone. A worrying trend for the eurozone is that export growth looks set to remain well below rates recorded before the global financial crisis hit in 2007. This situation is due, in part, to China's continued slowdown. In 2015, China's demand for imports grew by 0.5 per cent compared with 7.0 per cent in 2014.

Figure 2: Real GDP Growth, Eurozone and its Members, 2014 and 2015

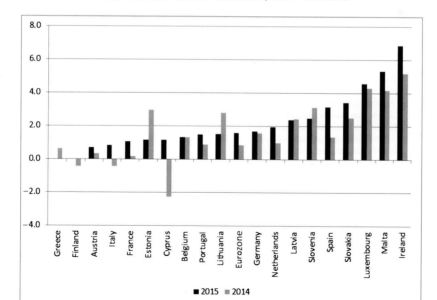

Source: European Commission AMECO database

As always, the economic performance of eurozone members varied (see Figure 2). Real GDP in France and Germany grew by 1.7 per cent and 1.1 per cent, respectively. France's recovery was long overdue, with real GDP expanding by more than 1 per cent for the first time since 2011. It is too soon to say whether the economic reforms pushed through by France's Economy Minister Emmanuel Macron were paying off, with low oil prices and a more favourable euro exchange rate the more obvious explanations for the country's improved short-term performance. Lithuania, which became the 19th EU Member State to join the eurozone in January 2015, saw real GDP growth slow from 3.0 per cent to 1.6 per cent, its exposure to Russia's troubled economy being a contributory factor.

Unemployment remains a chronic problem for the eurozone, although the unemployment rate fell from 11.6 per cent to 11.0 per cent in 2015 (see Figure 3). Within the eurozone, seven members recorded unemployment rates in excess of 10 per cent in 2015 and, of these, two, Greece and Spain, saw rates in excess of 20 per cent. In 2015, Ireland became the first country at the heart of the euro crisis to get its unemployment below 10 per cent. Of the 44,100 additional people who found themselves in employment in Ireland in 2015, 8.5 per cent gained employment in construction. This resurgence in construction mirrors an increase in Irish property prices after the house price crash of 2007, with the OECD warning against 'risks of another damaging property cycle' (OECD, 2015, p. 25).

The harmonized index of consumer prices remained static in 2015 (Figure 4). Falling energy prices added to deflationary pressures, with the cost of a barrel of Brent crude oil falling from over USD 100 in January 2014 to below USD 40 in December 2015. Among the factors that could continue to depress oil prices is the Iranian nuclear deal, announced

Figure 3: Unemployment Rate in the Eurozone and its Members, 2014 and 2015.

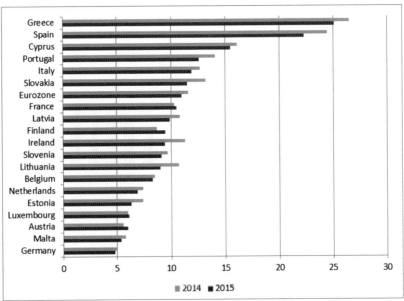

Source: European Commission AMECO database.
Note: Unemployment as a percentage of the civilian labour force.

Figure 4: Inflation Rate for the Eurozone and its Members, 2014 and 2015.

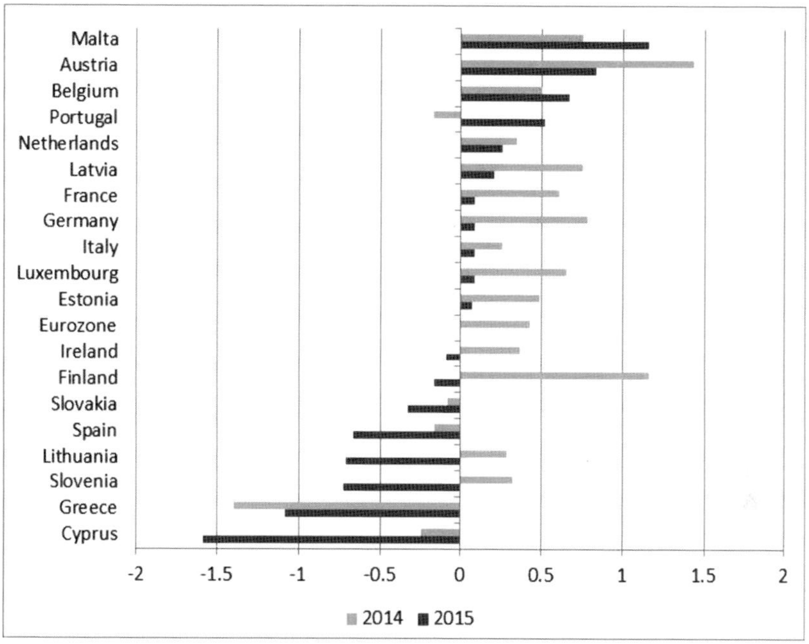

Source: European Commission AMECO database.
Note: Annual change in Harmonized Index of Consumer Prices.

in July 2015 and which the EU played a significant part in brokering.[5] In 2012, the EU imposed a ban on oil imports from Iran over concerns about its nuclear programme. The lifting of this ban in 2016 is expected to increase Iranian oil production by as much as 1 million barrels a day.

In the eurozone as a whole, the budget deficit as a percentage of GDP fell from 2.6 per cent to 2.2 per cent and government debt increased from 94.5 per cent to 93.5 per cent (see Table 1). Four out of 18 eurozone members found themselves with government borrowing above the excessive deficit procedure's 3 per cent of GDP threshold, and government debt as a percentage of GDP was in excess of 60 per cent in 14 countries. Posting a positive primary balance (a measure of government borrowing that excludes interest repayments) is a conventional indicator of a country's ability to reduce its government debt. In 2015, Ireland, Portugal and Cyprus all posted primary surpluses. Greece, in contrast, went from a primary surplus of −0.4 per cent to a primary deficit of −3.5 per cent in 12 months, underlining the devastating effects of the country's fiscal standoff with eurozone partners.

III. Monetary Policy: Quantitative Easing (At Last)

Facing persistent risks of deflation, the ECB Governing Council finally introduced a fully-fledged programme of quantitative easing in January 2015. This took the form of

[5] See Pomorska and Vanhoonacker's contribution to this volume.

Table 1: Governing Borrowing in the Eurozone and its Members as % of GDP, 2015

	Net Lending	Government Debt	Primary balance
Eurozone	−2.2	93.5	0.2
Austria	−1.6	85.9	0.7
Belgium	−2.9	106.1	0.0
Cyprus	−1.0	108.4	2.2
Estonia	0.3	10.1	0.4
Finland	−3.2	62.7	−2.1
France	−3.7	96.2	−1.6
Germany	0.5	71.6	2.1
Greece	−7.6	179.0	−3.5
Ireland	−1.8	98.4	1.5
Italy	−2.6	132.8	1.7
Latvia	−1.3	36.7	0.1
Lithuania	−0.9	42.7	0.7
Luxembourg	0.2	21.3	0.6
Malta	−1.6	64.0	1.0
Netherlands	−2.2	66.8	−0.9
Portugal	−4.2	129.1	0.5
Slovakia	−2.7	52.3	−1.2
Slovenia	−2.9	83.5	0.0
Spain	−4.8	100.7	−1.8

Source: European Commission AMECO database.

the expanded asset purchase programme (APP), which encompassed the existing asset backed securities purchase programme (ABSPP) and an expanded covered bond purchase programme (CBPP3) (see Hodson, 2015a) and a new public sector purchase programme (PSPP). The PSPP committed the Bank to buy bonds issued by national governments, EU institutions and EU agencies to a total of €60 billion per month until the end of September 2016. This step was significant because it entailed large-scale government bond purchases by the ECB for the first time. It also involved a much greater financial commitment on the part of the ECB, which had previously been spending €10 billion per month on covered bonds and asset-backed securities.

The European Central Bank enjoys a high degree of statutory independence under the Treaties but its independence does not remove it entirely from the sphere of national politics. National central bank governors outnumber members of the ECB Executive Board by a ratio of around 3:1 on the ECB Governing Council and while the national central bankers are independent, they are appointed by national governments to head a national institution. As a consequence, on major matters of eurozone monetary policy, national interests are never entirely absent. This point is clearly discernable in relation to the APP's provision on the purchase of bonds issued by national governments, EU institutions and EU agencies. Of these purchases, the eurosystem as a whole will guarantee only a small share of government bonds. This leaves the *Banque de France* exposed to any losses that might result from the purchase of French government bonds, the Bank of Greece exposed to losses from Greek government bonds and so on. As Armstrong *et al.* (2015) note, this arrangement discourages reckless fiscal policies by national authorities by leaving national central banks exposed to the risk from such recklessness. And yet, the authors note, this arrangement could undermine the effectiveness of crisis management in the eurozone. Under the APP, for example, the Bank of Greece could, in principle, find itself insolvent because of ECB purchases of Greek government bonds.

It is too soon to say whether the APP has been a success. Although inflation expectations – a forward-looking measure of inflation – increased in the first half of 2015, they fell back in the second half of the year. In December 2015, the Governing Council agreed to extend the APP to the end of March 2016 'or beyond if necessary' (ECB, 2015, p. 5). At the same time, the ECB Governing Council decided to extend its experiment in negative interest rates, cutting the interest rate on its deposit facility from -0.2 per cent to -0.3 per cent.

IV. Financial Supervision: The Single Resolution Board as a *De Novo* Body

The year 2015 was a fairly quiet one for financial supervision after the ECB's high-profile stress tests in late 2014 (Hodson, 2015a). Yet, in its first full year of operation, the SSM held 38 meetings and took around 1,500 decisions on various aspects of financial supervision. The SSM's most important act was the completion of a eurozone wide supervisory review and evaluation process (SREP), a stress test of the eurozone's 120 largest banking groups. As part of this exercise, the SSM set capital ratios for the banks under review, requiring some to set aside additional capital for 2016. Two such banks were Popolare di Vicenza and Veneto Banca, which were required to raise a combined €2.5 billion in additional capital amid concerns over the management of some Italian financial institutions and their exposure to non-performing loans. The SSM's involvement in matters that have traditionally been the preserve of national authorities seemingly rankled with some, including the Deputy Governor of the Bank of Italy who warned the SSM against 'arbitrary' and 'unwarranted' decisions that, by reducing banks' capacity to lend, could be harmful to growth (Henry, 2015). Such protests did not deter the SSM, which announced in December 2015 that it would launch an investigation into Italy's cooperative banks.

The launch of the SRB was another key development in 2015. A major pillar of european banking union alongside the SSM, the SRB is responsible for dealing with failing financial institutions in eurozone members and other participating members.[6] As of 1 January 2016, when it became fully operational, the SRB assumed overall responsibility for brokering the sale or resolution of failing banks, 'resolution' referring in this context to changes to the legal, operational and financial structures of a bank with the aim of preventing outright bankruptcy. Previously it fell to national taxpayers to bail out failing banks. This situation gave rise to the so-called 'doom loop' between banking and fiscal crises (Obstfeld, 2013), as occurred in Ireland where government support to banks bankrupted an otherwise solvent state. To break this doom loop, the SRB will facilitate bank resolution via the Single Resolution Fund (SRF), an instrument funded not by public funds but via levies from financial institutions that will reach €55 billion by 2023.

The SRB is an instance of what Bickerton *et al.* (2015) call a *de novo* institution, that is, EU bodies created by Member States to carry out specific policy-making tasks at arm's

---

[6] In April 2015, the government of Denmark, a non-eurozone member, announced its intention of joining european banking union. This decision has not yet been ratified at the time of writing 12 months later.

length from the traditional Community institutions. Under proposals put forward by the Commission in July 2013, the Commission would have been formally responsible for deciding whether a failing bank should be resolved. This proposal went too far for the ECOFIN Council, which decided that the decision on whether to resolve a bank should rest with the ECB and national representatives but not the Commission (see Howarth and Quaglia, 2014). Under the final regulation, which was adopted by ECOFIN and the European Parliament in July 2014, the SRB is empowered to decide on whether a bank is failing or at risk of failing but it can only do so after the ECB has been given an opportunity to make such an assessment. Thereafter, it falls to the SRB to determine whether and how the bank in question should be resolved and whether and how the SRF should be used for this purpose. In cases where the use of this fund requires more than €5 billion, this decision falls to the plenary rather than the executive body of the SRB. Whereas the executive board includes the chair and four full-time members of the SRB, the plenary includes representatives of each national resolution authority.

De novo bodies operate at arm's length from the European Commission and the SRB is no exception in this regard. The Commission's most important role here concerns its right to put forward nominees to the SRB executive, albeit on the basis of an open competition and with the final decision being taken by the European Parliament. Thereafter, the Commission plays a second order role in relation to the SRB, the former being entitled to attend meetings of the executive and plenary as a permanent observer rather than a full participant. The Commission can object to the use of the SRF on grounds of competition or public interest, but the SRB is required to alter its use of the fund in such cases only if the Council supports the Commission's objections. In short, the SRB illustrates Member States' willingness to extend the scope of EU decision-making into a highly sensitive policy domain but without giving new powers to the Commission along traditional lines.

V. Economic Policy Co-ordination: Reinterpreting the Growth Pact

At the beginning of 2015, seven eurozone members had excessive deficits. Of these, Malta saw its excessive deficit procedure closed in June 2015 after the EU finance ministers, acting on a recommendation from the Commission, agreed that the country's budget deficit was below 3 per cent of GDP and forecast to remain there. Five of the six remaining states – Cyprus, Spain, Greece, Ireland and Portugal – faced no additional steps under the excessive deficit procedure. France faced closer scrutiny, having been in a state of excessive deficit since 2009. After giving France an initial deadline of 2013 to correct this deficit, EU finance ministers decided to extend this deadline by two years in view of the 'unexpected adverse economic events' facing the French economy at this time (Council of the European Union, 2013). Two years later, with little prospect of this deadline being met, the ECOFIN Council agreed to give France until 2017 to correct its excessive deficit, this decision being based, in part, on a favourable assessment of the structural reforms underway in this country since 2012 (Council of the European Union, 2015).

The flexibility offered to France in 2015 provides further proof that the EU's reformed fiscal rules are more flexible than some of its fiercest critics allow. Further evidence in support of this interpretation can be seen in the Commission's January 2015 Communication *Making the Best Use of the Flexibility Within the Existing Rules of the Stability and Growth Pact* (European Commission, 2015). Through the ideas set out in this document,

Commission President Jean-Claude Juncker (2014) sought to make good on his 'manifesto commitment' to a more flexible interpretation of the Pact. Specifically, the Communication set out clauses relating to investment and structural reform and clarifications related to cyclical conditions designed to show how the Commission will use its leeway for interpretation under the stability and growth pact to promote growth and jobs. In the end, Juncker's move did not quite work as intended. In April 2015, the Council's legal service issued an opinion, which suggested that such questions of interpretation should be codified in the Economic and Financial Committee's (EFC) Code of Conduct on the Stability and Growth Pact rather than left in the hands of the Commission. This power play between the Commission and the national finance ministries that comprise the EFC had yet to conclude at the year's end as negotiations over a revised code of conduct continued.

VI. The Future of Eurozone Governance: The Five Presidents' Report

The claim that the EU is in dire need of reform is accepted by critics and champions of European integration alike. And yet the Union is almost always engaged in some institutional revision or another while simultaneously debating the need for new, more ambitious reforms. The publication of the Five Presidents' Report in June 2015 illustrates well the EU's infatuation with reform, this being the third high-level report on EMU since Member States began to reform the eurozone in 2010. The five presidents in question – heads of the Eurogroup, European Council, European Parliament, European Commission and European Central Bank, respectively – took their cue from the Euro Summit in October 2014, which called on four out of these five presidents 'to prepare next steps on better governance in the euro area' (Euro Summit, 2014). The unforeseen participant was European Parliament President Martin Schulz, whose eventual involvement reflected his close working relationship with Jean-Claude Juncker and the European Parliament's determination to play a greater role in eurozone affairs.

Mirroring the structure of the Delors Report on EMU, the Five Presidents' Report outlined three stages to complete EMU by 2025. The first stage (1 July 2015 – 30 June 2017) included tentative thoughts on a common deposit insurance scheme, designed to complete European banking union and proposals for the creation of a euro area system of competitiveness authorities and a European fiscal board. The system of competitiveness would involve the creation of national agencies to track macroeconomic imbalances. It can be understood as the latest in a series of initiatives designed to foster national ownership over EU economic surveillance rather than relying on the Commission to play the role of bad guy from Brussels (Deroose et al., 2008). The proposal for a European fiscal board envisaged a new independent agency empowered to issue opinions on Member States' stability programmes and draft budget plans. That the Commission saw this board as a potential threat is suggested by the speed with which it established a European fiscal board in October 2015 on its own terms and without involvement from EU finance ministers.

Stages 2 and 3 of the Five Presidents' Report were less detailed, the report suggesting only that the former should begin in June 2017 and that the latter should end by 2025. Among the ideas slated for stage 2 was the codification of 'commonly agreed benchmarks for convergence' (Juncker *et al.*, 2015, p. 5), a variation on the Euro Plus Pact, an inter-governmental agreement that tried (but ultimately failed) to encourage Member States to enact specific structural reforms in national law. More ambitious still was the report's call for a 'macroeconomic stabilization function for the euro area' designed to adjust to large macroeconomic shocks and the creation of a eurozone treasury. Detail on stage 3 was sketchier still, the report suggesting simply that it would begin when all other stages had been completed.

The weakest elements of the Five President's Report were its ideas on legitimacy. Here the report called for closer interaction between European and national parliamentarians in a revamped European semester, a modest procedural proposal that sat uneasily with the five presidents' grand visions of economic, fiscal, financial and political union. The report was also equivocal about the need for treaty change. Reference was made to the integration 'into the framework of EU law the Treaty on Stability, Coordination and Governance; the relevant parts of the Euro Plus Pact; and the Inter-governmental Agreement on the Single Resolution Fund' during the proposed 'deepening by doing' stage (1 July 2015 – 30 June 2017). But the report also emphasized the need to 'make the best possible use of the existing Treaties' during stage 1 (Juncker *et al.*, 2015, p. 5). Conveniently – and presumably deliberately – stage 2 was not set to begin until after the latest possible date for a British referendum on whether to remain in the EU, the question of whether the UK might be disadvantaged by deeper eurozone integration being a sensitive one in the Brexit debate.

It remains to be seen what impact the ideas contained in the Five Presidents' Report will have on the future of eurozone governance. Understandably preoccupied with the European migration crisis, EU heads of state or government delayed discussion of the report until December 2015, at which point the Council was instructed to address (although not necessarily agree to) Commission proposals stemming from the report without delay. Questions concerning 'the legal, economic and political aspects of the more long-term measures contained in the report', the European Council (2015) agreed, would be returned to before the end of 2017. This lack of urgency invites the question of whether the EU needed yet another ambitious high-level report on the future of EMU at this time.

VII. External Representation: The Eurozone and the IMF

The eurozone's fragmented system of external relations has been widely criticized in the scholarly literature. The Treaty on the Functioning of the European Union (TFEU) allows the Council to establish a unified representation in 'international financial institutions and conferences' (Article 138 TFEU), but the Commission's attempts to make use of this provision in 1998 were rebuffed. Since then Member States have adopted *ad hoc* and informal measures to coordinate the EU involvement in IMF, the World Bank, the Organization for Economic Cooperation and Development (OECD), the Group of 7 (G7) and the Group of 20 (G20). The result is that a variety of actors – including officials from the ECB, Eurogroup, European Council and Member States – speak for the euro in these international forums. The fragmented manner of these arrangements has been criticized by a number of scholars (for example, McNamara and Meunier, 2002; Cohen, 2009). And yet, eurozone members have shown themselves to be capable of speaking with one voice in the G20 and the IMF (Hodson, 2011, pp. 97–107).

Building on the Five Presidents' Report, the European Commission put forward a proposal in October 2015 on establishing a more unified representation for the eurozone on the international stage.[7] The proposal envisaged coordinated EU positions within the IMF being prepared by the Council, the Eurogroup, the Economic and Financial Committee (EFC), and its subsidiary body, the Eurogroup Working Group. Coordination across a range of institutions risks being bureaucratic and slow moving, thus raising concerns about the ability of a single eurozone constituency to respond rapidly to fast-changing events in the international monetary system.

Debates about the eurozone's fragmented system of external representation often overlook the fact that European influence within the Fund is considered to be disproportionately high by many commentators outside of Europe. This influence was seen in 2015 when calls by First Deputy Managing IMF Director David Lipton, an American, for a non-European to head the Fund failed to gain traction.[8] In February 2016, former French Finance Minister, Christine Lagarde secured a second term as IMF Managing Director, thus continuing Europe's informal grip over the leadership of the Fund for the time being.

The IMF's involvement in the euro crisis since 2010 has added a new dimension to debates about Europe's relationship with the Fund. What matters here is not only the €60 billion in loans that the IMF has contributed to eurozone members but also the Fund's new role within EU policy-making. This role goes beyond the pooling of resources by the EU and IMF to encompass a role for the Fund in monitoring the conditions attached to European loans and eurozone surveillance more generally. The IMF's emergence as a *de facto* institution of the EU (Hodson, 2015b) can be seen, for example, in the European Stability Mechanism Treaty, which states that the 'Commission – in liaison with the ECB and, wherever possible, together with the IMF – shall be entrusted with monitoring compliance with the conditionality attached to the financial assistance facility'.

This Europeanization of the IMF has caused tensions among EU Member States, as evidenced by Greece's aforementioned attempts to 'kill the *troika*', but also between the EU and the Fund. Striking in this respect was the fact that the IMF had not, at the time of writing, agreed to contribute to the €85 billion package of loans offered to Greece in August 2015, even though IMF officials were involved in negotiating the terms attached to these loans. Speaking in July 2015, Christine Lagarde suggested that the IMF would not lend to Greece unless eurozone members first agreed to restructure Greek debt.[9] On this point, the IMF emerged as an unlikely ally of Greece, even though Alexis Tsipras remained steadfast in his position about the need for a European solution to his country's fiscal crisis.

Conclusion

The word drama is overused in describing the EU's susceptibility to crises or, as Davis Cross and Xinru Ma (2015, p. 1053) put it, the overwhelming tendency of commentators to frame 'challenges and setbacks to EU integration as existential crises'. Theatrical metaphors lend themselves all too easily to Greece but this cannot mask the very real

---

[7] COM(2015) 603 final.
[8] *Emerging Markets*, 11 October 2015.
[9] *The Guardian*, 17 July 2015.

existential threats that surround the country's place in the eurozone. So dramatic was Greece's fiscal crisis in 2015, indeed, that the BBC staged *A Greek Drama*, a radio play that imagined tense behind-the-scenes discussions between Alexis Tspiras, Yanis Varoufakis, Angela Merkel and Jeroen Dijsselbloem. An unusual subject for a radio play, it offered further proof of the EU's public struggles to contain the effects of a sovereign debt crisis that has profound implications for the lives of ordinary Europeans and which, after six years, is still far from being resolved.

The deal struck by the euro summit in July 2015 kept Greece in the eurozone in the short term but it did so at the cost of imposing even tougher economic conditions on Greece and without addressing the root causes of its fiscal problems. The damage to the EU's legitimacy was also significant, the euro summit seeming to set aside the Greek people's opposition to austerity, as expressed in its referendum on negotiations with the EU and IMF and, more generally, in the rise of Syriza. The heads of state or government showed themselves to be capable, once again, of governing under pressure, but they did little to engender public trust in EU policy-making.

Concerns over the legitimation of eurozone governance were not confined to Greece in 2015. The eurozone's economic recovery picked up, but low growth remains a longstanding problem for EMU, alongside more recent challenges such as high unemployment and the risk of deflation. EMU's legitimacy is judged, in no small measure, on the euro's ability to deliver price stability (see Verdun and Christiansen, 2000; Hodson and Maher, 2002), which makes the threat of deflation politically as well as economically damaging. The ECB's new programme of quantitative easing offered a belated response to this problem, but it remains to be seen whether it will bring inflation back towards the Bank's target of 2 per cent. Concerns over legitimacy were seen too in the field of financial supervision, where the SSM, in its first full year of operation, delved deeper into the affairs of European banks and faced political pressure for so doing. The Commission treaded more carefully in the field of fiscal policy, offering a more flexible interpretation of the stability and growth pact, but encountering resistance from national officials as a result. Finally, the Five President's Report offered yet another vision of EMU's future, advocating economic, fiscal, financial and political union. These proposals varied in the detail provided but none grasped the question of how to legitimate a more complete EMU that would go well beyond the vision of its founding architects (Dyson and Maes, 2016).

References

Aiyar, S., Barkbu, B., Batini, N., Berger, H., Detragiache, E., Dizioli, A., Ebeke, C., Lin, H., Kaltani, L., Sosa, S., Spilimbergo, A. and Topalova, P. (2016) 'The Refugee Surge in Europe: Economic Challenges'. In *IMF Staff Discussion Note* (Washington, DC: IMF).

Armstrong, A., Caselli, F., Chadha, J. and den Haan, W. (2015) 'Risk-sharing and the Effectiveness of the ECB's Quantitative Easing Programme', *VoxEU Blog* 23 October. Available at at: http://voxeu.org/article/ecb-s-quantitative-easing-programme.

Bickerton, C.J., Hodson, D. and Puetter, U. (eds) (2015) *The New Intergovernmentalism: States and Supranational Actors in the Post Maastricht Era* (Oxford: Oxford University Press).

Chassany, A.-S., Barker, A. and Robinson, D. (2015) 'Greece Talks: "Sorry, but There is No Way You are Leaving this Room"', *Financial Times*, 13 July.

Cohen, B.J. (2009) 'Dollar Dominance, Euro Aspirations: Recipe for Discord?' *JCMS*, Vol. 47, No. 4, pp. 741–66.

Council of the European Union (2013) '*Council Recommendation with a View to Bringing an End to the Situation of an Excessive Government Deficit in France*', (10569/13).

Council of the European Union (2015) '*Council recommendation with a view to bringing an end to the excessive government deficit in France*' (6704/15).

Cullen, A. (2015) 'Schaeuble Popularity Soars as Germans Doubt Greece's Euro Future', *Bloomberg News* 3 July. Available online at: http://www.bloomberg.com/news/articles/2015-07-03/schaeuble-popularity-soars-as-germans-split-on-greece-in-euro.

Davis Cross, M.K. and Ma, X. (2015) 'EU Crises and Integrational Panic: The Role of the Media'. *Journal of European Public Policy*, Vol. 22, No. 8, pp. 1053–70.

Deroose, S., Hodson, D. and Kuhlmann, J. (2008) 'The Broad Economic Policy Guidelines: Before and After the Re-launch of the Lisbon Strategy'. *JCMS*, Vol. 46, No. 4, pp. 827–48.

Dyson, K. and Maes, I. (2016) *Architects of the Euro: Intellectuals in the Making of European Monetary Union* (Oxford: Oxford University Press).

ECB (2015) *Introductory Statement to the Press Conference (with Q&A) – 10 March* (Frankfurt: ECB).

Emerson, M. (1992) *One Market, One Money: An Evaluation of the Potential Benefits and Costs of Forming an Economic and Monetary Union* (Oxford: Oxford University Press).

Eurogroup (2015) 'Statement by the President of Eurogroup on Greece', 21 November. Available online at: http://www.consilium.europa.eu/en/press/press-releases/2015/11/21-eurogroup-greece/.

European Commission (2008) 'Emu@10: Successes and Challenges after Ten Years of Economic and Monetary Union', *European Economy*, No. 2/2008.

European Commission (2015) 'Making the Best Use of the Flexibility within the Existing Rules of the Stability and Growth Pact', COM(2015)12 final.

European Commission (2016) 'Winter 2016 Economic Forecast: Weathering New Challenges'. *European Economy Institutional Papers*, Vol. 20.

European Council (2015) 'Conclusions, 8 December', EUCO 28/15.

Euro Summit (2014) 'Euro Summit, 24 October', EUCO 28/15.

Euro Summit (2015) 'Euro Summit Statement Brussels, 12 July', SN 4070/15.

Evans, P.B. (1993) 'Building an Integrative Approach to International and Domestic Politics: Reflections and Projections'. In Evans, P.B., Jacobson, H.K. and Putnam, R.D. (eds) *Double-edged Diplomacy: International Bargaining and Domestic Politics* (Berkeley, CA: University of California Press).

Ghironi, F. (2015) 'Variable Geometry Bites Back: Schäuble's Motives', *Vox EU*, Vol. 18 July. Available at: http://voxeu.org/article/variable-geometry-bites-back-sch-uble-s-motives.

Henry, P. (2015) 'Bank of Italy Letter Slams `Arbitrary' ECB Over Capital Demands'. *Bloomberg* 21 September. Available online at: http://www.bloomberg.com/news/articles/2015-09-21/bank-of-italy-letter-slams-arbitrary-ecb-over-capital-demands.

Hodson, D. (2011) *Governing the Euro Area in Good Times and Bad* (Oxford: Oxford University Press).

Hodson, D. (2015a) 'Eurozone Governance: Deflation, Grexit 2.0 and the Second Coming of Jean-Claude Juncker'. *JCMS*, Vol. 53, No. s1, pp. 144–61.

Hodson, D. (2015b) 'The IMF as a De Facto Institution of the EU: A Multiple Supervisor Approach'. *Review of International Political Economy*, Vol. 22, No. 3, pp. 570–98.

Hodson, D. and Maher, I. (2002) 'Economic and Monetary Union: Balancing Credibility and Legitimacy in an Asymmetric Policy-Mix'. *Journal of European Public Policy*, Vol. 9, No. 3, pp. 391–407.

Howarth, D. and Quaglia, L. (2014) 'The Steep Road to European Banking Union: Constructing the Single Resolution Mechanism'. *JCMS*, Vol. 52, No. s1, pp. 125–40.

Juncker, J.-C. (2014) *A New Start for Europe: My Agenda for Jobs, Growth, Fairness and Democratic Change* (Brussels: European Commission).

Juncker, J.-C., Tusk, D., Dijsselbloem, J., Draghi, M. and Schulz, M. (2015) *Completing Europe's Economic and Monetary Union* (Brussels: European Commission).

Mac Fhearraigh, D. (2012) 'SYRIZA and the Rise of Radical Left-Reformism in Europe'. *Irish Marxist Review*, Vol. 1, No. 2, pp. 103–9.

Mason, P. (2015) 'As Greece Gives its Marching Orders to the Troika – Five Reactions'. *Paul Mason Blog*, 31 January. Available online at: http://blogs.channel4.com/paul-mason-blog/greece-european-troika-yanis-varoufakis-jeroen-dijsselbloem-syriza/3169.

McNamara, K.R. and Meunier, S. (2002) 'Between National Sovereignty and International Power: What External Voice for the Euro?' *International Affairs*, Vol. 78, No. 4, pp. 849–68.

Newman, A. (2015) 'Germany's Euro Experience and the Long Shadow of Reunification'. In Blyth, M. and Matthijs, M. (eds) *The Future of the Euro* (Oxford: Oxford University Press), 117–35.

Obstfeld, M. (2013) 'Finance at Center Stage: Some Lessons of the Euro Crisis'. *European Economy Economic Papers*, Vol. 493.

OECD (2015) *OECD Economic Surveys Ireland* (Paris: OECD).

Putnam, R.D. (1988) 'Diplomacy and Domestic Politics: The Logic of Two-level Games'. *International Organization*, Vol. 42, No. 3, pp. 427–60.

Verdun, A. and Christiansen, T. (2000) 'Policies, Institutions and the Euro: Dilemmas of Legitimacy'. In Crouch, C. (ed.) *After the Euro: Shaping Institutions for Governance in the Wake of European Monetary Union* (Oxford: Oxford University Press), 162–78.

JCMS 2016 Volume 54. Annual Review pp. 167–184   DOI: 10.1111/jcms.12413

Rising Hopes in the European Economy Amidst Global Uncertainties*

ISTVÁN BENCZES[1] and BALÁZS SZENT-IVÁNYI[2]
[1] Corvinus University of Budapest [2] Aston University

Introduction

After years of recession and stagnation, the European economy picked up speed slightly in 2014, and 2015 saw strong signs of recovery, with growth reaching almost 2 per cent. Driven by increasing consumption and rising real incomes due to historically low inflation rates, as well as the expansion of exports supported by weak currencies, this recovery came at a time when storm clouds were brewing in the global economy. In 2015 the US increased the benchmark interest rate for the first time since the eruption of the economic and financial crisis in 2007–08, Chinese growth began transitioning to a new, lower normal, and key emerging markets, such as Brazil and Russia were in crisis, not to mention the difficulties arising from geopolitical risks such as the huge inflow of refugees and migrants and the conflict in the Middle East. These external conditions make Europe's improving performance even more noteworthy, but also beg the question of just how sustainable the European recovery can be.

The aim of this contribution is to analyze Europe's economic performance, focusing on the developments in 2015, but also placing them in a broader context. Just like our contribution to the previous year's *Annual Review* (Benczes and Szent-Iványi, 2015), this piece on the European economy focuses not only on the performance of the EU as a whole, but also on its Member States. It demonstrates which countries managed to outperform the others and which needed to heat up their engines. EU-wide generalizations along with data on average-performance can be misleading for such a heterogeneous region; yet, there is clearly evidence of some convergence among EU countries in terms of economic performance.

Europe's economic recovery has had a clear impact on its labour markets as well. The second half of this contribution provides a more detailed overview of labour market developments in Europe in the post-crisis era. After several years of labour market turmoil, unemployment is once again decreasing across the continent. Nevertheless, Europe is not out of the woods yet as unemployment is still higher and the labour force participation rate is still lower than immediately before the crisis. A special emphasis is put on investigating the impacts of the crisis on labour markets and how labour market policies have reacted.

Section I presents the global economic and political context, which is then followed by a discussion of the main economic indicators and Europe's performance in Section II. Section III focuses on monetary and fiscal policy developments, while Section IV

*We are grateful to the Editors, Nathaniel Copsey and Tim Haughton, for insightful and constructive comments.

provides an analysis of post-crisis labour market trends. The final section offers some brief conclusions.

I. The Global Economic and Political Context

Global growth continued its decelerating trend in 2015, slowing to 3 per cent, which was well below the 5–6 per cent rates of the pre-crisis era. The collapse of the financial sector in 2007–2008 hit the developed economies unprecedentedly hard, while the developing world and the emerging markets proved to be more resilient to the negative effects of the crisis. By 2015, however, the situation had changed dramatically. Slowly but steadily, advanced economies managed to increase their growth performance from 1.8 per cent in 2014 to 2 per cent in 2015, while emerging and developing economies suffered a huge drop in growth momentum by slowing from 4.5 per cent in 2014 to 3.7 per cent (see Table 1). The year 2015 proved to be the fifth consecutive year of slowing growth performance in less developed countries.

The continued strong performance of the US, and the acceleration of growth in Japan and the EU all contributed to the relatively good performance of advanced economies. However, speculation that US monetary policy would be tightened, combined with an eventual interest rate rise by the Federal Reserve in December, as well as the accompanying reversal of capital flows, increasing volatility in financial markets, and the weakening of emerging market currencies all dampened the impact of the American economy on global growth.

The single most important factor for the relatively weak performance of developing and emerging economies was the continuous fall of commodity prices, which exerted highly negative impacts on most of these economies through several channels, leading to higher unemployment, lower tax revenues, increased government debt, intensified credit risk, rising current account deficits and falling profitability and investment activities. Although the deterioration in the (net barter) terms of trade was somewhat counterbalanced by the sharp depreciation of most emerging market currencies, the loss of value of national currencies, in turn, could cause serious currency mismatches in both

Table 1: The Global Economic Context – Global and Regional GDP Growth Rates

	2011	2012	2013	2014	2015*
World	4.1	3.5	3.2	3.3	3.0
Advanced economies	1.7	1.1	1.1	1.8	2.0
EU	1.8	−0.5	0.2	1.4	1.9
USA	1.6	2.2	1.5	2.4	2.5
Japan	−0.5	1.7	1.6	−0.1	0.7
Emerging and developing economies	6.2	5.4	4.9	4.5	3.7
Brazil	3.9	1.8	2.7	0.1	−3.8
China	10.3	9.6	8.0	7.4	6.9
India	7.9	4.9	6.9	7.1	7.2
Russia	4.3	3.4	1.3	0.6	−3.7

Source: European Commission (2016, p. 179).
* indicates forecast data.

the financial and the non-financial sector's balance sheets, making emerging markets more susceptible to shocks.

The most vulnerable region of the year was perhaps Latin America – the region from where several contagious financial crises had emanated in the last three and a half decades. The EU has devoted significant efforts over the last 15 years to strengthen its economic ties with the continent mostly by ratifying trade agreements. The EU has indeed become the leading investor and the second most important trading partner for the region, with Brazil alone accounting for more than half of European investments and one-third of trade. The deceleration of economic growth can significantly undermine Europe's efforts to further expand economic relations with the region.

From 2012 onwards, the Chinese economy has been slowing down, first to below 8 per cent, and by the end of 2015 to below 7 per cent. This slowdown was not simply the consequence of the business cycle, but a deliberate effort of the Communist government to make the country more resilient to external shocks, and reorientate the economy towards a more consumption-driven model, with slower but more sustainable growth rates (IMF, 2015b). Such a policy shift raises serious concerns in the rest of the world, including the EU, as a deliberate shift in the main driver of Chinese growth can lead to a slowdown in international trade.[1]

As in previous years, global political tensions meant serious drags on economic prosperity; suffice to mention the acute conflict between Russia and Ukraine (and as a consequence Russia and the advanced economies) or the Syrian crisis, which has led to unprecedented flows of refugees to Europe.[2] The migration crisis has tested the solidarity among Member States, which was also undermined by the British threat of exit – all issues raising serious concerns about the future of the European economy and even the integration project itself.

As a consequence, despite good growth performance of the advanced economies along with the recovery in Europe, long-term growth prospects have not improved. Due to serious macroeconomic imbalances such as record high public and private sector debt and structural deficiencies – particularly weak, undercapitalized financial markets, low investment activity, and negligible productivity increases (IMF, 2015a) – the capacity of the global economy to weather a potential downturn looks bleak.

II. Europe's Economic Performance: Growth, Inflation and External Balance

Despite the global tensions, the EU's economic recovery continued in 2015. After gaining momentum in 2014, growth further accelerated to 1.9 per cent in 2015, bringing Europe's business cycle in sync with the rest of the advanced world after several years. This relatively good growth performance was driven by a number of factors. Private consumption, subdued for years after the crisis, picked up significantly in 2015, surpassing its pre-crisis levels in real terms, fuelled in part by an increase in disposable incomes due to low oil prices. Investments and exports also grew significantly, reflecting renewed confidence in markets, although levels of investment in real terms still remain below their peak

---

[1] China, the world's second largest economy, has become the second most significant trading partner of the EU after the US, while the EU is carving out the highest share in China's foreign trade.

[2] On the migration crisis see Börzel's and Monar's contributions to this volume.

Table 2: Average EU Growth Rates (in per cent) and the Best and Worst Performing Member States

	2011	2012	2013	2014	2015*
EU average	1.7	−0.4	0.2	1.4	1.9
Standard deviation	2.9	2.4	2.2	1.7	1.6
Best performers	Poland (4.8)	Lithuania (3.8)	Luxembourg (4.5)	Ireland (5.2)	Ireland (6.9)
	Latvia (5)	Estonia (4.7)	Lithuania (3.5)	Luxembourg (4.1)	Malta (4.9)
	Lithuania (6.1)	Latvia (4.8)	Poland (3.5)	Hungary (3.7)	Luxembourg (4.7)
	Estonia (8.3)		Romania (3.5)	Malta (3.5)	Czech Rep. (4.5)
			Latvia (3.0)	Poland (3.3)	Sweden (3.6)
			Malta (2.6)		Romania (3.6)
					Poland (3.5)
					Slovakia (3.5)
Worst performers	Portugal (−1.8)	Portugal (−3.3)	Greece (−3.2)	Croatia (−0.4)	Finland (0)
	Greece (−8.9)	Greece (−6.6)	Cyprus (−5.9)	Finland (−0.4)	Greece (0)
				Italy (−0.4)	
				Cyprus (−2.5)	

Source: Authors, based on European Commission (2016, p. 152).
Notes: The 'best performers' are the countries which showed rates at least one standard deviation higher than the EU average. 'Worst performers' are at least one standard deviation lower. *indicates forecast data.

registered in 2007. The sharp fall in growth rates across the developing world is yet to have an impact on European exports, which were helped by the depreciation of the euro.

However, as in previous years, economic performance was highly uneven among Member States. The usual cleavages familiar from past years have remained: (1) countries outside the eurozone grew somewhat faster than those inside (1.9 per cent and 1.6 per cent, respectively); (2) newer Member States achieved higher growth rates than older ones, with Malta (4.9 per cent), the Czech Republic (4.5 per cent), Poland (3.5 per cent), Romania (3.6 per cent), Slovakia (3.5 per cent) and Latvia and Hungary (both 2.7 per cent) performing above the EU average (see Table 2). The faster growth of newer Member States may be evidence of strengthened convergence processes within the EU, severely halted by the crisis.[3] Among the older members, the performance of Ireland (6.9 per cent), Sweden (3.6 per cent) Spain (3.2 per cent) and the UK (2.3 per cent) are noteworthy. At the other end of the spectrum, Greece's economy stagnated (0 per cent) due to the uncertainties caused in the first half of the year around the extension of its bailout programme, and further austerity measures required after the extension.[4] Finland also stagnated, and three other countries (Austria, Italy and Estonia) registered very low growth rates below 1 per cent. The good news, however, is that after several years of harsh contraction in quite a few Member States, 2015 proved to be the first post-crisis year that saw no country with a negative growth rate.

Among the large economies, Germany maintained its momentum from 2014, achieving 1.7 per cent in 2015; driven mostly by consumption, but private investment and a strong current account surplus also played a role. France finally seems to have left its

---

[3] It is worth noting though that the newer Member States' growth record was rather diverse during the years of the crisis. Poland experienced a solid positive growth rate on the one hand, while Latvia suffered a cumulated loss of 25 per cent on the other.

[4] On the Greek experience see Featherstone's and Hodson's contributions to this volume.

Table 3: Average EU Inflation Rates (Harmonized Indices of Consumer Prices, in Percentages) and Countries with the Lowest and Highest Values

	2011	2012	2013	2014	2015*
EU average	3.1	2.6	1.5	0.6	0.0
Standard deviation	1.1	0.9	1.0	0.7	0.6
High inflation	Romania (5.8)	Hungary (5.7)	Estonia (3.2)	Austria (1.5)	Malta (1.2)
	Estonia (5.1)	Estonia (4.2)	Romania (3.2)	UK (1.5)	Austria (0.8)
	UK (4.5)	Poland (3.7)	Netherlands (2.6)	Romania	Sweden (0.7)
	Latvia (4.2)	Slovakia (3.7)	UK (2.6)	(1.4)	Belgium (0.6)
	Lithuania 4.1	Czech Republic (3.5)			
	Slovakia (4.1)				
Low inflation or deflation	Czech Republic (2.1)	Greece (1.0)	Bulgaria (0.4)	Slovakia (−0.1)	Spain (−0.6)
	Slovenia (2.1)	Sweden (0.9)	Cyprus (0.4)	Spain (−0.2)	Poland (−0.7)
	Sweden (1.4)		Portugal (0.4)	Portugal (−0.2)	Slovenia (−0.8)
	Ireland (1.2)		Sweden (0.4)	Cyprus (−0.3)	Bulgaria (−1.1)
			Latvia (0.0)	Greece (−1.4)	Greece (−1.1)
			Greece (−0.9)	Bulgaria (−1.6)	Cyprus (−1.6)

Source: Authors, based on European Commission (2016, p. 162).
Notes: Countries with 'low inflation or deflation' are the ones which showed inflation rates at least one standard deviation below the EU average. 'High inflation' countries are at least one standard deviation higher. *indicates forecast data.

close-to-stagnation state of the previous three years behind, although its growth rate of 1.1 per cent, fuelled by increased domestic consumption, is hardly spectacular. Italy is one of the countries in the EU which faced severe losses during and after the crisis. Nevertheless, 2015 proved to be a milestone for the Italian economy as it managed to record a positive, though still moderate, growth level of 0.8 per cent.

Levels of inflation remained subdued across the EU in 2015, continuing the trend of moderation seen in previous years. The EU's average harmonized consumer price index stood at exactly 0 per cent in 2015; approaching slowly the danger zone of deflation. Low energy prices, falling import prices and the still present output gap in the euro area were, nevertheless, counterbalanced by more dynamic economic growth along with the pick-up of consumer demand which caused core inflation, calculated without energy and food price changes, to rise steadily. Looking at individual cases it is striking that inflation remained weak even in countries which registered decent growth rates, such as Ireland (0.3 per cent), the UK (0.1 per cent), Poland (−0.6 per cent) or Spain (−0.5 per cent). As shown by these numbers, deflation was clearly a fact of life in many Member States in 2015, especially in Cyprus (−1.6 per cent) and Greece (−1.0 per cent), but a decrease in consumer price levels happened in a total of 11 economies. No country came close to the ECB's target rate of 2 per cent inflation with Malta's 1.2 per cent being the highest (see Table 3).

In terms of external balance, the trend of the previous years continued, with most creditor countries increasing their already huge current account surpluses even further (see Table 4). The number of Member States with current account deficits decreased to nine. Germany, the EU's largest creditor economy, has seen its current account surplus reach yet another record following the crisis: 8.8 per cent of its GDP or €267 billion. On the other hand, the UK continued to have the largest deficit, exacerbated by growing import

Table 4: Average EU Current Account Deficit (as Percentages of GDP) and Member States with Highest Deficits and Surpluses

	2011	2012	2013	2014	2015*
EU average**	−0.9	0.1	1.4	1.5	1.8
Standard deviation	4.4	3.9	3.6	3.7	3.8
Highest current account surpluses	Netherlands (8.8)	Netherlands (10.2)	Netherlands (11)	Netherlands (10.6)	Netherlands (10.4)
	Luxembourg (6.2)	Germany (7.2)	Denmark (7.2)	Germany (7.8)	Germany (8.8)
	Germany (6.2)	Sweden (6.5)	Germany (6.7)	Slovenia (6.5)	Denmark (7.1)
	Sweden (6)	Luxembourg (6.1)	Sweden (5.8)	Denmark (6.3)	Slovenia (6.9)
	Denmark (5.7)	Denmark (5.6)	Luxembourg (5.7)	Luxembourg (5.5)	
				Sweden (5.4)	
Highest current account deficits	Portugal (−5.5)	Greece (−4.3)	France (−2.6)	Finland (−2.2)	Latvia (−1.9)
	Slovakia (−5.5)	Romania (−4.3)	Cyprus (−3.8)	France (−2.3)	Czech Rep. (−2.4)
	Greece (−10.4)	Cyprus (−5.1)	United Kingdom (−4.5)	Greece (−2.9)	Cyprus (−4.8)
				Cyprus (−3.8)	United Kingdom (−5.0)
				United Kingdom (−5.1)	

Source: Authors, based on European Commission (2016, p. 176).
Notes: Countries with high current account deficits are ones which showed deficits at least one standard deviation below the EU average. Those with high surpluses are at least one standard deviation above. *indicates forecast data. **unweighted average of Member State current account balances.

demand. Strong economic growth and accelerating consumption contributed to the deficits both in the Czech Republic and Latvia. In some cases, current account surpluses can still be seen as a legacy of the crisis, with internal aggregate demand still being restricted, such as Italy (see Benczes and Szent-Iványi, 2015). But improving export performance has increasingly been emerging as a key driver of improving balances in 2015, with countries like Ireland, Germany, Spain, France, Croatia, Hungary and the Czech Republic experiencing substantial improvement in their export performance.

Changes in competitiveness can be best approximated by the movements of the real effective exchange rate (REER), which captures the cost competitiveness of a country. The REER of the EU as a whole appreciated in both 2013 and 2014, but 2015 saw a substantial depreciation, driven mainly by a weakening single currency (see Table 5). As explained in last year's contribution (see Benczes and Szent-Iványi, 2015, p. 172), Member State REERs can be more meaningful than that of the EU as a whole, which reflects the EU's changing competitiveness via its external trading partners. Most Member States saw substantial improvements in their REERs; only the UK and the Baltic countries saw deterioration. The unusually strong loss of 8.3 per cent in the UK was triggered by the appreciation of the pound (at least until the end of 2015) and the growth of wages in a relatively tight labour market, although according to the *Guardian*,[5] wage growth was

[5] *The Guardian*, 17 February 2016.

Table 5: Average Real Effective Exchange Rates, and Highest Appreciations and Depreciations (Unit Labour Costs Relative to a Group of Industrialized Countries, Percentage Change on Preceding Year)

	2011	2012	2013	2014	2015*
EU	0.5	−4.9	7.9	3.2	−8.4
Unweighted average of Member States	0.1	−2.0	1.6	0.0	−2.6
Standard deviation	2.7	2.8	2.9	2.8	3.2
Highest REER depreciation	Romania (−5.9)	Spain (−6.6)	Greece (−6.3)	Czech Rep. (−6.3)	Ireland (−8.0)
	Ireland (−3.5)	Greece (−6.2)	Croatia (−2.6)	Hungary (−4.2)	Greece (−6.5)
	Poland (−2.6)	Ireland (−6.2)	Czech Rep. (−2.6)	Sweden (−3.8)	Sweden (−5.7)
	Estonia (−2.5)	Croatia (−5.8)	United Kingdom (−2.5)	Croatia (−3.6)	
	Croatia (−2.5)	Portugal (−5.8)	Hungary (−1.6)	Cyprus (−3.2)	
		Romania (−5.2)			
Highest REER appreciation	Czech Republic (2.9)	Latvia (0.9)	Estonia (5.2)	Estonia (3.7)	Latvia (0.9)
	Malta (3.7)	Luxembourg (0.9)	Bulgaria (8.3)	Latvia (4.0)	Lithuania (1.1)
	Bulgaria (3.9)	Bulgaria (1.4)		Bulgaria (4.4)	Estonia (4.2)
	Sweden (7.5)	Sweden (3.0)		United Kingdom (5.3)	United Kingdom (8.3)
		United Kingdom (4.1)			

Source: Authors, based on European Commission (2016, p. 167).
Notes: countries with high REER depreciations are the ones which showed depreciations at least one standard deviation below the EU average. Those with high appreciations are at least one standard deviation above the average. *indicates forecast data.

slowing throughout the year and had dipped below 2 per cent in December 2015. Competitiveness rankings, especially the World Economic Forum's Global Competitiveness Index (World Economic Forum, 2015), show only minor changes compared to 2014 with some newer Member States improving their positions by five or more places. Besides the Czech Republic, Lithuania, Romania, Slovenia and Slovakia, Italy also managed to level up its competitiveness. The Greek deterioration in competitiveness finally came to a halt, but Greece still remained the least competitive country in the EU.

III. Economic Policies in Europe

By and large monetary policy was very accommodative both inside and outside the eurozone, while fiscal policies were generally neutral. Some countries were rather active in downsizing their mountains of debt that they accumulated over the past few years, which has become one of the most serious challenges in the EU.

The official lending rate of European Central Bank (ECB) remained close to zero in 2015, just like in most of the countries outside the eurozone. Although the Fed increased its benchmark rate after seven years from 0.25 to 0.5 in December 2015, the ECB did not follow suit. The nine non-EMU Member States were also reluctant to copy the Fed and either stuck to the previous levels (such as the UK and the Czech Republic) or administered a further easing of their monetary policy. The most aggressive cuts in 2015 were implemented in Hungary which lowered interest rates to a record low of 1.35 per cent down from 11.5 per cent in 2008 (see Table 6).

Table 6: Official Central Bank Rates (in Percentages) and Long-term Ratings

	Official central bank rate (lending rate)	Date of last rate decision	Long-term ratings (Standard and Poor's)
Bulgaria	0.01	February 2016	BBB–
Croatia	2.50	October 2015	BB
Czech Republic	0.05	November 2012	A+
Denmark	0.05	January 2015	AAA
Hungary	1.35	July 2015	BB+
Poland	1.50	March 2015	A–
Romania	1.75	May 2015	BBB-
Sweden	−0.35	July 2015	AAA
UK	0.50	March 2009	AA+
Eurozone	0.00	March 2016	various

Source: Central Bank and Standard and Poor's websites.

With rates close to zero, European central banks were forced to turn to unconventional measures in the last few years to support their economies and to provide the European markets with liquidity. By and large, unconventional policy tools meant the purchase of assets. Besides the ECB's schemes such as the securities market programme, the outright monetary transactions programme, and the more recent public sector purchase programme, other European central banks have also been heavily involved in applying different unconventional measures. The Bank of England engaged in government bond purchases as early as January 2009, and launched its funding for lending scheme three years later. The scheme was adopted by the Hungarian Central Bank as well. Hungary also set up a so-called 'bad bank' in 2015, which would have the responsibility of cleaning up other banks' balance sheets from toxic assets, especially mortgages. The Swedish and the Danish central banks decided to operate with negative deposit rates, while the Czech central bank started weakening the external value of the koruna more recently. On the other hand, the Bulgarian National Bank has become the target of harsh criticism for not being able to adequately supervise its financial system and for allowing the country's fourth largest commercial bank to collapse.

Taking into account the very lax monetary policy of the ECB and the weakening of the euro, none of the non-EMU countries seemed to gain too much in relative terms (that is, compared to countries paying with the euro) by sticking to their national currencies in the last few years. In fact, many of them, namely Bulgaria, Croatia, Hungary and Romania, continued instead to face low credit ratings (see Table 6) and highly volatile market rates. For these countries, adopting the euro would efficiently reduce the exposure of their currencies and economies to volatile and often hostile international markets.

While monetary policy continued to explore uncharted territories in order to boost aggregate demand, fiscal policy, in principle, can always be exploited by generating extra spending or lowering taxes – unless countries are strictly bound by legal restrictions to maintain sound fiscal positions, as they are in the EU. As for almost every single country embarked on large-scale spending programmes at the beginning of the global crisis, EU states were forced to start putting public finances back into shape as early as 2011. Fiscal space was, therefore, considerably reduced in the last couple of years. As a consequence, the average EU headline deficit ratio dropped to the threshold of 3 per cent by 2014. In

Table 7: Average General Government Budget Balances (in per cent of GDP) in the EU, and Best/ Worst Performers

	2011	2012	2013	2014	2015*
Mean	−4.6	−3.8	−3.5	−3.0	−2.5
Standard deviation	3.3	2.6	3.3	2.5	1.7
Best performers	Germany (−0.9)	Bulgaria (−0.5)	Germany (0.1)	Germany (0.3)	Estonia (0.3)
	Estonia (1.0)	Germany (0.1)	Luxembourg (0.6)	Estonia (0.7)	Germany (0.5)
	Luxembourg (0.3)	Estonia (−0.3)	Sweden (−0.9)		
	Finland (−1.0)	Luxembourg (0.1)			
	Sweden (−0.1)	Sweden (−0.9)			
Worst performers	Ireland (−12.6)	Ireland (−8.0)	Greece (−12.2)	Bulgaria (−5.8)	Croatia (−4.2)
	Greece (−10.0)	Greece (−8.6)	Spain (−6.8)	Croatia (−5.6)	Greece (−7.6)
	Spain (−9.4)	Spain (−10.3)	Slovenia (−14.6)	Cyprus (−8.9)	Portugal (−4.2)
	Lithuania (−9.0)	UK (−8.3)		Spain (−5.9)	Spain (−4.8)
				Portugal (−7.2)	UK (−4.2)
				UK (−5.7)	

Source: Authors, based on European Commission (2016, p. 169).
Notes: The 'best performers' are the countries which showed a budget position at least one standard deviation above the EU average. 'Worst performers' are at least one standard deviation below. *indicates forecast data.

2015 Member States managed to reduce the deficit ratio even further to 2.5 per cent (see Table 7).[6] This improvement was the consequence of the interplay of a multitude of factors, such as improved growth and reduced interest payments in particular.

The method of restoring fiscal discipline differed from country to country. In general countries relied heavily on both revenue-based and expenditure-based consolidations (or a mix of these two approaches) throughout the years 2010 to 2015. The substantial increase in revenues can be partly explained by the relative improvement of economic conditions, as cyclically adjusted total revenues had also increased recently. The most dramatic revenue-side consolidation was adopted by Greece, relying mostly on the increase of direct taxes (by one-third). Belgium, Finland, Slovakia and Portugal were also very active in collecting more income in order to stabilize their public finances. Besides Greece, direct taxes such as taxes on income and wealth, were drastically increased in Finland, Portugal, Malta and France. Indirect taxes were increased especially in the Czech Republic, Spain, Italy and Slovenia. A third group of Member States (Bulgaria, Hungary, the Netherlands, Poland and Slovakia) initiated a consolidation in their welfare system by raising net social contributions.

Spending-side consolidations were pursued mostly by countries outside the EMU: Poland, Bulgaria, Romania and the UK. They were joined by the crisis-hit economies at the periphery and the Baltic States. These countries were all very active in downsizing welfare spending and public sector salaries, which are claimed to be the two politically most sensitive items (Alesina and Perotti, 1995). Ireland, Portugal and Spain also cut public investment, reducing its size by roughly one half in five years.

The year 2015 was also a turning point in the post-crisis debt history of the EU. According to the European Commission's (2016) estimates, public debt-to-GDP ratios

---

[6] The eurozone average was even lower: 2.2 per cent.

seemed to be finally showing a declining trend. The average debt ratio peaked at a record high of 88.6 per cent in 2014, but dropped to 87.2 per cent in 2015. In 2015, the new lows in both deficit and debt ratios came along with more countries successfully leaving the excessive deficit procedure (EDP). As a consequence of the financial and economic crisis, 24 Member States were put under EDP in 2010 and 2011. By 2015, their number had decreased to nine: the crisis-hit countries such as Spain, Portugal, Greece and Ireland, along with Slovenia, Cyprus and France from the eurozone, plus Croatia and the UK.

IV. Employment and Labour Market Policies after the Crisis

During the years before the crisis, European labour market activity had shown an ever-improving trend. Unemployment remained constantly below 10 per cent, reaching its lowest in 2008 at 7 per cent. The labour force participation rate steadily approached the magical level of 70 per cent, eventually reaching it in 2008. The crisis, however, witnessed millions of Europeans losing their jobs, with unemployment jumping up by a dramatic 3.9 percentage points by 2013. The labour force participation rate also decreased significantly, showing that many people chose to withdraw from the labour market altogether. Youth unemployment has also increased, with the large numbers of jobless providing increasing competition for new labour market entrants.

The economic crisis has clearly put significant pressures on governments, provoking the adoption of a number of reforms. Fortunately, economic recovery in 2014 and 2015 had a noticeable impact on labour market tendencies, as demonstrated by Figure 1. The year 2015 saw the average rate of unemployment return to single-digit numbers, at 9.5 per cent, but with significant heterogeneity across the EU. This section of the contribution provides an overview of the EU's post-crisis labour market recovery, first by analyzing the impacts of the crisis, followed by details on the impact of the recovery on labour

Figure 1: Labour Force Participation and Unemployment Rates in the EU, 2005–15 (percentages).

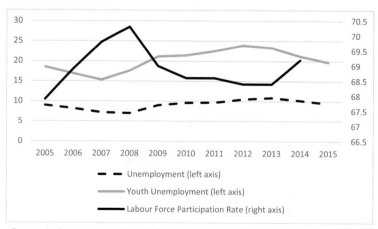

Source: Authors, based on Eurostat data.

Figure 2: Changes in Unemployment, 2008 = 100 per cent.

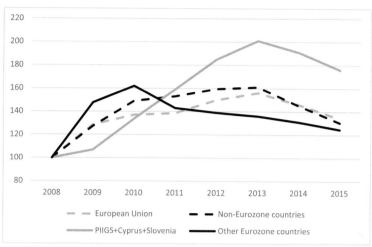

Source: Authors, based on Eurostat data.

markets, and finally government policies. It argues that any optimism must be of the cautious variety. Both internal and external factors can make the current trends not only highly vulnerable, but also easily reversible. Structural deficiencies are manifold. Most importantly, many EU countries are characterized by high levels of natural unemployment preventing the young and the chronically unemployed from entering the market.

The crisis has had differential impacts on the labour markets of Member States. By clustering the countries into three different groups (the nine non-eurozone Member States, the seven most heavily hit eurozone economies including Portugal, Italy, Ireland, Greece and Spain (the PIIGS countries) as well as Cyprus and Slovenia, and the remaining 12 EMU Member States), an interesting pattern emerges. For the EU as a whole, unemployment steadily increased between 2008 and 2013. However, the three groups showed very different developments. While the nine countries outside of the eurozone experienced a very similar pattern to that of the EU average, eurozone Member States had a very diverging and, in fact, puzzling experience. The two waves of the recession had very different impacts on the two clusters with EMU countries (see Figure 2). The seven countries which were most heavily hit by the crisis faced a much more moderate increase in unemployment (compared to their starting levels in 2008) in the first phase (the global stage) than their fellow EMU peers. Surprisingly, it was only in 2010 when these seven economies reached the average losses of the EU.[7] The other eurozone countries, on the other hand, were hit massively by the first wave, elevating their unemployment rates on average by 60 per cent in just two years. In the second phase, however, the situation dramatically changed. The European debt crisis phase led to a doubling of unemployment in the seven

---

[7] In 2008, the seven most heavily hit economies started at a relatively low level of 7.0 per cent, while the other 12 in the EMU had an average of 6.3 per cent. Non-EMU members recorded an average of 6.0 per cent in the same year. By 2010, the seven crisis hit economies had an unemployment rate of 11.5 per cent, while their EMU peers stood at 10.2 per cent. Non-EMU countries had quite a low level of 9.0 per cent.

Table 8: Average EU Unemployment Rates (in Per Cent of Total Labour Force) and the Best and Worst Performing Member States

	2011	2012	2013	2014	2015*
EU average	9.7	10.5	10.9	10.4	9.5
Standard deviation	4.3	5.2	5.6	5.3	5.0
Best performers	Austria (4.6)	Austria (4.9)	Germany (5.2)	Germany (5)	Germany (4.8)
	Luxembourg (4.8)	Luxembourg (5.1)	Austria (5.4)		
	Netherlands (5)	Germany (5.4)			
Worst performers	Ireland (14.7)	Portugal (15.8)	Portugal (16.4)	Cyprus (16.1)	Cyprus (15.6)
	Lithuania (15.4)	Croatia (16)	Croatia (17.3)	Croatia (17.3)	Croatia (16.2)
	Latvia (16.2)	Greece (24.5)	Spain (26.1)	Spain (24.5)	Spain (22.3)
	Greece (17.9)	Spain (24.8)	Greece (27.5)	Greece (26.5)	Greece (25.1)
	Spain (21.4)				

Source: Author, based on European Commission (2016, p. 163).
Notes: The 'best performers' are the countries which showed unemployment rates at least one standard deviation below the EU average. 'Worst performers' are at least one standard deviation higher. *indicates forecast data.

distressed economies by 2013. In the other 12 eurozone countries, however, the second wave did not push unemployment up. In fact, the ratio steadily declined following the peak year of 2010. From 2013 onwards, unemployment improved in each of the three groups, though the seven heavily hit economies were still very far away from their pre-crisis levels in 2015. Most worryingly, with the exception of Cyprus, the share of long-term unemployed (those without a job for 12 months or more) was at least 50 per cent in these countries in 2015,[8] reflecting serious structural deficiencies.

The analysis above reveals that the two phases of the double-dip recession had very different impacts on EU countries. While the collapse of the world economy in 2008 had a more pronounced impact on the core economies of the eurozone, the European debt crisis of 2010–12 had a toll in terms of jobs almost exclusively on countries in the periphery and left the core, by and large, intact. Countries without the single currency did not perform either better or worse in terms of job losses than the EU average, thus, adopting the common currency in itself was neither an amplifier of the crisis, nor a remedy to it, at least in terms of labour market outcomes.

From a country-by-country perspective, labour markets showed an even more profound heterogeneity (see Table 8). The most antinomic performance was produced by Germany. The country was severely hit by the first wave of the crisis, losing 5.6 per cent of its GDP in 2009, and found its unemployment rate peaking at 7.6 per cent in 2009. However, this rate was still much lower than Germany suffered just four years before that (11.2 per cent). The Hartz reforms, a series of tough labour market measures introduced between 2002 and 2005, seemed to pay off rather well for the former sick man of Europe.[9] In fact, the second

---

[8] Greece had an abnormally high share of 73.7 per cent in 2015. Long-term unemployment is posing a real challenge for other countries as well such as Croatia (67.5 per cent), Slovakia (67.0 per cent), Bulgaria (63.0 per cent), Belgium (51.0 per cent) and Latvia (50.6 per cent).
[9] Hartz IV bundled together all the previously segmented unemployment and social benefits and provided one single benefit package to those in need. Since beneficiaries had to experience a substantial cut in the net value of their welfare benefits, the reform plan made Germany the only country in the EU where labour earnings inequality actually increased in the last few decades (Koske *et al.*, 2012).

wave of the crisis found an improving labour market with an unemployment rate of 5.2 per cent in 2013 when the EU average was at its highest. The rate dropped below 5 per cent in 2015.[10] While the German labour market can be seen as relatively dualistic with a high share of atypical employment (Eurostat, 2015), the flexibility of the labour market as a whole, including those in permanent positions, has increased substantially since the turn of the Millennium (Eichhorst and Marx, 2011; Seeleib-Kaiser and Fleckenstein, 2007). This performance is especially impressive when seen together with a continuously rising labour force participation rate.

Most other Member States, however, were not so lucky and have mostly seen 2–3 percentage point increases in their unemployment rates following the crisis. It is no surprise that the countries hit most severely by the crisis were also the ones that experienced the biggest hikes in their unemployment rates. Greece, Spain and Cyprus were the most dramatically affected countries. The change in unemployment between 2008 and 2013 (the years when EU averages were the lowest and the highest) was 19.7, 14.8 and 12.2 percentage points, respectively. Bulgaria (7.4 percentage points), Ireland (6.7), Croatia (8.7), Italy (5.4),[11] Lithuania (6.0), Portugal (7.6) and Slovenia (5.7) could not be proud of the degree of deterioration either. These countries were all heavily impacted by both the global (2008–09) and the European (2011–12) phases of the crisis.

The Baltic countries on the other hand showed a rather different pattern from all other members. These small and markedly open economies were heavily beaten by the first wave of the great recession by experiencing a two-digit increase in the rate of unemployment in two years (between 2008 and 2010).[12] But from 2011 onwards, when the European public debt crisis took root and pushed several economies into the second dip, they all managed to return to growth and make up for the job losses. Table 8 details the recent performance of Member States, and lists the best and worst performing countries. It is beyond the scope of this contribution to speculate about either the causes or the consequences of such striking differences observed throughout the EU, but it reinforces analyses in the literature which argue that the eurozone is not an optimum currency area (Jager and Hafner, 2013; Handler, 2013).

At least in part labour market structures and policies can be blamed for the severe impacts of the crisis in many countries. European labour markets have often been accused of heavy regulation and rigidity (Barbieri and Scherer, 2009). Countries like Portugal, Italy, Spain, France, Germany, the Netherlands and Belgium all have systems of strong employment protection, which includes regulations on severance payments, and a set of complex legal restrictions and administrative processes on dismissing workers. While providing a degree of job security for those employed, these systems have the tendency to generate high unemployment, as they increase the cost of hiring workers, which in turn makes firms more reluctant to hire (Blanchard et al., 2014). In such situations, firms can be especially averse to hiring workers whose productivity can be difficult to assess, such as those of new entrants to the labour market, and those who have been unemployed for a long time. These problems have received much attention in the scholarly literature (see for example Saint-Paul, 1996), and European governments have been introducing measures

---

[10] The only country which managed to replicate the German trick was Malta: 6.9 in 2009, 6.4 in 2013 and 5.4 in 2015.
[11] Italy was an outlier in the sense that it also experienced a further deterioration of 0.4 percentage points in 2014.
[12] In numbers: Estonia: 5.5, 16.7; Latvia: 7.7, 19.5; and Lithuania: 5.8, 17.8 in 2008 and 2010 respectively.

to improve flexibility since the mid-1990s (Bentolila *et al.*, 2012a). The main thrust of re-forms focused on making the usage of part-time and fixed-term contracts easier (Eichhorst and Marx, 2011). These 'atypical forms' of employment have gained popularity in many continental countries and have resulted in the creation of dualized labour markets (Bentolila *et al.*, 2012a).

The spread of atypical employment however has only made European labour markets more flexible on the margins, and has not solved the underlying problem of rigidity and the high natural rate of unemployment (Blanchard and Tirole, 2003). It has also created new problems, ranging from social issues related to job insecurity and the inability of the atypically employed to access a number of services all the way to negative impacts on pro-ductivity growth, with firms being reluctant to invest in training non-permanent employees. Promoting atypical employment was, however, seen by governments as politically attrac-tive, as it did manage to create jobs in the short term, and allowed governments to avoid confrontation with trade unions representing 'insider' workers in permanent contracts.

The boom of the pre-crisis years masked the unfavourable effects of dualized labour markets. The economic crisis underlined that dualization might in fact be a dead end strat-egy for increasing labour market flexibility. With the onset of the crisis firms were quick to lay off temporary workers, but full adaptation took a long time as laying off insiders was difficult and expensive. The example of Spain shows that the extremely high levels of unemployment can clearly be ascribed to the lax rules surrounding atypical contracts. Employees with such contracts have taken the brunt of layoffs after the crisis hit, but due to the low productivity of those in insider positions economic recovery was not made eas-ier (Bentolila *et al.*, 2012b).

Reforming European labour market policies has thus become a priority since the crisis. The EU adopted the EU2020 growth strategy in 2012 with the goal of ensuring a 75 per cent labour force participation rate in the age group of 20 to 64 years (European Commis-sion, 2012a). No such ambitious target can be realistically achieved without bold struc-tural reforms that enhance productivity, mobility and job quality. The goals of EU2020 were translated into policy proposals by the Employment Package (European Commis-sion, 2012b), which aimed to help people find their way (back) to employment or find a higher quality and more rewarding job. It endorsed further internal flexibility and also called for active labour market policies. According to Ecorys and IZA (2012), active la-bour market measures such as (vocational) training or job-search assistance can be effec-tive in delivering benefits both in the medium and in the long term. Fixed-term contracts or employment incentives, however, provided rather mixed evidence. Employers can (mis)use the former to dismiss temporary workers; while the latter works only if targeted at specific groups and not general employment.

Member States have made some efforts to translate these and other policy frameworks into practice. The remainder of this section focuses briefly on two issues in labour market policy: increasing overall labour market flexibility and youth unemployment.

Instead of supporting further dualization, governments need to tackle the politically more sensitive issue of increasing the overall flexibility of their labour markets. The ex-ample of the Hartz reforms in Germany, as mentioned above, clearly shows that politi-cally sensitive, large scale overhauls of labour market policies can be successful in the long run. Table 9 lists the main reforms that selected European governments have carried out since the start of the crisis, focusing on the countries which enacted the most

Table 9: Labour Market Reforms in Selected European Countries, 2008–15

Country	Reforms
Belgium	2015: Increase of the notice period for redundancy dismissals. 2012: Increase in the severance payment obligation.
Czech Republic	2014: Abolition of the minimum wage for young workers. 2013: Increase in the maximum duration of fixed-term contracts and reduction in the severance pay applicable in cases of redundancy dismissals of employees with one year of service. 2009: Reduction of limitations on overtime work per week. 2008: Elimination of the obligation for retraining or reassignment in cases of redundancy dismissals.
Finland	2015: Elimination of the requirement to notify a third party before dismissing an employee or group of employees.
France	2015: Substantial amendment of labour market regulations, including the provisions dealing with large-scale collective redundancy processes.
Germany	2016: Introduction of a minimum wage.
Greece	2012: Decrease in the severance pay applicable in case of redundancy dismissals.
Ireland	2014: End of a 60 per cent rebate for employers on severance payments and elimination of the requirement for third-party notification when terminating a redundant worker.
Italy	2016: New Jobs Act, which simplifies redundancy rules and encourages out-of-court reconciliation, reducing the time and cost for resolving labour disputes. Also broadens the coverage of unemployment insurance. 2015: Relaxation of the conditions for using fixed-term contracts but reduction of their maximum duration to 36 months. 2010: Usage of fixed-term contracts permitted for permanent tasks. 2009: Increase in the notice period for redundancy dismissals.
Luxembourg	2010: Increase in severance payments applicable in redundancy dismissals.
Poland	2011: Reduction in the maximum duration of fixed-term contracts.
Portugal	2016: Introduction of priority rules for redundancy dismissals and new regulations for collective bargaining agreements. 2015: Reduction of the amount of severance pay per year of service and increase in the maximum cumulative duration of fixed-term contracts. 2014: Abolition of priority rules for redundancy dismissals. 2013: Increase in the maximum duration of fixed-term contracts and reduction in the severance pay applicable in cases of redundancy dismissals. 2012: Approval of new Labour Code: reduction in severance pay, reduction in overtime payment by 50 per cent, abolition of four paid public holidays, easier dismissal of workers. 2010: Increase in both the notice period for redundancy dismissals and the maximum cumulative duration of fixed-term contracts.
Spain	2014: Reduction of the maximum cumulative duration of fixed-term contracts and increase in the minimum wage. 2013: Unlimited duration of fixed-term contracts allowed temporarily. 2011: Reduction of the notice period applicable in case of redundancy dismissals.

significant reforms. The table shows that while many reforms have happened, a good number of them in fact entrench the dualistic nature of labour markets even further, for example by liberalizing the usage of fixed-term contracts even further as in the cases of the Czech Republic, Italy and Portugal. There is also clear evidence of back tracking, with governments making firing and hiring in insider positions even more difficult, as shown by reforms in Belgium, Ireland and Luxembourg. The two countries with the most anaemic labour markets, France and Italy, however, have finally initiated important reforms in 2015 and early 2016. It is nonetheless still too early to tell how these will play out.

In terms of youth unemployment, one of the seven flagship initiatives of the EU2020 strategy was called 'Youth on the Move' which aimed at strengthening the entry of young Europeans to the labour market. As part of EU's Employment Package, the Youth Employment Package called for support in the form of continued education, a traineeship or a new job after a four month waiting period for young people under 25 who lost their job or left formal education. As the scheme is mostly financed by Member States, each country should adopt its own implementation plan. Until recently, the scheme only managed to make a real breakthrough in the wealthier countries with a strong welfare state system and an otherwise moderate youth unemployment rate such as Sweden, Finland or Austria (ILO, 2012). Youth unemployment remains worryingly high, especially in the Southern and some Eastern Member States. Youth unemployment for the EU as a whole peaked at 23.8 per cent in early 2013 and by the end of 2015 decreased to just below 20 per cent. The highest values were recorded last year in Greece (48.4 per cent), Spain (47.5 per cent) and Croatia (44.9 per cent). Germany, on the other hand, had hardly any problem: youth unemployment was at 7.1 per cent in 2015. The efficient German labour market, but also the country's relatively unique system of vocational training and apprenticeships, seem to work well in absorbing young people.

Conclusions

The European economy continued its recovery in 2015, posting its highest growth rate since 2007, fed by strengthening domestic consumption, a weakening single currency and improving export competitiveness. Europe's decent growth performance was translated into decreasing unemployment, improving government budget balances, and reduction in public debt, all indicating that Europe has left behind the double-dip crisis. For the first time since the eruption of the financial and economic crisis, none of the EU-28 economies recorded negative growth. The economic performance of the EU was less heterogeneous in 2015 than in previous years.

Nevertheless, Europe's recovery is still obviously fragile due to both internal and external factors. The global economic and political environment is full of uncertainties and ambiguities. Every corner of the world might hold something in store. The transition to slower growth in China, the tightening monetary conditions in the US, the slowing of economic activity in emerging markets, and conflicts in the Middle East can expose the European recovery to unwanted shocks in the near future. In such a hectic external environment, one of the crucial questions is whether the EU can respond collectively. The external shocks might pose rather different challenges for Member States. While small open European economies are strongly dependent on the large ones, especially Germany, and to a lesser extent France, the UK or even the Netherlands, the economic performance of the big economies is directly linked to overseas markets. Anything that happens in the USA or China can have a dramatic effect on Germany for instance. At the same time, events in Russia, Turkey, Korea, Japan or the United Arab Emirates, all in the top 20 trading partners of Germany, will also have impacts. And the EU itself is not without internal troubles. Greece is still at zero growth which pushes the country further away from the EU average. And Finland, Austria and Italy have nothing to celebrate yet either. Additionally, the unusually low rate of inflation, and indeed deflation in some countries, the still huge debt burdens, the threat of recovery without jobs and so on are all major problems, with monetary and fiscal policy not having much real capacity and ability to impact any of these.

This contribution has also explored European labour markets and employment policies after the crisis. More than eight years after the financial and economic crisis, Europe is yet to return to pre-crisis levels of labour market performance. While European labour markets have reacted well to the economic upswing, unemployment is still above the level of the pre-crisis era. Countries which were hit by the crisis the most are still well behind their peers on the road to recovery in terms of employment. Most worryingly, it is not only short-term unemployment that seems to pose a burden on the PIIGS (along with Slovenia), but also long-term and structural unemployment. It seems that the inflexible and dualistic nature of European labour markets has made the impacts of the crisis unexpectedly painful in many countries. Germany being probably the only exception to this trend. Whether other countries should (or can) follow the German example is rather uncertain at this point, since Germany, the main market for most of the European countries, has become the most competitive economy in Europe, accumulating the largest surplus in its current account. Although the PIIGS countries did experience a recovery in their trade balance (with the exception of Spain), this happened mostly at the cost of reduced imports, while export capacity was barely strengthened. European countries should not be spared from much-needed structural reforms, yet it is quite often the case that such reforms do put an extra burden on societies in the short run which, coming so soon after the sufferings of the crisis years, is quite unacceptable for many.

References

Alesina, A. and Perotti, R. (1995) 'The Political Economy of Budget Deficits'. *IMF Staff Papers*, Vol. 42, pp. 1–31.

Barbieri, P. and Scherer, S. (2009) 'Labour Market Flexibilization and its Consequences in Italy'. *Europan Sociological Review*, Vol. 25, No. 6, pp. 677–92.

Blanchard, O.J., Jaumotte, F. and Loungani, P. (2014) 'Labor Market Policies and IMF Advice in Advanced Economies during the Great Recession'. *IZA Journal of Labor Policy*, Vol. 3, No. 2, pp. 1–33.

Blanchard, O. J. and Tirole, J. (2003) 'Contours of Employment Protection Reform'. MIT Department of Economics Working Paper, 03-35.

Bentolila, S., Dolado, J. and Jimeno, J. (2012a) 'Reforming an Insider-Outsider Labor Market: The Spanish Experience'. *IZA Journal of European Labor Studies*, Vol. 1, No. 4, pp. 1–29.

Bentolila, S., Cahuc, P., Dolado, J. and Le Barbanchon, T. (2012b) 'Two-Tier Labour Markets in the Great Recession: France *Versus* Spain'. *The Economic Journal*, Vol. 122, No. 562, pp. F155–87.

Benczes, I. and Szent-Iványi, B. (2015) 'The European Economy in 2014: Fragile Recovery and Convergence'. *JCMS*, Vol. 53, No. s1, pp. 162–80.

Ecorys and IZA (2012) *Analysis of Costs and Benefits of Active Compared to Passive Measures.* Final Report. END/NZ EI22101 (Rotterdam: Ecorys).

Eichhorst, W. and Marx, P. (2011) 'Reforming German Labour Market Institutions: A Dual Path to Flexibility'. *Journal of European Social Policy*, Vol. 21, No. 1, pp. 73–87.

European Commission (2012a) *Europe 2020: Europe's Growth Strategy* (Brussels: European Commission).

European Commission (2012b) *Towards a Job-rich Recovery* (Brussels: European Commission).

European Commission (2016) *European Economic Forecast Winter 2016* (Brussels: European Commission).

Eurostat (2015) 'Employment Statistics'. Available online at: http://ec.europa.eu/eurostat/statistics-explained/index.php/Employment_statistics.

Handler, H. (2013) 'The Eurozone: Piecemeal Approach to an Optimum Currency Area', WIFO Working Paper, 446.

ILO (2012) *Eurozone Job Crisis: Trends and Policy Responses* (Geneva: International Labour Organization).

IMF (2015a) *World Economic Outlook. Adjusting to Lower Commodity Prices* (Washington DC: IMF).

IMF (2015b) *'People's Republic of China. 2015 Article IV consultation'*, IMF Country Report 15/234 (Washington, DC: IMF).

Jager, J. and Hafner, K.A. (2013) 'The Optimum Currency Area Theory and the EMU'. *Intereconomics*, Vol. 48, No. 5, pp. 315–22.

Koske, I., Fournier, J. and Wanner, I. (2012) 'Less Income Inequality and More Growth – Are They Compatible? Part 2. The Distribution of Labour Income', OECD Economics Department Working Papers No. 925.

Saint-Paul, G. (1996) *Dual Labor Markets* (Cambridge, MA: MIT Press).

Seeleib-Kaiser, M. and Fleckenstein, T. (2007) 'Discourse, Learning and Welfare State Change: The Case of German Labour Market Reforms'. *Social Policy & Administration*, Vol. 41, pp. 427–48.

World Bank (2016) *Doing Business. Business Reforms for Labor Market Regulation*, (Washington, DC: The World Bank). Available online at: http://www.doingbusiness.org/reforms/overview/topic/labor/market/regulation. Last accessed: 10 June 2016.

World Economic Forum (2015) *The Global Competitiveness 2015–2016* (Geneva: World Economic Forum).

JCMS 2016 Volume 54. Annual Review pp. 185–203   DOI: 10.1111/jcms.12429

The Political Economy of European Capital Markets Union

LUCIA QUAGLIA,[1] DAVID HOWARTH[2] and MORITZ LIEBE[2]
[1]University of York [2]University of Luxembourg

Introduction

In September 2015 the European Commission put forward an Action Plan for Capital Markets Union (CMU) and two legislative proposals concerning securitization. Further legislative activity was to follow. The 'Five Presidents Report' of June 2015 had presented CMU as necessary to complement Banking Union and ultimately to complete Economic and Monetary Union (EMU). CMU was also considered by the Commission (2015a) as the 'new frontier of Europe's single market' with the aim of reducing fragmentation in financial markets, diversifying financing sources, strengthening cross-border capital flows and improving access to finance for businesses, particularly Small and Medium Enterprises (SMEs). More immediately, the CMU initiative was to encourage bank and other corporate securitization in the European Union, the level of which had plummeted since 2007 with the outbreak of the international financial crisis. CMU was also intended to boost the global competitiveness of European financial centres which over the previous decade had lost ground in global rankings (Deutsche Bank, 2015; FESE, 2015).

The CMU project was a potentially important development in the Single Market for two main inter-related reasons. First, full financial market integration had been a long-standing and rather elusive goal of the European Union. Second, the term Capital Market *Union* was deliberately chosen by the Commission to indicate that CMU was complementary to Banking *Union* and necessary for the completion of Economic and Monetary *Union*, which had been the focus of considerable intergovernmental debate and EU legislative activity from 2012 (Howarth and Quaglia, 2013, 2014, 2015). While it is argued below that the logic behind the link between the three unions is at best problematic, the Commission designed the CMU project to appeal to a range of EU Member States – both those in the euro area and outsiders.

This contribution undertakes a preliminary investigation of the 'making' of the CMU project, explaining what CMU is, its economic and political objectives, as well as its main drivers and obstacles. It is argued that the likely winners and losers of the project – both financial groups and specific Member State governments – largely formed the constituencies for and against CMU. The organization of national financial (and specifically banking) systems largely directed Member State government preferences on CMU. The potential winners were also influential in promoting a specific form of CMU, or at least specific priorities in the construction of CMU. The analysis below is organized as follows. Section I discusses the incomplete financial market integration in the EU as well as the variations in financial capitalism in its Member States, which sheds light upon national preferences on CMU. Section II explains the objectives and the main features of CMU. Section III examines the promoters of and 'foot-draggers' on CMU, with Member State government and economic interest group preferences gauged principally by written responses to the Commission's consultation on CMU and other public statements. Section IV focuses on the specific element of the CMU project which was prioritized by EU policy-makers – namely, securitization – and was the subject of the Commission's first explicitly CMU-linked legislative proposals of September 2015.

I. Incomplete Financial Market Integration in the EU

The impact of the international financial crisis and then the euro area sovereign debt crisis on the single market in financial services was devastating. The fragmentation of the financial services market in turn affected the European Central Bank's (ECB's) ability to operate effective monetary policy (ECB, 2012). Not only had banking markets become less integrated since 2008 on a range of measures, but also the cross-border bond holdings of euro area financial companies (as a percentage of the total) declined markedly from the middle of the 2000s. In 2005, of the government and corporate bonds held by financial companies, over 40 per cent were cross border. By 2011 this figure had dropped to 23 per cent. Similarly, the share of cross-border collateral used by euro area financial companies had dropped from over 50 per cent of the total to approximately 33 per cent. The euro area periphery (Italy, Portugal, Spain, Greece and Ireland) was most affected by this retreat to domestic debt given the declining confidence of non-periphery banks in the value of sovereign and corporate debt issued in the periphery (Howarth and Quaglia, 2013, 2016). A destabilizing sovereign debt–domestic bank loop was created in the periphery (BIS, 2011). Higher periphery government spending and rising debt burdens increased sovereign risk (Merler and Pisani Ferry, 2012) and threatened to disrupt the collateral function of sovereign debt, with a resultant damaging effect on bank funding conditions (BIS, 2011). Banking Union was a response to this (see Howarth and Quaglia, 2013, 2014), but it did not address the problem of capital markets.

Capital markets are financial market segments not involved in bank intermediation. They include corporate bond issuance, corporate debt securitization, private equity investment, public equity issuance and initial public offerings, venture capital, the direct purchase of loans by insurers and investment funds from banks and credit intermediation by specialized non-bank financial firms, including leasing companies and consumer finance companies (European Commission, 2015a). Compared to the US, European finance was considerably more bank based.[1] In 2015, bank credit formed approximately 80 per cent of total financial assets in the EU with the remaining 20 per cent as corporate debt and equity. The reverse was the case for the US. EU public and private equity markets were approximately half the size of those in the US (in 2013 as a percentage of Gross Domestic Product (GDP)). In 2013, stock market capitalization reached 64.5 per cent in the EU versus 138 per cent of GDP in the US. Even stock market capitalization in China (at 74 per cent) exceeded that of the EU. EU non-financial company debt securities markets (which refers to debt issued by a government or corporation that may be traded on secondary markets, such as bonds, notes or money market instruments) was only a third as large as in the US relative to GDP (12.9 per cent of GDP in the EU). The EU markets for both private placements (a form of direct lending typically between

[1] All figures here are drawn from the Infographics produced by the Commission. Available online at: http://ec.europa.eu/finance/capital-markets-union/index_en.htm. Last accessed: 1 October 2015. See also Véron and Wolff (2015) for an examination of the different US and EU financial sectors and different national financial sectors.

institutional investors and mid-sized firms) and venture capital also lagged massively behind US markets in real terms and relative to GDP (European Commission, 2015a).

In the EU compared to the US, non-financial companies – especially SMEs – relied far more on bank credit and this greater dependence made the European economy more vulnerable when bank lending conditions tightened in a number of Member States during and following the international financial crisis. In the EU there was a significant increase in corporate debt issuance by non-financial companies over the half decade following the crisis – which in part reflected a favourable market environment for bond issuers due to low interest rates. Bonds, however, were principally issued by large companies rather than SMEs (European Commission, 2015a). Both equity and debt markets were characterized by a strong home-country bias (prior to and after the international financial crisis). Shareholders and buyers of corporate debt rarely went beyond their national borders when they invested. Significant differences in financing conditions between Member States remained with differing rules and market practices for products such as securitized instruments or private placements (European Commission, 2015a).

The heavy reliance on bank credit also demonstrated the importance of securitization to stimulate bank lending in a number of EU Member States (Hardie and Howarth, 2013). However, the international financial crisis took its toll on securitization issuance in Europe, dropping rapidly from a high of €594 billion at the end of 2007. Figures began to rise again in 2011 but remained well below the pre-crisis level, reaching €216 billion at the end of 2014. The Commission and the ECB placed great emphasis upon reviving both bank and non-financial company securitization in the EU. The Commission argued that if the SME securitization market could be revived safely, it could generate some €20 billion of additional funding (European Commission, 2015a, p. 2). Changes to international capital requirements and EU banking regulation in the aftermath of the international financial crisis also hit bank lending.

Variation in Financial Capitalism in the EU and National Preferences on CMU

EU Member State financial systems largely determined national government policies on CMU as they had on previous efforts to integrate EU financial markets (Story and Walter, 1997; Quaglia, 2010). There are two main ways to measure different financial systems: the main categories of financial assets as a percentage of all financial assets and to GDP; and the sources of non-financial company external funding (Allen and Gale, 2000). There was wide variation in financial system development across EU Member States (see ECMI, 2015). Figure 1 considers the significance of financial intermediaries other than banks in national financial systems. On this measure only nine Member States had non-bank financial intermediation above 50 per cent of GDP while only three – Luxembourg, Ireland and Sweden – were higher than 100 per cent. More specifically, Table 1 locates 27 Member States into groups based on the relative size of their stock market capitalization (to national GDP) and distinguishes between larger and smaller markets (in terms of total size). Taking the extremes, at the end of 2013 domestic stock market capitalization exceeded 125 per cent of GDP in Luxembourg and 121 per cent in the UK compared to less than 10 per cent in Cyprus, Slovakia, Latvia and Lithuania (European Commission, 2015a). The main hypothesis tested in this contribution is that Member States with large non-bank-based financial sectors – notably, the UK,

Figure 1: Financial Intermediation in EU Member States via Markets (per cent of GDP, 2015).

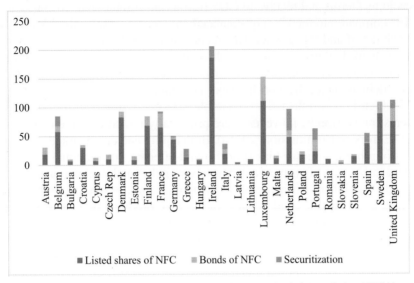

Source: Eurostat, ECB, European Private Equity and Venture Capital Association (EVCA), Securities Industry and Financial Markets Association (SIFMA).

Luxembourg, Sweden, Ireland and the Netherlands – were the most energetic in promoting CMU and supporting financial sector liberalization more generally in the EU. Greater caution on CMU was to be expected on the part of Germany, Italy and Austria (among others). The smaller, Central and Eastern European Member States potentially had the least to gain in terms of improved market access for their smaller financial sector firms.

Table 1: Varying Stock Market Capitalization in the European Union (as per cent of GDP, End 2013 Figures, EU-27, excluding Croatia)

	High (+90 per cent)	Moderately high (60–89 per cent)	Moderate (30–59 per cent)	Low (10 to 29 per cent)	Very low (<10 per cent)
Larger economies (GDP above EU national average)	United Kingdom (121) Netherlands (98) Sweden (112)	France (81) Spain (79) Belgium (71)	Germany (51) Italy (35) Austria (38) Poland (38)		
Smaller economies (GDP below EU national average)	Luxembourg (125)	Denmark (71)* Ireland (75) Finland (84)	Portugal (35) Greece (33) Malta (45)	Romania (13) Hungary (15) Czech Rep. (15) Bulgaria (13) Slovenia (15) Estonia (10)	Slovakia (6) Cyprus (9) Lithuania (8) Latvia (4)

Source: ECMI (2015).
* End 2012 figure.

Regarding the second measure of financial systems, the access of firms and individuals to capital markets also differed significantly. Figure 2 demonstrates considerable national variation in terms of the external funding of non-financial companies (equity versus bank credit as a percentage of total company liabilities). Non-financial company reliance on equity issuance exceeded reliance on bank credit in only the UK and Denmark. Non-financial company reliance on *both* equity and debt issuance exceeded reliance on bank credit in external company finance (excluding private equity) in only the UK, Denmark, Finland, France and Germany, and only exceeded 30 per cent of the total in half the Member States. Bond issuance was concentrated in larger markets and exceeded 10 per cent of the total only in seven Member States (European Commission, 2015a). It is more difficult to use this factor (external funding of non-financial companies) to predict Member State preferences on CMU. Member States in which non-financial companies relied more heavily on bank credit might be expected to seek further to develop alternative sources of funding and thus support the market liberalization objectives of CMU.

Other financial system features were of potential relevance in terms of shaping Member State preferences on CMU: first, the openness of national banking systems might have encouraged support for CMU. On the one hand, a number of EU Member States had banking systems that were dominated by home banks and relatively closed to foreign operations (see Table 2). This was the case in all six of the largest economies, with the exception of the UK. On the other hand, in about half the EU Member States – including most of the smaller economies – the banking system was very open to the subsidiaries and branches of banks headquartered in other EU Member States, with levels rising to above 90 per cent

Figure 2: Liability Structure of Non-financial Companies in EU Member States (end 2015) (Bank credit, listed shares, bonds, as a percentage of total of the three).

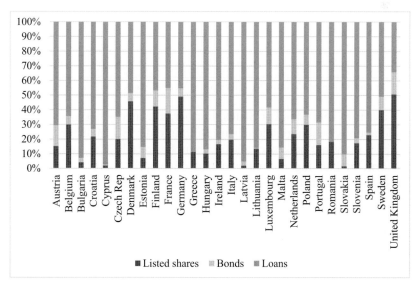

Source: Eurostat

Note: *Figures exclude other liabilities, including non-listed equity, trade credit and other.

Table 2: Foreign Penetration into EU-27 Banking Systems End 2013 (per cent of Total Banks Assets Held by Subsidiaries and Branches of Foreign EU and 'Rest of World' Banks)

	European Union	Rest of World	Total
Very High (above 90 per cent)			
Estonia	91	5	96
Slovakia	96	0	96
Luxembourg	74	18	92
High (60–89 per cent)			
Czech R.	86	5	91
Malta	26	49	75
Lithuania	72	2	74
Bulgaria	73	0	73
Romania	71	1	72
Poland	56	9	65
Belgium	51	14	65
Finland	64	0	64
Latvia	45	15	60
Moderate (30–59 per cent)			
Hungary	54	5	59
Ireland	37	11	48
United Kingdom	17	28.5	45.5
Cyprus	13	16	29
Slovenia	31	0	31
Low (10–29 per cent)			
Austria	16	6	22
Portugal	19	0	19
Denmark	16	2	18
Italy	12	0	12
Germany	9	2	11
Sweden	7	3	10
Very low (0–9 per cent)			
Netherlands	7	2	9
France	7	1	8
Spain	7	0	7
Greece	3	0	3

Source: ECB (2014); national central bank data for non euro area Member States.

of total bank assets in four Member States. Further, a related – but more difficult to measure – consideration is banking nationalism. Both in older EU Member States, where foreign banks had a marginal presence, and in a number of CEECs – notably Hungary and Poland – a form of banking nationalism had developed (Barnes and Johnson, 2015; Epstein, 2014; Howarth, 2013). The second hypothesis tested in this contribution is that the governments of Member States with more open banking systems – and thus lower levels of banking nationalism – were more likely to support financial liberalization and diversification measures promoted by the CMU project.

II. The CMU Project

In a speech to the European Parliament in May 2014, Jean-Claude Juncker – then candidate for Commission President – launched the idea of CMU (Juncker, 2014). In

November 2014, the Commission's Communication 'An Investment Plan for Europe' explicitly called for a European Long-term Investment Funds (ELTIF) regulation, 'high-quality' securitization, standardized credit information on SMEs, the promotion of private placements markets and the review of the Prospectus Directive. In February 2015 the Commission published the Green Paper 'Building a Capital Markets Union' and launched a three-month consultation on its contents, with a view to elaborating an Action Plan setting out a roadmap and timeline for establishing a CMU by 2019. The Commission's stated objectives were to 'promote stronger capital markets that would complement banks as a source of financing, improving access to financing for all businesses across Europe, especially for [SMEs] and infrastructure'; 'to increase and diversify the sources of funding from investors in the EU and all over the world'; and 'to improve market efficiency, making the financial system more stable by opening up a wider range of funding sources'. Two additional consultations on 'high-quality' securitization and the 'Prospectus Directive' were also launched in February. The Commission argued that it supported market-driven solutions when they were likely to be effective, and regulatory changes only where necessary (European Commission, 2015a, pp. 4–5).

The Commission estimated that the EU needed between €1 trillion to €2 trillion to finance its infrastructure needs by 2020 (European Commission, 2015a). To this end, the Commission proposed the ELTIFs which were designed to bring together investors seeking to place their money into companies and projects for the long term with enterprises in need of 'patient' long-term money. As such ELTIFs were presented as an integral part of the drive to improve the long-term funding of the EU's economy which is embodied by the European Fund for Strategic Investments (EFSI), the creation of which was proposed by the Commission in January 2015 and adopted through a Regulation by the Council in June 2015 (European Parliament and Council, 2015; see also European Commission, 2015a).

There were more than 400 written responses to the consultation on CMU. While unscientific, an analysis of the home Member States and sectors of these respondents suggests varying levels of interest in CMU. Almost a quarter (22 per cent) were from the UK, 16 per cent from Belgium (Brussels), 13 per cent each from France and Germany and 4 per cent each from Italy and the Netherlands. This pattern of responses suggests a particularly strong interest in CMU by the UK. The high figures for Belgium reflect the location of EU-level financial associations. Thirty-six per cent of respondents were from the financial sector; 20 per cent were non-financial companies and their representative associations, 5 per cent were NGOs and only 1.6 per cent were consumer organizations. This suggests that CMU mainly elicited the interest of the financial industry – seeking new opportunities for expansion – and less that of companies (including SMEs, which were actively targeted given their perceived need for improved access to external funding). Within the financial industry, the respondents were 26 per cent banks and their representative associations, 16 per cent insurers, 11 per cent pension providers, 2 per cent investment management firms (including hedge funds, private equity funds, venture capital funds, money market funds, and securities firms), 15 per cent market infrastructure operators (for example, Central Counter Parties (CCPs), stock exchanges), and 18 per cent other financial services (for example, advice and brokerage) (European Commission, 2015c).

The summary of the responses, which was compiled by the Commission, emphasized that the majority supported all five priorities for early action set out in the Green Paper. In addition, the respondents suggested a number of additional priorities including the agreement of a harmonized definition of SMEs in EU legislation; the development of crowd-funding, business angels, venture capital and loan-originating funds; the finalization of the European Money Market Funds reform; the improvement of corporate bond market liquidity; the reduction of the capital charge for infrastructure investments by insurance undertakings under Solvency II; and the lowering of the remaining legal barriers to support efficient post-trade processes for cross-border securities transactions. In September 2015 the Commission presented an Action Plan for CMU (European Commission, 2015b) and two proposed directives on securitization: the first legislative building-block in the construction of CMU. In his speech, the Commissioner responsible for financial services, Jonathan Hill, listed his top six priorities which largely followed those of the Green Paper with the addition of a priority specifically focused on support for venture capital and equity financing, and an assessment of existing regulation with the aim of streamlining.

III. Promoters of and 'Foot-draggers' on CMU

The Commission and the ECB

As in earlier initiatives concerning financial market integration in the EU (see Egan, 2001; Jabko, 2006), the European Commission was the main driver of CMU, with strong support from the ECB. The new Commission President, Jean-Claude Juncker – who was both former Prime Minister and Finance Minister of Luxembourg – a country whose economy relied heavily on the financial sector – had a very good understanding of the issues at stake. The British national put in charge of the project was Jonathan Hill, who became the Commissioner for 'Financial Stability, Financial Services and Capital Markets Union', one of the few examples in European Union history where a Commissioner's job title matched that of a specific project. Similarly, reflecting the great importance attached to the CMU project, the European Commission was also reshuffled to form a new 'Directorate-General for Financial Stability, Financial Services and Capital Markets Union' (DG FISMA). The Commission deliberately framed CMU as an initiative to complement Banking Union and ultimately to complete EMU. Hence it was presented as a way to address the concerns of the repercussions of 'differentiated integration' – linked to EMU and, more recently, Banking Union – on the single financial market. The ECB supported the project as a way to provide funding to the real economy, notably to SMEs, and to ensure the 'smooth and homogenous transmission of monetary policy and [to] help foster financial stability' (ECB, 2015).

The Member States

The two hypotheses outlined above largely hold with a couple of partial exceptions: those Member States with more diversified financial systems and more open banking systems were more likely to support CMU. Of all EU Member States, the UK had potentially the most to benefit from the financial liberalization and diversification promised in the CMU project, given the diversity of its financial sector and, in particular, the high concentration of wholesale market activity, private equity and hedge funds (Véron, 2014). CMU was enthusiastically supported by both the UK government (2015) and the City

(TheCityUK, 2015). Commissioner Hill stressed the huge investment flows from UK-based banks and other financial companies to the continent (Hill, 2015b). Some commentators (for example, Ringe, 2015b, p. 5) interpreted CMU, in part, as an attempt to repair the strained relations between the UK and the EU / euro area by giving 'a political signal to strengthen the Single Market as a project of all 28 Member States', not only to the euro area countries, and in an area where the UK had a clear competitive advantage. As predicted above, the broadly enthusiastic response of the UK government was joined principally by those Member States with the most well-developed and diversified financial sectors, including Ireland (2015), the Netherlands (2015), Sweden (2015) and Luxembourg.[2] However, the very low foreign bank presence in the Netherlands and Sweden contradicts the second hypothesis.

In the UK, given the fact that CMU would also involve new EU regulation and further centralization, there was some reluctance on the basis of national sovereignty-related concerns (Véron, 2014), which might also explain the somewhat different views of Commissioner Hill and Commission President Juncker as to the institutional content of CMU. Commissioner Hill and DG FISMA officials did not discuss institutional reform in their presentations on CMU. By contrast President Juncker in the Five Presidents' Report (2015) argued that CMU 'should lead ultimately to a single European capital markets supervisor'. However, the strong UK government opposition to further centralization helps explain the absence of institutional measures in both the February 2015 Green Paper and the September 2015 Action Plan (Véron, 2015).

While broadly supportive of Commission efforts to improve financing to the real economy, the German and French governments demonstrated greater caution on CMU (Germany, 2015; Gouvernement français, 2015). German government reticence on CMU reflects the importance of bank credit in the country, the comparatively limited developments of alternative finance, the closed banking (and broader financial) system, the absence of a credit crunch since the outbreak of the international financial crisis and the reliable provision of credit to SMEs notably by smaller savings banks and cooperatives. French reticence is somewhat more surprising given the country's more developed financial sector. However, French reluctance can be explained by a long-standing policy of national champions in the banking sector (see Howarth, 2013) and the lowest foreign presence of all EU financial systems (see Table 2). On the demand side, as in Germany, there was limited perceived need for developing alternative finance: France did not suffer a credit crunch following the outbreak of the international financial crisis. However, large banks still dominated the French financial sector. Despite the presence of private equity firms and hedge funds in both countries, there was longstanding opposition to foreign 'alternative' investment companies and the full liberalization of capital markets more generally (Buckley and Howarth, 2011; Zimmerman, 2010). Most hedging activity was managed by large banks. Earlier in the decade, the French and German governments had fought to impose tough transparency and other conditions on the operation of these 'alternative' investment funds and their managers.

Wolfgang Schäuble and Michel Sapin, respectively the German and French finance ministers, sent a letter to Commissioner Hill in July 2015, expressing scepticism about copying the financial model of the United States (Schäuble and Sapin, 2015). They demanded that a level

---

[2] Interview with senior official from Luxembourg Ministry of Finance responsible for CMU, Luxembourg, 15 April 2016.

playing field between the various capital and bank-based financial instruments be maintained and that banks be central to all efforts to improve financing businesses, especially SMEs. The two finance ministers also made reference to the 'proportionality principle', an indication that they were ready to challenge the Commission's efforts to promote financial liberalization and diversification if they undermined national policy preferences.

Given their more limited development, the financial sectors of Southern, Central and Eastern European Member States were generally in a weaker position to gain advantage from CMU (see Figure 1; Table 1). Nonetheless, the minority of euro area and EU periphery governments and public bodies that provided written responses to the Commission's consultation (six of 16) were broadly positive – see, for example, Italy (2015). The principal interest for most of these countries was to enhance the provision of finance, especially to SMEs, the relative economic importance of which was much greater than in Northern EU Member States (TheCityUK, 2015). The Commission designed CMU to appeal to EU and euro area periphery countries, which had been hit hard by the international financial and then sovereign debt crises with the explicit promise of improved financial flows to their economies which would help to kick-start growth and create jobs (Ringe, 2015a). However, the very limited number of respondents from Southern Europe to the Commission's consultation suggests that neither the public institutions nor the private stakeholders in these countries were heavily involved in the CMU policy debate. Furthermore, the Commission-proposed ELTIFs were of particular interest to euro area periphery countries faced with significant cuts to public investment due to high debt burdens. Moreover, the French government, struggling with low growth and a rapidly rising debt burden, was similarly keen to emphasize the 'investment' dimension of CMU (Gouvernement français, 2015).

Economic Interest Groups

In terms of the positioning of different economic (and specifically financial) sectors, non-bank investors, including private equity and venture capital firms, were also likely to benefit from CMU. These firms and their representative associations were the most unreservedly positive about the CMU project in their responses to the Green Paper consultation – see, for example, the Association for Financial Markets in Europe (AFME, 2015); and the Alternative Investment Management Association (AIMA, 2015). A number of national associations representing non-bank financial firms came out strongly in favour of CMU including the *Association Française de la Gestion financière* (AFG, 2015) and German *Bundesverband der Wertpapierfirmen* (2015) which argued that 'attractive and sustainable capital markets need a diverse "eco system" of variegated market structures and [financial] firms of different size'. Furthermore, a range of large EU-headquartered universal banks, which were likely to benefit substantially from CMU, were strongly positive on the project and were particularly supportive of the relaunch of securitization (BNP Paribas, 2015; Intesa, 2015; Lloyds, 2015; Société Générale, 2015; Unicredit, 2015; see also Mügge 2010).

Other financial groups were positive but also expressed some caution. In its response to the Commission's consultation, the European Banking Federation – which represents 32 national banking associations and a range of bank types – expressed its broad support for the CMU project (EBF, 2015). However, the EBF also expressed its concern that banks should not be placed at a disadvantage in efforts to liberalize other market sectors and that CMU should ensure a level playing field among different financial institutions.

The main 'foot-draggers' on CMU were smaller domestically-focused banks and protected financial 'national champion' market infrastructure firms in some Member States, which disliked the prospect of competition from alternative financing channels (Turner, 2015; Véron, 2014). The important position of small bank lenders in a number of EU Member States – notably Germany – contributed to national government caution. These banks and their representative associations – including the European Savings and Retail Banking Group (ESBG) and the European Association of Cooperative Banks (EACB) – were particularly critical of the CMU project, arguing that they were better suited than capital markets to provide funding to the real economy, especially to SMEs (EACB, 2015; ESBG, 2015). These banks argued for loosening the conditions that had been imposed on small banks after the crisis, and notably reducing capital requirements (EACB, 2015; ESBG, 2015; Turner, 2015).

The impact of CMU would also likely be different amongst stock exchanges across the EU but it was clear that CMU would increase pressure to consolidate in the sector. Despite significant consolidation over the previous three decades, there remained 16 stock exchanges in the EU – in comparison to two in the US – protected by national governments (Deutsche Bank, 2015, p. 7). Initial Public Offers (IPOs) tended to take place on domestic exchanges and smaller firms had a tendency to focus on the local stock market. The large number of exchanges had the potential effect of limiting the investor base for IPOs and for smaller companies' stocks. Consolidated exchanges that operated in more than one country were subject to harmonized EU rules, such as the Markets in Financial Instruments Directive (MiFID), and non-harmonized national rules (often, due to gold-plating) concerning local markets. These national rules would be harmonized in CMU, reducing operational costs and encouraging consolidation among stock exchanges (Deutsche Bank, 2015). Business would likely move towards the largest and most competitive financial centres, first and foremost London, but also Frankfurt and Paris. The Federation of European Stock Exchanges (FESE, 2015) was positive on CMU and the encouragement of capital markets but also expressed caution and the need to respect the crucial role played by national exchanges, the 'diversity of ecosystems' (FESE, 2015, p. 4) and the 'level playing field' between stock exchanges and other financial services.

Outside the financial sector the main responses from the real economy came from companies' and employers' organizations in Germany and to a more limited extent in France. Their responses were somewhat more general than those submitted by the financial industry The German Chamber of Commerce (Deutscher Industrie- und Handelskammertag, 2015) was comparatively hostile to CMU arguing that 'a bank-based financial system fulfilled the needs of the European economy' and questioning the logic of building up capital markets to replace banks.[3] The Federation of German Industry, *Bundesverband der Deutschen Industrie* (BDI, 2015) and its French counterpart, the *Mouvement des entreprises de France* (MEDEF, 2015), placed emphasis on the need for a regulatory level playing field in the EU and internationally with rules that were uniformly applied to all financial instruments having the same function. Despite the purported importance of improving SME financing, associations specifically representing SMEs did not respond to the Commission's consultation.

Pesendorfer (2015) argues that the consultation was framed in such a way as to marginalize more radical responses and encourage those focused on deepening capital

---

[3] Authors' own translation.

markets, reinforcing securitization and promoting the Commission's better regulation agenda. Later, in response to the Commission's Action Plan, 29 trade unions, economic and civil society associations and think tanks prepared a critical statement on the likely effectiveness of the CMU project (*Finance Watch*, 2015). The statement argued that by focusing on the supply of credit – which was not perceived as a serious problem – the CMU project ignored the pressing demand-side policies that were needed to promote sustainable growth and employment in the EU. While the statement welcomed some initiatives of the CMU project, it argued that several others would create additional risks for the economy, including efforts to revive securitization which was too complex and expensive to help SMEs raise finance without subsidies. The statement noted that the EU's biggest banks 'arguably' stood to gain the most from CMU.

IV. The First Building Block of CMU: Securitization

It is revealing that the first CMU-related legislative proposals officially put forward by the Commission in September 2015 concerned securitization: a draft Regulation set out criteria for Simple, Transparent and Standardised Securitisations; and a draft amendment to the Capital Requirements Regulation sought to make the capital treatment of securitizations more risk-sensitive (and thus, effectively, to lower capital requirements on securitized assets) (European Commission, 2015e, 2015f). The Commission and ECB were keen to assuage market and public concerns about securitization, which had a bad reputation as a consequence of the crisis.[4] In its explanatory document for the draft legislation the Commission (2015d) distinguished between massive losses on securitized products produced by US banks and the very small losses on securitized products in the EU. The focus on securitization reflected the reality of Europe's bank-dominated financial systems, which could use securitization to get around tighter European capital requirements and increase lending – notably to SMEs. As noted above, the issuance of securitization by financial firms (notably banks) in the EU had plummeted since the outbreak of the international financial crisis, although levels started rising again in 2011. However, the focus on securitization was also about encouraging SMEs to bypass banks in their efforts to raise external funding, by securitizing their own assets and selling these on corporate debt markets. The issuance level of SME securitized products was €36 billion in 2014, less than half its peak level of €77 billion, and only a small part of overall securitization. Commission and ECB efforts to encourage non-financial company securitization were also about stimulating further the development of European corporate bond markets. The focus on securitization also reflected ongoing international, Commission and ECB efforts distinct from the CMU project (see, for example, BCBS, 2011; BCBS and IOSCO, 2015; ECB and Bank of England, 2014; EBA, 2015). Commissioner Hill was at pains to point out that EU efforts were part of a broader international effort.[5]

The Commission's push on securitization was also facilitated by national financial sector developments. In all four Member States with the highest issuance of securitized products in 2007 – the UK, Netherlands, Spain and Italy – amounts had plummeted in the aftermath of the financial crisis and were still dropping rapidly during the 2013–15 period (Table 3). The largest absolute decline was in the UK: approximately €100 billion or 22

[4] *The Telegraph*, 19 February 2015.

per cent over the two years. The governments of these four Member States were particularly keen on EU legislative developments to encourage securitization and reverse the fall (see, for example, Netherlands, 2015). The largest absolute increases in securitization over the two-year period were in France and Germany. In France, the issuance of securitized products reached record levels in 2015. While still far below the total and relative-to-GDP levels found in several other Member States, this significant increase suggests that the French and German governments were also open to Commission and ECB efforts to encourage securitization – as confirmed in positive French and German government statements (Gouvernement français, 2015; Germany, 2015) – and that a consensus could be found among the large Member States on the issue.

The Commission received 120 written responses to its consultation on securitization launched in February 2015 with almost a quarter from the UK and almost a half from financial companies. The relatively limited response from non-financial companies (including associations representing SMEs) suggests again a significant imbalance in interest. UK-based companies led the way on securitization in the EU (almost a quarter of the EU total issuance in 2014) and UK-based investors provided almost half of total EU investment in securitized products (UK Government, 2015) (see also Table 3). These UK-based companies had a strong interest in improving their access to other EU Member State markets. On the whole, the respondents to the consultation indicated that the priority should be to develop an EU-wide framework for simple, transparent and standardized securitization. Furthermore, many respondents to the Commission's consultation (including the UK Government, 2015) argued that to promote securitization, the disparity in regulatory treatment between securitization and other asset classes should be reduced.

Conclusion

Although the Commission presented Capital Market Union as complementary to Banking Union, there were very few similarities and three main differences between these two projects. First, with regard to CMU, the term 'union' was somewhat misleading because, *de facto*, the project involved 'an incremental improvement of the existing regulatory framework governing the integration' of different EU Member State capital markets (Ringe, 2015a, p. 6). Second, Banking Union applied not to the entire EU, but only to EMU Member States and others that decided to opt in. No euro area outsider by spring 2016 had opted into Banking Union. CMU applied to all EU Member States. Third, and most important, while Banking Union centralized banking supervision and resolution for euro area Member States, in CMU centralization was not the main objective. On the contrary, Commissioner Hill (2015a) pointed out that CMU involved building 'a single market for capital from the *bottom up*, identifying barriers and knocking them down one by one' (italics added). However, some 'centralization' or harmonization through EU re-regulation would be needed in the CMU project, as in the case of previous initiatives designed to promote financial market integration in the EU. Véron (2014) argues that: '[a]n EU-wide approach [was] the best way to overcome entrenched political economy constraints that [had] repressed the development of capital markets and non-bank finance'. Indeed, many of the measures proposed in the Commission's Green Paper were

---

[5] *Euractive*, 19 February 2015.

Table 3: Securitization Outstanding by Country of Collateral*, 2013–15 (third quarter, € billions)

Member State	2013	2014	2015	Change 2013–15 (percentage)
Austria	2.1	2.2	1.8	−14.3
Belgium	85.2	76.6	65.8	−22.8
Finland	0.2	0.8	1.0	+500
France	37.8	69.3	69.6	+84.1
Germany	78.2	74	88.2	+12.8
Greece	29.3	25.1	21.4	−27.0
Ireland	44.0	35.3	33.5	−23.9
Italy	189.4	164.4	153.1	−19.2
Netherlands	281.6	258.2	240.3	−14.7
Portugal	39.5	35.8	32.1	−18.7
Spain	181.6	167.6	162.9	−10.3
United Kingdom	447.5	402.2	347.3	−22.4

Source: AFME (2015).
* Only EU Member States with outstanding issuance over €1 billion.

not bottom up, they involved top-down EU legislation concerning the harmonization of certain EU capital market rules (Ringe, 2015a). The main intersection between Banking Union and CMU was that the consolidation of supervision and resolution policies in the Banking Union area created a spill-over dynamic encouraging policy integration in related activities – for example accounting and auditing policies – which fell within the CMU remit (Véron, 2014).[6]

This contribution examined the politics and political economy of the CMU project, which was still very much in progress at the time of writing in spring 2016. It argues that – up to the end of 2015 at least – CMU was a lot of hype surrounding a policy – namely the promotion of securitization – which was difficult to sell to sceptical European publics in the years following the financial crisis. The Commission and the ECB argued that securitization was a policy that was essential to re-start the flow of credit to the real economy in the EU, especially given the limited development of financial services other than banking in most Member State financial systems and the heavy reliance of non-financial companies (notably SMEs) on bank credit. The CMU project and the financial liberalization and diversification that it promised had likely winners and losers – both Member States and specific sectors of the economy – which therefore acted as pace-setters or 'foot-draggers' in discussions and negotiations on the project. The main winners were the City of London – with its diverse financial sector – and specifically alternative investment companies. Many big internationally active universal banks engaged in investment banking activities would also likely do well out of the liberalization of EU financial markets. The main losers were likely to be the less competitive, domestically-oriented parts of the financial sector and the less competitive market infrastructures (notably stock exchanges) found in several EU Member States. Thus, the UK, Irish, Swedish, Netherlands and Luxembourg governments unambiguously supported the market liberalization agenda in CMU, whereas the main continental Member States – notably

[6] A number of powerful economic interests and the German federal government (Germany, 2015) were explicit in their on-going opposition to the harmonization of accounting and auditing policies.

France and Germany – expressed their reservations. The French and German governments supported the CMU project, while stressing the importance of banks to European economies and rejecting both the inherent desirability of the US financial model – promoted by the Commission and the ECB – as inappropriate for the EU.

References

AFG (Association Française de la Gestion financière) (2015) 'Response to the Commission's Consultation on the Green Paper on CMU'. Available at https://ec.europa.eu/eusurvey/publication/capital-markets-union-2015?language=en. Last accessed: 13 March 2016.

AFME (Association for Financial Markets in Europe) (2015) 'Response to the Commission's Consultation on the Green Paper on CMU'. Available at https://ec.europa.eu/eusurvey/publication/capital-markets-union-2015?language=en. Last accessed: 13 March 2016.

AIMA (Alternative Investment Management Association) (2015) 'Response to the Commission's Consultation on the Green Paper on CMU'. Available at https://ec.europa.eu/eusurvey/publication/capital-markets-union-2015?language=en. Last accessed: 13 March 2016.

Allen, F. and Gale, D. (2000) *Comparing Financial Systems* (Cambridge, MA: MIT Press).

Barnes, J. and Johnson, J. (2015) 'Financial Nationalism after the Crisis: The Hungarian Experience'. *Review of International Political Economy*, Vol. 22, No. 3, pp. 535–69.

BCBS (Basel Committee on Banking Supervision) (2011) 'Report on asset securitisation incentives', The Joint Forum, July, Basel: BIS. Available at http://www.bis.org/publ/joint26.htm. Last accessed: 16 July 2016.

BCBS (Basel Committee on Banking Supervision) and IOSCO (International Organization for Securities Commissions) (2015) 'Capital treatment for "simple, transparent and comparable" securitisations', 10 November, Basel: BIS. Available at http://www.bis.org/press/p151110a.htm. Last accessed: 16 July 2016.

BIS (Bank for International Settlements) (2011) 'The Impact of Sovereign Credit Risk on Bank Funding Conditions'. In *Committee on the Global Financial System Paper 43* (Basel: BIS).

BNP Paribas (2015) 'Response to the Commission's Consultation on the Green Paper on CMU'. Available at https://ec.europa.eu/eusurvey/publication/capital-markets-union-2015?language=en. Last accessed: 13 March 2016.

Buckley, J. and Howarth, D. (2011) 'Regulating the So-Called "Vultures of Capitalism"'. *JCMS*, Vol. 49, No. s1, pp. 123–43.

BDI (Bundesverband der Deutschen Industrie) (2015) 'Response to the Commission's Consultation on the Green Paper on CMU'. Available at https://ec.europa.eu/eusurvey/publication/capital-markets-union-2015?language=en. Last accessed: 13 March 2016.

Deutsche Bank (2015) 'Capital Markets Union: An Ambitious Goal But Few Quick Wins', EU Monitor, Global Financial Markets, 2 November (Frankfurt: Deutsche Bank Research). Available online at: https://Www.Dbresearch.Com/PROD/DBR_INTERNET_EN-PROD/PROD0000000000371611/Capital_Markets_Union%3A_An_Ambitious_Goal,_But_Few_.Pdf. Last accessed: 15 January 2016.

Deutscher Industrie- und Handelskammertag (2015) 'Response to the Commission's Consultation on the Green Paper on CMU'. Available at https://ec.europa.eu/eusurvey/publication/capital-markets-union-2015?language=en. Last accessed: 13 March 2016.

EACB (European Association of Cooperative Banks) (2015) 'Response to the Commission's Consultation on the Green Paper on CMU'. Available at https://ec.europa.eu/eusurvey/publication/capital-markets-union-2015?language=en. Last accessed: 13 March 2016.

EBA (European Banking Authority) (2015) 'EBA Report on Qualifying Securitisation: Response to the Commission's call for advice of January 2014 on Long Term Financing' (London: EBA). Available at https://www.eba.europa.eu/documents/10180/950548/EBA+report+on+qualifying+securitisation.pdf. Last accessed: 14 March 2016.

EBF (European Banking Federation) (2015) 'EBF Response to the Commission's Green Paper on the Capital Markets Union', EBF 014896, 13 May. Available at http://www.ebf-fbe.eu/wp-content/uploads/2015/05/EBF_014896-EBF-response-to-CMU-Green-Paper1.pdf. Last accessed: 3 March 2016.

ECB (European Central Bank) (2012) *Financial Integration Report* (Frankfurt: ECB).

ECB (European Central Bank) (2014) *Banking Structures Report* (Frankfurt: ECB). Available at https://www.ecb.europa.eu/pub/pdf/other/bankingstructuresreport201410.en.pdf. Last accessed: 2 March 2016.

ECB (European Central Bank) (2015) *Building a Capital Markets Union – Eurosystem Contribution to the European Commission's Green Paper* (Frankfurt: ECB). Available at https://www.ecb.europa.eu/pub/pdf/other/150521_eurosystem_contribution_to_green_paper_-_building_a_cmuen.pdf?d45301c62386a193f81154659fe87345. Last accessed: 2 March 2016.

ECB (European Central Bank) and Bank of England (2014) 'The Case for a Better Functioning Securitization Market in the European Union', Discussion Paper, 29 May. Available at https://www.ecb.europa.eu/pub/pdf/other/ecb-boe_case_better_functioning_securitisation_marketen.pdf. Last accessed: on 2 February 2016.

ECMI (European Capital Markets Institute) (2015) 'ECMI Statistical Package', CEPS. Available at http://www.eurocapitalmarkets.org/statistics. Last accessed: on 15 June 2016.

Egan, M. (2001) *Constructing a European Market* (Oxford: Oxford University Press).

Epstein, R. (2014) 'Assets or Liabilities? The Politics of Bank Ownership'. *Review of International Political Economy*, Vol. 21, No. 4, pp. 765–89.

ESBG (European Savings and Retail Banking Group) (2015) 'ESBG Response to the European Commission's Green Paper on "Building a Capital Markets Union"'. Available at http://www.savings-banks.com/press/positions/Pages/capital-markets-union.aspx. Last accessed: 2 March 2016.

European Commission (2015a) 'Green Paper: Building a Capital Markets Union', COM(2015) 63 final, 18 February. Available at http://eur-lex.europa.eu/legal-content/EN/TXT/PDF/?uri=COM:2015:63:FIN&from=EN. Last accessed: 8 February 2016.

European Commission (2015b) 'Action Plan on Building a Capital Markets Union', COM(2015) 468 final, 30 September. Available at http://eur-lex.europa.eu/legal-content/EN/TXT/PDF/?uri=CELEX:52015DC0468&from=EN. Last accessed: 3 March 2016.

European Commission (2015c) 'Feedback Statement on the Green Paper "Building a Capital Markets Union": Accompanying the Document Communication from the Commission to the European Parliament, the Council, the European Economic and Social Committee and the Committee of the Regions Action Plan on Building a Capital Markets Union', COM(2015) 468 final, SWD(2015) 183 final, 30 September. Available at http://ec.europa.eu/finance/consultations/2015/capital-markets-union/docs/summary-of-responses_en.pdf. Last accessed: 1 November 2015.

European Commission (2015d) 'Simpler Securitisation', 30 September. Available at http://ec.europa.eu/finance/capital-markets-union/docs/simpler-securitisation_en.pdf. Last accessed: 3 March 2016.

European Commission (2015e) 'Proposal for a Regulation of the European Parliament and of the Council Laying Down Common Rules on Securitisation and Creating a European Framework for Simple, Transparent and Standardised Securitisation and Amending Directives 2009/65/EC, 2009/138/EC, 2011/61/EU and Regulations (EC) No 1060/2009 and (EU) No 648/2012', COM(2015) 472 final, 2015/0226 (COD), 30 September. Available at http://eur-lex.europa.eu/legal-content/EN/TXT/PDF/?uri=CELEX:52015PC0472&from=EN. Last accessed: 12 February 2016.

European Commission (2015f) 'Proposal for a Regulation of the European Parliament and of the Council amending Regulation (EU) No 575/2013 on Prudential Requirements for Credit Institutions and Investment Firms', COM(2015) 473 final, 2015/0225 (COD), 30 September 2015. Available at http://eur-lex.europa.eu/legal-content/EN/TXT/PDF/?uri=CELEX:52015 PC0473&from=EN. Last accessed: 12 February 2016.

European Parliament and Council (2015) 'Regulation on the European Fund for Strategic Investments, the European Investment Advisory Hub and the European Investment Project Portal and amending Regulations (EU) No 1291/2013 and (EU) No 1316/2013 — the European Fund for Strategic Investments'. Available at http://eur-lex.europa.eu/legal-content/EN/TXT/PDF/? uri=CELEX:32015R1017&from=EN. Last accessed: 12 December 2015.

FESE (Federation of European Stock Exchanges) (2015) 'Response to the Commission's Consultation on the Green Paper on CMU'. Available at http://www.fese.eu/images/documents/position-papers/ 2015/FESE-Response_CMU-Green%20Paper-150513.pdf. Last accessed: 13 March 2016.

Finance Watch (2015) 'Who Will Benefit from the Capital Markets Union?' 29 September. Available at http://www.finance-watch.org/informer/blog/1150-who-will-benefit-from-cmu-fr?lang=fr. Last accessed: 2 March 2016.

Five Presidents' Report (2015) 'Completing Europe's Economic and Monetary Union', Available at https://ec.europa.eu/priorities/sites/beta-political/files/5-presidents-report_en.pdf. Last accessed: 13 September 2015.

German Bundesverband der Wertpapierfirmen (2015) 'Response to the Commission's Consultation on the Green Paper on CMU'. Available at https://ec.europa.eu/eusurvey/publication/ capital-markets-union-2015?language=en. Last accessed: 13 March 2016.

Germany (Federal Government of Germany, represented by the German Federal Ministry of Finance) (2015) 'Green Paper of the European Commission on a Capital Markets Union German Comments'. Available at https://ec.europa.eu/eusurvey/publication/capital-markets-union-2015. Last accessed: 13 March 2016.

Gouvernement français (2015) 'Response to the Commission's Consultation on the Green Paper on CMU: Priorités et objectifs de la France pour l'Union des marchés de capitaux'. Available at https://ec.europa.eu/eusurvey/files/99621bcb-cbc1-4673-ae30-da39f4e0b61e. Last accessed: 13 March 2016.

Hardie, I. and Howarth, D. (eds) (2013) *Market Based Banking and the International Financial Crisis* (Oxford: Oxford University Press).

Hill, J. (2015a) 'Unlocking Funding for Europe's Growth – European Commission consults on Capital Markets Union', Press Release IP/15/4433, date. Available at http://europa.eu/rapid/ press-release_IP-15-4433_en.htm. Last accessed: 12 November 2015.

Hill, J. (2015b) 'For a Financial Sector that Promotes Investment', Speech to the City of London Corporation Policy Committee, London, 15 July. Available at http://europa.eu/rapid/press-release_SPEECH-15-5380_en.htm. Last accessed: 1 February 2016.

Howarth, D. (2013) 'France and the International Financial Crisis: the Legacy of State-led Finance'. *Governance*, Vol. 26, No. 3, pp. 369–95.

Howarth, D. and Quaglia, L. (2013) 'Banking Union as Holy Grail: Rebuilding the Single Market in Financial Services, Stabilizing Europe's Banks and "Completing" Economic and Monetary Union'. *JCMS*, Vol. 49, No. s1, pp. 119–41.

Howarth, D. and Quaglia, L. (2014) 'The Steep Road to Banking Union: the Setting Up of the Single Resolution Mechanism'. *JCMS*, Vol. 50, No. s1, pp. 125–40.

Howarth, D. and Quaglia, L. (2015) 'The Political Economy of the Euro Area's Sovereign Debt Crisis: Introduction'. *Special Issue of the Review of International Political Economy*, Vol. 22, No. 3, pp. 457–84.

Howarth, D. and Quaglia, L. (2016) *The Political Economy of Banking Union* (Oxford Oxford University Press).

Intesa (2015) 'Response to the Commission's Consultation on the Green Paper on CMU'. Available online at: https://ec.europa.eu/eusurvey/publication/capital-markets-union-2015?language=en. Last accessed: 13 March 2016.

Ireland (2015) 'Irish Department of Finance Response to the Commission's Consultation on "Building a Capital Markets Union"'. Available at http://www.finance.gov.ie/sites/default/files/15-05-13%20Irish%20Department%20of%20Finance%20response%20to%20the%20Commission%20consultation%20on%20Building%20a%20Capital%20Markets%20Union.pdf. Last accessed: 2 March 2016.

Italy (Italian Ministry of the Economy and Finance) (2015) 'Building a Capital Markets Union: Italy's views on the Commission Green Paper', 21 May. Available at https://ec.europa.eu/eusurvey/publication/capital-markets-union-2015. Last accessed: 13 March 2016.

Jabko, N. (2006) *Playing the Market*: *A Political Strategy for Uniting Europe, 1985-2005* (Ithaca: Cornell University Press).

Juncker, J-C. (2014) 'Political Guidelines for the Next Commission', 15 July. Available at http://www.eesc.europa.eu/resources/docs/jean-claude-juncker--political-guidelines.pdf. Last accessed: 15 January 2016.

Lloyds (2015) 'Response to the Commission's Consultation on the Green Paper on CMU'. Available at https://ec.europa.eu/eusurvey/publication/capital-markets-union-2015?language=en. Last accessed: 13 March 2016.

MEDEF (*Mouvement des entreprises de France*) (2015) 'Response to the Commission's Consultation on the Green Paper on CMU'. Available at https://ec.europa.eu/eusurvey/publication/capital-markets-union-2015?language=en. Last accessed: 13 March 2016.

Merler, S. and Pisani-Ferry, J. (2012) 'Sudden Stops in the Euro Area'. *Bruegel Policy Contribution*, No. 2012/06.

Mügge, D. (2010) *Widen the Market, Narrow the Competition: Banker Interests and the Making of a European Capital Market* (Colchester: ECPR Press).

Netherlands (2015) 'Response of the Netherlands – European Commission Green Paper – Building a Capital Markets Union'. Available at https://www.rijksoverheid.nl/binaries/rijksoverheid/documenten/kamerstukken/2015/05/13/the-netherlands-response-to-ec-green-paper-capital-markets-union/the-netherlands-response-to-ec-green-paper-capital-markets-union.pdf. Last accessed: 2 March 2016.

Pesendorfer, D. (2015) 'Capital Markets Union and Ending Short-Termism: Lessons from the European Commission's Public Consultation'. *Law and Financial Markets Review*, Vol. 9, No. 3, pp. 202–9.

Quaglia, L. (2010) *Governing Financial Services in the European Union* (London: Routledge).

Ringe, W.G. (2015a) 'Capital Markets Union for Europe: A Commitment to the Single Market of 28'. *Law and Financial Markets Review*, Vol. 9, No. 1, pp. 5–7.

Ringe, W.G. (2015b) 'Capital Markets Union for Europe - A Political Message to the UK', Oxford Legal Studies Research Paper No. 26/2015, March. Available online at: http://papers.ssrn.com/sol3/papers.cfm?abstract_id=2575654. Last accessed: 2 March 2016.

Schäuble, W. and Sapin, M. (2015) 'Letter'. Available at http://www.economie.gouv.fr/files/files/PDF/2015-07-06_letter-about_capital-markets-union_6-july-2015.pdf. Last accessed: 10 September 2015.

Société Générale (2015) 'Response to the Commission's Consultation on the Green Paper on CMU'. Available at https://ec.europa.eu/eusurvey/publication/capital-markets-union-2015?language=en. Last accessed: 13 March 2016.

Story, J. and Walter, I. (1997) *Political Economy of Financial Integration in Europe*: *The Battle of the System* (Manchester: Manchester University Press).

Sweden (2015) 'The Swedish Government and the Swedish Authorities' Common Answer to the Commission Green Paper on Building a Capital Markets Union'. Available at http://www.fi.se/upload/43_Utredningar/30_Remissvar/2015/svenskt-svar-kapitalmarknadsunion-150513.pdf. Last accessed: 2 March 2016.

TheCityUK (2015) 'Capital Markets Union: The Perspective of European Growth Companies', October. Available at http://www.ey.com/Publication/vwLUAssets/ey-capital-markets-union-the-perspective-of-european-growth-companies/$FILE/ey-capital-markets-union-the-perspective-of-european-growth-companies.pdf. Last accessed: 23 February 2016.

Turner, Z. (2015) 'Money Matters: a Capital Markets Union Primer: Low-profile Commissioner Quietly Prepares Blockbuster Financial plan', *Politico*, 27 July. Available at http://www.politico.eu/article/moving-money-a-capital-markets-union-primer/. Last accessed: 4 March 2016.

Unicredit (2015) 'Response to the Commission's Consultation on the Green Paper on CMU'. Available at https://ec.europa.eu/eusurvey/publication/capital-markets-union-2015?language=en. Last accessed: 13 March 2016.

UK Government (2015) 'UK Response to the Commission Green Paper on Capital Markets Union: Building a Strong Capital Markets Union'. Available at https://ec.europa.eu/eusurvey/files/634a485d-8dd9-41e6-af91-030013307436. Last accessed: 12 December 2015.

Véron, N. (2014) 'Defining Europe's Capital Markets Union', *Bruegel Policy Contribution*, Working Paper No. 2014/12. Available online at: http://bruegel.org/2014/11/defining-europes-capital-markets-union/. Last accessed: 10 September 2015.

Véron, N. (2015) 'Europe's Capital Markets Union and the New Single Market Challenge', 30 September. Available at http://bruegel.org/2015/09/europes-capital-markets-union-and-the-new-single-market-challenge/. Last accessed: 5 November 2015.

Véron, N. and Wolff, G. (2015) 'Capital Markets Union: A Long-Term Vision', Prepared for the informal ECOFIN meeting in Riga, Latvia on April 25. Available at http://www.iie.com/publications/papers/Véron20150425.pdf. Last accessed: 2 February 2016.

Zimmerman, H. (2010) 'Varieties of Global Financial Governance? British and German Approaches to Financial Market Regulation'. In Helleiner, E., Pagliari, S. and Zimmerman, H. (eds) *Global Finance in Crisis* (London: Routledge), 121–38.

JCMS 2016 Volume 54. Annual Review pp. 204–217   DOI: 10.1111/jcms.12430

Europe as a Global Actor: Searching for a New Strategic Approach

KAROLINA POMORSKA and SOPHIE VANHOONACKER
Maastricht University

Introduction

The one image of 2015 that depicts a dramatic interaction between the EU and the rest of the world is the world-famous picture of the Syrian toddler Alan Kurdi, who together with at least 12 other Syrians, drowned in an attempt to reach the Greek island of Kos. Apart from symbolizing the human tragedy of the refugee crisis unfolding at the EU's external borders, the picture is also illustrative of broader developments and challenges for European foreign policy. It shows that crises in the neighbourhood and in seemingly faraway regions like Iraq and Afghanistan cannot simply be ignored as they can have an immediate impact on the EU's domestic situation. A second telling illustration of how internal and external security have become increasingly intertwined are the November terrorist attacks in Paris. After having been trained in Syria by representatives of the Islamic State of Iraq and the Levant (ISIS), radicalized EU nationals returned home to commit suicide attacks in the French national capital.

The acute crises of migration and terrorism have not only created the need for a revision of internal and external policies, they also revealed the necessity for new synergies between actors that used to operate in separate professional worlds. At the national level for instance, the blurring of borders between internal and external security required increased co-operation between the Ministries of the Interior and those of Foreign Affairs. As these two players have traditionally been driven by different agendas, this interaction is far from self-evident.[1] At the European level, it has created new room of manoeuvre for the European Commission, traditionally a rather marginal player in the field of European diplomacy but active in the area of Justice and Home Affairs.

Against this turbulent background, it was the task of the High Representative/Vice President (HRVP) Federica Mogherini to move forward with the development of a new Global Strategy. After presenting a strategic assessment of the EU's role in the world at the European Council in June 2015 (EEAS, 2015a), she spent the rest of the year consulting with the Member States and different stakeholders. Although the unstable international context gives a sense of urgency to the discussion, the cacophony in Brussels and amongst the Member States in the above-mentioned crises, indicates that coming up with a shared strategic outlook will be a challenging exercise.

In the same format as last year, this contribution consists of four sections. We first focus on the performance of the institutional actors involved in the EU's external relations. Because the post-Lisbon institutional setting is still relatively new, it is worthwhile

---

[1] This point was made by Geoffrey Edwards during his lecture at Maastricht University on 19 April 2016.

investigating how different actors have carved out their new roles and interacted with each other. In addition, we analyze how the new players such as Federica Mogherini, Donald Tusk and Jean-Claude Juncker have brought new dynamics into the Brussels institutional game. As a second step, we review the three key dimensions of the EU's external action: trade, security and diplomacy. In contrast to the 2014 review, when the section on security dealt primarily with the Common Security and Defence Policy (CSDP), this year it focuses on security in the broad sense of the word, including internal security.

I. Institutional Dynamics in Brussels and Beyond

The year 2015 was the first full year in office of European Council President Tusk, the HRVP Mogherini and Commission President Juncker. Although these new players have in many respects followed in the footsteps of their predecessors, there are also marked differences, both in terms of style and substance. During the term of Herman Van Rompuy and Catherine Ashton (2009–15), the attention of the President of the European Council and the HRVP was focused predominantly on internal affairs: dealing with the financial crisis and setting-up of the European External Action Service (EEAS). The leadership role of the previous Commission President Barosso had overall been rather limited, certainly in comparison with President Juncker.[2] The arrival of multiple ambitious characters in Brussels, each intending to play a role in external relations was bound to result not only in agenda-setting initiatives and activism but also in some rivalries. As we have seen from the examples of the Ukrainian crisis and negotiations with Turkey, European Council President Tusk convincingly fulfilled his early commitment to get involved in the EU's external relations. A European Council official was quoted saying that 'Tusk sees his role as going beyond that of only being a broker of compromises as that of being someone who can and should lead the way, when necessary, which sometimes also means more forceful statements'.[3] Tusk often spoke up in favour of sanctions against Russia and rallied support among the Member States. At the same time, his relationship with the 'Southern' Member States and the High Representative still left plenty of room for improvement, and this was not only due to their different positions on EU–Russia relations. For example, Tusk decided to play an active role in the refugee negotiations with Turkey and embarked on a visit to Ankara in September, against the advice of the EEAS and to the surprise of the service.[4]

Commission President Juncker has been remarkably active in the field of external action, gaining legitimacy from the increasing significance of policies such as migration, energy and enlargement, areas where the Commission has a well-established role and expertise. He was a visible face of the EU's foreign policy and did not hesitate to widely express his views on the EU's relations with Russia, Turkey and Syria. The Commission played a key role in searching for a plan to deal with the refugee crisis and Juncker did not shy away from political statements and putting pressure on the Member States. He occasionally found himself on a collision course with Tusk such as on the issue of migration quotas. Juncker stood up for a controversial policy plan insisting that he was 'perfectly aware that there is a large part of the public who does not want this, but it

[2] See Dinan's and Hodson's contributions to this volume.
[3] *Politico*, 22 October 2016.
[4] *Politico*, 10 February 2016.

has to be done'.[5] The reinforced role of the Commission was also highlighted in the ongoing debate on the Nord Stream 2 project. In December, 10 Member States[6] sent a letter to President Tusk, in which they claimed that 'the position of the European Commission on the Nord Stream 2 project will … influence the perception of the EU's common foreign and security policy among its core allies'.[7]

In the attempt to strengthen the role of the European Commission in external relations, President Juncker requested the new HRVP prioritize her role within the European Commission (Pomorska and Vanhoonacker, 2015, p. 218). Mogherini moved to the Berlaymont building and hired staff from the European Commission for the posts in her cabinet, a step towards more efficient co-operation between the Commission and the EEAS and a more 'joined-up' European foreign policy. Mogherini has been more media-friendly and visible than her predecessor. She has engaged in a dialogue with think-tanks and civil society, being present also on social media platforms like Twitter, often answering personally to her critics. However, even observers who generally praised her performance admit that there had been criticism inside the EEAS suggesting that Mogherini has been rather slow when taking decisions and did not embark on a more radical reform of her service as had been requested for example by the European Parliament (Cameron, 2015).

The need for reform and proposals for concrete changes had been recommended in the 2013 EEAS Review (EEAS, 2013). One of them was to re-balance the structure of the organization, which was very top-heavy, by reducing the number of senior posts. The restructuring took place in the summer but only partially addressed the criticism, as the number of managerial jobs merely decreased from 34 to 30 (Novotna, 2016, p. 2). Even though the Corporate Board with its four members was abolished, the service now has one Secretary General with three deputies. The CSDP part of the EEAS, mainly the EU Military Staff (EUMS), which were always thought to be somewhat disconnected from the rest of the service, were put on the same level as other Directorates General. The Eastern Member States have remained generally underrepresented in the EEAS. Poland, for example, was left with no comparable substitution for Deputy Secretary General Maciej Popowski. It is clear that the Italian presence in crucial positions has been very much strengthened, as was the case earlier with the British nationals serving under Catherine Ashton.

Ashton had also been criticized for not fully engaging as a co-ordinator of the external relations portfolios in the European Commission and in the EEAS. Even on the rare occasions when she was present at the co-ordination meetings it was the Commission President Barosso who insisted on taking the lead. With Juncker's guidance, Mogherini set out to change this state of affairs by leading the reactivated Commissioners Group on External Action. The Brussels-based Centre for European Policy Studies (CEPS) assessed that this move 'undoubtedly improved the Union's track-record in terms of the Union's coherence and visibility', introduced an element of pragmatism to the HRVP's actions and became 'a logical counterpart for the Foreign Affairs Council' (Blockmans and Russack, 2015, p. 13). However, this clear improvement in the working relationship

---

[5] *The Telegraph*, 9 September 2015.
[6] Bulgaria, the Czech Republic, Estonia, Greece, Hungary, Latvia, Lithuania, Poland, Romania and Slovakia.
[7] *Reuters*, 27 November 2015.

and coordination with the European Commission came with a risk of straining the relationship with the Member States. Indeed, some members of the Council questioned the role of the EU officials in international relations, but also informally complained of not being sufficiently consulted for example in the process of re-thinking the EU's Global Strategy.

After Mogherini's successful performance during her hearings at the European Parliament (EP) in 2014, the expectation was that she would prioritize the relationship between the EEAS and the Parliament, which indeed evolved positively in 2015. An agreement was signed in November that detailed how the EU delegations could provide assistance to the EP delegations (EEAS, 2015c). This was agreed on the basis of Article 5.7 of the Decision establishing the EEAS, which stipulated that the Union delegations should 'have the capacity to respond to the needs of other institutions of the Union, in particular the European Parliament, in their contacts with the international organisations or third countries'. The agreement clarified, for example, how the EP can make use of the premises of the EU delegations or how the delegations would provide support to Members of the European Parliament (MEPs) visiting third countries (including political and press expertise). There is now also a short assignment programme in place that resembles a staff exchange, which also facilitates the relationship between the EEAS and the EP.

One of the key priorities for the EEAS and the HRVP in 2015 was the preparation of the new EU Global Strategy. During the term of the first HRVP, the efforts by several Member States to push for a new security strategy failed. There were multiple reasons, not least the lack of enthusiasm on the part of the HRVP and some of her staff. In contrast, Mogherini had already showed a more positive and enthusiastic approach to this issue during her hearing in the European Parliament in October 2014. Based on a general mandate from the European Council in December 2013 (European Council, 2013), the HRVP and her closest staff worked throughout 2015 on the new strategic assessment of the EU's role in the world (EEAS, 2015a). The document was presented to the European Council in June. Several working methods were tried out, including an informal working group bringing together representatives of the EEAS, the Commission, Council Secretariat and the European Council. In turn, European leaders asked Mogherini to prepare an EU Global Strategy on Foreign and Security Policy by June 2016. In addition, Mogherini engaged in a consultation process over the new strategy through multiple events, co-organized with think-tanks, policy institutes but also with the broader public. She criticized the current agenda of the Foreign Affairs Council (FAC) for mainly being driven by crises, and advocated an EU foreign policy that is not merely reactive to global events. This strategic exercise, just like the European Security Strategy in 2003 when the EU was divided over Iraq, serves the internal function of overcoming divisions between the Member States who should agree on common priorities (Tocci, 2015, p. 116). Critics were quick to point out that such an approach may be dangerous and 'lull policy-makers into a false comfort zone', arguing the EU should move beyond seeing its foreign policy in terms of process and not outcomes and opt for a comprehensive goal-oriented approach (Raik et al., 2015, p. 7; Youngs, 2015).

While the HRVP has shown a very pro-active attitude with regards to the strategy, some Member States have complained they had not been consulted to a sufficient extent. There was a danger that the document would not be endorsed by the Council or that it would remain 'on paper with no follow-up' (Kaca, 2015). In addition, some capitals

perceived Mogherini as focusing too much on her own agenda with regards to the strategic review, which may in the end enlarge the role and power of the European Commission
and the EEAS. The fate of the 2003 strategy clearly shows that the commitment of the
Member States is crucial. While there is no final text agreed upon yet (at the time of writing), from what Mogherini presented in June 2015 it is clear that it will be a fundamentally different document than the previous strategy.

II. The European Union as a Market Actor

Parallel to the above-mentioned attempts to give a more strategic direction to EU external
action in general, the year 2015 also saw a parallel debate on the future direction of EU
trade policy. In October 2015, the European Commission adopted a new trade and investment strategy under the title 'Trade for all: Towards a More Responsible Trade and Investment Policy' (European Commission, 2015a). By proposing to base the policy on
the three pillars of effectiveness, transparency and values, the strategy tries to address
the challenges raised by newly emerging markets and the public perception of EU trade
policy being unresponsive to the demands of small businesses and the broader public.
In response to the economic recession of the past years, the document pleads for increased
responsiveness to new international developments such as digital trade and a better integration of EU trade policy with other dimensions of EU external action. The latter is in
line with the Lisbon Treaty's ambition to establish a more coherent European foreign policy as also expressed in the 2013 joint communication by the European Commission and
the HRVP on the comprehensive approach advocating a better use of the various instruments at the disposal of the EU in a more strategic and effective way (European Commission and HRVP, 2013).

A second key objective of the new strategy is to address the increasing public
disenchantment with the common commercial policy and its emphasis on deregulation
(European Commission, 2015b). This objective is to be realized by paying more attention
to the impact of trade liberalization processes on the job market and the European social
model. In response to the criticisms of the lack of transparency, it is proposed that key negotiation texts of international trade negotiations are made publicly available. The latter
may be a nice gesture but may also prove to be very good news for competing powers
rather than for the average European citizens themselves. A first step towards more
openness was made in December 2015 when, in the frame of the negotiations of the
Transatlantic Trade and Investment Partnership (TTIP), the European Commission agreed
to give every MEP access to all categories of confidential documents, including the draft
consolidated texts (European Parliament, 2015).

The strategy's third pillar on the importance of values is far from new but the Commission found it important to reaffirm its commitment to be 'a force for good' (Council of the
EU, 2003). It is indeed the case that close cooperation with players such as China who
turn a blind eye to human rights, have increasingly raised questions about the EU's sin-
cerity as a 'normative power' and led to the allegation that it is after all not that different
from traditional national foreign policies with their key focus on interests (Hyde-Price,
2006). In her foreword to the new strategy, Trade Commissioner Cecilia Malström emphasized that EU trade policy is not just about interests but also about values (European
Commission, 2015a). The fact that she deems it necessary to reaffirm this point, is an

indication of the fact that the rhetoric about 'normative power' Europe is met with increasing scepticism.

The 'Trade for All' document is also interesting as it gives insight into the EU's response to the crisis in the multilateral trade system. While still emphasizing the centrality of the WTO, it advocates a parallel strategy of investing in the conclusion of bilateral and regional agreements. As such, this merely confirms the EU's increased reliance on bilateral trade and investment agreements of the past years, as we also pointed out in our 2014 contribution to the *JCMS Annual Review* (Pomorska and Vanhoonacker, 2015). An illustration of this in 2015 was the conclusion of the Free Trade Agreement with Vietnam, which built on a Partnership and Cooperation Agreement (PCA) signed in 2012. Although Vietnam is a relatively small player, the agreement is also of broader relevance in three respects. Through its emphasis on sustainable development in fields like labour, the environment and natural resources, it is considered to also serve as an example for future agreements with other developing countries. Secondly, it is expected to be a stepping stone for the conclusion of a region-to-region agreement with the Association of Southeast Asian Nations (ASEAN), the EU's largest trading partner outside Europe after the US and China. Earlier attempts to negotiate such a regional agreement had given way to a bilateral approach in 2009. In 2014, the EU had already set up an Free Trade Agreement (FTA) with Singapore and negotiations with Thailand and Malaysia were still ongoing. Thirdly and most importantly, the FTA includes a new approach to investment protection and more particularly a permanent investment dispute resolution system including an appeal mechanism rather than *ad hoc* arbitration panels. As is well known, the dispute settlement issue is one of the most heavily contested issues of both the EU–Canada Comprehensive Economic and Trade Agreement (CETA) and the ongoing TTIP negotiations.

As a matter of fact, the CETA text, which still needed to be ratified by the Council and the EP at the time of writing, has been adjusted in line with the new Investor State Dispute Settlement (ISDS) clauses of the FTA with Vietnam (European Commission, 2016). At the core of the concerns are the provisions for investment arbitration. The original set-up with temporary arbitration panels bypassing domestic courts, led to fears about the possibility of massive corporate litigations against the EU or its Member States. One of the big concerns was that in order to prevent such litigations, states would become more reluctant to introduce stringent rules in the field of health, the environment or other policy fields, and would prioritize private interests of big firms over those of the general public (Barlow, 2015).

The new approach to dispute settlement has also been extended to the TTIP negotiations but it is doubtful whether this will be enough to convince the increasingly loud critics of the agreement. By November 2015, only 53 per cent of EU citizens still supported TTIP, a further decrease of 3 per cent from May and 5 per cent lower than in 2014 (European Commission, 2014, 2015b). At the same time, the numbers against TTIP rose from 28 (May 2015) to 32 per cent (European Commission, 2015b). The fall in support has been particularly marked in the Netherlands, Ireland, Malta and several central European countries (Bulgaria, Czech Republic, Hungary). It may not be accidental that, in many of these states, right-wing populist parties have been on the rise, successfully exploiting domestic fears for the further opening up of markets and the negative impact of globalization. The fiercest opponents against TTIP, however, were to be found in

Austria (70 per cent against) and Germany (59 per cent against). In these countries, NGOs and civil society organizations have been very successful in mobilizing public fears, especially in sensitive fields such as food security, environmental issues as well as the earlier mentioned ISDS. Stories about American chlorinated chickens ('*Chlorhühnchen*') conveyed the picture of TTIP as a threat to the high European food safety standards and did little good to its overall image (Hamilton, 2014; Hamilton and Blockmans, 2015). The national debates about TTIP clearly illustrate that, even if the Commission is the key negotiator of this international trade deal, domestic politics still matter greatly. This is especially the case since the agreement will most probably be earmarked as a mixed agreement, which would imply that it would not only have to be ratified by the Council and the EP but also at the national level. With 28 Member States, each with their own sensitivities and political particularities, it remains very difficult to predict how the negotiations will develop in the future. As we have seen in the Netherlands with the non-binding referendum on the association agreement with Ukraine, disenchanted citizens do not hesitate to take every opportunity to express their dissatisfaction, even if this implies holding the entire EU hostage. Although the EU needs the economic boost that could be triggered by TTIP, it remains to be seen whether the economic rationale will be able to outweigh the more cultural and social concerns that it has raised. The change of government in the US in 2017 is a further complicating factor for the negotiations and the ratification process.

III. The EU as a Security Actor

With the ongoing crises in Ukraine and Syria, the massive wave of refugees and the bloody terrorist attacks in Paris in November, 2015 was a very challenging year for European security. If it were still alive, the hope that the post-Cold War period would be one of long peace and stability was definitely shattered. The above-mentioned events and the EU's response (or lack of it) gave the debate on an EU Global Strategy on Foreign and Security Policy a lot of food for thought, both with regards to the changing nature of international security challenges as well as the future shape of the EU's role as a security provider. As the responses to the conflicts in Ukraine and the Middle East are covered elsewhere in this volume, this section mainly focuses on the refugee crisis and the jihadist terrorist threat, two examples of how the traditional divide between external and internal security is dissolving and how security can no longer be reduced to just military security.

The refugee crisis, which is in the first place a humanitarian crisis, has confronted the EU with a real test. While in 2014 the number of people that had lodged an asylum claim in one of the Member States amounted to 600,000, in 2015 it had already risen to more than 1 million (Eurostat, 2016). Although this is still much lower than in Turkey and some of Syria's other neighbours, the chaos caused by the massive arrival in a concentrated number in southern and eastern European locations, meant that the initial sympathy for those fleeing from war zones did not last long. Populist appeals thriving on the widespread malaise since the euro crisis, exploited the refugee wave to further nurture simmering emotions of anxiety and xenophobia. With the massive inflows in Greece and Italy, the Dublin regulation whereby asylum applications need to be handled by the Member State where an asylum seeker first enters, had become unsustainable. Many Member States, especially in Central and Eastern Europe, were extremely reluctant to move towards a sharing scheme whereby the absorption of refugees would be organized on a proportional basis. The agreement of September 2015 to relocate 160,000 refugees across the EU was reached only due to the exceptional use of a qualified majority vote.[8]

By the end of the year only 272 refugees had been welcomed by another Member State (European Foreign Policy Scoreboard, 2016). These figures were disappointing but not surprising. Despite the EU's rhetoric about its normative ambitions and chancellor Merkel's efforts to engage the other EU leaders in a more welcoming approach, Member States in the first place resorted to national measures such as the temporary closure of borders. At the European level, the Commission and the European Council mainly invested in the control of the EU's external borders and in cooperation and reliance on third countries (Carrera and den Hertog, 2016). The first was well illustrated by the launching of the military naval operation EUNAVFOR MED (Council Decision, 2015) and the revamping of Frontex by transforming it into a European Border and Coast Guard with increased competencies, staff and equipment (European Commission, 2015c). EU EUNAVFOR, which has its operational headquarters in Rome, aims to stop human smugglers in the Mediterranean by identifying their networks and seizing their assets (Carrera and Den Hertog, 2016). The second strategy of relying on third countries was exemplified by the fierce attempts to reach a deal with Turkey, one of the main gateways used by the migrants and refugees used to reach the EU. In late November 2015, the EU and Ankara reached an agreement whereby the latter would help to stem the flow of migrants by tackling people smugglers and policing its sea borders. In exchange, Brussels consented to provide humanitarian and financial support (€3 billion) to accommodate the refugees, to revitalise the stalled accession talks, and to ease the visa rules for Schengen countries by October 2016 (European Council, 2015a, 2015b).

Next to the refugee crisis, the second key security threat that proved to be a challenging test for the EU's role as a security provider in 2015 was that of terrorism.[9] Falling under the scope of EU internal security and being handled in the frame of EU justice and police co-operation, it is a case traditionally handled outside the frame of CSDP. In January, 12 cartoonists of the Paris-based satirical weekly magazine *Charlie Hebdo* were killed by Islamist gunmen and on 13 November the mass shooting by Islamic fundamentalists in the same city, catapulted counter-terrorist co-operation to the top of the EU agenda. Although both events led to widespread popular outrage all over the EU and all Member States backed the French UN resolution urging countries to adopt all necessary measures against the self-declared Islamic State, the events also showed the limits of EU cooperation. Following the November attacks, French President Francois Hollande 'Europeanized' the aggression and elevated it to a security problem, beyond that of justice and home affairs by invoking for the first time the EU's mutual defence clause (Article 42.7 of the Treaty on European Union (TEU)) (Faleg, 2015). In the absence of a common European army, the response to the French demand for assistance was organized on a bilateral basis. The UK joined the US-led airstrikes against IS on Syria and Germany committed planes and personnel while abstaining from joining the air strikes (European Council on Foreign Relations, 2016).

---

[8] *The Guardian*, 23 October 2015. See also Monar's contribution to this volume.
[9] See also Monar's contribution to this volume.

The ease with which some of the terrorists returned easily to their homes in Brussels well illustrated the broader vulnerability of a border-free EU to terrorism and highlighted the need for better intelligence-sharing and police co-operation to identify networks of terrorists and foreign fighters. On 20 November the EU ministers of Justice and Home Affairs agreed to step up external border controls and to take new steps in information sharing. An important initiative was the decision to establish a European Counter Terrorist Centre (ECTC) within Europol. The main aim of the centre, which became operational in January 2016, is to increase the information exchange between law enforcement centres, provide analysis and co-ordinate action in case of major terrorist attacks (European Council and Council of the European Union, 2015).

In short, 2015 was an extremely challenging year for the EU as a security provider, confronting it with new challenges for which it was only partially equipped. While the multiple extraordinary European Councils showed that most national governments recognized the need for European solutions to the trans-boundary problems they were facing, nationalist reflections against a background of increasing support for populist parties were never far away and the track record of European solidarity after more than 60 years of European integration was rather weak.

IV. The EU as a Diplomatic Actor

While in the area of trade the emphasis has primarily been on bilateral interaction, in the field of diplomacy we have seen a combination of both bilateral as well as multilateral dealings. Possibly the most significant diplomatic achievement in 2015 was the finalization of the nuclear deal with Iran in July. The joint comprehensive plan of action stipulated that Iran would convert and reduce its nuclear facilities and that the long imposed economic sanctions would be lifted. The agreement owed much to Mogherini's predecessor and the US which took a leading role in the last stages of negotiations. This success story sharply contrasts with that of the poor progress in the resolution of the Syrian crisis. It is only since mid-2015, partly due to the changed relationship with Iran, that we witnessed intensification in diplomatic efforts aimed at finding a political settlement. The EU was certainly not in the lead but was involved alongside other actors such as the US, Iran, Saudi Arabia and Russia. Prior to the Foreign Affairs Council in Luxembourg in October 2015, Mogherini took a cautious approach to Russia's aggressive air strike campaign in Syria, claiming that it was 'neither positive nor negative' but a 'game-changer' with worrying aspects (Mogherini, 2015). The EU was represented by Mogherini during the Vienna peace talks that started in November 2015 bringing together 20 participants under the umbrella of the International Syria Support Group (ISSG). Those in the lead, however, were primarily the US and Russia.

Another major international crisis that continued throughout 2015 took place in Libya. Mogherini was involved in looking for ways to build a new unity government, for example, trying to mount diplomatic support in the United Nations. The first half of the year she discussed in the Foreign Affairs Council the introduction of sanctions such as travel bans and freezing of assets, against individuals, which were introduced during the summer. For the EU, the UN-brokered unity government was particularly important as it was hoped that it would be able to combat the self-declared Islamic State in the north of the country and contribute to the reduction of African migrants to the EU. Still, amidst these activities, the EU was criticized for remaining merely a 'payer not a player' when it came to the Middle East (Hiltermann, 2015).

The example of Turkey showed that the formal division of tasks is not easily translated into practice and different actors compete with one another. The Commission was active with Vice President Frans Timmermans being given the task of acting as the main negotiator in the relationship with Turkey, in co-operation with the Commissioner for Neighbourhood Johannes Hahn and Christian Danielsson, Director General for the Neighbourhood and Enlargement. While Mogherini agreed to be the one taking care of overall foreign policy co-ordination, it is no secret that the co-ordination between the European Council President Tusk and the EEAS left much room for improvement. For example, Tusk's arrival in Ankara in the autumn was not well-coordinated with the External Action Service.

One of the most positive achievements in 2015 was that the Member States remained united on the issue of sanctions against Russia. The restrictive measures were linked to the second ceasefire agreement, called 'Minsk II', which had been negotiated in the so-called Normandy format involving Russia, Ukraine, France and Germany. The latter two countries represented the EU, without the active participation of the EEAS. Chancellor Merkel played a key role in the process and the role of both Member States was largely seen in a positive light. Member States' diplomats reported being kept in the loop by the German negotiators. While the EEAS was absent in the Normandy format of the negotiations it had been active in its support for the involvement of the Organisation for Security and Cooperation in Europe (OSCE) (see, for example, EEAS, 2015b). Both the HRVP and the Commission President undertook initiatives that took even some insiders by surprise. On 14 January, Mogherini circulated a letter to the Member States proposing a possible conditional 'roll-back' on sanctions against Russia and engaging in an informal dialogue on technical issues, such as customs or transit of goods with the Euroasian Economic Union.[10] The initiative was not endorsed by the Member States, however, following Russia's non-compliance with the Minsk agreements. Several states were unhappy, seeing it as going back to 'business as usual', while the paper was criticized for misunderstanding the driving factors of Russia's foreign policy (Liik, 2015). Commission President Juncker wrote a letter to the Russian President Putin on 16 November praising the idea of an 'integrated trade area linking Lisbon to Vladivostok' as an important and valuable objective. Those Member States advocating a tough stance towards Russia, like Poland and Lithuania, raised their concerns over this initiative and emphasized that the opinion expressed in the letter was a personal view of the Commission President and certainly not the opinion of the European Union. In a common letter sent to the High Representative and the Trade Commissioner on 11 December, both Member States demanded that the EU stopped sending optimistic and encouraging signals to Moscow at 'a sensitive moment' in their relations.[11]

In terms of multilateral diplomacy, the positive news in 2015 came from Paris, where at the UN Climate Change conference the first ever global and legally binding deal on the reduction of climate change was reached. Under the leadership of its Foreign Minister Laurent Fabius, France played the leading role of an effective host enjoying support from

[10] *EU Observer*, 14 January 2015.
[11] *EU Observer*, 15 December 2015.

the other EU Member States. The EU received well-deserved praise for its performance and its more pragmatic approach, adjusted after the failure in Copenhagen in 2009. Less positive signals, however, came from the Review Conference of the States Party to the Treaty on the Non-Proliferation of Nuclear Weapons (NPT) held in May. No agreement was reached and the EU's performance was very much undermined by the disagreement among the Member States on the issues of nuclear disarmament and the use of nuclear energy. This stood in contrast to the EU's more effective past performances in the NPT Review Conferences. The fact that the EU's Council Working Group was unable to find a common language in the run-up to the Conference was already worrying (Dee, 2015, p. 600). The lack of internal agreement limited the actions that could have been taken by the EEAS, which was officially representing the Union in the negotiations. The requests by EEAS officials to attend closed room sessions with Member States' officials were denied (Dee, 2015, p. 602). Finally, the EU's diplomacy in the United Nations was confronted by a powerful opposition, mostly on the part of Russia, who vetoed a resolution for an investigation of the MH17 flight, twice vetoed a British proposal for commemoration of the Srebrenica massacre and opposed the EU's efforts for obtaining a UN authorization for anti-trafficking operations in the Mediterranean (ECFR, 2016, p. 26). On the more positive side, the EU Member States contributed to the signing of the Sustainable Development Goals (SDGs) (ECFR, 2016, p. 27).

Conclusion

While traditionally the external action of the EU was all about the Union reaching out to the world, in 2015 the dominant picture was one of the world coming to the EU, forcing the Union and its Member States to take positions on a couple of very challenging issues. On the institutional level, the new players provided new dynamics in their interactions and revived struggles for influence. President Tusk clearly took a more active role in European foreign policy than his predecessor whose attention had been totally absorbed by the eurozone crisis. For HRVP Mogherini, an important difference with Ashton, her predecessor, was that she privileged the 'VP part' of her job much more, symbolized by her move to the Berlaymont. As we have seen, however, this novel direction was not always appreciated by the Foreign Ministers in the Council. Last but not least, we also saw a much more active role by the European Commission and its President Juncker. While on the one hand this is certainly linked to his personality and vast experience in EU policy-making, on the other hand, many important foreign policy issues such as the conflict in Ukraine or the migration crisis had direct links with policy areas such as energy and enlargement that fall within the Commission competences.

One of the most interesting developments confirmed in this review was the increasing blurring between what is internal and external to the EU. A successful conclusion of the TTIP negotiations will depend as much on the capacity of the Member States to address a critical public opinion as on the interaction between negotiators in Brussels and the US. The firm opposition by civil society organizations illustrates that 'foreign policy can never be abstracted from the domestic context from which it springs' (Hill, 2016, p. 43). The refugee crisis was both addressed with traditional Justice and Home Affairs instruments as well as with the CSDP instrument of a military operation. Also in the case of jihadist terrorism, we saw a combination of internal policy measures such as increased information exchange and a revamped Frontex with external actions such as a more active diplomatic role in the Syria crisis. The inside and the outside became profoundly linked with each other, without a clear demarcation line. For a Union characterized by fragmented policy-making procedures between internal and external policies this need for joined-up policy-making is a real challenge.

Luckily 2015 was not merely one of doom and gloom for EU external action. Successes like the Iran nuclear deal and the important role during the climate negotiations underlined the strengths of the EU as an international player. Decades of co-operation and increased institutionalization made the Union a respected foreign policy actor with an impact on the international scene. However, as we can observe in the case of the problematic negotiations on the Treaty on the Non-Proliferation of Nuclear Weapons, such accomplishments still depend on a minimum level of agreement amongst the Member States who continue to have the last word.

The rapidly changing European and international context gave Mogherini and her staff plenty of input for the draft of the Global Strategy. At least two lessons can be drawn at the conclusion of 2015. Firstly, the ESS 2003 picture of 'a secure and prosperous Europe in a better world' no longer corresponds with what we see today. Secondly, it no longer makes sense to make an external (Council of the EU, 2003) and internal security strategy (European Council, 2010) as was the case in the past. It is therefore to be hoped that the revised document will present an integrated approach and novel ideas about the policy and governance challenges raised by the increasingly overlapping internal and external challenges.

References

Barlow, M. (2015), 'Fighting TTIP, CETA and ISDS: Lessons from Canada'. Available online at: http://www.globaljustice.org.uk/resources/fighting-ttip-ceta-and-isds-lessons-canada. Last accessed: 20 March 2016.

Blockmans, S. and Russack, S. (2015) 'The Commissioner's Group on External Action – Key Political Facilitator', *CEPS Special Report No. 125* (Brussels: CEPS).

Cameron, F. (2015) 'Mogherini: Dousing the Flames of a Baptism by Fire', *EUObserver*, 6 October 2015. Available online at: https://euobserver.com/opinion/130574. Last accessed: 4 April 2016.

Carrera, S. and Den Hertog, L. (2016) 'A European Border and Coast Guard: Fit for Purpose?' *CEPS Commentary*, 24 February. Available online at: https://www.ceps.eu/publications/european-border-and-coast-guard-what's-name. Last accessed: 27 April 2016.

Council of the EU (2003) 'A Secure Europe in a Better World. European Security Strategy', 12 December, Available online at: http://www.consilium.europa.eu/uedocs/cmsUpload/78367.pdf. Last accessed: 28 April 2016.

Council Decision (CFSP) (2015) '2015/972 of 22 June 2015 Launching the European Union Military Operation in the Southern Central Mediterranean (EUNAVFOR MED)', *Official Journal of the EU*, L 157, 51, 23 June.

Dee, M. (2015) 'The EU's Performance in the 2015 NPT Review Conference: What Went Wrong'. *European Foreign Affairs Review*, Vol. 20, No. 4, pp. 591–608.

EEAS (2013) 'EEAS Review'. Available online at: http://eeas.europa.eu/library/publications/2013/3/2013_eeas_review_en.pdf. Last accessed: 2 March 2016.

EEAS (2015a) 'Strategic Review – The European Union in a Changing Global Environment. A More Connected, Contested and Complex World'. Available online at: https://europa.eu/ globalstrategy/en/strategic-review-european-union-changing-global-environment.   Last accessed: 16 April 2016.

EEAS (2015b) Statement by High Representative/Vice-President Federica Mogherini at the OSCE Ministerial Council in Belgrade, 3 December. Available online at: http://eeas.europa.eu/state-ments-eeas/2015/151203_01_en.htm. Last accessed: 2 April 2016.

EEAS (2015c) 'EEAS Guidelines for visits by the European Parliament Delegations (July 2015)', Brussels, Ref. Ares(2015)4800543, 3 November.

European Commission (2014) 'Public Opinion in the European Union, First Results', *Standard Eurobarometer*, 82. Available online at: http://ec.europa.eu/public_opinion/archives/eb/eb82/ eb82_first_en.pdf. Last accessed: 20 March 2016.

European Commission (2015a), 'Trade for All: Towards a More Responsible Trade And Invest-ment Policy'. Available online at: http://trade.ec.europa.eu/doclib/docs/2015/october/ tradoc_153846.pdf. Last accessed: 20 April 2016.

European Commission (2015b) 'Public Opinion in the European Union. First Results', *Standard Eurobarometer*, 83. Available online at: http://ec.europa.eu/public_opinion/archives/eb/eb83/ eb83_first_en.pdf. Last accessed: 20 April 2016.

European Commission (2015c) 'Securing Europe's External Borders. A European Border and Coast Guard'. Available online at: http://ec.europa.eu/dgs/home-affairs/what-we-do/policies/securing-eu-borders/fact-sheets/docs/a_european_border_and_coast_guard_en.pdf. Last accessed: 17 June 2016

European Commission (2016) 'Joint Statement Canada-EU Comprehensive Economic and Trade Agreement (CETA)', 29 February. Available online at: http://trade.ec.europa.eu/doclib/docs/ 2016/february/tradoc_154330.pdf. Last accessed: 17 April 2016.

European Commission and High Representative of the European Union (2013) 'Joint Communi-cation to the European Parliament and the Council: The EU's Comprehensive Approach to external Conflict and Crises', JOIN (2013) 30 final, 11 December.

European Council and Council of the European Union (2015) 'Conclusions of the Council of the EU and the Member States meeting within the Council on Counter Terrorism', 20 November. Available online at: http://www.consilium.europa.eu/en/press/press-releases/2015/11/20-jhaconclusions-counter-terrorism/. Last accessed: 27 April 2016.

European Council (2010) 'Internal security strategy for the European Union. Towards a European security model (Brussels: Council General Secretariat)'. Available online at: https://www.consilium. europa.eu/uedocs/cms_data/librairie/PDF/QC3010313ENC.pdf. Last accessed: 17 June 2016.

European Council (2013) 'Conclusions', 20 December. Available online at: https://www.consilium. europa.eu/uedocs/cms_data/docs/pressdata/en/ec/140245.pdf. Last accessed: 4 April 2016.

European Council (2015a) 'Conclusions', 19 March. Available online at: http://www.consilium. europa.eu/en/press/press-releases/2015/03/conclusions-russia-ukraine-european-council-march-2015/. Last accessed: 5 April 2016.

European Council (2015b) 'Meeting of Heads of State or Government with Turkey – EU-Turkey Statement', 29 November. Available online at: http://www.consilium.europa.eu/en/press/press-releases/2015/11/29-eu-turkey-meeting-statement/. Last accessed: 27 April 2016.

European Council on Foreign Relations (2016) 'European Foreign Policy Scorecard 2016'. Available online at: http://www.ecfr.eu/scorecard/2016. Last accessed: 5 April 2016.

European Parliament (2015) 'All MEPs to Have Access To All Confidential TTIP Documents'. Available online at: http://www.europarl.europa.eu/sides/getDoc.do?pubRef=-%2F%2FEP% 2F%2FTEXT%2BIM-PRESS%2B20151202IPR05759%2B0%2BDOC%2BXML%2BV0% 2F%2FEN&language=RO. Last accessed: on 20 April 2016.

Eurostat (2016) 'Asylum Quarterly Report'. Available online at: http://ec.europa.eu/eurostat/statis-tics-explained/index.php/Asylum_quarterly_report. Last accessed: 27 April 2016.

Faleg, G. (2015) 'European Security after the Paris Attacks', *CEPS Commentary*, 24 November. Available online at: https://www.ceps.eu/publications/european-security-after-paris-attacks. Last accessed: 27 April 2016.

Hamilton, D. (2014) 'Transatlantic Challenges: Ukraine, TTIP and the Struggle to be Strategic'. *JCMS*, Vol. 53, No. s1, pp. 25–39.

Hamilton D. and Blockmans, S. (2015) 'The Geostrategic Implications of TTIP', *CEPS Report No.105* (Brussels: Centre for European Policy Studies).

Hill, C. (2016) *Foreign Policy in the Twenty-First Century* (London: Palgrave Macmillan).

Hiltermann, J. (2015) Europe's Middle East Myopia, Crisis Group, http://www.crisisgroup.org/en/regions/middle-east-north-africa/op-eds/hiltermann-europe-s-middle-east-myopia.aspx Last accessed: 4 April 2016

Hyde-Price, A. (2006) '"Normative" Power Europe: A Realist Critique', *Journal of European Public Policy*, Vol.13, No. 2, pp. 217–34.

Kaca, E. (2015) 'The Labours of HR Federica Mogherini: Her Pursuit of a Strategy and Effectiveness', PISM Strategic File No. 14(77), Warsaw. Available online at: https://www.pism.pl/files/?id_plik=20163. Last accessed: 15 April 2016.

Liik, K. (2015) 'The Real Problem with Mogherini's Russia Paper', *ECFR Commentary*. Available online at: http://www.ecfr.eu/article/commentary_the_real_problem_with_mogherinis_russia_paper402. Last accessed: 15 March 2016.

Mogherini, F. (2015) 'Doorstep Remarks before the Foreign Affairs Council in Luxembourg', 12 October. Available online at: https://youtu.be/QMa8Q1pQ3N4. Last accessed: 10 April 2016.

Novotna, T. (2016) 'Not a Leap but a Step in the Right Direction: Mogherini's Structural and Personnel Reform of the EU's Diplomatic Service', EUROPEUM, March 2016. Available online at: http://europeum.org/data/articles/novotna-eeas-appointments.pdf. Last accessed: 14 April 2016.

Pomorska, K. and Vanhoonacker, S. (2015) 'Europe as a Global Actor: the (Un)Holy Trinity of Economy, Diplomacy and Security'. *JCMS*, Vol. 53, No. s1, pp. 216–29.

Raik, K., Helwig, N. and Iso-Markku, T. (2015) 'Crafting the EU Global Strategy. Building Blocks for a Stronger Europe', FIIA Briefing Paper No. 188.

Tocci, N. (2015) 'Towards an EU global strategy'. In Missiroli, A. (ed.) *An EU Global Strategy: Background, Process, References* (Paris: EU Institute for Security Studies), pp. 115–20.

Youngs, R. (2015) 'Will the EU's Global Strategy Meet the Foreign Policy Challenges of the Future?' Carnegie Europe. Available online at: http://carnegieeurope.eu/2015/10/15/will-eu-s-global-strategy-meet-foreign-policy-challenges-of-future/ij51. Last accessed: 5 April 2016.

JCMS 2016 Volume 54. Annual Review pp. 218–224   DOI: 10.1111/jcms.12405

Chronology: The European Union in 2015

CHARLOTTE GALPIN
University of Copenhagen

At a Glance

Presidencies of the EU Council: Latvia (1 January–30 June) and Luxembourg (1 July–31 December).

January

1	Lithuania adopts the euro, bringing the number of eurozone members to 19.
7	A terrorist attack takes place at the Paris office of French satirical newspaper *Charlie Hebdo*. Twelve people are shot dead by Islamist gunmen, including the editor and several cartoonists.
11	In a run-off election, Kolinda Grabar-Kitarović of the Croatian Democratic Union (HDZ) becomes the first female president of Croatia.
11	New EU rules for the protection of domestic violence victims come into force, allowing easier recognition of restraining orders.
14	Having previously announced his intention to resign on account of his age, Italian president Giorgio Napolitano steps down.
19	The Commission and European Investment Bank (EIB) launch fi-compass, an advisory service on financial instruments, part of the EU Investment Plan.
21	German, French, Russian and Ukrainian foreign ministers agree to establish security zones during talks on the Ukraine crisis in Berlin.
22	The European Central Bank (ECB) launches a bond-buying programme of €60 billion per month to support the eurozone economy.
25	In a snap general election in Greece, anti-austerity party Syriza wins the most seats but falls just short of an absolute majority. Alexis Tsipras becomes Greek Prime Minister, replacing Antonis Samaras of New Democracy.
26–27	The first European Migration Forum takes place in Brussels.

February

2	Centre-left candidate Sergio Mattarella is elected President of Italy in the fourth round of parliamentary voting.
5	NATO sets up command centres in Central and Eastern Europe, including Poland, Romania, Bulgaria, Latvia, Lithuania and Estonia.
8	Representatives of 190 countries meet for climate negotiations in Geneva ahead of the 21st Conference of the Parties (COP) to be held in Paris in November.
11	The Greek parliament votes to support Prime Minister Tsipras' plan to cancel Greece's EU/IMF bailout programme.
12	At talks in Minsk, leaders of Belarus, Ukraine, Russia, France and Germany agree to a ceasefire in Ukraine to take effect on 15 February.

12	At an informal European Council summit in Brussels, EU leaders discuss the conflict in Ukraine, counter-terrorism measures, the Greek crisis and improving economic and monetary union (EMU).
17	The EU announces €234 million in development aid to Zimbabwe for the first time since the introduction of sanctions in 2002, as part of the National Indicative Programme (NIP) for Zimbabwe.
23	In a breakdown of the Minsk ceasefire agreement, two people are killed in an explosion in the eastern Ukrainian city of Kharkiv.
24	The Eurogroup approves an extension of Greece's bailout programme by four months, after the Greek government accepts new reform measures.
25	The Commission publishes a Communication on its strategy to create an Energy Union, including a blueprint for a global climate change agreement.
27	Boris Nemtsov, a Russian opposition leader, is shot dead in Moscow.

March

1	In a parliamentary election in Estonia, the centre-right Reform Party comes first and Prime Minister Taavi Rõivas is re-elected.
6	The EU announces further sanctions against Syria, freezing the EU assets of supporters of President Bashar al-Assad and barring their entry into the EU.
10	EU finance ministers agree to extend the deadline for France to reach EU budget deficit limits. They also approve Commission President Juncker's Investment Plan Fund.
10	The Parliament votes to limit interchange fees on European card payments.
12	Iceland officially withdraws its application for EU membership.
15	Romanian Finance Minister Darius Vâlcov resigns amid corruption allegations.
18	The Commission proposes a Tax Transparency Package to deal with corporate tax avoidance.
19–20	At the European Council, EU leaders agree to move towards an Energy Union. Other topics discussed include external relations, including eastern partnerships, Russia and Ukraine, Libya and the European economy.
24	The EU lifts restrictions on development cooperation with Guinea-Bissau.
29	The conservative opposition party UMP and its allies come first in run-off local elections in France. The National Front wins more than 60 seats but no councils.

April

1	The EU lifts milk quotas for dairy farmers that had been in place since 1984.
9	The Nordic nations (Denmark, Sweden, Norway, Finland and Iceland) announce increased defence cooperation and solidarity with Baltic countries.
12	Italian authorities announce 3,791 migrants have been rescued by the Italian coastguard in one day, the highest number of the year so far. On 19 April, at least 800 people die in a boat that capsizes off the coast of Libya, bringing the total number of deaths in the Mediterranean Sea up to that point in 2015 to 1,500.
13	French, German, Russian and Ukrainian foreign ministers meet in Berlin to discuss the ceasefire in eastern Ukraine.
14–15	G7 foreign ministers meet in Lübeck.
14	The European Parliament approves an agreement on legislation limiting how the EU's 10 per cent target for renewable energy in transport fuels can be met. The contribution of crop-based biofuels is capped at 7 per cent, with the remaining 3 per cent deriving from alternative biofuels and renewable electricity.

19   In parliamentary elections in Finland, the opposition Centre Party comes first, followed by the Eurosceptic Finns Party and Prime Minister Alexander Snubb's National Coalition in third place. After forming a centre-right coalition, the Centre Party's Juha Sipilä becomes Prime Minister on 29 May.

23   A special meeting of the European Council is held to discuss the loss of life in the Mediterranean Sea. EU leaders agree to measures intended to limit illegal migration flows, increase funding for the EU's search and rescue Operation Triton, fight traffickers and ensure internal EU solidarity on asylum.

26   In a run-off presidential election in Northern Cyprus, left-wing moderate Mustafa Akıncı beats incumbent Derviş Eroğlu with 60 per cent of the vote.

27–28   17th EU–Ukraine summit is held in Kyiv, as violence intensifies in the conflict zone.

28   The Commission publishes its European Agenda on Security to cover the period 2015–20.

May

5   The EU agrees to withdraw surplus pollution allowances under the EU's emissions trading system (ETS) and to place them in a new market stability reserve from 2019.

6   The Commission publishes its Digital Single Market Strategy.

7   In parliamentary elections in the United Kingdom, the Conservative Party wins an outright majority and David Cameron is re-elected Prime Minister. Cameron promises to hold a referendum on Britain's EU membership by the end of 2017.

13   The Commission announces a European Agenda on Migration to respond to the growing crisis in the Mediterranean.

15   Romania's Regional Development Minister, Liviu Dragnea, is convicted on corruption charges relating to the 2012 impeachment of former Romanian President Traian Băsescu.

21–22   The Eastern Partnership summit is held in Riga. The EU signs a Memorandum of Understanding with Ukraine for its third macro-financial assistance programme.

24   In local and regional elections in Spain, the left-wing anti-austerity Podemos and pro-market Ciudadanos draw support away from the mainstream parties.

25   In a run-off presidential election in Poland, Andrzej Duda, the conservative candidate, beats incumbent President Bronisław Komorowski with 51.5 per cent.

27   The Commission puts forward proposals to relocate 40,000 asylum-seekers from Italy and Greece and 20,000 people from outside the EU to other EU Member States through a quota-based distribution scheme.

29   EU–Japan summit takes place in Tokyo.

31   In local and regional elections in Italy, the right-wing Northern League and and populist Five Star movement increase their overall support, with the centre-left governing Democratic Party (PD) gaining just 23 per cent of the vote.

June

3   The Latvian parliament elects Defence Minister and Green Party member Raimonds Vējonis as President, replacing Andris Bērziņš.

5   Romanian Prime Minister Victor Ponta is placed under criminal investigation for corruption. His government wins a vote of no confidence on 12 June and Ponta is charged with corruption offences on 13 July.

7	Turkish President Tayyip Erdoğan's ruling AK Party wins 40 per cent of the vote in a general election but fails to win a majority.
7–8	A G7 summit is held at Schloss Elmau in Germany. Leaders discuss sanctions against Russia, the Greek debt crisis and global warming.
10	The speaker of the Polish parliament, Radosław Sikorski, and the treasury and sports ministers resign in the wake of an eavesdropping scandal.
10–11	The EU–CELAC summit takes place in Brussels.
12	The EU–Mexico summit takes place in Brussels.
12	The Prime Minister of Moldova, Chiril Gaburici, resigns amid questions over the authenticity of his school certificates.
18	In a general election in Denmark, right-wing parties win a majority in parliament and the far-right Danish People's Party becomes the second largest party. The Liberal Party forms a minority government and Liberal leader Lars Løkke Rasmussen replaces Helle Thorning-Schmidt as Prime Minister.
22	The Commission publishes the 'Five Presidents' Report' on completing economic and monetary union, which calls for deeper integration in the eurozone.
25–26	At the European Council, EU leaders agree on a voluntary relocation and resettlement programme for 60,000 refugees, and discuss Greece, security and defence and economic policy.
27	At a Eurogroup meeting, creditors refuse to extend Greece's bailout programme until after the referendum on the bailout. Greek officials announce banks will remain closed from 29 June.
29	EU–China summit takes place in Brussels.
30	Greece defaults on a €1.6 billion debt repayment to the IMF and the country's second bailout programme expires.

July

5	In a referendum in Greece, 61 per cent vote against the terms of a new bailout deal.
7	Following the resignation of the Prime Minister, the EU freezes financial aid to Moldova until the formation of a new government.
8	The Parliament votes to support the Transatlantic Trade and Investment Partnership (TTIP) but calls for a replacement for the controversial investor-state dispute settlement (ISDS) mechanism.
12–13	At an emergency euro summit, eurozone leaders agree 'in principle' on a third bailout programme for Greece. Dutch Finance Minister Jeroen Dijsselbloem is re-elected Chair of the Eurogroup.
14	P5 + 1 world powers (Britain, China, France, Russia, the United States plus Germany) reach a nuclear deal with Iran. Under the joint comprehensive plan of action, Iran agrees to limit its nuclear programme in exchange for the lifting of economic sanctions.
15	The Commission proposes a climate and energy summer package, including calls for better energy efficiency labelling.
16	The Greek parliament votes to support the reforms required to secure agreement on a third bailout package and the EU approves bridge loans to Greece. On 20 July, Greek banks re-open three weeks after closing, although some restrictions remain. A second package of reforms is approved two days later.

August

3	The Greek stock market re-opens after five weeks of closure following the imposition of capital controls.

3   Kosovo's parliament votes to create a war crimes court to be located in The Hague in the Netherlands.
4   The EU and Vietnam reach a deal on a free trade agreement.
10–11   Violence in eastern Ukraine escalates, risking the Minsk ceasefire agreement reached in February.
14   After the terms of the new bailout are agreed on 11 August, the Greek Parliament and Eurogroup ministers approve the deal worth up to €85 billion.
20   France and Britain sign a deal to cooperate on border security at the Channel Tunnel.
20   Macedonia announces a state of emergency at its border with Greece.
20   After the Commission signs a Memorandum of Understanding with Greece for the new three-year bailout programme, Greek Prime Minister Alexis Tsipras resigns and calls new elections for September.
21   Germany announces the suspension of the Dublin rules for Syrian refugees.
27   The Western Balkans summit takes place in Vienna.
31   Greek authorities announce that the coastguard has rescued 2,500 refugees arriving at Greek islands in the past three days. Thousands of people start to arrive in Austria and Germany by train from Hungary.

September
2   A photo of drowned Syrian toddler Alan Kurdi on a Turkish beach sparks renewed calls for action on refugees in the EU.
4   1,000 people leave Budapest by foot in order to walk to the Austrian border. During the next two days, over 11,000 refugees arrive in Germany by train.
6   Thousands protest in the Moldovan capital of Chişinău calling for President Nicolae Timofti to resign over a US$ 1 billion corruption scandal.
7   The Commission announces a €500 million aid programme for EU farmers suffering from a growing food crisis.
15   EU–Republic of Korea summit takes place in Seoul.
15   The Court of Auditors finds serious errors in the tendering process for the award of €349 billion of EU cohesion funds.
16   The Commission proposes a special public Investment Court System to replace the private investor-state dispute settlement tribunals proposed as part of the TTIP negotiations with the US.
20   In a general election in Greece, Syriza comes first ahead of the conservative New Democracy and forms a coalition government with the Independent Greeks. Alexis Tsipras is returned as Prime Minister.
22   Despite opposition from Central and Eastern European Member States, the Council agrees to a plan to resettle 120,000 refugees across the EU.
23–24   At an informal European Council meeting, leaders agree to set up EU 'hotspots' for processing requests for asylum, to better protect the EU's external borders and to help the most affected Member States and the Western Balkans. They also agree to financial assistance including €1 billion for humanitarian agencies, funds to support Lebanon, Jordan and Turkey and to strengthen co-operation with Turkey.
26   Strict EU standards for home boilers come into force which are expected to lead to significant energy efficiency savings.
27   In a regional election in Spain, separatist parties win a majority in the Catalonian parliament.
30   The Commission presents its Capital Markets Union action plan.

October
2   A summit on the Ukraine conflict is held in Paris between Russia, Ukraine, France and Germany, who agree to extend the Minsk peace plan agreement.
4   In a general election in Portugal, the governing centre-right coalition, Portugal Ahead, comes first ahead of the Socialist opposition but fails to achieve a parliamentary majority. A centre-right minority government is sworn in on 30 October, returning Pedro Passos Coelho as Prime Minister.
6   The Court of Justice rules that the Safe Harbour data sharing agreement between the EU and US is invalid.
6   EU finance ministers approve a directive requiring the automatic exchange of information about cross-border tax rulings.
11   In a presidential election in Belarus, President Alexander Lukashenko is returned for a fifth term. On 12 October, the EU suspends sanctions against Belarus.
14   The Commission issues a Communication on its trade strategy entitled 'Trade for All'.
15   At the European Council, EU leaders discuss EU migration policy, including cooperation with third countries and strengthening the EU's external borders.
18   In Federal Assembly elections in Switzerland, the right wing Swiss People's Party (SVP) wins the most votes and increases its number of seats. In the Federal Council election on 9 December, the SVP wins its second seat in the Swiss cabinet.
25   In a parliamentary election in Poland, the opposition conservative Law and Justice Party wins an outright majority ahead of the governing party Civic Platform. Beata Szydło is elected Prime Minister.
25   At a mini summit in Brussels on the Western Balkans migration route, leaders of Albania, Austria, Bulgaria, Croatia, Germany, Greece, Hungary, Macedonia, Romania, Serbia and Slovenia agree to a 17-point plan of action.
27   The European Parliament passes the telecoms single market legislation without amendments to its provisions for net neutrality. The bill will also abolish mobile roaming charges by 2017.
27   The EU and Kosovo sign a Stabilisation and Association Agreement.

November
1   In the second parliamentary election of the year in Turkey, the Justice and Development Party (AKP) wins a majority with 49.5 per cent of the vote.
4   Following national protests in response to a fire in a nightclub in Bucharest that killed 32 people, Romanian Prime Minister Victor Ponta resigns.
8   Parliamentary elections in Croatia result in a hung parliament, with the centre-right HDZ's Patriotic coalition winning the most seats ahead of the governing centre-left SDP's Croatia is Growing coalition.
10   In a letter to Council President Donald Tusk, British Prime Minister David Cameron sets out four key priorities for his reform of the UK's EU membership.
11–12   The Valletta Summit on migration between the EU and Africa takes place in Malta. On 12 November, EU leaders discuss migration at an informal European Council meeting in Valetta.
12   Sweden announces the imposition of temporary border controls with Denmark in order to reduce the number of refugees arriving in the country.
13   Terrorists kill 130 people in a series of suicide bombings and mass shootings in Paris. The seven attacks take place at the Bataclan concert hall, where 89 people are killed, the Stade de France, and restaurants and bars. Islamic State of Iraq and the Levant (ISIL) claim responsibility.

15–16   The G20 summit takes place in Antalya, Turkey.
21   After the terror threat is raised to the highest level, Brussels goes into a six-day lockdown in the wake of the Paris terror attacks.
24   Turkey shoots down a Russian fighter jet that reportedly strayed into Turkish airspace on the border with Syria.
25   After the conservative minority government falls, the Socialist Party forms a government in Portugal. The Socialist Party leader, António Costa, replaces Pedro Passos Coelho as Prime Minister.
29   At the EU–Turkey summit, the EU agrees to a €3 billion Refugee Facility to support Syrian asylum seekers and refugees in Turkey.
30   The COP21 UN Climate Change Conference opens in Paris.

December
2   The Commission proposes its Circular Economy Package designed to create a more sustainable and competitive economy.
2   The Commission proposes a Directive on Terrorism which would criminalize preparatory acts such as travelling or organizing travel for terrorist purposes.
3   In a referendum in Denmark 53 per cent of voters reject an opt-in to EU Justice and Home Affairs policies.
7   Latvian Prime Minister Laimdota Straujuma resigns following internal struggles in the governing coalition.
7   The EU agrees a deal on the Network and Information Security Directive, the EU's first cybersecurity law.
9   Bulgarian Justice Minister Hristo Ivanov resigns after the parliament rejects some of his proposed reforms of the judiciary.
12   The COP21 Climate Change Conference results in a historic international agreement between 195 countries. The Paris Agreement pledges to keep global warming well below 2 degrees and to work towards a limit of 1.5 degrees above pre-industrial levels.
13   In run-off regional elections in France, the centre-right Les Républicains (formerly UMP) win the most votes and seven regions. With 6.8 million votes, the National Front wins council seats in all regions but no control of any councils.
14   Serbia opens the first two chapters of its EU accession negotiations.
17–18   At the European Council, EU leaders agree to speed up the implementation of measures to deal with the migration crisis and reaffirm the need for improved information-sharing to fight terrorism. They also discuss the UK referendum on EU membership, EMU, external relations, the internal market and energy union.
20   Parliamentary elections in Spain result in a hung parliament, with the governing centre-right People's Party winning the most votes but failing to come close to a majority.
21   The Parliament and Council agree to reforms of the EU's data protection rules that give citizens greater access to, and more control over, their personal data.
22   The Polish parliament approves a controversial amendment to the country's constitutional court law which would require rulings to achieve a two-thirds majority and the presence of at least 13 judges.
23   Pharmaceutical executive Tihomir Orešković is nominated Prime Minister of Croatia following a hung parliament in the country's November elections.

JCMS 2016 Volume 54. Annual Review pp. 225–232   DOI: 10.1111/jcms.12465

Index

Note: Italicised page references indicate information contained in tables.